Our Lives – Our Stories: Life Experiences of Elderly Deaf People

Sign Languages
and Deaf Communities

Editors
Annika Herrmann, Markus Steinbach, Ulrike Zeshan

Editorial board
Carlo Geraci, Rachel McKee, Victoria Nyst,
Marianne Rossi Stumpf, Felix Sze, Sandra Wood

Volume 14

Our Lives – Our Stories: Life Experiences of Elderly Deaf People

Edited by
Roland Pfau, Aslı Göksel and Jana Hosemann

The SIGN-HUB project has received funding from the European Union's Horizon 2020 research and innovation program under grant agreement No. 693349.

ISBN 978-3-11-110462-1
e-ISBN (PDF) 978-3-11-070190-6
e-ISBN (EPUB) 978-3-11-070201-9
ISSN 2192-516X
e-ISSN 2192-5178

Library of Congress Control Number: 2020949175

Bibliographic information published by the Deutsche Nationalbibliothek
The Deutsche Nationalbibliothek lists this publication in the Deutsche Nationalbibliografie; detailed bibliographic data are available on the Internet at http://dnb.dnb.de.

© 2022 Walter de Gruyter Inc., Boston/Berlin and Ishara Press, Lancaster, UK Typesetting: Integra Software Services Pvt. Ltd.
This volume is text- and page-identical with the hardback published in 2021.
Printing and binding: CPI books GmbH, Leck

www.degruyter.com

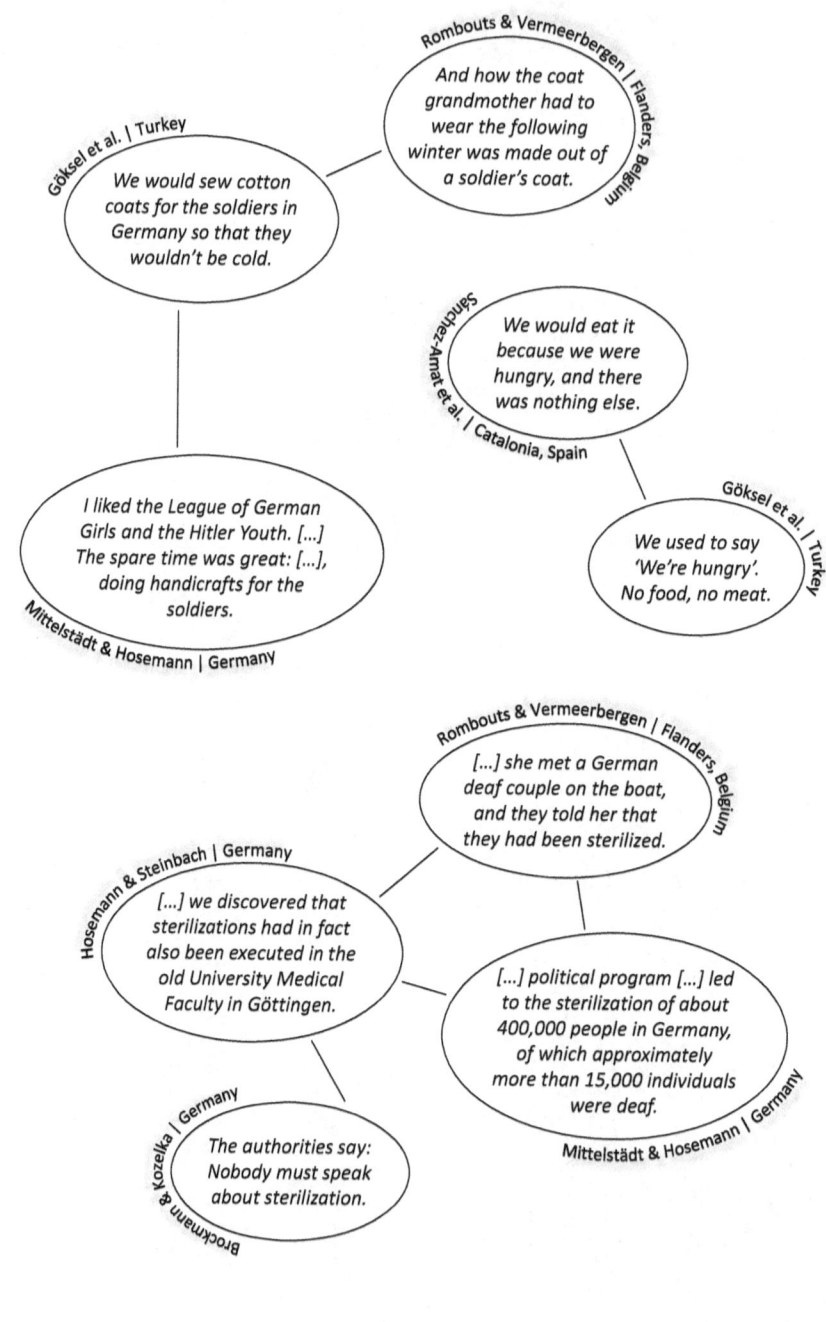

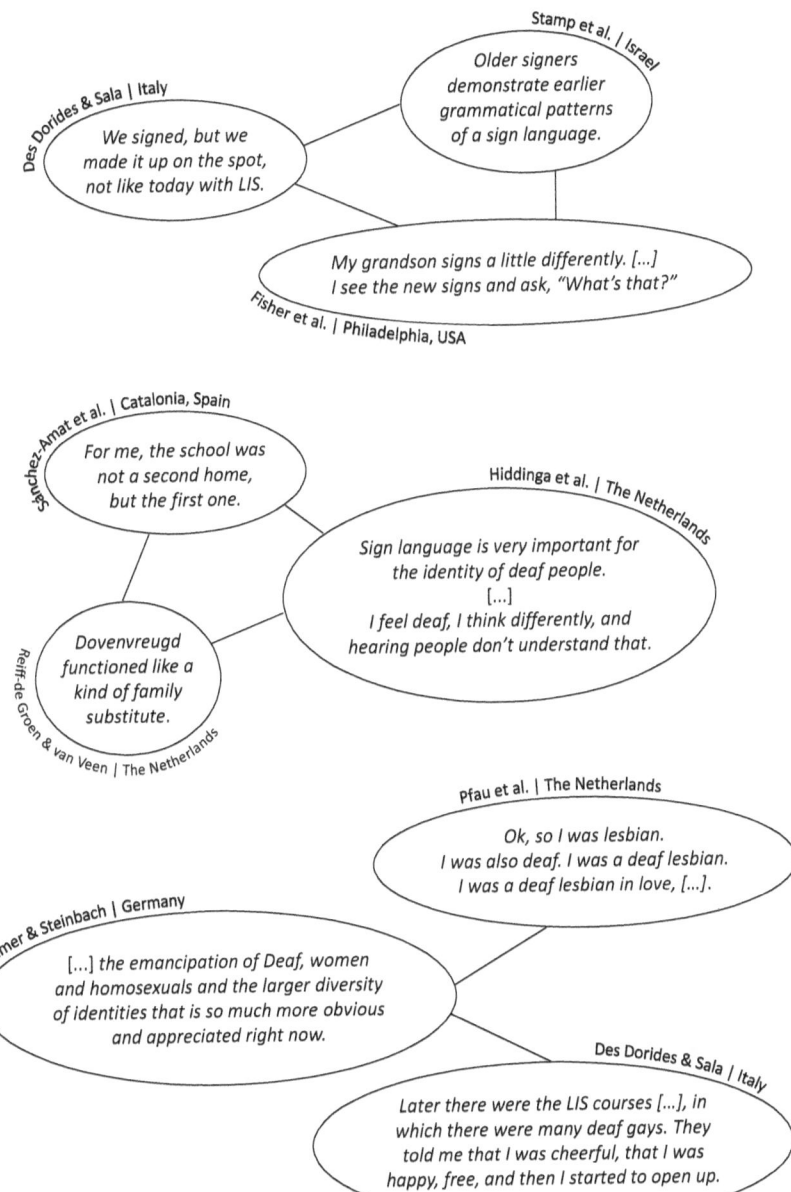

Contents

Roland Pfau, Aslı Göksel, and Jana Hosemann
Much more than a treasure: the life stories of elderly Deaf people —— 1

Part I: **"For this experience, I am grateful to the elderly Deaf people": Collecting and disseminating life stories**

Jens-Michael Cramer and Markus Steinbach
Conducting interviews with elderly Deaf people: opportunities and challenges —— 19

Jana Hosemann and Markus Steinbach
Making the life stories of Deaf seniors visible: a students' exhibition —— 45

Part II: **"I found out that deaf people could do many things": Issues of culture and identity**

Luca Des Dorides and Rita Sala
Once upon a time: history and memory of Italian Deaf elderly signers —— 65

Aslı Göksel, Süleyman S. Taşçı, Buket Ela Demirel, Elvan Tamyürek Özparlak, Burcu Saral, and Hasan Dikyuva
Deafness in Turkey 1930–2020: administrative, social, and cultural aspects —— 91

Roland Pfau, Annemieke van Kampen, and Menno Harterink
Pink sign: identity challenges, choices, and changes among elderly Deaf homosexuals in the Netherlands —— 129

Part III: "Apparently, one could hear airplanes, but we knew nothing": Deaf lives in times of conflict and oppression

Annika Mittelstädt and Jana Hosemann
Impairment vs. *disability*: The paradoxical situation of deaf people during the German Nazi Regime —— 171

Elisabeth Brockmann and Elena Kozelka
Forced sterilization of deaf people during the German Nazi Regime – a trauma and its compensations after 1945 —— 197

Lisa Rombouts and Myriam Vermeerbergen
Surviving a war of silence: Deaf people in Flanders during the Second World War —— 217

Jordina Sánchez-Amat, Raquel Veiga Busto, Xavi Álvarez, Santiago Frigola, Delfina Aliaga, Miguel Ángel Sampedro, Gemma Barberà,
and Josep Quer
The Francoist dictatorship through the Deaf lens —— 247

Part IV: "He signs like me, we are the same": Linguistic and educational perspectives

Jami Fisher, Julie A. Hochgesang, Meredith Tamminga, and Robyn Miller
Uncovering the lived experiences of elderly Deaf Philadelphians —— 277

Rose Stamp, Svetlana Dachkovsky, and Wendy Sandler
Time will tell: time and discourse as 'motion through space' in early Israeli Sign Language (ISL) —— 323

Part V: "Goodbye, hearing world!": Creating a safe environment for the elderly Deaf

Judith Reiff-de Groen and Peter van Veen
De Gelderhorst: a home full of signs —— 359

Anja Hiddinga and Research Collective 'Beyond Hearing. Cultures Overlooked'
Growing old together: aging deaf people and the politics of belonging —— 383

List of contributors —— 403

Subject index —— 407

Name index —— 413

Roland Pfau, Aslı Göksel, and Jana Hosemann
Much more than a treasure: the life stories of elderly Deaf people

1 Introducing 'elderly Deaf signers'

The documentary *We were there . . . We are here*, one of the outputs of the SIGN-HUB project (see Section 2.2), begins with the signed comment "History tells the stories of HEARING communities". Following this, the film title appears (in written English and in sign language), setting the stage for an impressive series of signed fragments from the life stories of elderly Deaf signers. Similar in spirit to the documentary, the present volume can be seen as a modest contribution to filling the gap that is alluded to in the above quote. Without doubt, the life stories of members of the Deaf community are a treasure – or "much more than a treasure", a phrase that we borrowed from the title of the beautiful poem, composed by Miguel Ángel Sampedro Terrón in International Sign, which concludes the documentary.

None of the over two hundred sign languages that are presently in use around the globe has a written form. A direct consequence of this is that sign language communities are traditionally "oral" communities (Byrne 2016), which implies that their culture – including cultural productions – is transmitted "orally" (i.e., in a non-written, visual form) via sign language and has therefore, for the longest time, not been documented. The oldest document that shows the actual use of a sign language, rather than just offering a description and/or dictionary in printed form (e.g., Mallery 1881), is probably the 1913 film *Preservation of the sign language*, in which George Veditz, the president of the National Association of the Deaf, famously expresses in American Sign Language "As long as we have deaf people on earth, we will have signs". This and a few subsequent recordings are now considered some of the most significant documents in Deaf history (cf. Supalla & Clark 2015). In addition, there are intriguing recordings from the 1930s of Plains Indian Sign Language (Davis 2010).[1] However, while being undoubtedly of significant historical value, these documents tell us little about the lived reality and experiences of signers at the time.

---

[1] These recordings can be viewed on Youtube; search, for instance, for "George Veditz" or "Indian Sign Language Council".

https://doi.org/10.1515/9783110701906-001

When elderly signers are included in recent studies, it is usually for the purpose of studying sociolinguistic variation (e.g., Schembri & Johnston 2012) or to track diachronic changes in a sign language based on synchronic data. In both types of studies, productions of older signers – be they spontaneous or elicited – are compared to productions of younger signers with respect to a certain lexical or grammatical feature (see, e.g., Meir (2012) for the evolution of verb agreement). However, given the nature of these studies, it is clear that they focus on the form rather than the content of the signed productions. A publication type that does offer insights into the lives of Deaf people across the centuries are (auto)biographies, such as, for instance, the fictionalized autobiography of the French Deaf teacher Laurent Clerc (Carroll 1991), which focuses on his early years in Paris in the late 18th century; the biography of American Deaf pioneer Edmund Booth, who lived in the 19th century (Lang 2009); Herring Wright's (1999) memories of her life as an African American Deaf woman from the 1920s to the 1940s, which offers an intriguing account of her family life and education in North Carolina; and Vasishta's (2006) memoir of growing up deaf in India in the 1950s – to give just a few examples.

Most of the contributions to this volume are based on information extracted from interviews with elderly Deaf signers; that is, they are based on autobiographical information and are thus similar in spirit to the latter two works mentioned in the previous paragraph. However, each contribution includes information from various signers from a specific country and thus, the chapters make an effort to sketch a broader picture and present a more kaleidoscopic view of a certain period, event, or development – often offering different perspectives on the subject matter. In this way, the volume as a whole hopes to contribute to the preservation of the unique memories and experiences of elderly Deaf people, and thus, their history, culture, and language – a treasure that would otherwise be lost forever.[2]

2 The SIGN-HUB project – and beyond

The present volume is an output (a so-called "deliverable") related to the project "The SIGN-HUB: preserving, researching, and fostering the linguistic, historical, and cultural heritage of European Deaf signing communities with an integral resource"; this four-year project (2016–2020) has received funding from the European Union's Horizon 2020 research and innovation program (grant agreement No. 693349). We will describe the goal and the content of the project

---

[2] For the importance of digital Deaf histories, see also Legg (2016).

in more detail in Section 2.1, before zooming in on the project component dedicated to the life stories of elderly Deaf signers in Section 2.2. However, the volume does not only contain investigations based on information gathered in the context of SIGN-HUB. It also includes studies by research groups from outside the project that work on related topics; these will be briefly introduced in Section 2.3.

2.1 The SIGN-HUB project

As stated in the grant proposal, the main goal of the SIGN-HUB project was to provide "the first comprehensive response to the societal and scientific challenge resulting from the generalized neglect of the cultural and linguistic identity of signing Deaf communities in Europe". From a strictly geographic perspective, the project went beyond Europe, as the participating countries were France, Germany, Israel, Italy, The Netherlands, Spain, and Turkey. The core output of the project – next to this volume – is an open access digital platform (www.sign-hub.eu/), an innovative resource hub for the documentation of the linguistic and cultural heritage of Deaf communities on the one hand, and for sign language assessment on the other hand. The content part of the project encompassed the following four components (so-called "tasks"), which are represented on the platform (see also Geraci et al. 2019).

(i) *digital sign language grammars* – task leaders: Meltem Kelepir (Boğaziçi University, Istanbul) and Josep Quer (University Pompeu Fabra, Barcelona);
(ii) *an interactive digital atlas of linguistic structures of the world's sign languages* – task leaders: Jana Hosemann (University of Cologne) and Markus Steinbach (University of Göttingen);
(iii) *online sign language assessment instruments for use in clinical intervention and school settings* – task leaders: Caterina Donati (University Paris Diderot – Paris 7) and Naama Friedmann (Tel Aviv University);
(iv) *digital archive of life narratives by elderly Deaf signers* – task leader: Roland Pfau (University of Amsterdam).

Besides the "task leaders" mentioned in this list, other important administrative tasks were performed by the following project members: Carlo Cecchetto (University Milano-Bicocca), together with Meltem Kelepir, was responsible for coordinating the four content components, Chiara Branchini (Ca' Foscari University, Venice) managed the dissemination activities, and Carlo Geraci

(Institut Jean Nicod, Paris) bridged the content and the technical part, that is, the implementation of the content on the digital platform. Josep Quer was the Project Coordinator.

The present volume is a deliverable related to component (iv). However, before describing this component in more detail in the next section, we provide below some information on the other three components.

(i) Digital sign language grammars

In the course of SIGN-HUB, comprehensive (yet not exhaustive) grammars have been written for five sign languages: Catalan Sign Language, German Sign Language, Italian Sign Language, Sign Language of the Netherlands, and Turkish Sign Language. All grammars follow the exact same structure, that is, a fixed table of contents that has been developed in a previous European project ("SignGram"). The table of contents together with a detailed manual and a glossary of linguistic terms constitutes the *SignGram Blueprint* (Quer et al. 2017).[3] The online grammars contain numerous visuals (images and videos) and are downloadable from the platform. Most of the grammars have been written by teams including PhD students and (Deaf and hearing) senior researchers.

In addition to the five comprehensive grammars, certain domains of grammar have been described for French Sign Language and Spanish Sign Language. Crucially, the platform is expandable in order to add sections to existing grammars and grammars of other sign languages in the future (following the structure of the Blueprint).

(ii) Digital atlas of linguistic structures of the world's sign languages

Next to linguistic descriptions of individual sign languages, the project created an atlas of linguistic structures, inspired by existing atlases for spoken languages like the *World Atlas of Language Structures* (WALS, Dryer & Haspelmath 2013). The Atlas allows the user to get an overview of the typological variation across sign languages in the domains of phonology, lexicon, morphology, syntax, pragmatics, and socio-history. To this end, four questionnaires were developed and distributed among sign language experts. The questionnaires address approximately 200 grammatical features in total. To date, information from about 100 different sign languages has been implemented in the Atlas. On interactive maps, the users can search the Atlas by grammatical feature (e.g., types of

---

[3] The *SignGram Blueprint* is an open access publication available at: doi.org/10.1515/9781501511806.

two-handed signs, position of wh-sign) and by sign language. Data collection for this part of the project will continue, with additional sign languages to be added in the future.

Clearly, the grammatical description and the typological study of sign languages have an important positive impact both at the community and the scientific level (cf. Pfau & Zeshan 2016), as both efforts "will likely reinforce (or even initiate) the process of language awareness, upon which Deaf identity is built" (Geraci et al. 2019: 34). In general, the linguistic study of sign languages has a lot to contribute, as it adds to our understanding of the possible variation across and within languages.

(iii) Online sign language assessment instruments
The third component of SIGN-HUB has been dedicated to creating a variety of assessment tests to detect lexical impairment and to measure proficiency in various grammatical domains (see Mann & Haug (2014) for an overview of assessment tests in sign language). One key aspect of the project has been to standardize the tests across healthy populations of signers with various levels of sign language exposure. Subsequently, the tests can be systematically used for early diagnosis and identification of language pathologies both in Deaf adults and Deaf children. The tests are available for free; detailed descriptions of each test as well as detailed guidelines on how to use the assessment tools can be downloaded from the platform.

So far, the tests, which evaluate comprehension and production of isolated signs and of full sentences, have been used to assess the linguistic skills of signers of four sign languages: Catalan Sign Language, French Sign Language, Italian Sign Language, and Spanish Sign Language. Data has been collected from three groups of Deaf participants: native signers (exposed to sign language from birth), early signers (exposed to sign language before the age of 6), and late signers (exposed to sign language between the age of 6 and 15).

2.2 Life stories of elderly Deaf signers

We now present in somewhat more detail the project component dedicated to creating a digital archive of life narratives by elderly Deaf signers. First, and foremost, we conducted interviews with elderly Deaf signers (age range 66–97) in five countries in six sign languages: Catalan Sign Language, German Sign Language, Italian Sign Language, Sign Language of the Netherlands, Spanish Sign Language, and Turkish Sign Language. All interviews were conducted by

Deaf interviewers and followed a pre-defined questionnaire; however, the questionnaire was only meant as a guideline to allow for comparison across countries, and the addition of country-specific questions was actually encouraged. In the end, we conducted a total of 137 interviews with 142 interview partners, which amounts to approximately 175 hours of material (see Cramer & Steinbach, this volume, for details on the questionnaire, the procedure, and the interviewers' experiences).

The interviews collected in the context of the SIGN-HUB project are available on the project platform (www.sign-hub.eu/, under the tab "Life stories") – provided that the interviewee has given consent. Moreover, at least a fragment from each interview has been subtitled in English and the local spoken language (e.g., German subtitles for the signers interviewed in Germany). These subtitled fragments can also be viewed on the project platform.

Next to the interviews, project partners in France and Israel digitized pre-existing materials. In France, these were three documentary movies: (i) *1939–1945 Que Faisaient Les Sourds?* ('1939–1945 What did the Deaf do?'), which reports on an event organized by the Académie de la Langue des Signes Française ('Academy for French Sign Language') held in March 2004, which dealt with the situation of Deaf people during World War II; (ii) *La Vie Des Sourds Pieds Noirs Et Juifs D'Algérie* ('Life of the Deaf *Pieds Noirs* and Jews of Algeria'), which reports on a similar event (date unknown) about the war in Algeria (1954–1962); (iii) *Quel Avenir Pour Les Personnes Agées Sourdes?* ('What is the future of the elderly Deaf?'), a collection of interviews with elderly Deaf people in France conducted in the early 2000s. What makes these movies a unique contribution to the documentation of Deaf history is the fact that they have been realized either entirely by Deaf people or under the direct supervision and direction of Deaf people in an effort to preserve their own memories.

As for Israel, a number of life stories from the Deaf archive of the University of Haifa have been digitized. This archive is an impressive collection of roughly fifty narratives compiled over the past 20 years by the late Irit Meir, Wendy Sandler, and assistants (see also Stamp et al., this volume). The signers in the selected recordings are representative of different backgrounds in Israel, and the content of their stories is varied (e.g., Holocaust, immigration, experiences at a school for the Deaf).

Based on the interviews, as well as the materials from France and Israel, a second important deliverable has been created: the 40-minute documentary *We were there . . . We are here*. The movie is based entirely on memories of elderly Deaf signers, and thus offers an unprecedented perspective on their experiences regarding family, education, work, war, and identity issues. The movie does not contain any spoken language as a voice over; it only features the signed accounts of signers from all participating countries, thematically organized into chapters, and with subtitles. It ends with the above-mentioned poem by Miguel Ángel Sampedro Terrón. Just like the interviews, the documentary is available on the project platform (there are versions with English subtitles, with subtitles in the local spoken languages, and with interpretation in Catalan Sign Language and International Sign).

The third project output is the volume that you are holding in your hands. The volume contains 13 chapters; eight of these chapters are authored by project members and five are written by researchers from outside the SIGN-HUB project (see Sections 2.3 and 3 for details). There are a total of 37 authors, 14 of whom are Deaf.

Together, the four project components, sketched in this and the previous section, will (i) help in exploring and valuing the identity and the cultural, historical, and linguistic assets of Deaf communities, (ii) advance linguistic knowledge on the natural languages of the Deaf, and (iii) impact on the diagnosis of language deficits within these minorities. In this way, the project as a whole showcases and boosts that largely unknown part of our common heritage.

2.3 Contributions from outside SIGN-HUB

Once we had a rough idea regarding the topics to be covered in the contributions based on SIGN-HUB interviews, it was decided to make an effort to complement these chapters by reaching out to colleagues working on topics related to the experiences and the lives of elderly Deaf signers. Using our network, as well as information drawn from online resources, we contacted eight researchers / research teams. Six of them agreed to contribute, and in the end, five of them submitted a chapter.

We are very excited that this effort allowed us to include two chapters from countries that were not part of SIGN-HUB, namely Belgium (Rombouts & Vermeerbergen) and the United States (Fisher et al.), next to additional contributions from Germany (Brockmann & Kozelka) and the Netherlands (Reiff-de Groen & van Veen and Hiddinga et al.). We are grateful to these authors for enriching the present volume with their interesting perspectives on historical, social, cultural, and linguistic issues related to elderly Deaf signers. An overview of all chapters included in the volume is presented in the next section.

3 Overview of chapters

The chapters in this volume are organized thematically into five parts. The two chapters that make up **Part I** report on hands-on experiences related to the interviews and their dissemination. In the opening chapter, *Jens-Michael Cramer* and *Markus Steinbach* introduce the backbone of many of the contributions to this volume, which is the procedural aspects of the interviews conducted with the elderly Deaf in the five countries that have taken part in this component of the SIGN-HUB project. Their survey spans many aspects of the interviewing process, both the preparation for the interviews and the interviews themselves. Among these are the semi-structured questionnaire, how the interviewees were found, what the setting was, how the consent form was introduced, how the interviews were conducted, and what the attitude of the interviewees was to being approached and interviewed. Based mostly on Germany as a case study, the authors also discuss the country-based differences concerning locations of the interviews, the levels of compliance of the interviewees, and the selection of memorable events. They also highlight the challenges encountered in interviewing the Deaf, in particular their reluctance to be recorded (in a few cases), and the mistrust of some of their hearing relatives. They conclude that all in all, the experience was positive for the interviewees as well as for the interviewers.

The second chapter, co-authored by *Jana Hosemann* and *Markus Steinbach*, describes a one-year project at the University of Göttingen, Germany, in which a group of 13 students together with three supervisors created an exhibition based on the interviews with elderly Deaf signers. In the first semester, the students faced the challenge of understanding the content of the interviews; at the same time, they had to select and investigate topics that are representative of the life of elderly Deaf people. In the second semester, the group worked on transforming the content of their research into visual pieces appropriate for an exhibition that was going to attract a broad and heterogeneous audience. The chapter takes the reader through the process of creating an exhibition, starting with the content, leading past the challenges in actually designing and building the pieces and the exhibition, and finishing with the opening event and the outcome of the team's journey.

Part II focuses on social life, education, Deaf culture, and issues of identity drawn from interviews made in Italy, Turkey, and the Netherlands. In the first chapter in this section, *Luca Des Dorides* and *Rita Sala* draw upon the interviews made with elderly Deaf Italians born in the first half of the 20th century and explore various aspects of Deaf identity. Their investigation is informed by Deaf Studies as a political activity and biographical method. Within this context, they take issue with the assumed binary nature of power relations between the hearing and the Deaf, and couch their observations within the idea that the relation between the Deaf community and the hearing community is dynamic, rather than merely focusing on the oppressive aspects in the history of the Deaf. Against this background, the authors discuss marginalization and oppression on the one hand, but on the other hand, the notion of power as an element that is inherent in every individual. To this end, the chapter reveals attitudes towards language and signing in public, the practices at deaf schools and institutions, and the case study of a deaf dressmaker who went from a functioning professional to a woman who was admitted to an asylum. The chapter also addresses the double discrimination against Deaf women, as typical gender roles are repeated within the Deaf community.

The next article in this section is by *Aslı Göksel, Süleyman S. Taşçı, Buket Ela Demirel, Elvan Tamyürek Özparlak, Burcu Saral*, and *Hasan Dikyuva*, who discuss the administrative, social, and cultural aspects of Deafness in Turkey in the last 90 years, predominantly through the eyes of the Deaf elderly signers. The chapter, also based on archival material, presents a panoramic view of Deaf lives, ranging from reporting negative encounters with hearing people to highlighting the positive aspects of their productive lives. There are sections on participation in the Deaflympics, the beauty contest for Deaf young women in which the Turkish candidate in 1969 became Miss Deaf World, and the social life and educational practices in schools. Most notable is the section on Deaf activists, educationalists, and association directors, of whom Süleyman Gök (1904–1979) was the most prominent. The interviewees who personally knew Gök, founder of the fingerspelling system in Turkish Sign Language (TİD) and director and founder of the Yıldız School for the Deaf, remember his disciplinarian but care-giving attitude. The whole article is peppered with anecdotes about personal lives, but also about various dignitaries and state officials of the time.

In the final chapter of this part, *Roland Pfau, Annemieke van Kampen*, and *Menno Harterink* address the issue of identity and intersectionality in a specific group within the Deaf community in the Netherlands: Deaf people who identify as homosexual/LGBTIQ. Drawing information from interviews conducted within the SIGN-HUB project, conversations with younger Deaf people, and information from published sources, the authors sketch some of the challenges that Deaf homosexuals were faced with – within their families and the Deaf community – and how these challenges impacted their identities. Special attention is given to *Roze Gebaar*, the Dutch Association for Deaf LGBTIQ people, which was founded in 1982. The interviews reveal that *Roze Gebaar* played an important role in shaping identity, as it allowed Deaf homosexuals for the first time to interact with like-minded people from within the Deaf community and thus to transition, at least to some extent, from the hearing to the Deaf world. Thanks to societal changes, for younger Deaf LGBTIQ people, it is easier to embrace their sexual identity, and therefore, they tend to give more importance to their Deaf identity. The discussion of identity issues is complemented with an overview of queer terminology from Sign Language of the Netherlands.

Part III comprises four chapters that center around deafness during World War II, the Spanish Civil War, and the Francoist regime, with two chapters on Germany, and one each about Belgium and Spain (Catalonia).

The first two chapters in this section focus on the theory and practice of forced sterilization in pre-war and war-time Germany and occupied Europe. *Annika Mittelstädt* and *Jana Hosemann* place in the center of their investigation the ambivalent behavior of the National Socialist practices towards the Deaf, as well as the ambivalent interpretation of that era by the Deaf. They note that, on the one hand, the Deaf were being discriminated, persecuted, and forcibly sterilized, but that, on the other hand, they were recruited in the branches of the youth organization *Hitlerjugend*, and that some of the interviewees report pleasant memories of those times. They study this ambivalence in the light of one of the recent tools used in disability studies, that of the difference between 'impairment', a biological state, and 'disability', a social construct. The attempt of the Nazi party to recruit Deaf people in the branch of the *Hitlerjugend* and to educate Deaf children could then be explained as an attempt to see Deaf people as 'disabled' and to 'integrate' them into the society (purely for economic reasons). In contrast, the victims of sterilization and euthanasia would be deemed 'impaired', that is, as having a dysfunction that should be resolved or eliminated. Another significant aspect of the chapter is a detailed exegesis into the laws of the Third Reich concerning the disabled. The content of the laws and the discussion surrounding them, together with public acceptance, are given chronologically, thereby forming a coherent background to how primarily the Deaf, but also other individuals falling under these laws, were perceived and treated during the unfolding of the war.

The previous chapter sets the stage for *Elisabeth Brockmann* and *Elena Kozelka*, who report on earlier interviews made with victims of forced sterilization and forced abortions and their families. The laws and regulations as well as the post war reparations are discussed in this chapter. The authors note that of the 400,000 people who had been forcibly sterilized, 15,000 were deaf, and of these, 1,600 were killed under the *Euthanasia* program. The Hereditary Health Courts decided who would be sterilized and who would be spared, and although individuals with acquired deafness were also among the victims of sterilization and euthanasia, the Deaf community suffered through the division between those who would be sterilized and those who would be spared. But the most traumatic source of suffering was without doubt the experience of being sterilized, conducted sometimes under unhygienic conditions which caused long-lasting physical and psychological pain. Phrases like "I went completely silent", ". . . no longer felt a normal man", "there was no happiness in love anymore", ". . . have broken me" speak for the depth of the psychological scars that were endured. The authors also discuss the post-war lack of recognition and acknowledgement, which went on for several decades. They note that today, victims of forced sterilizations are compensated by the allocation of an allowance to the victims on a monthly basis. However, an official and legal acknowledgement that forcibly sterilized (deaf) people have the status of 'persecuted by National Socialism' has not yet been accomplished.

Lisa Rombouts and *Myriam Vermeerbergen* also provide information about the Deaf in Nazi Europe. In their chapter, which covers the time of the German occupation of Belgium, they uncover memories of Deaf individuals who have witnessed the war from the beginning to the end. Some of these people have been interviewed within the scope of the *Seniorenproject*, and the others have been interviewed by one of the authors. These individuals share vivid memories about the war, from where they were when they first became aware of the war, to how they fled, sometimes barely escaping the soldiers looking for them, and then to how they returned. The chapter centers around the memories of two Jewish girls, one of whom, Anna van Dam, has also been the main character in a movie. It emerges that among all of the interviewees, these two girls are the only ones who have heard of the sterilization of the Deaf in Germany. Aware of the fact that memory does not necessarily reflect facts as they happened, the authors draw a picture of the life of Deaf Belgians during the war. The most prominent aspect that the interviewees share is the overwhelming feeling of being left in the dark. Thus, this chapter does not only provide us with anecdotes about the war, but also offers a crucial insight about the experiences of the Deaf who live among the hearing.

In the final chapter in this part, *Jordina Sánchez-Amat, Raquel Veiga, Xavi Álvarez, Santiago Frigola, Delfina Aliaga, Miguel Ángel Sampedro, Gemma Barberà,* and *Josep Quer* report on the experiences of the individuals during the Francoist dictatorial regime following the Civil War in Spain (1936–1939). The interviewees mention different aspects of their lives which were marred by the values and fear dominating the society: education, communication, family and marriage, professional lives, and their associations. The interviewees express their frustration with forced oralism and show ambivalence towards their school days during which, on the one hand, they were inordinately punished, but on the other, found a haven for expressing themselves among their peers. The chapter contains vivid memories about the shelters and about the scarcity of food and the acts of solidarity towards those who were suffering throughout these hard times. The section on Deaf activists during the dictatorship is particularly telling regarding the problems of being deaf, which were compounded by their stance (as communists) against the regime.

Part IV focuses predominantly on linguistic aspects of two sign languages, the Philadelphian variety of American Sign Language (ASL) and Israeli Sign Language (ISL), both of the elderly, and inevitably linked to Deaf identity.

Jami N. Fisher, *Julie Hochgesang*, *Meredith Tamminga*, and *Robyn Miller*'s chapter is based on the memories of Deaf elderly Philadelphians, extracted from the Philadelphia Signs Project. It begins by introducing two prominent schools in Philadelphia, currently the Pennsylvania School for the Deaf and W.H. Martin School, and moves on to discuss three main themes that underlie the experience of the interviewees. One of these themes is their experience on their first days at school. For some, the experience was terrifying, but the overall feeling is one of happy memories due to being surrounded by Deaf peers. The second theme covers the Philadelphian variety of ASL, the attitude of the interviewees towards ASL, and the lexical differences between the pan-regional variety of ASL and the Philadelphia dialect, as well as the differences between old and new signs and the attitude towards these. The third theme revolves around Black Deaf Philadelphians, whose experiences have been hitherto left out of historical accounts. The authors highlight the systemic racism in the educational institutions especially in the pre-1960s period, and acknowledge the imminence of future studies in unraveling the experiences of Black Deaf Philadelphians.

Drawing on the productions of elderly signers who are the first generation of signers of ISL, *Rose Stamp*, *Svetlana Dachkovsky*, and *Wendy Sandler* explore a time expression (TIME-PASS), which broadly refers to the passage of time. They observe that this sign has two different prosodies. It may constitute its own intonational phrase, or it may introduce an intonational phrase. Coupled with these are differences in the rhythmic pattern in the cyclic manual part of the sign, all of which furthermore tend to co-occur with a cluster of non-manual markers. Based on these observations, the authors claim that the two different exponents of this time expression in fact signal two different discursive functions. One (TIME-PASS1) demarcates background information, evaluation, and connection between larger units. The other (TIME-PASS2) is more temporal in nature, is similar to perfective aspect, and is followed by time adverbials. The authors draw our attention to the cyclic gesture referred to in the literature as embodying 'time as motion through space', and suggest that this metaphor can be expanded to 'motion through discourse'.

Part V, the final section of the book, is devoted to a care home for the elderly Deaf, *De Gelderhorst* in Ede in the Netherlands. The first chapter in this part is by *Judith Reiff-de Groen* and *Peter van Veen* and provides a history of the care home, starting with its predecessor, *Dovenvreugd*, established in the early 1950s. In 1972, as a result of an initiative of the board, who tried to solve the overcrowding problem, this care home gave way to *De Gelderhorst*. Both of these institutions were run by hearing people, and communication was through spoken language accompanied by gestures. The principles were initially laid down by hearing people, then to be revised following the input from Deaf people. The situation began to change in the 1980s. The authors highlight the momentum in favor of Deaf identity and Deaf culture in later years, which resulted in informed care for the psychological well-being of the residents. The chapter continues with expounding the mission and the core tasks of *De Gelderhorst*, the primary ones being self-reliance, and establishing sign language as the medium for communication. The chapter ends with a vision for the future and activities of the residents of *De Gelderhorst*, one of which is to build bridges with the hearing world.

The second article about *De Gelderhorst* is by *Anja Hiddinga* in collaboration with a Research Collective. This chapter complements the previous one by building upon interviews conducted with the residents, their attitudes towards living in a home away from the hearing world, and by couching these in an ethnographic study of the significance of socialization among the Deaf, cultural identity, and the feelings of belonging to one's kindred group. The notion of a carescape was the underlying source for an environment in which Deaf people can feel cared for and understood. The patronizing behavior of the hearing towards the Deaf and the controlling tendencies that come with this are said to create an environment in which the Deaf felt and still feel isolated. Institutions such as *De Gelderhorst* counter this attitude because it gives self-reliance to the Deaf, caters for different communicative needs, and in a language, i.e., sign language, that they are familiar with, even though some of the residents are not fluent in NGT. The authors also discuss the diversity among Deaf people and different senses of belonging, which are linked to different motivations for wanting to move into *De Gelderhorst*.

4 Notation conventions

In the text and in examples, signs are presented in SMALL CAPS. Obviously, these glosses do not tell us anything about the form of the sign, they only function as an approximation of the sign's meaning (using written English as language of representation). When necessary, the form of a sign is explained in the text or illustrated by means of an image. The gloss IX refers to a pointing sign (index finger extended); when two words are necessary to gloss a single sign, they are separated by a hyphen (e.g. TIME-PASS).

Most of the contributions to this volume make use of quotes from interviews with signers. As for the chapters by SIGN-HUB authors, these come, for the most part, from interviews with elderly signers that have been conducted in the context of the project. All quotes – no matter whether they stem from interviews conducted by the authors themselves or from previously published interviews – are presented in italics; shorter quotes appear in the running text between double quotation marks, longer ones in a separate indented paragraph. Most of the original quotes are accompanied by a source code between square brackets, which usually includes at least a participant code (e.g., M10 for a male interview partner), the date of the interview, and a time stamp. However, some quotes are only accompanied by a pseudonym or a code for the signer.

Note finally that in studies on deafness and sign language, a distinction is commonly made between the use of lower-case 'deaf', referring to the audiological status, and upper-case 'Deaf' to indicate an affiliation with Deaf culture. We emphasize that we left it to the contributors whether they wanted to follow this convention or not, and some of them explain their choice in a footnote. When referring to a particular elderly signer, for instance, it may not even be clear whether this individual identified as culturally Deaf or not, that is, whether use of 'Deaf' would be appropriate. This implies that not all uses of 'deaf' throughout the volume necessarily exclude affiliation with Deaf culture.

Acknowledgements:

 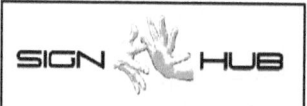

The SIGN-HUB project has received funding from the European Union's Horizon 2020 research and innovation program under grant agreement No. 693349. We are indebted to Markus Steinbach for encouragement and guidance from the very beginning of the editing journey. A special thanks to Michaela Göbels from De Gruyter Mouton for her friendly and professional assistance.

References

Byrne, Andrew. 2016. Sign language literature. In Genie Gertz & Patrick Boudreault (eds.), *The SAGE Deaf studies encyclopedia*, 832–835. London: SAGE Publishing.

Carroll, Cathryn. 1991. *Laurent Clerc: The story of his early years*. Washington, DC: Gallaudet University Press.

Davis, Jeffrey. 2010. *Hand talk: Sign language among American Indian nations*. Cambridge: Cambridge University Press.

Dryer, Matthew S. & Martin Haspelmath (eds.). 2013. *The world atlas of language structures online*. Leipzig: Max Planck Institute for Evolutionary Anthropology. Available online at: http://wals.info.

Geraci, Carlo, Roland Pfau, Pietro Braione, Carlo Cecchetto & Josep Quer. 2019. Hidden languages in a digital world: the case of sign language archives. *Journal of the Italian Association of Speech Sciences (Studi AISV)* 6. 31–47.

Herring Wright, Mary. 1999. *Sounds like home. Growing up Black and Deaf in the south*. Washington, DC: Gallaudet University Press.

Lang, Harry G. 2009. *Edmund Booth: Deaf pioneer*. Washington, DC: Gallaudet University Press.

Legg, Jannelle. 2016. Exploring the promise of digital deaf histories. *Sign Language Studies* 17(1). 42–58.

Mann, Wolfgang & Tobias Haug. 2014. Mapping out guidelines for the development and use of sign language assessments: Some critical issues, comments and suggestions. In David Quinto-Pozos (ed.), *Multilingual aspects of signed language communication and disorder*, 123–139. Bristol: Multilingual Matters.

Mallery, Garrick. 1881. *Sign language among North American Indians*. Washington, DC: Smithsonian Institution [Re-printed 2001, Mineola, NY: Dover Publications].

Meir, Irit. 2012. The evolution of verb classes and verb agreement in sign languages. *Theoretical Linguistics* 38(1–2). 145–152.

Pfau, Roland & Ulrike Zeshan. 2016. Positive signs: How sign language typology benefits deaf communities and linguistic theory. *Linguistic Typology* 20(3). 547–559.

Quer, Josep, Carlo Cecchetto, Caterina Donati, Carlo Geraci, Meltem Kelepir, Roland Pfau & Markus Steinbach (eds.) 2017. *SignGram Blueprint: A guide to sign language grammar writing*. Berlin: De Gruyter Mouton.

Schembri, Adam & Trevor Johnston. 2012. Sociolinguistic aspects of variation and change. In Roland Pfau, Markus Steinbach & Bencie Woll (eds.), *Sign language. An international handbook*, 788–816. Berlin: De Gruyter Mouton.

Supalla, Ted & Patricia Clark. 2015. *Sign language archaeology*. Washington, DC: Gallaudet University Press.

Vasishta, Madan. 2006. *Deaf in Delhi. A memoir*. Washington, DC: Gallaudet University Press.

Part I: **"For this experience, I am grateful to the elderly Deaf people": Collecting and disseminating life stories**

Jens-Michael Cramer and Markus Steinbach
In collaboration with Delfina Aliaga, Xavier Álvarez, Buket Ela Demirel, Luca Des Dorides, Francesca Di Meo, Hasan Dikyuva, Santiago Frigola, Annemieke van Kampen, Miguel Ángel Sampedro, and Elvan Tamyürek Özparlak

Conducting interviews with elderly Deaf people: opportunities and challenges

1 Introduction

In this chapter, we document the work and the experiences of the Deaf interviewers that conducted interviews with elderly Deaf people to create an archive of the life stories of these seniors for six different sign languages, i.e., Catalan Sign Language (LSC), German Sign Language (DGS), Italian Sign Language (LIS), Sign Language of the Netherlands (NGT), Spanish Sign Language (LSE), and Turkish Sign Language (TİD). We document the work of the interviewers from the first step, the recruitment of elderly Deaf seniors for the interviews, until the final step, the archiving and documentation of the interviews. We also discuss expectations the Deaf interviewers had before conducting the interviews and some of the challenges they were faced with. It has to be kept in mind that the Deaf interviewers have a close relation to the Deaf community. Some interviewers are even members of Deaf families. Hence, they are an integral part of the Deaf community and thus share the wish to preserve and foster the linguistic and cultural heritage of their respective community by documenting important aspects of the (in)visible lives of elderly Deaf people.

The chapter is structured as follows: First, we set the stage by describing the background of this enterprise (Section 2). Then we explain the procedure of preparing and conducting the interviews with Deaf seniors (Section 3), followed by a sketch of important technical aspects (Section 4). In Section 5, we report some of the experiences of the Deaf interviewers, for instance, concerning the recruitment of interviewees, problems encountered during the interviews, and memorable moments. Section 6 concludes this chapter with an outlook on the scientific and social potential the life stories collected in this project have for future research.

https://doi.org/10.1515/9783110701906-002

2 Behind the scenes

Collecting the life stories of elderly Deaf seniors was not only a highly interesting and rewarding experience but also a very responsible task for the Deaf interviewers in the five countries (and for the six sign languages) of the SIGN-HUB project which participated in this task. For some of the six sign languages in this project (e.g., DGS), one interviewer was responsible for all interviews. For other sign languages (e.g., LIS), an interviewer team consisting of more than one interviewer conducted the interviews. We come back to this issue below.

The common basis for the interviews was a questionnaire developed at the beginning of the project by all partners in close collaboration. Although common guidelines have been developed for all interviews, the specific historical and cultural situation of the six sign languages required, of course, also particular attention. Therefore, the local teams prepared additional specific questions for their sign language. In the end, the interviewers had at their disposal a preprepared questionnaire with 20 identical questions to be asked for all six sign languages and five or more additional sign language-specific questions. The basic equipment (two videocameras and one floor lamp, see Section 4) was also the same for all six teams.

Conducting the interviews in the years 2016–2018 allowed us to reveal not only general tendencies in the lives of elderly Deaf people that could be observed for all six sign languages and Deaf communities but also interesting differences between the languages and communities of this project and their obvious specific historical and cultural aspects. For example, it was easier to acquire elderly Deaf seniors in the southern countries than in the northern countries. Possibly, the stereotype that people in the south are more extroverted and communicative than people in the north might be responsible for this difference. Another reason for differences between the countries and regions can be found in the history of each country and region. In Germany, for instance, most of the Deaf seniors grew up without a socially and politically accepted and recognized sign language and without good school education. As a consequence, many elderly Deaf people do not have a strong self-confidence. In addition, the way of living of Deaf seniors also differs to a certain extent across the five countries and regions. In Turkey, many of the Deaf seniors who were interviewed live in an urban area (e.g., in Istanbul). By contrast, in Germany, Spain, and Catalonia, the Deaf seniors we interviewed live more widespread and very often in smaller villages. A final reason for differences may be found in the family background, that is, whether a Deaf senior grew up in a hearing or a Deaf family. This last factor, however, is not specific for a country or sign language but has been observed for each country and sign language.

Despite the fact that the interviewers worked with a questionnaire that served as a guideline, the organization, structure, and conducting of the interviews was different for each sign language. This was necessary to account for culture-specific characteristics of the Deaf communities and to address such aspects as optimally as possible. A general tendency was, however, that, for all six sign languages, Deaf seniors with positive experiences and memories generally happily agreed to be interviewed, while many Deaf seniors with negative experiences and memories were more hesitant and reserved. Therefore, as a result, it is not unlikely that the interviews collected in this project do not make all dimensions of the life stories of elderly Deaf people equally accessible to us. Nevertheless, it was an important aim of this project to receive a balanced view of the lives of elderly Deaf people and to interview as many elderly Deaf people with as many diverse backgrounds as possible to make the archive maximally representative.

3 Preparing and conducting the interviews

In this section, we will describe how the interviews were prepared and conducted by taking the interviews collected in Germany as an example. Once the interviewer had made an appointment with a Deaf senior and had received the address of the interviewee, the visit to the senior was prepared carefully. The interviewer went through the questionnaire several times, considered various possible transitions, continuations, as well as additional topics to be discussed and refreshed his knowledge of the historical events that might turn out to be important for a particular interview. Furthermore, the cameras had to be checked, and the relevant documents – information sheet, consent form, privacy statement, and personal data sheet – had to be prepared. Finally, an envelope with 50 Euro allowance for participation at the interview was prepared.

Subsequently, the interviewer put together the equipment and drove by car or train to the senior. Typically, the procedure would start with an informal conversation after a welcome coffee. The seniors were usually very interested in the background of the project and often asked for more information about the project in particular and the field of sign language research and Deaf studies in general. On many occasions, the partner or a confidant of the Deaf senior was involved and participated in this first informal conversation. Then the interviewer introduced himself in more detail to the participant(s) and described his personal family background including the fact that he himself has Deaf parents. In this context, the possibility was often considered that the senior might know the interviewer's parents, or that the parents of the interviewer and the interviewee him- or herself had attended the same school for the Deaf. These questions were asked mainly out of pure curiosity and were not relevant for the interview itself. However, whenever it turned out that the senior was familiar with the interviewer's parents, or that some institution has been visited by both, the relationship between the interviewer and the interviewee became immediately more familiar and relaxed. If this was not the case, an attempt was made to create a trusting atmosphere during a longer preparatory conversation.

After this first informal phase of getting to know each other, the privacy policy was discussed in detail with the Deaf senior. In this context, the interviewer always offered the senior to show him or her a video of the German Sign Language (DGS) translation of the privacy policy and the questionnaire on the laptop. Almost all seniors rejected this and preferred to either read the privacy policy themselves and/or get it explained by the interviewer. The joint answering of all questions of the metadata and the consent form (see Figure 1) always took quite some time. Occasionally, the senior needed a short break in between.

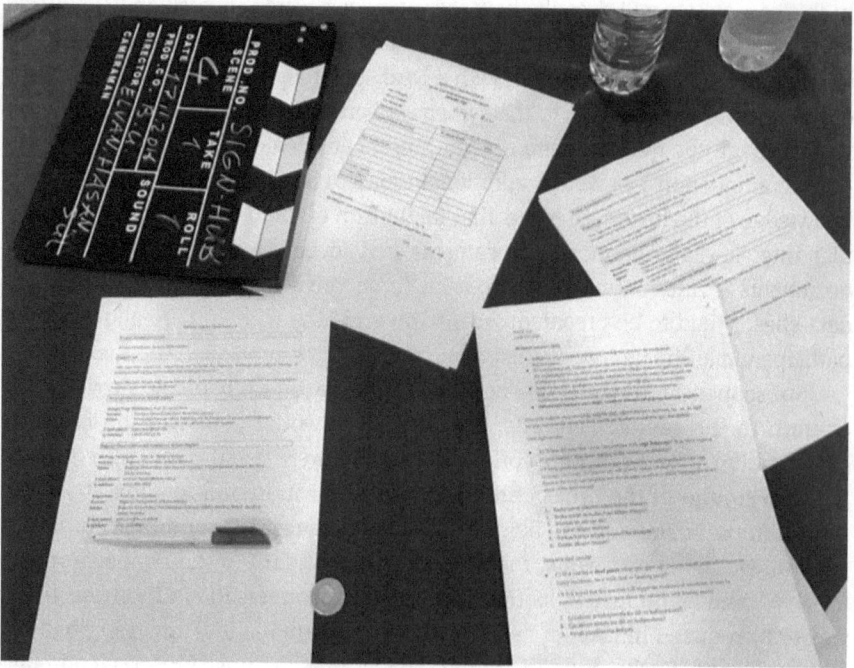

Figure 1: Preparatory materials (metadata sheet, privacy policy, consent form, . . .) used in Turkey.

Afterwards, the interviewer decided together with the senior in which room the interview should take place. Finally, the interviewer set up the two cameras and the floor lamp and arranged, if necessary, also the seating.

After the setup was complete, the interview started. Before switching on the cameras, the senior was informed about the approximate sequence of questions (childhood – youth – work – Deaf club – etc.) and the questions that will open the interview. In this way, the interviewer tried to create a relaxed atmosphere and to reduce the initial nervousness of the interviewee.

The first question in all interviews in Germany was always "What's your name, and where were you born?" After this general opening, the main part of the questionniare was discussed step by step. As mentioned above, this part had been developed in close collaboration within the SIGN-HUB project as a general guideline for the interviews with elderly signers. The main aim was to achieve optimal comparability for later evaluation of the interviews and comparisons between different sign languages. The following list gives an overview of the most important questions that have been asked during each interview:

- When did you first come into contact with sign language? Did (members of) your family use sign language in daily communication? Was sign language used at the school you attended?
- Are there any memories of your schooldays you would like to share?
- Did you have any Deaf peers when you grew up? Do you recall any adventures or funny incidents with Deaf or hearing peers?
- Are you/have you been married? How did you and your partner meet?
- What kind of profession did you (and your partner) practise?
- Do you have family? How often do you see your children, grand children, and other relatives?
- Are you an active member of a Deaf club, or have you been in the past? How important are/were these activities for you? Do/did you have a special role in the club?
- Have you been a member of a club, e.g., a sports club, organized by hearing people or by hearing and Deaf people? What were your experiences? Did hearing members make any effort to integrate you and to communicate with you?
- What was/is your favorite time in the past? Do you have any hobbies? How do you spend an ordinary day?
- What was the life like in {name of city} when you were young? Did you move to a bigger city for education or to join the Deaf community?
- In everyday life, were you often faced with problems because you were Deaf? Do you think life is easier now for Deaf people?

- Do you have experiences with Deaf art such as Deaf theatre companies or sign language poetry? Do you know any 'Deaf jokes'?
- Do you have any specific memories of life during wartime/post-war/cold war and other important historical events?
- Deaf people are a specific minority within the society you live in. Do/did you have contact with members of other minorities, no matter whether they were Deaf or hearing, for instance, homosexuals or members of certain religious or ethnic groups?
- Do you think that participation of Deaf people in political and social life has changed over the years?
- Do you have contact with Deaf people outside your region/country? Have you travelled abroad? How is your experience of meeting Deaf people in/of other countries?
- Do you use digital media (Internet, Facebook, video conferencing, . . .)? If so, do you think that digital media have changed your social and/or personal life?

All questions of the general part of the questionnaire have been asked for all six sign languages documented in this project. The list above illustrates that this part includes questions on the family background of the Deaf seniors, their educational path, sign and spoken language acquisition, the social life during school, possibly at a boarding school with foster parents, the social life in Deaf clubs, job training and profession, friends, family formation, private life, communicative, cultural and social barriers in daily life, the use of modern media, and the relationship to other minority groups.

In the second part of the interview, language- and culture-specific aspects were discussed. In Germany, for instance, this part included questions on personal experiences during the Second World War, the post-war period, the economic developments in the 1950s in Germany, and the political and cultural changes in the 1960s. The interviewer also asked the seniors about the division of Germany, the reunion in the 1990s, and the political, economic and cultural developments till today.

Finally, the senior was asked to recollect memories of elderly Deaf people she or he had met in her or his youth and to remember the way these people had lived and, if possible, lost signs these people had used. Sometimes the interviewees could remember some older signs that nowadays are almost extinct in their sign language.

After the first interviews, the interviewer step by step gained more experience in how to conduct the interviews. As a consequence, she or he internalized the questions and could thus more easily adapt the structure of the interview spontaneously to the conversational setting. The interviewer no longer had to tick off question by question but was able to organize a more natural and fluent conversation with the interviewee. As a consequence, the interviewee felt more comfortable, and in many cases, the seniors began to talk more freely about their life after the first question and also introduced additional topics and interesting experiences. A general rule for the interviewer was to never interrupt the senior during the interview but to develop strategies to take notes which questions of the questionnaire had already been answered by the senior. The remaining (unanswered) questions were then asked at a later stage of the interview.

4 Technology and preparation

The technical equipment consisted of two cameras with the respective tripods, one high floor lamp, and one laptop with the sign language translations of the privacy statement, the consent form, and additional informations about the SIGN-HUB project. All six teams used the same equipment. On the basis of the general questionnaire, the responsible local team developed a questionnaire in the corresponding spoken language as a guideline for the interviews. In addition, the local teams translated the general consent form, which was, if necessary, adapted to regulations specific for the respective country or region. This consent form was given to the interviewer together with a hard disk containing all materials necessary for conducting the interviews. For some sign languages, the interviewers prepared the country- and culture-specific questions and aspects of the consent form together with the local team. Each team composed a translation of the consent forms into the local sign language that could be shown before the interviews if necessesary (see Figure 2). Alternatively, the interviewer translated parts of the consent forms into the local sign language at the beginning of the session with an elderly Deaf person.

Depending on the sign language variety the Deaf senior was using and the senior's communication skills, the interviewer adapted his or her use of sign language before and during the interviews to establish an optimal communicative setting for the senior. This adaption could involve the use of more basic signs, local variants of a sign, explanations in combination with specific signs, mouthings, a different system of fingerspelling, or signs from the signed system based on the surrounding spoken language. In almost all participating countries and regions, the existence of different Deaf institutes and schools for the Deaf has led to the development of a certain degree of lexical and grammatical variation and correspondingly different varieties of each sign language

Figure 2: Deaf seniors in Turkey are watching the video with the Turkish Sign Language translation of the consent form.

(cf. Geraci et al. 2011; Eichmann & Rosenstock 2014). In addition, for many sign languages, national or regional standards have either not yet been developed or these standards are not used by elderly Deaf signers (for standardization, cf. Schermer 2012, 2016; Jaeger 2017). Therefore, some elderly Deaf persons were using a specific local variety of their sign language, which implied that the language used in the interviews had to be adjusted to the interviewee in order to establish a common basis for communication. Other specific adaptions were at times necessary when Deaf seniors used older varieties of the local sign language, were orally oriented because of oral education at school, or suffered from some problems with concentration or memory lapses.

5 Experiences of the interviewers

5.1 The interviewer teams

At the very beginning of the SIGN-HUB project, a Deaf person with close connections to the Deaf community was selected as responsible interviewer. Three of the interviewers were working at the universities participating in the project, the others were freelancers. In Germany, for instance, the interviewer grew up with Deaf parents and DGS as his first language. Thanks to his parents, he became integrated into the Deaf community at an early age. He was and still is in close contact with the older Deaf generation that was interviewed in the project, and he is familiar with linguistic and cultural characteristics specific of this generation. Hence, he was able to adapt himself to the communicative preferences of the seniors easily, for instance, by using different varieties of DGS and/or

'Lautsprachbegleitende Gebärden' (LBG), a signed system used in Germany, by adjusting the degree of mouthing and the speed of signing, and by using the two-handed DGS fingerspelling system preferred by the older generation instead of the one-handed system used by younger signers (for variation and change in finger spelling, cf. Sutton-Spence, Woll & Allsop 1990).

The Deaf interviewers of the other sign languages investigated in this project have a similar linguistic and cultural background. Most of them have Deaf family members and grew up with the sign language of their family as their first language. A few of the interviewers grew up in hearing families but acquired sign language at a very early age. Sign language is thus the native language of all interviewers and also the language used in daily communication. Also, all interviewers are strongly involved in the national Deaf communities. In addition, all interviewers had access to higher education and have excellent skills in the local written language. This bilingual competence was important for the preparation and translation of the questionnaire as well as for the synopsis, translation, subtitling, and annotation of the interviews. And, last but not least, they had previous experience and expertise in data collection procedures and in conducting the interviews, one of the most important skills for such an ambitious project.

For three sign languages (DGS, LSE, and NGT), one and the same interviewer conducted all interviews. For the other three sign languages (LIS, LSC, and TİD), more than one interviewer was involved in the project. Italy, for example, implemented a more complex procedure including various local interviewers, one principal interviewer, and one general coordinator, who were all responsible for conducting the interviews. At the beginning of the project, the general coordinator instructed the local interviewers about the project, the structure of the interviews, and how to conduct them. The main task of the local interviewers was then to manage the recruitment of the Deaf seniors since they all knew the elderly Deaf people in their region very well and could thus easily approach the seniors and ask them whether they were interested in participating in an interview. All local interviewers were teachers of LIS and already had experience in conducting interviews. The principal interviewer received additional intensive training on the history of LIS and the Italian Deaf community organized by the National Deaf Institute, the Italian Association of Oral History, and the Institute of Cognitive Science of the Italian Center for Scientific Research (*Consiglio Nazionale delle Ricerche*, CNR). Both, the local interviewers and the principal interviewer formed the interviewing teams. Typically, while the local interviewer was the contact person and the confidant of the Deaf seniors, the principal interviewer was the more experienced supervisor of the interviews.

5.2 Recruitment of interview partners

In Germany, the interviewer designed a flyer and a circular e-mail with detailed information about the project in general and the interviews in particular. In a first step, the e-mail and the flyer were sent to the German Deaf Society (*Deutscher Gehörlosen-Bund*, DGB), Deaf senior representatives in each state, and various social and church institutions taking care of elderly Deaf people. In a second step, the interviewer contacted several organizers of regular meetings of elderly Deaf people and asked them if he could personally introduce himself and the project at one of these meetings. The general interest in the project was huge, and the interviewer got the opportunity to visit several senior meetings in different states of Germany. In his presentations, he briefly introduced the SIGN-HUB project, described the aim and structure of the interviews, and explained the privacy policy, that is, that the data would be anonymized and treated confidentially, and that each interviewee could decide on the use and distribution of his or her interview. After the presentation, the interviewer answered questions from the seniors and had short discussions with individual people interested in the project.

Although elderly Deaf people were very interested in and positive about the project, these presentations did not always guarantee interview appointments with Deaf seniors. Therefore, the organizers of senior meetings were asked to enquire again whether seniors who have previously expressed interest in participating were now ready to make an interview appointment. Very often, appointments were also made through local contact persons, as many seniors are not familiar with modern media. In many cases, dedicated contact persons such as pastors, caregivers, and senior representatives reminded the seniors to make an appointment with the interviewer. Some seniors were also recruited with the help of the Deaf parents and Deaf coda friends of the interviewers.

5.3 Advertisement and dissemination

At various big events such as cultural festivals of the Deaf and local and national senior meetings, the interviewers (sometimes together with other members of the SIGN-HUB team) gave presentations and distributed flyers advertising the project. Besides that, the interviewers gave many short presentations at various smaller local events for the Deaf and also for hearing people to inform not only elderly Deaf people but also family members and friends, as well as a general audience about this important project fostering the linguistic and cultural heritage of elderly Deaf people. Even at events not directly related to the Deaf community, for instance, specific scientific dissemination events for a general audience or for children, the interviewers introduced the project, described the unique linguistic and cultural background of elderly Deaf people in Europe, and explained the importance of this project for archiving and documenting their cultural and linguistic heritage.

The situation in the Netherlands was different from the other countries because many elderly Deaf people live together in *De Gelderhorst*, a special apartment complex for elderly Deaf people (see chapters by Reiff-de Groen & van Veen and by Hiddinga et al., this volume). Therefore, many interviews have been conducted there. The interviewer and the coordinator presented the goal of the project at *De Gelderhorst* together with a local contact person; about 20 elderly Deaf people attended this meeting. After the presentation, the interviewer already made individual appointments with seniors that were interested in the project. In addition, the interviewer also went to a recreational meeting where she gave another presentation. Again, individual appointments were made after the presentation.

The networks of Deaf friends and family members of the interviewers generally provided strong support to the project and especially to the recruitment of interview partners. A general aim of all interviewers was to make appointments with as many and as diverse Deaf elderly people as possible, including male and female seniors, seniors from different ethnic groups if possible, Deaf people from different Deaf institutes and from different regions, as well as hetero- and homosexual people (among other groups). Another important aspect for the recruitment of Deaf seniors was schooling: Some elderly Deaf people went to boarding schools, others stayed at home or lived with host families. The interviewers were also looking for elderly Deaf people who had Deaf parents or even grew up in a Deaf family with many Deaf family members across different generations. And finally, some of the elderly Deaf people who participated in the interviews were very active members of the Deaf community while others did not participate much in Deaf activities and Deaf organizations.

5.4 Challenges

In most countries and regions, the recruitment of Deaf seniors was faced with two main challenges. On the one hand, it was not easy to get in contact with Deaf seniors, especially with seniors living in more rural areas. On the other hand, many elderly Deaf people turned out to be quite camera-shy, that is, they were interested in participating in the interviews but did not want to be videotaped. In some areas, Deaf seniors live quite isolated in smaller villages in a mostly hearing neighborhood and have only limited contact to other people. In addition, modern media such as e-mail, Facebook, Twitter, or facetime are not familiar to many Deaf seniors. Hence, getting in contact with Deaf seniors was at times difficult. Another hindering aspect was that most elderly Deaf people do not have higher education. Therefore, it is quite understandable that some seniors were insecure and suspicious of sharing personal stories and presenting private information in front of a camera. Moreover, sometimes it was difficult for the interviewer to explain the meaning of the project's privacy policy and confidential data handling according to the national data protection law.

Furthermore, some Deaf seniors did not want to present parts of their lives in front of the camera. Instead, the interviewer was asked if it was possible to document the interview in written form rather than on videotape. This means that the Deaf seniors were keen to tell their life stories and to share details of their biography but not in front of a camera. In many cases, a careful explanation of the importance of videos for the documentation of life stories told in sign language convinced the seniors, and they agreed that their individual life story could only be told in their sign language and that video recording was thus necessary to document the interview. In a few cases, the interview could, however, not be conducted.

Compared to the other sign languages, the LIS interviewers were faced with the greatest challenges in organizing the interviews in each region because of limited availability of Deaf seniors and suitable locations for the interview, issues with managing technical requirements, and limited time and funding for travelling of the general coordinator, the principal interviewer, and the cameraman.

In the Netherlands, like in Germany, the interviewers spent quite some time to get in contact with elderly Deaf people and to make individual appointments for the interviews. In the Netherlands, however, modern media like Whatsapp with video messages and facetime turned out to be very helpful because some people who did not respond to the e-mails of the interviewer actively used video-based communication systems.

After the interview, some elderly Deaf people asked the interviewers whether he or she could send them immediately a copy of the interview video because they wanted to show it to family members and friends. In this case, it was hard for interviewers to put the seniors off until the end of the project and to explain why at this stage of the project, preparing and distributing additional videos for family members and friends was difficult or almost impossible.

5.5 Meeting with Deaf seniors

As soon as a Deaf senior had agreed to participate in an interview, the interviewer arranged with the senior the appropriate location and time for the interview. If possible, the interviewer always met the requests and wishes of the Deaf seniors. In most cases, the interview took place at the Deaf senior's home, mostly in their living room or in their kitchen (see Figure 3).

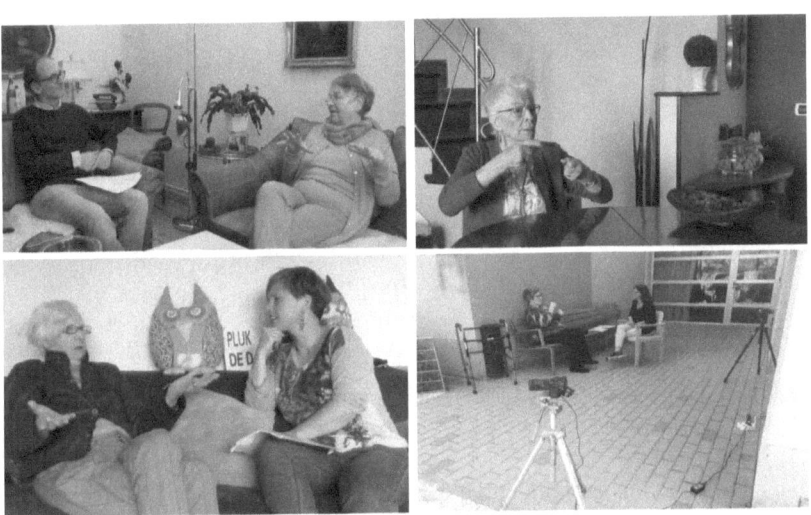

Figure 3: Typical settings of interviews: in the living room (top left: Germany; bottom left: The Netherlands), in the kitchen (top right: Italy), or on the terrace (bottom right: Catalonia) of the Deaf senior.

Some interviews took place at the building of the local Deaf association or a facility where religious services for Deaf seniors usually take place (see Figure 4). In case the interview took place in a public facility, the interviewers typically prepared a coffee corner for the interviewee. For interviews at the senior's home, the interviewers would bring along a cake or some other sweets.

As already mentioned above, for three sign languages (DGS, LSE, and NGT), the interviewers went to the interviews alone, bringing along two cameras, a laptop, and the metadata and consent forms on paper. In Italy, the interviewer team consisted of three people. In the beginning, the Italian interviewers were prepared to show the sign language version of the consent form on a laptop. Later, however, they did not need the laptop anymore because the Deaf seniors typically did not want to see the videos on the laptop. Instead, as already mentioned above, the seniors preferred to discuss and, if necessary, go through the written consent form together with the interviewers, who translated the form into sign language. One advantage of this procedure was that the interviewers could already adapt their sign language to the needs of the interviewee before the interview

Figure 4: Typical setting of an interview in a public building (Italy).

started, that is, when explaining the consent form to the elderly Deaf person. In Turkey, some seniors asked for support by hearing family members, who were present in the room when discussing and signing the consent form. For the other sign languages, the Deaf seniors discussed and signed the consent form usually without consulting family members (see Figure 5).

In order to establish a collaborative and intimate atmosphere between the participants and the interviewers, the first half hour of each visit was spent with free, informal conversation while the camera and the floor lamp were set up (see Figure 6).

Ideally, the setup was carried out by other members of the team, if available, so that the interviewer could attend to the senior. When the interview started, the research assistants waited in another room, alone or with other family members of the interviewee, to avoid any distraction from and influence on the interview. That is, research assistants (especially hearing members of the research team) were only present during the camera setup to avoid any negative influence on the naturalness of the communicative setting. During the interviews, the Deaf interviewer asked research assistants for help only when she or he was the only interviewer, and one of the cameras was used to record pictures or objects that were important in the conversation (see Figure 7).

An interesting constellation emerged when Deaf couples were interviewed. Usually, the interviewers complied with the seniors' wishes to participate in the interview as a couple. This situation was particularly challenging for the

Conducting interviews with elderly Deaf people: opportunities and challenges — 33

Figure 5: Deaf senior is signing the consent form (Italy).

Figure 6: The interviewer team explains the interviewee the technical setup (Turkey).

Figure 7: Photographs presented by interviewees during the interviews (top left: Turkey; top right and bottom: The Netherlands).

interviewer. In Turkey, for instance, an illiterate female participant was faced with the disapproval of her husband during the interview, expressed in a judgmental and accusing manner, for misrepresenting events. In another interview in Turkey, the husband expressed his discomfort about his wife telling too much about their private life. In general, the wife was the more talkative part of the couple and obviously enjoyed sharing anecdotes from the past.

In Turkey, like in Germany, Italy and Spain, most interviews took place at the senior's home. Only a few interviews were conducted in a studio in Ankara, a Deaf club in İzmir, and in a hotel in Diyarbakır. Some participants opted for an interview outside their homes. One reason was that they did not want to cause any inconvenience to hearing members of the family. One Deaf senior stated this explicitly to the interviewer.

Interviews at a senior's home sometimes caused practical problems when the interviewer had trouble setting up the cameras and the light in a small room and establishing an optimal setting for documentation. In addition, the interview sometimes had to be paused since the interviewee was interrupted by or had to take care of family members during the interview. On the other hand, the interviewers observed that the interviewees who were recorded at home generally felt more comfortable when answering the questions. Obviously, the interviewees could remember the past more easily in a familiar environment, as their homes are filled with memories. Therefore, it was generally an advantage to visit a Deaf senior at his or her home. The language used in a studio or a Deaf club was somewhat more formal and restrained in comparison to the cozy communication atmosphere that emanated in a private environment. In the latter enviroment, the interviewers automatically preferred to also use a more informal and affable register.

5.6 Communication with Deaf seniors

The communication with the Deaf seniors usually worked very well. Only in a few situations was it difficult for the interviewer to understand a Deaf senior. Reasons for such communicative problems were, for the most part, either of a linguistic (e.g., variation in the sign language used, especially the use of older, dialectal, and uncommon varieties of signs, as well as atypical use of mouthings) or cognitive nature (e.g., problems with concentration or memory lapses and poor involvement of the interview partner). Especially the first factor, that is, the linguistic variation and change of sign languages, is now well documented for many different sign languages (cf. Herreweghe & Vermeerbergen 2004; Adam 2012; Hillenmeyer & Tilmann 2012; Janzen 2012; Schembri & Johnston 2012; Jaeger & Heßmann 2016; Hanke et al. 2017; Macht & Steinbach 2019).

In Germany, the linguistic situation in the interviews was quite diverse. On the one hand, some interviews took place in LBG (*Lautsprachbegleitende Gebärden*), the signed system typically used in Germany in educational settings, accompanied by clear mouthings of the corresponding spoken words (cf. Boyes Braem & Sutton-Spence 2001). Most seniors grew up in an orally dominated educational environment and were only taught in spoken and written German at school. Additionally, Deaf seniors would sometimes ask the interviewer not to sign the questions too fast and to use mouthings if possible. On the other hand, some Deaf seniors preferred to use DGS. It was striking that in such interviews, the interview partners were typically children of Deaf parents, that is, despite the oral tradition in Deaf education in Germany, these people grew up with DGS as their first language (for the history of Deaf education, cf. Moores 2010; Plaza-Pust 2012; Borgwaldt 2012). Sometimes, communication problems during the interviews were not caused by language use but were simply due to weaker motor skills of Deaf seniors, which resulted in manually reduced forms of signs.

In the Netherlands, in Spain and in Catalonia, a few elderly people were also strongly orally oriented. Again, the interviewers adapted their sign language by using mouthings much more frequently, and also more explicitly, than usually. Sometimes interviewers and interviewees wrote things down on paper for a better understanding. An important strategy, used in many interviews to achieve a better mutual understanding, was for the interviewers to repeat part of what an interviewee told them. These repetitions did not only show the interviewee that the interviewer had understood him or her, but it also encouraged the interviewee to continue and to share more stories.

During some interviews, very specific problems arose. In the Netherlands, for example, two elderly women did not want the interviewer to record the interview on video. They also did not give their consent to making the video publicly available on the project's platform. Instead, they were more interested in chatting and gossiping with the interviewer. However, the interviewer discovered that both seniors were sharing really interesting life stories, which she would have loved to record on video. But since the two elderly women did not give their consent, the interviewer strictly followed their wish and did not record the interviews.

In another situation, the interview had to be stopped half-way because the elderly woman was sick and could not continue. The interviewer made a new appointment but sadly, shortly afterwards, the interviewee passed away, and the interviewer could not complete the interview with this person. On another occasion, a very old lady gave the interviewer first the permission to use the videos, but changed her mind during the interview and asked the interviewer not to make the gossip included in the interview available to other people. This caused a dilemma for the interviewer because he wanted to respect her request but also wanted to make the interview available for research as complete as possible. Hence, the interviewer discussed the issue with the responsible project leader when preparing the annotations and subtitles for this video. At that point, the old lady unfortunately had already passed away. Since the interviewer knew her family very well, he asked the daughters of this lady what to do with the interview. The daughters agreed on not making the interview publicly accessible but gave permission to use the video at least internally for research purposes, that is, projects investigating the life stories, the language, and the culture of elderly Deaf people.

In Turkey, many seniors emphasized that they were very happy to have been invited for the interviews since they were aware that they had important topics to talk about and could thus make an important contribution to a research project documenting their language and culture. The Turkish team assumed that they felt honored to be consulted as an expert, and that this was a welcome opportunity for them to share their lives, memories, and experiences. In addition, the interviews were an important opportunity for the Deaf seniors to show their hearing family members that the local sign language and Deaf culture as well as the specific life experiences of Deaf family members are an important contribution to the linguistic and cultural heritage not only of the Deaf minority but also of the hearing mainstream society. The interviews thus had the potential to directly improve the recognition of the Deaf senior in his or her family and of the 'cultural heritage' of Deaf people in general.

Some interviewees had difficulties in understanding the concept of 'cultural heritage'. The interviewer explained that the interviews are an essential part of a bigger project that aims at a documentation of the linguistic and cultural heritage of the sign language community. During the interviews, the interviewees frequently asked when they would get the opportunity to watch the interviews. Many seniors assumed that they will be broadcast on television. During the interview, the interviewers usually promised to address this issue at the end of the interview and made an effort to bring back the attention of the senior to the topic of the interview.

Most family members of the interviewees had a supporting and positive attitude towards the research team during the whole interview process. Both Deaf and hearing family members assisted the interviewer team in explaining the consent form and in preparing the setup. This experience was evidence that the general descriptions and explanations provided at the outset by the interviewers were found satisfactory. While hearing family members of some of the interviewees left the interviewee alone with the interviewer, others stayed in the room during the interview. In the latter case, no questions were directed to the (hearing) family members in order to maintain the focus on the Deaf participants of the interview.

Because of some miscommunication before one interview in Diyarbakır, Turkey, the hearing family members of the interviewee did not expect the visit of the interviewer team. Because the family had been deceived in the past by people who wanted to take advantage of them, the family members did not allow the interviewer team in. The interviewers had to convince the family members with explanations about the purpose of their visit at the home of the Deaf relative.

5.7 Problems encountered during the interviews

Most of the interviews proceeded harmoniously and without problematic incidents. In a few cases, an interviewee, who had asked her/his spouse or caregiver to stay in the room during the interview, interacted with this additional person in the middle of the interview, although it had been agreed that neither the spouse nor caregiver should be involved in the interview. However, such moments did not pose a huge problem for the interviewer and were always accompanied with humor. Only in one case, an interview had to be stopped prematurely because the Deaf senior was no longer willing to continue the interview and sign in front of the camera despite the consent given before the interview.

Sometimes, it happened that during the interview, interviewees either started to scold spouses, to talk negatively about former life companions, relatives, superiors, or to tell very personal anecdotes. In such cases, the interviewer asked again whether this information could also be made available to the public. Often such episodes were then 'censored' on request of the Deaf senior. In one case, a Deaf senior asked to divide the interview into two parts: a public part, which can be made available to the general public, and a confidential part, which may only be used internally for project-related studies.

In Italy, the interviewers had to cancel two interviews out of a total of thirty interviews. Almost all of the Italian Deaf seniors were happy to tell about their lives and to answer questions, even though only three of them had previous experience with biographical interviews. A few questions were not well understood by some seniors. The answers to those questions were, thus, rarely exhaustive. The preferred topics of the interviews were family, school, relationships with other Deaf people, and work – this holds true for LIS as well as for the other sign languages.

In Turkey, the interviewers decided to ask the questions of the questionnaire in strict order. However, when the interviewees connected two different subjects, the interviewer felt free to ask a related question which would have come later in the order of the questions. Moreover, if necessary, the interviewers asked additional closed or open questions and provided clarifications about the content of a specific question in order to provide a context for the topic addressed by the question. Occasionally, one of the interviewees did not understand the main idea of the question and talked about irrelevant details. In such situations, interviewers followed different strategies. They either waited for the interviewee to finish the story and then made an effort to clarify the question, or they asked another question and returned to the question not answered properly later.

5.8 Memorable moments

Each individual interview was a very special and memorable moment for the interviewer. When the interview took place at an interviewee's home, interviewers usually brought a cake or sweets, but often the Deaf seniors themselves had already prepared a warm welcome with coffee and home-baked cake for the interviewers. They typically gave them first a short guided tour of their home and were full of pleasant anticipation of the visit. On the one hand, many seniors had joyful events and positive experiences to report. On the other hand, they also remembered negative experiences and let the interviewer participate in the emotions that came back when sharing such experiences. The interviewers were touched by the fact that many seniors said after the interview that they "had rarely had such a good conversation about their own person". Some seniors said that the interview had made them more aware of specific aspects of their own personal circumstances, and that some situations and issues had become more understandable. In many cases, the seniors asked the interviewer for another visit. For the interviewers, the interviews were also moving for the reason that they gained better and clearer insight into their own history as a member of the Deaf community and in the life of older Deaf family members.

In Italy, especially in interviews with women, a Deaf companion attended the interview sometimes. The interviewers felt that it was not appropriate to insist and ask the companion to wait outside during the interview (or at least to remain out of sight of the interviewee). During an interview in Turin, the interviewees' dog managed to enter the room and to jump immediately on the interviewee's lap. Typically, the interviewers spent quite some time at the interviewee's home before and after the interview to talk to the elderly Deaf persons and their families. This additional time spent together was not only important for the success of the interviews but was also a very nice experience, not only for the interviewees but also for the interviewers. In some cases, the interviewer even made friends with the senior and his or her family. In Turin, the Italian team interviewed a prominent member of the Deaf Association, who was an expert in Deaf history. During the interview, it became apparent that he was a highly impressive person, very smart, educated, very kind, and always actively involved in the Deaf community. Unfortunately, he died shortly after the interview. His death is a grievous loss for the Deaf community in Italy. In Salerno, the interviewer team conducted the interviews in the venue of the Deaf Association, but they had not been warned that there was another event in the next room. Therefore, some interviewees, who wanted to participate in this event, were in a hurry to leave. Because of this coincidence, two interviews scheduled for that day could not take place.

In the Netherlands and Germany, the interviewers were very touched by stories about the long and painful segregation of children from their families when attending a boarding school. The Dutch interviewer reports that now, when walking through the old Deaf institute, her thoughts are always with the elderly Deaf people who have experienced this painful separation from their parents.

In Turkey, the interviewees were eager to share memorabilia at their homes such as photographs, old magazines, newspapers, and other objects (see Figure 8). One participant in İzmir shared brochures of national and international Deaf events. Another interviewee, who used to be a tailor, showed the dresses she had made herself. As a general tendency, the interviewees were more talkative and had more vivid memories when it came to personal life stories and school experiences than when reporting on social and political events.

Figure 8: A Deaf senior is presenting a photo album with old pictures to the interviewer (Italy).

It was also very interesting to observe that some interviewees were brave enough to talk about very negative memories and would even come back to these negative topics during the interview over and over again. Some participants requested certain portions of the interview to be deleted because they got carried away and realized they had shared too intimate personal details. When talking about persons and places, the interviewers realized that the interviewees knew the signs for these people and places very well. Sometimes the interviewees remembered the corresponding name signs but could not remember the Turkish names.

In general, the interviewees were more attentive at lunchtime than in the evening. Almost all participants enjoyed the interviews and were eager to continue the interview even after three hours. Only in some places, e.g., in İzmir, the interviews had to be kept short because the goal was to interview as many people as possible. In these interviews, the interviewees therefore were not able to address the questions in great detail.

6 Conclusion

Through the effort of all teams involved in this important project, and especially thanks to the local Deaf interviewers, an impressive number of life stories of elderly Deaf people could be collected for six different sign languages. Only the close cooperation of Deaf seniors and Deaf interviewers made this project a huge success. The interviews provided many interesting new insights, not only for the interviewers but also for the Deaf seniors, and they will be the central building blocks of a new international archive that allows us to discover a new and so far partly invisible world. This unique archive can now be studied in a variety of ways, not only by scientists but also by the interested Deaf and hearing public. We hope that, in the long run, the resulting studies will give the impetus for many different linguistic, historic, cultural, and sociological documentations of the unique experiences and memories of this generation of Deaf people.

The interviews will hopefully contribute to a better understanding of the fascinating Deaf culture in Europe and its history. A first evaluation of the interviews reveals that despite many individual as well as cultural and historical differences between individual countries and regions, the life stories of Deaf seniors also reveal many interesting similarities, even across national and regional borders. All Deaf seniors constitute a unique linguistic and cultural minority in their country and region, living in a hearing environment in which the use of spoken language is dominant. Because of the ignorance of many hearing people, most Deaf seniors have had unpleasant experiences and, as a consequence, felt different from the hearing majority. In the Netherlands, the Deaf interviewer described the communicative barriers and cultural isolation she had experienced as a little girl as follows:

> When I was a little girl, I missed a lot of life stories from my hearing grandparents but my mother often made an effort to interpret for me when I asked my grandparents about something like, for example, their experiences during the Second World War. But I still felt different. When I talked with the elderly Deaf people, I felt more of the same thing: 'We are Deaf so we

share experiences as Deaf persons.' So, I listened to their life stories, also understanding more about how they experienced the Second World War, and more of other stories. My awareness about the huge differences between the past and the present has grown; how the present has developed from the past: for instance, the emancipation of Deaf, women and homosexuals and the larger diversity of identities that is so much more obvious and appreciated right now. For this experience, I am grateful to the elderly Deaf people who have been fighting for this.

[Annemieke van Kampen, 5 April 2019]

Additionally, the Deaf seniors all belong to an impressive local, regional, national, and international Deaf community with a comparable history as well as similar experiences and hopes.

Acknowledgments: This contribution has been possible thanks to the SIGN-HUB project, which has received funding from the European Union's Horizon 2020 research and innovation program under grant agreement No 693349, and the project "(Un)sichtbare Lebensgeschichten", funded by the Ministry for Science and Culture of Lower Saxony (MWK). We would like to thank everyone who contributed to making this project a huge success, especially the interviewers, coordinators, and research assistants: Claudio Baj, Kadir Gökgöz, Aslı Göksel, Gabriella Grioli, Jana Hosemann, Emiliano Mereghetti, Chiara Di Monte, Dorothee Nyga, Roland Pfau, Susanna Ricci Bitti, Jordina Sánchez Amat, Burcu Saral, and Süleyman S. Taşçı. Without the extremely committed interview teams, the documentation of the life stories of elderly Deaf people, a unique linguistic and cultural heritage, would not have been possible. And last but not least, we would like to thank the responsible editor Roland Pfau for his helpful comments on different versions of the manuscript.

References

Adam, Robert. 2012. Language contact and borrowing. In Pfau, Roland, Markus Steinbach & Bencie Woll (eds.), *Sign language: An international handbook*, 841–862. Berlin: De Gruyter Mouton.

Boyes Braem, Penny & Rachel Sutton-Spence (eds.) 2001. *The hands are the head of the mouth: The mouth as articulator in sign languages*. Hamburg: Signum.

Borgwaldt, Christian. 2012. Gebärdensprachpädagogik: DGS im bilingualen Schulunterricht. In Eichmann, Hanna, Martje Hansen & Jens Heßmann (eds.), *Handbuch Deutsche Gebärdensprache*, 325–342. Hamburg: Signum.

Eichmann, Hanna & Rachel Rosenstock. 2014. Regional variation in German Sign Language: The role of schools (re-)visited. *Sign Language Studies* 14. 175–202.

Geraci, Carlo, Katia Battaglia, Anna Cardinaletti, Carlo Cecchetto, Caterina Donati, Serena Giudice & Emiliano Mereghetti. 2011. The LIS Corpus Project: A discussion of sociolinguistic variation in the lexicon. *Sign Language Studies* 11. 528–574.

Hanke, Thomas, Reiner Konrad, Gabriele Langer, Anke Müller & Sabrina Wähl. 2017. *Detecting regional and age variation in a growing corpus of DGS*. Poster presented at the Workshop Corpus-based Approaches to Sign Language Linguistics: Into the Second Decade, Birmingham.

Herreweghe, Mieke Van & Myriam Vermeerbergen (eds.) 2004. *To the lexicon and beyond: Sociolinguistics in European Deaf communities*. Washington, DC: Gallaudet University Press.

Hillenmeyer, Margit & Savina Tilmann. 2012. Variation in der DGS. In Eichmann, Hanna, Martje Hansen & Jens Heßmann (eds.), *Handbuch Deutsche Gebärdensprache*, 245–270. Hamburg: Signum.

Jaeger, Hanna. 2017. Modality matters: On social forces determining what is a standard in German Sign Language (DGS). *Linguistik Online* 81. 45–58.

Jaeger, Hanna & Jens Heßmann. 2016. Mikrovariation in Gebärdensprachen. In Ulrike Domahs & Beatrice Primus (eds.), *Handbuch Laut, Gebärde, Buchstabe*, 321–334. Berlin: de Gruyter.

Janzen, Terry. 2012. Lexicalization and grammaticalization. In Pfau, Roland, Markus Steinbach & Bencie Woll (eds.), *Sign language: An international handbook*, 816–841. Berlin: De Gruyter Mouton.

Macht, Claudia & Markus Steinbach. 2019. Regionalsprachliche Merkmale in der Deutschen Gebärdensprache. In Joachim Herrgen & Jürgen Erich Schmidt (eds.), *Sprache und Raum. Ein internationales Handbuch der Sprachvariation*, 914–935. Berlin: De Gruyter Mouton.

Moores, Donald F. 2010. The history of language and communication issues in deaf education. In Marc Marschark & Patricia E. Spencer (eds.), *The Oxford handbook of deaf studies, language, and education, vol. 2*, 17–30. Oxford: Oxford University Press.

Plaza-Pust, Carolina. 2012. Deaf education and bilingualism. In Pfau, Roland, Markus Steinbach & Bencie Woll (eds.), *Sign language: An international handbook*, 949–979. Berlin: De Gruyter Mouton.

Schembri, Adam & Trevor Johnston. 2012. Sociolinguistic aspects of variation and change. In Pfau, Roland, Markus Steinbach & Bencie Woll (eds.), *Sign language: An international handbook*, 788–816. Berlin: De Gruyter Mouton.

Schermer, Trude. 2012. Language planing. In Pfau, Roland, Markus Steinbach & Bencie Woll (eds.), *Sign language: An international handbook*, 889–908. Berlin: De Gruyter Mouton.

Schermer, Trude. 2016. Language variation and standardization. In Anne Baker, Beppie van den Bogaerde, Roland Pfau & Trude Schermer (eds.), *The linguistics of sign language*, 279–298. Amsterdam: Benjamins.

Sutton-Spence, Rachel, Bencie Woll & Lorna Allsop. 1990. Variation and recent change in fingerspelling in British Sign Language. *Language Variation and Change* 2. 313–330.

Jana Hosemann and Markus Steinbach
In collaboration with Christa Gaisbichler, Rieke Giese, Franziska Karger, Annika Mittelstädt, Dorothee Nyga, and Benita Pangritz.

Making the life stories of Deaf seniors visible: a students' exhibition

1 How the idea of an exhibition came into being

When the SIGN-HUB project was in its second year, at the beginning of 2018, the SIGN-HUB team in Göttingen, Germany, had already collected the first 25 interviews with Deaf elderly signers. Jana Hosemann, Jens-Michael Cramer (who conducted the interviews), and Markus Steinbach were sitting in a team meeting discussing the latest deliverable and our first major step of collecting the interviews. We were also planning how we could proceed with the annotations and subtitles of the interviews, when it struck our minds: Why don't we present our first results to a broader public in an exhibition? Well, developing an exhibition, just the three of us, seemed unrealistic. But, what if we could find a group of enthusiastic students? Students who have basic knowledge of German Sign Language (*Deutsche Gebärdensprache*, DGS) and the Deaf community, students who are energetic and would not mind investing time into a course beyond the compulsory curriculum. Luckily, just at that time, a group of students was creating and directing a unique bilingual theater performance (Dickens' *Christmas Carol*), presenting the play simultaneously in German and DGS. Hence, these were the first students we asked. Also, we knew a few students who had already been involved in some of our other projects on sign language; and additionally, we could contact enthusiastic students in the DGS classes offered at Göttingen University. Consequently, we soon had an excited crew of 13 students to start this ambitious project.

2 First steps: getting everyone organized

Creating an exhibition requires content, creative ideas how to present the content, (wo)manpower, and quite some financial support. In February 2018, we applied for the students' research and teaching fellowship *Forschungsorientiertes Lehren und Lernen (FoLL)* ('research-oriented teaching and learning'), who supported our

https://doi.org/10.1515/9783110701906-003

idea with about 3,000 €, additional to project money we had already budgeted for dissemination activities. However, money is no help without people who stand behind the idea and are willing to put a lot of effort, brain power, and creativity into creating the exhibition. Hence, getting organized and becoming a team was one of our first goals. We stretched the course over two semesters, four hours of meetings every week. We needed weekly DGS-German interpreting and were lucky to find a highly committed team of interpreters who accompanied us from the very beginning until the opening of the exhibition. Once the times and course structure had been fixed, we just needed to get everyone motivated to commit to the idea and to the work that would come. The 12 credit points for the course provided by the curriculum surely didn't seem enough to compensate for the effort.

So, how did we start? At the very beginning, we met in a pub and got to know each other. We established a personal connection, shared quality time, and became a group. Instead of 'teaching' the students, Jana, Jens and Markus rather coordinated the meetings and acted like supervisors of this creative scientific process. The plan was to use the first semester to fix the content of the exhibition, in other words: watch and understand the interviews with the Deaf elderly signers, find relevant topics for the exhibition, and visit schools and archives to collect additional materials to make the exhibition more accessible and vivid. The second semester was scheduled to transform the content into pieces for the exhibition; that is, thinking about creative ways how to present the contents defined in the first semester, in order to avoid boring posters with a lot of text that nobody would bother to read. An exciting year lay ahead of us.

3 First semester (April to July 2018): content

The first challenge we faced was in fact understanding the interviews. The students' DGS competence was based on DGS courses between level 1 and level 4. However, Deaf elderly seniors, aged 70 and above, sign rather differently compared to what is generally taught in DGS introductory courses. To exemplify this discrepancy: We invited five seniors to visit our class, so we could get to know each other and learn directly about their life experiences. In order to break the ice, every student and supervisor was supposed to introduce her- or himself by spelling their name in the manual alphabet. Polite as the seniors were, they nodded friendly after each person introduced themselves. Until we noticed a little hesitation and some frowned eye brows. It turned out that the one-handed manual alphabet the Deaf community is using nowadays was not familiar to the seniors. Spelling proper names is rather a 'modern' phenomenon that is used by younger signers, but is not common to signers who grew up in the 1930s and 1940s. Conversely, elderly signers use a two-handed manual alphabet that is not known by many younger signers today. Fortunately, Jens, who had conducted the interviews, could help us to bridge this communication gap by translating the DGS signing of the seniors into DGS we would understand. Similarly, he helped us understand the interviews by preparing pre-transcriptions of the content of the interviews. Only through this, we were able to understand what the seniors were telling in the interviews. (Note, at that time of the project, we did not yet have full translations of the interviews; these only came at a later point.)

The second challenge we faced was the lack of knowledge about sign languages and Deaf culture in the hearing majority, that is, the potential visitors of our exhibition. Like in many countries all over the world, the Deaf community in Germany represents a cultural and linguistic minority, about which the majority of the hearing population has very limited knowledge. Since very little knowledge about DGS and the Deaf community is made publicly accessible to a broader audience, prejudices about Deaf people and sign languages persist. The resulting lack of knowledge leads to an intensification of the existing communicative barriers for both Deaf and hearing people. Consequently, for our exhibition, we had to select topics that are representative of the life of Deaf elderly people. In addition, we had to find ways to display these topics in a way that would be transparent to a broad (hearing) audience (see Figure 1).

Figure 1: Part of the group working on their research topics.

We decided on six main topics for our exhibition: (1) *family life*, (2) *school education*, (3) *professional education and work life*, (4) *Deaf clubs and associations*, (5) *Deaf people in Nazi Germany*, and (6) a short *introduction to German Sign Language*. With these topics, we aimed to raise awareness not only about the experiences of Deaf people in Germany but also about how their language and culture has developed. In addition, we wanted to illustrate that the Deaf community is an integral and important part of the history of each society, and that sign language and Deaf culture enrich (multilingual and multicultural) societies as a whole. One overarching goal of this project was to address prejudices against the Deaf community and to create awareness that the life of Deaf people in Germany was sometimes very hard in the past – and unfortunately sometimes still is in the present days.

In order to delve deeper into the topics, we conducted round table discussions and invited experts on different topics: for example, Elisabeth Brockmann, a historian with a hearing-impairment, who has a large private collection of documents on the sterilization of Deaf people during Nazi Germany (see Brockmann & Kozelka, this volume). Other guests were Martina Bergman, who is one of the few professional museum tour guides offering integrative tours for Deaf and hard-of-hearing people, Helmut Vogel, who is a Deaf historian and president of the German Deaf Association, and Jürgen Wolf, an expert on genealogy and the aging of minorities in Western societies.

At the end of the first semester, each group presented the results of their research in a short presentation to the whole group. Whatever each group had accomplished at that time became the foundation for the next step: transforming the content into visual pieces appropriate for an exhibition that was going to attract Deaf and hearing people, old and young people, students and non-academics, as well as people with and without knowledge about the Deaf community, Deaf history, and sign languages.

In the following, we briefly summarize the main findings for four of the six topics we prepared for the exhibition: *school education, professional education and work life, Deaf clubs and associations,* and *Deaf people in Nazi Germany*.

3.1 School education

The main points of interest about the topic *school education* were: (i) the development of schools for the deaf (from the very beginning in the 14th century until today); (ii) the educational methods that were used in the schools; (iii) what Deaf elderly people remembered in the interviews about their own school and educational experiences; (iv) how these educational landscapes and settings (with a focus on methods and didactics) have changed in the last 60 years.

The study of this topic turned out to be more difficult, challenging, and frustrating than expected. Historical documents, books and articles, private photo albums and documents, the interviews with the Deaf elderly people, and movie documentaries from different European countries helped us with the first three research questions. It was interesting but also touching to see and read the personal experiences of Deaf people with oral education, suppression of sign language, and the deprivation of their communicative abilities. The fourth research question turned out to be especially difficult because there is very little documentation on the history of the existing schools for the Deaf in Germany. The schools in each federal state and region had to be investigated separately, and most of the information had to be gathered from the individual website of each school, which, however, varied significantly in their informative quality. Fortunately, most of these websites had a section on the history of the school, thus at least making it possible to put together an approximate puzzle of the schools for the Deaf in Germany at the time when the Deaf seniors had been pupils, i.e., around the 1950s. We were interested in information about when the schools were founded, whether they concentrated on oral or bilingual teaching methods, and if it was/is possible to finish the school with the general qualification for university entrance (i.e., "Abitur"). The data we were able to collect about the situation in the 1950s and today should, however, be treated with caution, because most of the data rely on statements and information provided by the schools themselves. Interestingly, many schools provided the requested information only very cautiously and reluctantly, and sometimes even used euphemistic terms about the teaching methods they use. Sometimes, the name of the school revealed the focus of education such as, for instance, *Special School for Hearing and Communication*, indicating an orally centered education. Other schools that either have started a bilingual program, or that considered the implementation of a bilingual program, or that at least introduced sign language classes in their program, typically emphasized this aspect on their website. They referred to this educational strategy as "a sign language component" or "a bilingual focus" of education. We defined the former as *somewhat oral* schools and the latter as *somewhat bilingual* schools.

It was surprising to see that the school landscape and the teaching methods used in Germany have not changed much over the last 60 years (see Figure 2). Recent educational approaches such as bilingual bimodal education and inclusion only enter this field slowly. The oral tradition is still a heavy burden for many Deaf children and adults (including the seniors), who were and are expected to lip-read for hours, receive excessive training in oral articulation, and at the same time were and are not allowed to use their sign language in class. Also, the separation of hearing and non-hearing children into different school systems

Figure 2: Schools for the Deaf in Germany, around 1950 and 2018 (poster displayed at the exhibition). Dark circle: somewhat oral school; light circle: somewhat bilingual school; dark triangle: somewhat oral "Abitur"; light triangle: somewhat bilingual "Abitur".

is still the standard in the educational scenery in Germany. A widespread modern bilingual and inclusive education for Deaf children is not in sight, as only a few schools show a tendency towards this important educational goal.

3.2 Professional education and work life

Their experiences during their work life was one of the most prominent topics in the interviews with the Deaf seniors. The discussion with the five seniors who had been invited to our seminar and the analysis of the interviews revealed that certain professions kept re-occurring in the lives of Deaf people: for example, tailor, cobbler, carpenter, draftsman, and gardener. However, many of the Deaf seniors mentioned during the interviews that these professions were not what they wanted to learn in the first place. Rather, they had been told that these were the only professions they could learn and practice due to their deafness and their school education. Another experience that many Deaf people report, and that has also been emphasized in the interviews with the Deaf seniors, is the disappointing lack of communication with hearing colleagues at the workplace. Most hearing colleagues, in former times but still today, are not able or willing to communicate in sign language, which leads to social isolation of the Deaf person in their work environment. Sitting alone at a desk, not knowing what is talked about while colleagues chat over coffee is a common experience for Deaf people.

Therefore, one group of students prepared the topic *professional education and work life* for the exhibition, with a focus on opportunities and barriers for Deaf people, especially in the last 60 years. During a research visit at the *Education Center for the Deaf* in Osnabrück, we discovered in an archive a list of occupations suggested for Deaf people in Nazi Germany in 1942. We realized that since then not much has changed in this respect. The list of typical professions and corresponding job trainings for Deaf adolescents (for example offered at a vocational training center for the Deaf) is still very limited compared to professions accessible for hearing people (see Figure 3). For the exhibition, we created a fictional character called "Tommy", representing a young Deaf person searching for his profession. Tommy's situation made the visitors of the exhibition aware of the fact that Deaf people in Germany still face many limitations in their job opportunities. Although legally Tommy has the same rights to pursue all kinds of professions and to attend all kinds of educational programs, just like his hearing peers, he is still confronted with many barriers and prejudices. The most challenging barriers are the lack of access to higher education, communicative barriers, problems in finding professional interpreters and funding interpretation, among others. The situation for Tommy nowadays has not significantly improved compared to the situation of the Deaf seniors back in the 1960s.

3.3 Deaf clubs and associations

Another topic that stood out in all interviews with the Deaf seniors are Deaf clubs and associations. These associations had and still have a huge impact and a tremendous importance for the daily life of Deaf seniors in Germany. Since almost every interviewed person was (or still is) actively involved in at least one Deaf club, it was immediately obvious that this aspect of Deaf culture should become an independent part of the exhibition. However, despite the importance of Deaf associations for the Deaf community, we had a tough time finding a sufficient amount of appropriate sources and historical information, mainly because this topic is poorly documented due to a lack of research and archiving. Hence, we mostly evaluated the interviews for personal stories and experiences that are related to Deaf clubs. During an excursion to the library of the *Institute of German Sign Language and Communication of the Deaf* (IDGS) at

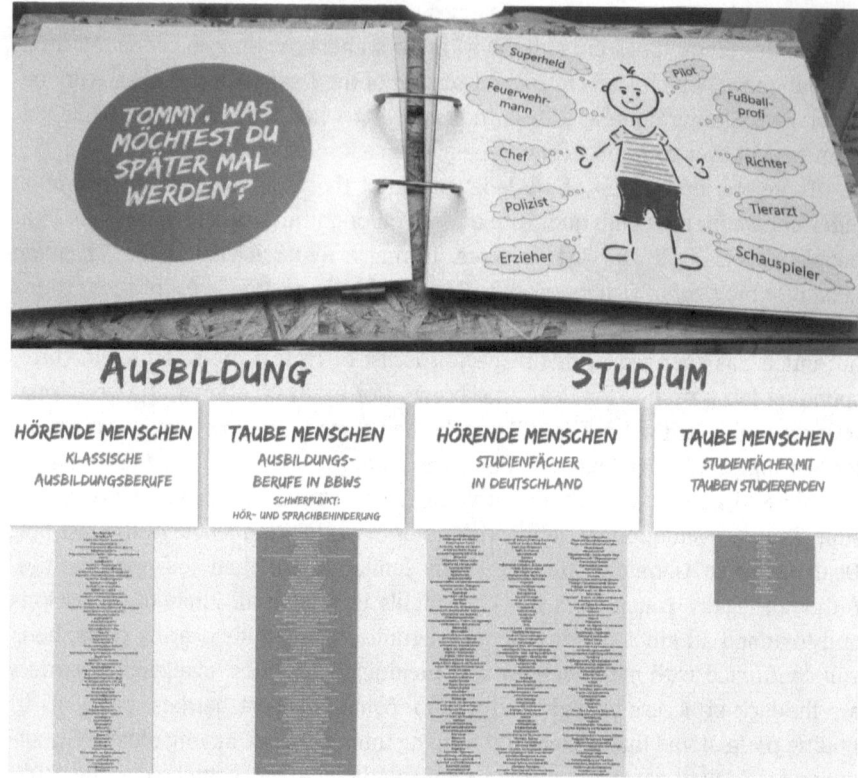

Figure 3: Top: Tommy and his dreams of professions "Tommy, what do you want to become?": pilot, soccer player, judge, veterinarian, actor, teacher, officer, boss, firefighter, hero. Bottom: Comparison of job opportunities for hearing (light columns) and Deaf people (dark columns). In this exhibition poster, each line is the name of one job opportunity. On the left-hand side, traditional job trainings ("Ausbildung"): approx. 340 job training opportunities for hearing people vs. 170 for Deaf people at a vocational training center. On the right-hand side, options for academic studies ("Studium"): approx. 1460 different fields of study for hearing people vs. about 20 different fields of study actually studied by Deaf people. Here, you only see the upper quarter of the complete poster.

Hamburg University, we found interesting collections of gazettes and journals written by and for Deaf people. These documents gave us a vivid insight into the community, the organizations, the life, and the zeitgeist of Deaf people in Germany over time. For the exhibition, we prepared a collection of different articles from 1885 to 2016 to show the visitors which topics were and to some extent still are important to the Deaf community (see Figure 4).

Making the life stories of Deaf seniors visible: a students' exhibition — 53

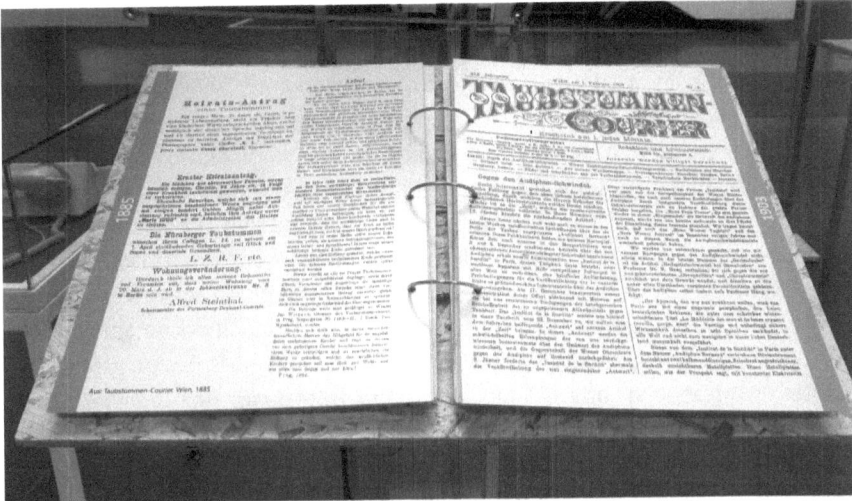

Figure 4: The exhibition hands-on book on Deaf associations: a collection of interesting and remarkable journal articles published between 1885 and 2016, which reflect the zeitgeist of Deaf people in Germany. Here, on the left page: proposals of marriage.

3.4 Deaf people in Nazi Germany

Most of the Deaf interviewees grew up in the 1930s and 1940s. Therefore, the time of Nazi Germany and life as a Deaf person during that time was an important topic in our exhibition. For obvious reasons, investigating this topic and preparing it for the exhibition was emotionally challenging. Reading about the different laws that had been passed between 1933 and 1945 in Nazi Germany, how these laws had been enforced in practice, and how this affected the personal lives of Deaf people was very distressing. For example, in 1935 abortion was legalized and enforced if one of the parents was hearing-impaired. Officially, it was required to get the consent of the pregnant woman to perform the abortion. However, we spoke to contemporary witnesses and read multiple interviews, in which the women reported that they had never consented to the abortion, but it had been performed on them nevertheless.

It was also upsetting and disturbing how formal and in clinical terms these cruel incidents were described in the historical documents. While Deaf people experienced discrimination, harassment, and persecution during their lives in Nazi Germany, we were shocked by the 'scientific' justification of this injustice. We read legislative texts and 'scientific' papers from the 1930s, in which hearing people propagandistically argued that Deaf people were inferior to hearing people. These hearing 'scientists' justified the sterilization of Deaf people by arguing that it was for the benefit of the society (for a detailed analysis of sterilization and the lives of Deaf people in Nazi Germany, see the chapters by Brockmann & Kozelka and Mittelstädt & Hosemann, this volume).

Another example of emotionless reports on the sterilization of Deaf people are clinical reports, in which doctors who performed the procedure described their actions. During our investigations, we discovered that sterilizations had in fact also been executed in the old *University Medical Faculty* in Göttingen, in other words: right next to the place where our exhibition was to be shown. Hence, we assumed that we should be able to find historical documents on sterilizations somewhere in the medical faculty of Göttingen University. Since we wanted to present an original medical report from 1940, one member of our team visited the archives of the university hospital. However, tracking down a sterilization document in this archive turned out to be a mission impossible. First, the documents were stored in the basement with a cold flickering, and somewhat creepy, lighting. Second, the rooms were infested by mold. Because of this health hazard, the team member had to wear a protective suit and a breathing mask to avoid any personal risks. Third, the documents were not archived chronologically or thematically, but were stored rather unsystematically. Our team member was told that the different rooms contained documents of different medical fields and that anything with regard to gynecology was stored in a room on the right-hand side. In this room, she found many aisles with a vast number of unorganized folders. However, she was on her own and no support or guidance was available. In this dark and moldy archive, she read many documents about different groups of people on whom sterilizations and abortions had been performed, but finding documents specifically on sterilization procedures on Deaf people during the Nazi period was impossible.

These were just some of the experiences our groups had when researching about the different topics relevant in the lives of the Deaf seniors. The next step was to analyze the content and to turn it into exhibition pieces.

4 Second semester (October 2018 to January 2019): design and construction

As opposed to the first semester, in which the students could work in an academic context familiar to them, by investigating and presenting a topic in a scientific way, the second semester brought a totally new challenge to all members of the team: working and thinking creatively, as an artist, as a constructor, as a

PR manager, and as a guide. We all had to learn how to transfer our knowledge into visually appealing and informative pieces that could be displayed at the exhibition. In order to come to a successful result, we had to fight the temptation of putting our results into scientific texts, which would be difficult (if not impossible) to read for non-academics. After four to seven semesters of training in how to write a scientific text, it was a challenge for everyone to overcome this habit and to think about how to present the content in a visual, non-textual manner. Hence, two of the most frequently uttered sentences in the second semester were: "This is too much text" and "This is too difficult to read".

Fortunately, we were smart enough to reach out for help and invited Julia Debelts, a manager for planning and creating exhibitions. She was of great help in giving us ideas on how we could present the content not only on posters but also in the form of hands-on pieces (such as the fictional character Tommy or the 'book' of journal articles, shown in Figures 3 and 4 above) and how we could set up and display the pieces (see Figure 5).

Figure 5: A construction plan of the exhibition space, including the positions of our three exhibition 'islands'.

In the second semester, we thus had to work on two main tasks simultaneously: first, each content group – *family life, school education, professional education and work life, Deaf clubs and associations, Deaf people in Nazi Germany,* and *introduction to German Sign Language* – had to create their posters and exhibits; second, we needed to build and set up everything around the exhibition. Consequently, we put together new working groups for the construction tasks: the design team, the building team, the sponsor and PR team, and the integration team. This is why each student participated in two different groups now, in a content group as well as in at least one construction group.

The opening of the exhibition was scheduled for January 15th, 2019. Hence, around Christmas and definitely in January, the workload got quite intense: posters had to be finalized and printed, building materials had to be purchased, invitation postcards and advertising posters had to be printed, and especially DGS videos had to be recorded. One of our main goals was to make the exhibition accessible to Deaf visitors by presenting all content in written German as well as in DGS and International Sign (IS). Hence, the (short) texts on the posters and on the illustrative objects had to be translated into DGS/IS, recorded on video, and then be made available via QR codes placed next to the objects and German texts.

Three days before the opening, we started to set up the exhibition. The exhibition did not only include informative posters with our research results, but also featured hands-on displays, which encouraged visitors to engage even more closely with the Deaf community. Next to 45 individual posters displayed in three different 'islands', we also had three television screens showing film material: excerpts from the interviews with Deaf seniors, as well as excerpts from major film productions by the Deaf community (all videos subtitled). These film excerpts provided additional visual input illustrating that our research project and the corresponding exhibition are based on real life experiences. In addition, we had four display cases with historic objects (e.g., old school journals, old telecommunications devices for the Deaf such as, for instance, a teletypewriter, and old hearing aids), two big books, a 'wheel of fortune' with DGS-related questions, and a 'communication box'. The latter was a hands-on object, in which two visitors could practice their lip-reading skills (see Figure 6).

In addition to the concrete construction of the exhibition, we also had other assignments to complete. First, we set up a website in German and DGS with additional information about the project and the exhibition (https://www.uni-goettingen.de/de/ausstellung/598123.html). Second, we prepared an official opening of the exhibition at Göttingen University (see next section). Finally, we designed postcards with letters of the DGS manual alphabet and the ILY ('I love you') sign on the front and information about the exhibition on the back (see Figure 7). In order to invite people to the exhibition, these postcards were distributed at different places at Göttingen University as well as in shops, cafés, and restaurants in the city center.

Making the life stories of Deaf seniors visible: a students' exhibition — 57

Figure 6: The "communication box". One visitor is wearing noise-canceling head phones (person on the right) and has to guess the question or task the other visitor is orally articulating (person on the left).

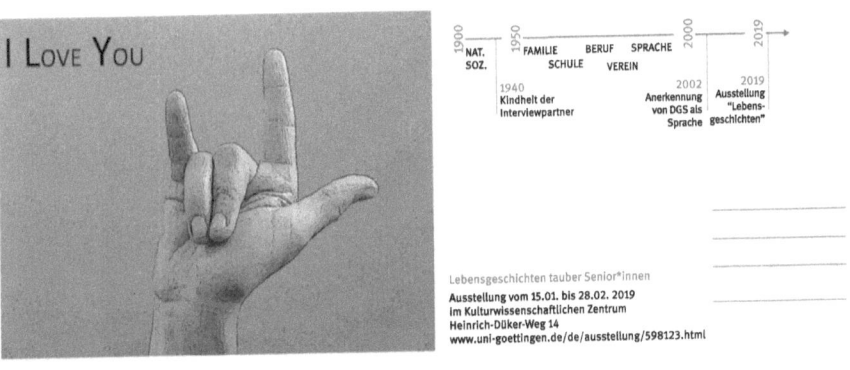

Figure 7: Advertising postcard of the exhibition. Next to the ILY sign, we also had postcards with each letter of the DGS manual alphabet.

5 The opening of the exhibition

As is true for many projects, the days prior to the deadline (i.e., for us prior to the opening) can get crazy. And indeed, they were. Right when we put together the first poles for the display framework, which would hold together our posters and exhibits, one of the poles broke, and the construction collapsed – so did our motivational spirit. This was an absolute low, and anxiety started to spread among the group. If we couldn't fix this weak point in the construction, none of our posters could actually be presented. We therefore immediately drove to a hardware store, bought everything we needed to fix those weak spots, and found a good solution that worked. In fact, the structure remained stable, and we could continue building the islands (see Figures 8 and 9).

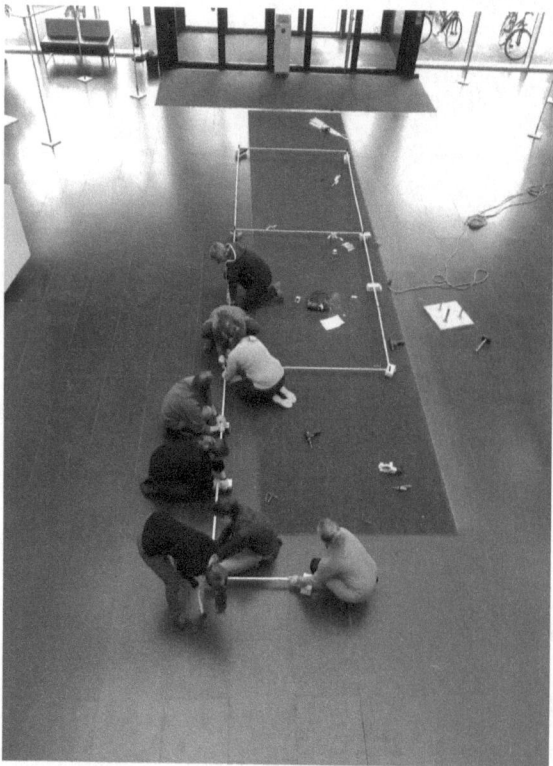

Figure 8: Assembling the poles of the big 'island'.

Figure 9: After 14 hours of building, the basic frameworks of the islands were set up.

After three days, or 36 hours, of intense building work, figuring-out things, discussions, and emotional ups-and-downs, the exhibition was finally set up and the opening night was about to start. On January 15th, 2019, at 6 pm, our first guests arrived at the opening. It was an honor that next to approximately 60 hearing, Deaf, and hard-of-hearing guests, we also had some prominent visitors: Christian Rathmann (Professor for sign language interpreting and Deaf studies at Humboldt University, Berlin), who gave a presentation in DGS on language attitudes, Andrea Bührmann (Vice president of Göttingen University), who said the opening words, and Helmut Vogel (President of the German Deaf Association) all supported our project. The local Deaf community and the local newspaper were present (see Figure 10), and many people even came from more distant cities like Hannover, Magdeburg and Hamburg. The evening was a total success, and during the following weeks, our team was booked multiple times to give a guided tour around the exhibition.

6 Summary: what we all took from that

Similar to other projects, we did not only experience the excitement and enthusiasm right before and during the opening event, but also the exhaustion right afterwards. For six weeks, the exhibition was open to the public in the *Cultural*

Figure 10: Article in the local newspaper *Göttinger Tageblatt*: "Exhibition about the life of Deaf people in Germany" (published January 17th, 2019). Picture taken at the opening event.

Studies Center at Göttingen University. During this time, we organized guided tours for the local Deaf community, local student groups, and visitors from the University of Magdeburg, who had not been able to attend the opening. We also produced a short video (https://www.uni-goettingen.de/de/virtuelle+tour/603648.html) and had an article published in the *Deutsche Gehörlosen Zeitung* ('German Deaf Journal').

But the two major outcomes of this experience were the following. First, our exhibition travelled to the *Information Center for the Deaf* in Osnabrück in February 2020, where it was presented in their communication center for five weeks in the context of their 50th anniversary. Second, and maybe even more significant, we all truly grew from this experience. We learned to overcome challenges, to find creative solutions and, most importantly, to support each other and to work as a team (see Figure 11).

Making the life stories of Deaf seniors visible: a students' exhibition — 61

Figure 11: The exhibition team.

Acknowledgements: The whole exhibition adventure would not have been possible without the courageous seniors, who were willing to share their life experiences with the public. We thank all the elderly Deaf signers for sharing their stories. Thanks to everyone in the course, who gave all their brain and muscle power in order to build this exhibition: Sonja Dietschi, Hannah Fecht, Christa Gaisbichler, Rieke Giese, Viktoria Sidonie Hänsch, Wei Huang, Judith Kalinowski, Franziska Karger, Elena Kozelka, Isa Kroeschell, Annika Mittelstädt, Dorothee Nyga, Benita Pangritz, and Franziska Tießen.

A special thanks to the wonderful DGS interpreter team including Karina Knipping, Andrea Knipping, and Lena Aßhauer (from *ViaManum Sign Language Interpreting*) for helping us with the cross-modal communication and accompanying us from the first course until the opening. Thanks to Tom Röber and Laurenz Kötter for helping us in setting up the exhibition in Göttingen, as well as in Osnabrück.

Thanks to our guests Martina Bergman, Elisabeth Brockmann, Anneliese Cramer, Michael Cramer, Julia Debelts, Karin Kallus, Eva-Maria Simon, Helmut Vogel, and Jürgen Wolf for their assistance and valuable input.

Finally, a special thanks to Susanne Wimmelman and the students' research and teaching fellowship *Forschungsorientiertes Lehren und Lernen (FoLL)* for the non-bureaucratic support. This contribution has been possible thanks to the SIGN-HUB project, which has received funding from the European Union's Horizon 2020 research and innovation program under grant agreement No 693349, and thanks to the project "(Un)sichtbare Lebensgeschichten", funded by the Ministry for Science and Culture of Lower Saxony (MWK).

Part II: "I found out that deaf people could do many things": Issues of culture and identity

Luca Des Dorides and Rita Sala
Once upon a time: history and memory of Italian Deaf elderly signers

1 Introduction

This chapter results from the analysis of a corpus of 69 interviews with deaf people born in the early twentieth century and has the aim to illustrate the cultural, social, and power dynamics experienced by these generations of signers.[1]

The debate on power has played a central role in reflections on the past of the Deaf Community, and a large body of literature agrees to describe Deaf people as an oppressed group (Lane 1992; Baynton 1996; Branson & Miller 2002; Burch 2002; Ladd 2003). This focus revolves around the two far-reaching incidents in the history of the deaf, both in Italy and worldwide, over the last 150 years: first, the Milan Congress in 1880, symbol of colonization (Lane 1992; Ladd 2003), and second, the "Deaf Resurgence" (Ladd 2003) triggered by the pioneering linguistic studies of Stokoe in the 1950s (USA) and appreciated by Italian researchers since the late 1970s (Volterra 1978, 1981; Manfredi Montanini et al. 1979; Volterra & Stokoe 1985).

The sense of a common past of oppression, mostly exercised through the educational system, has had the merit of revealing the actual existence of oppressive practices. However, it has not always prevented the temptation of following a binary logic, which opposes a powerful hearing majority to a powerless deaf minority (Lane 1992). Authors such as Paddy Ladd and Harlan Lane, although in different ways, have underestimated the productive aspect of these power relations, confining themselves to more or less fiercely denouncing their oppressive aspects. Only in recent years, this approach, partially shared with other authors (e.g., Baynton 1996; Burch 2002), has suggested a more dynamic perspective on the relations that deaf people used to have with the

---

[1] Two different projects based on oral sources were carried out between 2016 and 2019 by Luca Des Dorides: *"Ti segno la storia"* ('I sign history') for the General Directorate of Archives – MIBACT, and *"Task 2.4 Interview with elderly deaf signers"* for the SIGN-HUB project (with Rita Sala). In the context of these projects, which involved different approaches and purposes, 49 interviews were conducted, resulting in a total of about 80 hours of collected video material. A further 24 interviews were collected and analyzed as part of Rita Sala's bachelor and master theses in Sociology (Sala 2005, 2010). This chapter has been possible thanks to the SIGN-HUB project, which has received funding from the European Union's Horizon 2020 research and innovation programme under grant agreement No 693349.

https://doi.org/10.1515/9783110701906-004

hearing world (Edwards 2012). In concordance with Michele Friedner, we believe that the Deaf Community should be considered "as something produced by and through, and not in spite of, the existence of power" (Friedner 2010: 337). By making it the object of our study, we can reflect upon the productive relations with power, even the oppressing ones.

In order to regain this dynamic view of power relations, it is necessary to investigate the idea of Deaf Identity and to become aware that "it is critical to maintain the perspective that DHH [Deaf and Hard-of-Hearing] identities are among a multitude of identities interacting with each other to form the uniqueness of each individual" (Leigh 2010: 196). Therefore, adopting such a complex approach means to reject the idea that Deaf Identity is an ahistorical fact – both individual and collective – and to break the bond that all too often ties and subjugates the deaf history to hearing people's oppression. Deaf people have been oppressed and have fought against their oppression, but their history is more than that.

Even the use of a focal lens calibrated to the concept of marginality is not risk-free. Deaf people have been perceived as marginal, but the very concept of margin is a subtractive and intrinsically unidirectional perspective. We believe that the concept of marginality is inadequate for conveying the complexity of connections, relations, and cultural and identity-making stratification of real life. Marginality is tied to the ability to manage symbolic representation, and it is an ethnocentric concept that overlooks the capability of strategic decision and the interaction of "marginal people" (Perlman 1976; Forgacs 2014).

This kind of tension has recently led some authors to reflect on the idea that the Deaf Identity has to be considered an end point and encouraged them to think that it is necessary to highlight the differences inside the Deaf World (Friedner & Kusters 2015). The impression is that nowadays academics and members of the Deaf World are open to a more mature relationship with the plural dimension of their identity, by recalling their connection with essentialism (Kusters & De Meulder 2013; Ladd 2015) and facing, more or less frankly, the intersectionality problem (Barpaga 2015; Ruiz-Williams et al. 2015).

We believe, then, that the concepts of oppression and marginalization are essential in approaching the past of deaf people, but cannot be considered exhaustive. As we have seen, these concepts tend to underestimate the complexity of social, cultural, and identitarian stratifications that concern deaf people, whereas we think that the relationship with power should be investigated more thoroughly. Actually, power is not something that some people hold and some people don't, but rather *a ubiquitous* element that is inherent in everyone, because it is implicit in the relationships among individuals (Foucault 1991). Because of this characteristic, power allows us to take part in the never-ending process by which it is generated and reproduced in social environments. The utilization of methodological frameworks borrowed from Foucaldian theories of governmentality is not a novelty in the study of deaf people's past. However, their use has mainly aimed at denouncing the oppression as a socially constructed fact, while very little effort has been made to understand the role of the deaf in the incessant production and reproduction of power relations inside and outside the community (Lane 1992; Branson & Miller 2002; Ladd 2003; Siisiäinen 2016).

In order to approach the complexity of reality, we therefore think that it is more appropriate to focus on deaf people's life stories and their ability to avoid the binary interpretations of power relations. Our aim is to analyze the way we, as academics, look backwards by investigating the knowledge reflected in Deaf people's narrative world and their subjectivity. In fact, as Alessandro Portelli wrote, what people think is not only a historical fact, but it is also what guides the way people live (Portelli 2007).

Therefore, the first part of this chapter deals with the topic of oral sources and their ability to restore the 'power to speak' to those who do not have it. The history of Deaf people, like that of other groups considered 'marginal', has been built for a long time from written sources, produced by those who had the skills to make them as well as the power to impose them. But written sources are not the only way to access past events and their interpretations. Section 2.1, therefore, compares some autobiographical stories of Deaf elderly people and written sources relating to the internment in an Asylum of a young deaf girl at the beginning of the twentieth century. The comparison shows how these are not neutral testimonies of the past, but rather the result of the peculiar way individuals and institutions see and interpret reality at a given moment. The autobiographical narratives used in this chapter, however, are sources produced by the interest of researchers, and are affected by the particular way in which they were produced. This is why a large part of Section 2.2 is dedicated to the analysis of the methodologies of collection and interpretation of this type of sources.

Section 3 addresses the analysis of the stories in regard to school experiences, the relationship with the language and the Deaf Community. This is the unique and now unrepeatable memory of those who lived the long century following the Congress of Milan in Italy and who saw that same world crumble due to the combined effect of three important events: the progressive break-up of great special schools for the deaf as a result of the Law 517/1977 (the so-called *Mainstreaming Law*), the emergence of a new awareness about sign language and Deaf identity starting from the early 1980s, and the end of social connections related to the Deaf Club, which arose from the spread of new communication technologies.

Finally, in Section 4, we deal with the issue of gender relations within the Deaf Community by introducing the point on double discrimination suffered by Deaf women. In fact, from the collected autobiographical narratives, a substantial consistency of values between deaf and hearing people emerges in defining the boundaries between genders and the role of patriarchy.

2 The narrative world of the Deaf Community

The narrative world that this paper wants to share is that of the Deaf Community. Italian Deaf people have a history and a language that few people know, they constitute a group within the larger national community that only few people are part of, but they have stories to tell and a language to tell them. The Deaf Community, from which we collected the stories, does not represent the totality of deaf people in Italy. Deaf people who talk about themselves in this chapter are part of that bilingual and bimodal community that developed and uses Italian Sign Language (LIS) as a natural language and as the language of its own community. The Italian Deaf Community has a history that bases its origins on those of Italian culture and that has inevitably been influenced by the cultural aspects of Italy and by the historical and social events that have influenced the country. However, it also has its own educational, cultural, and social history, which is intertwined with that of the larger community. Yet, to date, little has been said about it, a path that is at the same time parallel to and different from that of the hearing majority, and that is inextricably linked to the visual language that characterizes it: "Cultural representations and language are tools with which we construct meanings of lived experience" (Hole 2007: 699).

In the text *Biografia, storia e società*, Maria Immacolata Macioti tells how, in the 1960s, the use of oral history/narrative interview derived from a conscious choice of the social scientist, who aimed at making the protagonists of her own study no longer "figures that cover places of power, or somehow eminent, [. . .] but the common people, the one until then ignored, the one that suffers the institution" (Macioti 1986: 12).

The everyday life of Italian Deaf people is no exception, and still today, with few exceptions (Pinna et al. 1990; ENS 2004), the Italian Deaf history is mainly a history of teaching methods or deaf institutes (Sani 2008; Morandini 2010; Debè 2014). This is due to a heterogeneous set of factors, including the difficulty in finding archival sources helpful for a different kind of research. It is therefore necessary to consider the question of sources in order to tell everyday life stories.

2.1 Speaking for oneself: the case study of Zelinda

Zelinda S. was born in Rome in 1871.[2] We know almost nothing about her family, except that her parents were poor and hearing. When she was admitted to the *Santa Maria della Pietà* ('Saint Mary of Pity') asylum in Rome, on October 3rd 1891, Zelinda was 20 years old, she was a dressmaker, and still lived with her parents, with whom she had not got along for some time. The diagnosis of psychiatrists at *Santa Maria della Pietà* was merciless: Zelinda was an idiot. At the time, the institution looked at her life to find a consistent logic for her presence in the asylum. It was at that moment that doctors and nurses left evidence of an existence which we would otherwise barely have heard of:[3]

> Till she was six, she lived with her family, from six to eleven years old, she stayed at the Deaf-mute Institute in Rome, then she went back to her family. [. . .] When she was five, she got meningitis and lost her hearing. [. . .] Even-tempered until she was eighteen. [. . .] a mediocre intelligence, in fact, she was a dressmaker. [. . .] The first symptoms came on suddenly when she was eighteen, she closed herself off in the room, refused any food, tore everything and pounced on the household. [. . .] Insanity changed her character, she didn't obey her parents and she railed against her mother.
>
> [ASMP, *Cartelle Cliniche*, Zelinda S. 1919][4]

So, Zelinda was deaf. She was one of the many deaf people committed to Italian asylums between the 19th and 20th century because of suffering from mental illness, or simply because they disturbed the environment where they lived. They were usually people from poor families and unwilling to adapt to discipline, frequently deaf children out of the school system or unemployed deaf adults. In their committals, deafness was usually considered as a clinical characteristic secondary to an alleged psychic anomaly, and Zelinda's diagnosis was no exception to that approach: "(Deaf-mute) Idiocy". However, neither of those elements determined her committal, as is, once again, revealed by an observation made by the segregating institution:

> It seems that she grew fond of a deaf-mute for a couple of years; during this period, the symptoms of mental illness began to show up. [. . .] For several days, the insane (woman) has been refusing food, not sleeping, crying and despairing, threatening her relatives. Suffering from lypemania, she is dangerous to herself and others.
>
> [ASMP, *Cartelle Cliniche*, Zelinda S. 1919]

---

2 Zelinda's story was collected in the context of Luca Des Dorides' PhD dissertation in Historical Sciences (Des Dorides 2010).
3 Translation from Italian sources into English by the authors of this chapter.
4 All quotations came from Zelinda's personal medical record (*Cartella Clinica*) kept in the historical archive of the Santa Maria della Pietà [ASMP], the psychiatric hospital active in Rome from the sixteenth to the twentieth century.

Zelinda was internalized because her parents did not agree with her relationship with a deaf man, and that created tension in her household. Containment to a psychiatric asylum as a regulator of family conflicts, even in the absence of real psychic diseases, was a common practice in Italy, and studies on committal in mental hospitals in Liberal and Fascist Italy tend to highlight how institutions applied this practice (Fiorino 2002; Babini 2009; Valeriano 2017). Apparently, she was committed because she was a young woman who refused to submit to the patriarchal authority. But this interpretation, though correct, cannot explain her case completely.

In April 1913, over twenty years after her first committal, Zelinda was subjected again to a routine examination because of an internal transfer. In meetings with new doctors, she showed up as a very different woman; an adult, uncultured, and illiterate woman. Psychiatrists' reports reveal that they could not and did not want to study her case in more depth because "the patient being a deaf-mute, the psychic test cannot concern attitude and behavior" (ASMP, *Cartelle Cliniche*, Zelinda S. 1919). During her twenty-five years of institutionalization, Zelinda's presence in the asylum left close to no trace. As almost always happened, her deafness was treated neither at a communicative level nor through any efforts by the staff. The staff only noted communication difficulties as a deficiency of the patient, but did not involve people external to the institution to help them. Zelinda, being female and deaf, could not oppose the logic of exclusion and was weighed down by the heterogeneous set of discourse, institutions, and power relations that Michel Foucault set as the basis of what he called *dispositifs*.

Zelinda's is one of the many stories of marginalization showing that different marginalized identities are often present in one and the same person, and that it is difficult to disentangle one from the others. But Zelinda's voice is still missing. Her story is transmitted to us through the perspective of the other, the one of institutions and of those who, to say it with Bourdieu, hold the power to create symbolic representations (Bourdieu 2001). This institutional point of view allows us detect rejects, lacks, and inconsistencies of the institutions involved, but it does not solve the question of how to let people speak for themselves.

Carlo was 66 when, in May 2016, he came to the office of one of the authors with a clear request: "I want to tell you my story, let's have an interview."[5] Those who deal with oral history know well, as Alessandro Casellato wrote, that oral sources have legs, and sometimes they come looking for you (Casellato 2010).

---

5 All names used in this paper are invented, in order to eliminate any reference to the interviewed people.

Actually, interviewees are not inactive, they have their own motivations and goals, which can be different from those of the researcher.

Given the interviewee's initiative, the interview was conducted keeping the directivity level low. It was an unstructured interview, in which the contributions of the interviewer were reduced to a minimum. During the interview, Carlo made full use of the power to tell his story given him by his interviewer. From the very beginning, his story was deeply based on his homosexuality: the refusal of toys for boys in early childhood, his first sexual experiences, the difficulty of defining his homosexual identity, the discrimination experienced in the Deaf Community, and then, eventually, the love for his partner.

> *The reason I like men and I stay with them is because as a three or four year old child, I already felt like a girl. My mom always gave me toy-horse to play with but I gave them back because I wanted a doll [. . .] My mom said 'no' and that I had to play with car toys because I was a boy, but I told her I was a girl.* [DGA, 18/07/2016, 01:17–01:48]

> *Then, from 18–19 until 20, I started to be more free [. . .] I went to the club, I knew people and they called me 'pansy'. I felt very offended.* [DGA, 18/07/2016, 08:39–09:07]

> *In the 90s, thanks to theater, the situation began to open up. Later there were the LIS courses, some workshops, in which there were many deaf gays. They told me that I was cheerful, that I was happy, free, and then I started to open up.*
> [DGA, 18/07/2016, 37:12–37:47]

The real nature of his desire to tell his story with such a strict logical order became clear a few months later, when Carlo and his partner were joined in one of the first civil unions for same-sex couples celebrated in Rome. Their marriage finally closed the circle opened many years earlier, and Carlo, before tying the knot, felt the need to entrust someone with the story of the toilsome journey he had undertaken so many years before. After putting this last piece into place, the retrospective coherence of autobiographical reconstruction becomes transparent and solid within its narrative system. Such narration, directly led by the protagonist, does not result from a recovery of objective experiences, as if memory was an organized archive of real events, but rather from a process of re-signification of the past realized in order to meet the present needs.

Maria, too, accomplished a similar goal in the narration of her past. In her life, she has had three different name signs: the first one was given to her back in school and was related to her habit of tapping fingers; the last one, the name she still uses today, is related to the artistic activity she started when she was young. While describing the first years following the appearance of her deafness, between three and six years old, she soon makes clear what sense she wanted to give to her past:

> Then we went back to the village, and I couldn't talk or hear anymore, I couldn't hear the dogs barking, they wanted to play but it was hard for me to enter in communication. I was very upset and nervous, aggressive, I didn't know what to do, my mum was desperate and didn't know how to feed me. My maternal grandfather, he was a very smart man . . ., decided to send me to a nursery school run by the nuns, together with hearing children. Thanks to a very good nun, I walked in silence and looked at the old boards with alphabet letters, A for ant, B . . . those with animals, C for cat, and many other pictures, I was curious and fascinated by looking at them. There it is the visual communication for the Deaf! Instead of hearing, I looked . . . In the afternoon, in my father's bakery, I used to take some charcoal and draw and write on the wall. This made me happy, so I used to write everywhere, on the floor, on the walls, everywhere, it was full of signs. My aunt reproached me, also mum and dad got mad, and told me my face was all dirty. I stood still with the charcoal pencil in my hand, I didn't know to have such passion, but my parents didn't realize how this was important for my life. My father told me that I became an artist thanks to all those scribbles that stained his wall, they were similar to Egyptian figures. That was the beginning of my passion.
> [SH, 17/02/2017, 03:36–04:42]

Memory, both individual and collective, is not just a place where past events persist, it is actually the place where the sense of the past sustains the sense of the present. It is an area of turbulence where the lived and the unlived often merge.

Maria recalls the traumatic events that caused her deafness with a very detailed account. The scene is very clear in her head, although the events occurred 67 years ago, when she was only three years old:

> I was born hearing, I heard noises, birds, dogs. I lived near a farm. There were dogs, ducks, various noises, it was very nice. I was three and a half years old when I became deaf. At the mill, at the wash house, women used to go wash their clothes, carrying them in baskets on their head. In that meadow, there was a mill. I used to play in the sun with my hearing brother. We were there playing. I was wearing a small hat that my mother had sewed. It was itchy, and I threw it away. My mother had sewed it, as people used to do at that time, but it was itchy, nevertheless I continued playing in the sun. When I went back home with my brother, I started to tremble and I was hot. My mum got angry and told me that was because I stayed in the sun all day. The fever was very high, and chamomile tea didn't help. So, we went to the local doctor, but the situation was very serious. There was no cure. They took me to Genoa for some clinical tests, but nothing. Eventually, we went to Turin by train, and after an extensive research, they found out I became deaf. [SH, 17/02/2017, 01:42–04:30]

Emilia, instead, remembers the day of her diagnosis as if it was a personal memory, although she was only a few months old. Hence, that memory is very likely the result of the settling of family memories:

> I'm the only deaf-mute in my family. My mother used to call me "Emilia! Emilia!", but I didn't reply. She couldn't understand why, she thought I couldn't hear or something

> happened. So, she took me to the hospital to have a hearing check. The doctor had an instrument that emitted a whistle, you know? I was seated, I was very little, only 9 months old. My mum was there, and the doctor made a half turn around me and said: "This little girl is deaf." My mother fainted . . . She was upset . . . I was deaf-mute!
> [SH, 09/06/2017, 01:15–01:55]

While remembering the moment of diagnosis, elderly deaf people frequently report scenes of despair, shame and denial when parents find out that their children cannot hear. Filippo, deaf since his early childhood, describes his experience as follows:

> My parents were worried, having a deaf-mute son was a real problem, they couldn't handle it. When I was a child, my father used to call me, but I didn't reply. My mother used to call me, too, "Filippo!", but I didn't hear, and they asked themselves why. [. . .] So, we went to the doctor, and he told him that maybe I was deaf-mute. My father was surprised, because in our family nobody was deaf, so the doctor explained to him what it meant to be deaf-mute, I could neither hear nor speak . . . and I would have to attend school in a specialized institute. My father got upset, he almost threw himself off the balcony, but thankfully my grandmother grabbed him. [DGA, 15/02/2017, 04:03–05:04]

These narratives about reported experiences can affect the meaning of social spaces where people have lived and not only with regard to the role of deafness:

> There were all hearing people in my family. [. . .] When my mother was pregnant with me, in 1940, during the war period, a deaf-mute woman lived opposite our house, and my mother used to talk with her with gestures because she loved her. This woman used to come to our house to talk with my mother, and together they played the clap game. My mother was so impressed with this woman that, eventually, she passed deaf-mutism on to the child she was pregnant with. [DGA, 15/02/2017, 00:31–01:18]

In the Southern Italy of the early 1940s, the same culture that refuses deafness puts the responsibility in women's bodies. So, in the memory of the past, the imagination may take over the reality, as is evident from the below dialogue, which comes from the same interview as the previous quote.

> Filippo: *This was what my grandmother used to say, while my mother said I was deaf because of meningitis. [. . .]*
>
> Interviewer: *Whom did you believe?*
>
> Filippo: *I think my grandmother was right. [. . .]*
>
> Interviewer: *Therefore, if your mother hadn't met that woman, would you have been born hearing?*

> Filippo: *Yes, and also because as a precaution, thinking I could get angry, my mother always said I was deaf because of meningitis and because of the war . . . But it wasn't true, my grandmother always told me it wasn't true, it was because she spent her time with that woman, and since my mother was very compassionate, she loved that woman, she felt bad for her, she was empathic, and that's why I was born deaf-mute.*
>
> [DGA, 15/02/2017, 02:04–03:26]

2.2 Oral sources and Deaf people

Biographical interviews are a mode of inquiry that allows people to tell the story they experienced and to share the meaning they make out of that experience without being "quizzed" about specific aspects of their own life. The turning point in research methods towards non-standard, qualitative methods is linked to the communicative turn of sociology starting from Schutz, Goffman, Garfinkel, Habermas, and others. We are now in a period in which, due to an increased awareness of their relationship, the observer and the observed are no longer in an asymmetrical relationship but rather in an equal, or almost equal, relationship. Daniel Bertaux, one of the users of the biographical method, inserts life stories into the context of ethno-sociological research, a scientific field that intends to study a part of cultural reality, a *situation category*, a particular social world made up of a group of people who share a specific social situation.

> By relating many testimonies on the lived experience of the same social situation, for example, their singularities can be overcome and the progressive construction of a sociological representation of the social (collective) components of the situation can be attempted.
>
> (Bertaux 2003: 53)

In the narrative interview, a trusting relationship is built between the interviewer and the interviewee, leading to an interactive story of life, an "emotionally non-neutral relationship" (Bertaux 2003: 61), in which the interlocutors together construct the story according to their respective roles, negotiating the story itself according to the rules of every social action.

"Telling is *putting a story together*" (Jedlowsky 2000: 187). The story the interviewee will tell, the one (s)he will deliver to the researcher, exists within a dialectic where meaning will be constructed, co-constructed, both by and through a language. In our stories this is a sign language, whose history is a founding part of the narration. The understanding of a story takes place, according to Jedlowski (2000), because the narrator and the "listener" share *a conceptual device* that allows them to understand each other. This device is not constituted only by the language but by all the semantic competence that concerns acting, without which it would not be possible to understand a story.

"If we understand the actions that the stories tell, it is because we pre-understand the world of the action to which they refer in a way that we can call *pre-narrative*" (Jedlowsky 2000: 187f).

Here, the importance of having members of the Deaf Community conducting the interviews becomes obvious, as they share the same world or at least the experience of being deaf or of being part of a minority that still struggles to be recognized as a community with a specific cultural identity, and not only as being deficient. Hence, the interviews that we are talking about in this chapter have been conducted by Deaf interviewers, and the methodological framework of reference for the *rules of engagement* has been largely borrowed from the one developed for the compilation of linguistic corpora and the study of sign language variation (Lucas et al. 2001; Cardinaletti et al. 2011; Schembri et al. 2013; Stamp et al. 2016). Although these researches had the purpose of checking linguistic accommodation between informer and interviewer, a necessity that also applies to our collection, we supposed that the presence of deaf interviewers would help to create a "comfort zone", where interviewees can express themselves more freely.

The interpersonal exchange that is established between the two protagonists of the interview leads to the recognition of the interviewee as a person and not as an object of study. It also allows the researchers to make themselves known by initiating this basic interpersonal relationship for the construction of a complex social action, which is based on dialogue and has its own specific syntax.

The main goal was to use the overwhelming power of oral sources, which, when set free, can change the focus and subvert the researcher's horizon of meaning. In order to manage these needs, which are typical in qualitative research, reference has been made to methods of oral history, especially to the use of a creative type of interview, and its potential to go beyond the hegemonic reproductive approach, whether in a context of sign languages or not (Passerini 1978; Thompson 1978; List 1993; Hirsch 1995; Freebody & Power 2001; Ryan & Schuchman 2002; McCleary 2003). However, the importance of involving Deaf people went beyond simply recruiting a Deaf interviewer.

Speaking for oneself is not the act of expressing an unheard voice but, as Bourdieu wrote (Bourdieu 2001), the act of mastering the tools of narrative production. Allowing the unheard voices to be heard is not enough, since the untold narratives need to emerge. To make this possible, both Deaf people and sign language must be involved at all levels in the transmission of their own history. Following the deaf researchers Annelies Kusters and Maartje De Meulder, we think that doing Deaf Studies is an inherently political activity (Kusters et al. 2017). This compels the researchers to consider how to overcome the supremacy of *written scholarship* on the symbolic representations of the Deaf Community and sign languages (this is the paradox of Oral History and Deaf Studies). Involving Deaf academics and members of the sign language community and using sign language during the entire research and interpretation process is of utmost importance, because, as Paulo Freire wrote, liberating consists in acts of cognition, not transferals of information (Freire 1971).

Deaf people belong to an oral culture that, like all oral cultures, "does not have texts in which to preserve the collective memory; they only have the mnemonic abilities of the elderly that are refined with the exercise" (Montesperelli 2003: 9). Thanks to technology, these non-written languages – sign language in this case – can now be collected on video, and thus the specific linguistic expressions characteristic of the sign language, with all its communicative and cultural characteristics, can be captured.

3 Oppression and beyond

As we have seen in the previous paragraphs, studying memory through people's life stories implies looking for the personal and collective meaning that individuals and groups give to themselves as well as to their own past and present. The main operation involves connecting subjective and recurring aspects in narrative structures. In order to carry out such an operation, social spaces to which these memories can be applied are often sought out. These spaces can be quite large, as in the case of the memory of the Milan Congress, which involves the entire international Deaf Community, or they can be smaller in size, like an individual's family, political group, or school.

In accordance with an extensive body of literature, we give great importance to educational experiences in deaf life history (Nikolarizi & Hadjikakou 2006; Quinn 2010; McIlroy & Storbeck 2011). When we talk about institutes for the deaf, we refer to those schools that included a boarding school. Some institutes, which lacked such facilities, relied on external institutions. We can refer to deaf schools, following Erving Goffman's (1961) definition of the concept of an asylum as a total institution: "a place of residence and work where a large number of like-situated individuals, cut off from the wider society for an appreciable period of time, together lead an enclosed, formally administered round of life" (Goffman 1961: 17). At the same time, these institutes could also draw on the social status of those who were part of it, "however enjoyable or lax these pursuits may be" (Goffman 1961: 15). In fact, what kind of residents where living there and their gender was highlighted in the majority of the denominations of deaf schools in Italy, as *female deaf-mutes* or *male deaf-mutes*. In some of them, we also find a further indication of the economic status of the attending students, such as in Bologna, where the *Pio Istituto delle Sordomute Povere* ('Pious Institute for Poor Female Deaf-mutes') existed until 1975, in Crema, where the *Opera Pia Sordomute Povere* ('Pious Institution for Poor Female Deaf-mutes') welcomed girls until 1970, and in Milan, where we find the *Pio Istituto per Sordomuti Poveri di Campagna* ('Pious Institute for Poor Deaf-mutes from the Countryside'), which changed name in 1967 and became the *Pio Istituto Sordomuti di Milano* ('Pious Institute for Deaf-mutes of Milan'), a name more suited to the sensibility of the sixties.

Taking the appropriate distance from the total institutions analyzed by Goffman in *Asylums* (i.e., mainly psychiatric asylums), we can consider the institutes for the deaf semi-total places. In fact, as we can see in many testimonies later in the chapter, in most cases, and especially in the 20th century, deaf children entered school at a very young age and remained there for a long time, following rules imposed inside the schools, which were different from those within a family environment or in a non-boarding school. Like many total institutions, deaf schools had not only an educational role but mainly a rehabilitative mission, as they were set up with the aim of not just instructing the deaf but of returning them to society with the capacity to speak, so that they would no longer be stigmatized as *dumb*. To achieve this, the schools established a rule that prevented the use of signs, a preference for the oral method and lip-reading, and exhausting speech therapy sessions, all of which have marked the life of many deaf students. The history of what it was like to live inside the institutes is a shared history for Italian deaf people, especially until the 1970s and 1980s of the 20th century, when Law 517/1977, best known as the *Mainstreaming Law*, came into effect, leading to the closure of the majority of deaf schools in the 1980s. This happened because many parents, mostly hearing, preferred to keep their children close to home and in a "school for all", instead of sending them to special schools far from the family.

This big change in the history of Italian deaf education brought an end to these schools, thereby putting at risk the memory of an important part of Deaf Community life and Deaf Culture, that is, the memory of a past that tells about the schools where deaf people grew up, where they were formed, where the sign language was banished but where, at the same time, the community continued to develop its own cultural and linguistic peculiarities.

There are many publications that talk about these institutes as institutions per se, but only few actually report on the life in these institutions from the point of view of those who lived inside them, not as educators or teachers, but as children who spent their childhood and adolescence there. Their life "remains, therefore, a suspended chapter, a gap that can begin to be filled by giving voice to the social strata up to here neglected" (Montesperelli 2003: 39). This chapter contributes to the need for legitimacy that the Deaf Community and its history deserve within the Italian educational and social context.

Harlan Lane wrote that with the decision taken during the International Conference of the Educators of the Deaf in Milan in 1880 began "the Middle Age for the Deaf communities of the western world" (Lane 1995: 57). As we have already mentioned, we believe that this point of view, despite highlighting the obvious oppression endured by deaf people and sign languages, should undergo further evaluation. Before 1880, we find texts written by Italian deaf educators or teachers – like the one that a deaf educator named Giacomo Carbonieri (1814–1879) addressed to the distinguished professor Giovanni Gandolfi of the Royal University of Modena – claiming the value of sign language, which takes nothing away from the deaf's intellectual abilities (Gandolfi considered the hearing as the main gate of intelligence following Aristotle's philosophy).[6] However, it is not possible to find written testimonies of deaf authors written after the congressional resolution. This lack is probably linked to the fact that from that moment on, education has focused more on the ability to speak rather than to write.[7]

Making the necessary distinctions, we can compare what happened to the Deaf during the period from the end of the 19th century until the second half of the 20th century to the linguistic drama that Memmi (1965) notes during the colonial occupations.

> [T]he colonized's mother tongue, that which is sustained by his feelings, emotions, and dreams, that in which his tenderness and wonder are expressed, thus that which holds the greatest emotional impact, is precisely the one which is the least valued. It has no stature in the country or in the concert of peoples. If he wants to obtain a job, make a place for himself, exist in the community and the world, he must first bow to the language of his masters. In the linguistic conflict within the colonized, his mother tongue is that which is crushed. He himself sets about discarding this infirm language, hiding it from the sight of strangers. In the linguistic conflict within the colonized, his mother

---

[6] For further information on Carbonieri's work, the interested reader is referred to Pigliacampo (2000).

[7] The books written by deaf people have been discovered thanks to the Italian word for "deaf-mute" indicated next to the name of the author, as is true for the texts by Giacomo Carbonieri, Paolo Basso, and Giuseppe Minoja. After 1880, there are no more texts with this specification, which might lead one to think that there were no more deaf people who were able to write or publish books (see Corazza 1995).

tongue is that which is crushed. He himself sets about discarding this infirm language, hiding it from the sight of strangers. (Memmi 1965: 107)

Without going into details regarding the colonizing question, we report a testimony, made years ago and, about the worst consequence that the Milan Congress has had: the rejection of their natural language.

> Giuseppe: *My mom (deaf) didn't want me to sign in public. [. . .] Walking down the street, every time I tried to tell her something resulted in an elbowing and a "Is not good!", so I used to start running to get home as soon as possible and sign with her.* (Sala 2005: 51)

And again:

> Mario: *In my village, when I went out shopping, I was referred to as "the dumb", I knew it. Outside the house, it was not possible to sign because everyone stared at us, the signs are visible, and people stopped to look at us. My mom was more ashamed than my father* [both were deaf; authors' note]. *In the family, there were no problems but out of the house, to sign was troublesome!* (Sala 2005: 38)

Therefore, there can be no doubt that discrimination against sign languages deprived entire generations of deaf people of sign language, that is, it imposed a sort of subtractive bilingualism, to the extent that sign language was seen by deaf people themselves as a language of lesser value or something to be ashamed of. Emilia was born deaf at the peak of the Fascist era. When doctors diagnosed her with deafness, her mother fainted (see quote above). About twenty years later, after another world war, it was her turn to face the prospect that her daughter could be born deaf like her:

> Emilia: *When my daughter became deaf . . . no, she didn't become deaf, she was deaf from birth . . . my mother used to call her, and my father used to clap his hands, but nothing, she didn't turn around. So, they told me: "E. is deaf-mute". And I replied: "Fuck you, it isn't true!" At first, I was desperate, but then, little by little, I got accustomed to it, and everything went on normally. Besides, she was smart and learned to sign very quickly. When she grew up, she was eight or nine, she was always there signing, and I didn't like it, I felt ashamed, so I used to hold her hands, I used to drag her around by the hand. She wanted to sign and fidgeted while I held her hands because I didn't want her to sign. Then, in a natural way, everything went well.*
>
> Interviewer: *Why were you so embarrassed?*
>
> Emilia: *Because everybody looked at her, and I didn't want that. People who saw her fidgeting in that way didn't understand why she moved her hands so much, so I held her. Then, that moment passed, too.* [SH, 09/06/2017, 38:31–39:44]

Grazia, who was also from a Deaf family, was severely punished in deaf school because of her persistence in signing. After a punishment that forced her to stay overnight alone in a dark room, which resulted in her wetting herself, she decided not to sign anymore, disregarding her own and family language, in order to align herself to what at that time was required, namely "speak and behave well" (which implied not signing). But at some point, she had the chance to rediscover her language at another place, where Deaf identity was raised and sign language was preserved, that is, inside the Deaf association:

> *Then my father decided to bring me to the Deaf association to find a man to marry, "just to have a look". It was my first trip to a Deaf association with other Deaf people. We arrived by train, the local ENS* [Italian Deaf Club; authors' note] *was in a small room, around me everybody was signing, moving hands, and then I started to laugh, I couldn't stop laughing! They were not possibly signing, that was not admitted! Oh my God, they really are signing – I tell myself – and I keep laughing like crazy. My brother was with me, too, and scolded me because I was laughing. "This is the Deaf way, deaf-mutes sign, don't laugh", he said, but I kept doing it. After a while, an uncle from another town, who was visiting ENS, told me "You don't have to laugh if you see people signing, deaf people communicate with their hands* [the sign used was SIGNING, but mouthing was "parlare con le mani" ('talk with the hands'); author's note], *don't laugh". So, I was scolded by him, and this made me think a lot the night after. In bed, under the blankets, I began to think over what he said . . . the deaf talk with their hands, but what does it mean? Oh yes, it's true . . . so, he went on saying, that afternoon "Aren't you deaf, too? Hearing people can hear what others say, you can't, you are deaf, but you can see what deaf tell you by hand", and he was right. So, from that moment, I started signing again, but not outside in public. I was already shocked, and I was so restrained to use sign language to the point that tears ran down my face only thinking of using sign language, I was so ashamed, really ashamed. After that, I started to sign little by little, even when the deaf around me urged me to do that. They couldn't understand how much I was stuck in the position that signing wasn't possible for me. I really couldn't.*
>
> [SH, 08/07/2017, 19:48–21:20]

As these stories confirm, knowledge of (and curiosity towards) sign language that was common before the 20th century, had diminished, and with it the awareness that those *gestures,* as they were named in the past, were a true language. There were only few *free zones* where deaf people were able not to align with "normality". Therefore, essentially bilingualism disappeared, and this choice resulted in a generation of deaf who often had no competence in either Italian or LIS.

In Italy, as already mentioned, prejudices and indifference only began to be overcome at the end of the 1970s, when linguistic studies on sign language started to develop, thus making a crucial contribution to the general attitude toward sign languages. Up until that point, the language used by deaf people did not even have a name. Fabrizio, deaf and son of deaf parents, describes the beginning of his collaboration on the draft of the most complete Italian Sign Language dictionary (Radutzky 1992):

> *Elena Radutzky chose me because she found out that I signed properly. [. . .] I accepted willingly. They offered to me a work on LIS, I was eighteen, and I knew nothing about research or LIS. LIS . . . I don't know . . . Then I discovered many things. [. . .] I got very interested and began working on it.* [SH, 22/02/2017, 10:30–11:20]

The importance of that "Copernican revolution" (Fontana et al. 2015) can also be found in the stories of elderly Deaf people, who often remember 'their' sign language as something different from the one used today.

> Federica: *Today, there are many occasions when hearing people can sign. Today there are many, not before. These things have increased. [. . .] That's all changed!*
>
> Interviewer: *At the time, how did people sign? Were there signs? Did people sign enough?*
>
> Federica: *We signed, but we made it up on the spot, not like today with LIS. [. . .] We signed as it came . . .* [SH, 26/05/2017, 08:32–09:15]

From the testimonies collected, we can also infer the emergence of linguistic pride in those participants that grew up during the 1980s.

> Giovanna: *My parents* [both deaf; authors' note] *used to sign, and at home, signing was possible [. . .] but my obsession was that I had to speak well, in those days, everyone thought so, my parents too, [. . .]. I absolutely had to pronounce sentences in proper Italian. [. . .] When I discovered that my language* [Italian Sign Language; authors' note] *was a real language, I told to myself, between me and myself, "Fuck to everybody, I had to be aware of this before!"* (Sala 2005: 40)

But the institutes for the deaf have not only been the institutional and social space of oppression. At the end of the 19th century, attending a deaf school was still a privilege that concerned only a quarter of deaf children of school age (Raseri 1880). At the beginning of the following century, the *Population Census of the Kingdom of Italy* (1903) revealed that 73% of Italian deaf people were neither able to read nor write. Therefore, deaf schools, notwithstanding their limitations, were an opportunity for the deaf students who could attend them and had a major role in the education of the Italian Deaf Community. Even regarding the discrimination of sign language, we should look further into the matter. Already in 1892, during the second national congress of *deaf-mute* educators, Giulio Ferreri, one of the most important names in the education of the deaf in Italy, lamented the partial failure of Milan's resolutions: "We merely banned gesture from classes, but it was still accessible in the school, so that students and teachers would pick it up again at the end of school activities" (Congresso Nazionale degli Educatori dei Sordomuti 1893: 100).

Sign language continued to be used, not only among deaf people as a tool of communication and exchange, but also to communicate with teachers and assistants. Therefore, deaf schools, teachers, and social networks connected to them, despite their paternalistic approach, were also a fundamental strategic resource deaf people drew from, in order to improve their conditions.

> Francesca: *Instead, in Turin, I remember that deaf people didn't work and stayed with nuns, who hired them. The "Daughters of Charity" nuns had an association called 'Dame di compagnia'* ['Lady-in-waiting'; authors' note]. *[. . .] In this association, there were women of wealthy families who provided assistance and helped people in need. They helped people who needed a house, who needed a job, and I know that some deaf people found a job thanks to these "ladies in waiting". One deaf person found a job as an employee, and another became a chef considering that he was good at cooking, and this gave him great satisfaction. I remember they told me it wasn't easy for deaf people to find a job, because of the usual problem of communication. When I moved to Rome, I discovered a different reality, I found out that deaf people could do many things. The ENS* [Italian Deaf Club; authors' note] *handled this, so between the 1950s and 1970s, the situation improved.*
> [SH, 20/10/2017, 24:40–26:54]

From the interviews, it emerges that the role of the institutes is considered by all deaf interviewees to have been fundamental for their socialization and for meeting other children like them. It was also extremely important for educational purposes, although not enough to satisfy the *hunger for culture* they expected.

4 Crossing the barriers

Deaf communities in Italy are, of course, part of the Italian culture and share many cultural aspects. Deaf people went through the same history and cultural changes as the Italian hearing population. Studying the Deaf, we can study broader aspects of the Italian mainstream culture such as gender roles and socio-economic relations between classes.

Nowadays, Italian women are encouraged to be independent and to obtain a high level of education, despite some still existing sexist stereotypes that imply that women should be responsible for the majority of house duties and should aspire to a good marriage and motherhood. In the past, such stereotypes were seen as normal and were widely accepted within society and family. During the fascist regime, in order to strengthen the male domination and gendered hierarchies at the workplace, women were no longer allowed to access some specific professions which they had had access to during the First World War, when men were at the front (Toffanin 2014).

The history of the Italian patriarchy, which sharpened male dominance and female subordination, is reflected in a broader literature, including the history of the feminist movement and Italian novels. This cultural heritage emerges also from the analysis of the interviews conducted with elderly Deaf people in the context of our study, for instance, in the interview with Beatrice:

> I was a seamstress in my house, and I wanted to find a permanent job. They had promised me that I would get a telegram for a job, but my husband, then my fiancé, totally disagreed. He complained about the future, that I would not be able to look after my sons should I have one or two. And even if I explained to him that my mother could take care of them, as she was still young, he replied that his wife had to stay at home, cook, look after the house, and that this was how our relationship should be. And so, I did.
> [SH, 01/08/2017, 07:45–08:09]

Beatrice goes on telling why, at some point, she decided to get married despite the fact that she felt she was too young:

> I wasn't ready, it was too fast, I was 21, and it was too early to get married, but he kept coming to visit me, coming to my house and bother me, and you know why? He kept coming because he was an orphan, both his mother and father had died, so he was the little child, and all his brothers and sisters had moved away in search of a job in Switzerland and in Rome. So, I started a "non-binding" relationship with him at first, just to know him and see whether I liked him. We stayed together for a while but he kept asking me to marry him, he really wanted it because he was by himself at home and had to cook, to do everything, and it was impossible for him, how could he do it? So, I agreed to marry him but after explicit agreement of his brothers and sisters; [. . .] his older brother then came to me asking me to marry his brother as soon as I could, because he did not want to be worried about his deaf brother since he was living so far away.
> [SH, 01/08/2017, 11:35–12:50]

We also see in other interviews how the need to marry was considered a legitimate choice by those men who, once they had left the institute, no longer had anyone who would take care of and cook for them. In fact, it emerges from many testimonies that, in institutions that hosted both males and females – of course separated in the dorms and at other moments of the day – the girls were in charge of the role of "housekeeper" of the home-institution.

Since endogamy was rather common in the Deaf communities, as it generally is within minorities, examples of exogamy are very few in the interviews we conducted and are often attributed, as in the following example, to the *natural helping nature* of women, in this case, as "interpreter":

> Giacomo: I started working in the family business, things went very well, and in 1970, I decided to get married, but Mom and Dad absolutely didn't want me to, they were against it because she was poor, and they didn't want me stay with her because we were rich, we

were "signori". But I didn't care, I needed her, so she could interpret for me, help me. I needed her, I would teach her to sign.

Interviewer: *Was she hearing?*

Giacomo: *Of course, she was hearing! I taught her to sign . . .*

[SH, 03/01/2018, 09:40–10:02]

Although society is accustomed to read and think about minorities, it is not always obvious to everyone that one person can even be associated with more than one disadvantaged group. Being a woman and being deaf represents an identity that could result in double discrimination, as Francesca explains:

When I turned 20, my grandmother gave me a car as a gift. I remember when it arrived with a van directly from Turin. My uncle worked at Fiat, so he could buy a car at a reduced price, and he bought a Fiat 500 for me and sent it to my village. That day, the van arrived and parked right in front of my house, and my family said that there was a present for me inside. I see this big van, they open it, and inside I found a Fiat 500, and it was mine. I was so thrilled! People in my village instead thought it was crazy that I owned a car, someone who's deaf that can drive, it was not possible! For them, the deaf couldn't drive at all. That was the story in the whole village. Obviously, I could not hear all these rumors, and my grandmother disregarded them, as did my mother. After all, my grandma said "If they give you the driving license, if you got it, it means you can drive, that's enough!"

So, I started to drive around the village with my grandmother by my side, and the village gradually got used to the idea that a deaf woman could drive. Later on, I realized that a similar thing happened to my sister. At that time, she had a job. I have to say that in my village, women couldn't work but had to stay at home, at most they could be seamstress but working at home. My sister did not like dressmaking, so she found a job as a librarian at the City Hall. I've heard part of this story only recently, this is what happened: Every time she went to work, she was insulted by other villagers. They told her that she should be ashamed going to work, that she had to stay at home, that she shouldn't go to work, and she was insulted harshly. It was just another mentality, but we were in the 70s, not so many years ago. However, my sister decided to continue working [. . .]. Here in the city, it was different compared to my village, there were many more working women here, not a lot but it was more common, although when I started working in my office, out of 60 employees only two were women, my colleague and I. [SH, 20/10/2017, 24:14–26:45]

We already wrote about the importance attributed to teaching deaf children how to speak. This was the reason to ban sign language from schools, summarized in the slogan "gestures kill the word" that was spread all over the country after the Milan Congress in 1880. From many interviews, it emerges that women were more controlled in their signing compared to men, and that they were pushed more than the men to learn to speak properly. Having good speaking skills was considered charming and increased a woman's chance to become a "citizen's wife" (Cretella & Sanchez 2014: 30), as is evident from Beatrice's story:

> This deaf guy was looking for me in the village asking where the deaf-mute woman was living [. . .]; then this boyfriend [they only started dating after this episode; authors' note] rang at my door [. . .]. At that time, I was babysitting children for those women of the village who were working on the olives harvest, so I had no time to talk with him until 4 pm, when I finished working. [. . .] then he asked me whether I was deaf-mute, and I answered "Yes". [. . .] There was a hearing man with him, and he suggested to him to take me because I was good in speaking, to take me soon. [SH, 01/08/2017, 10:37–11.34]

The fact that his girlfriend had good speaking skills, and the need to have someone who could take care of all household chores, convinced Fulvio to get married, as he tells in the interview:

> Then I went to the Deaf Club, and I saw her, it was the first time, she was beautiful and she had good speech. [. . .] Yes, I liked her, but I wasn't thinking about getting married, I was just thinking about my job and playing football and nothing specific. She, too, wasn't really thinking about marrying me, she was just courting me, so we kept seeing each other. I really wasn't sure about my feelings for her, so we stayed together for a while, then we broke up, then back again. I didn't know what to do. At some point, I started thinking that I was living by myself, taking care of my laundry, always had to eat outside. Yes, I had to wash my clothes. At that time, I was renting a room in a house, and I didn't want to give my clothes to the landlady. She was a married woman with a son. So, I used to wash my clothes in the bathroom, and left them there to get dry. [. . .] After two years this way, always alone, by myself, I was thinking, and then she asked me to get married, and I accepted, and here we are. I was 26, and she was 25. [SH, 31/07/2017, 29:44–32:11]

This comment does not only highlight the double discrimination that women were faced with, but also the importance of speech and Fulvio's audistic attitude.

The interview with Laura offers another glance at the mainstream Italian culture of the 1950s and 1960s. In Italy, there was a long history of internal immigration from the South to the North during the so-called "boom", a period characterized by strong economic growth and technological development, which did not only bring a wave of immigrants in the North, but also resulted in a mutual distrust between southerners and northerners. Laura was from the South, and she moved to the North in order to escape from a very strict father, who never let her go out because she was deaf. Therefore, she left and moved to her sister's house. She met a deaf man and decided to get married. He was the first man she dated, she did not have any previous experience. Her parents and her sister did not want her to date a deaf man, so she escaped again, this time from her sister's house, saying that she would stop sending money home if they forbid her to date a deaf man. Scared of losing money, they accepted, so she started going out with this man. They got married, but things did not go well; he left her for a very close friend. They divorced and Laura, for the first time, agreed with her mother when she strongly discouraged Laura to marry a man from the North because she *"had to find a man from the South, a man like her, like us"* [SH, 20/04/2017, 23:25–24:30].

This brief excerpt hints at two pieces of common wisdom, shared both outside and inside the specific Deaf Culture: first, the one well-expressed in the Italian proverb "Moglie e buoi dei paesi tuoi" (lit. "Wife and oxen of your village", which corresponds to the English proverb "Better wed over the mixen than over the moor", meaning 'It is better to marry a neighbor than a stranger'); second, the fact that dating or marrying a deaf person was not considered a good choice by hearing parents.

We agree with Collu & Balit (1999), who wrote that the most common disagreement between parents and deaf daughters concerning marriage is the fear that a deaf child could be born should the daughter marry a deaf man (as mentioned by 12% of the married women interviewed for Collu & Balit's report). Despite this, the authors also state that the majority of the interviewed women preferred a deaf partner (78.2%). In the same study, Collu & Balit mention that marriage between deaf people is a modern trend. This claim, however, requires more in-depth analysis since, at least from the interviews we have gathered, it appears that there were very few exogamous marriages. What Luigi tells us about marrying a deaf woman is instructive:

Interviewer: *You married a deaf woman, why? How long have you been married?*

Luigi: *I married a deaf woman because hearing people speak, and I could not follow anything. I risked being isolated, but with a deaf wife, we could communicate through signs and understand each other better; with a hearing person the communication would not have been complete. If she talked to others, I could not participate and hear what they're saying. I do not remember how many years I have been married . . . so many!*

(Sala & Sala 2006: 37)

5 Conclusion

In this chapter, we examined the narrative world of elderly Deaf signers to investigate their experiences of oppression and marginalization, both in school and social life. The chapter demonstrates that Italian deaf people undoubtedly share a common past of oppression and discrimination, but that their history is more than that.

Deaf schools have not only been a place of oppression but rather a dynamic space where Deaf people have created themselves and built their community through the comparison and the collaboration with the hearing world. Moreover, the very idea of Deaf Community that emerges from the narrations of elderly Deaf people is more open to interpretation and thus less suitable for models of interpretation that "exacerbate the differences promoting the exclusion in the name of an alleged authenticity" (Fontana 2017: 248).

Italian elderly Deaf signers constitute a very heterogeneous language community, and it seems very difficult to solve "the riddle of deaf identity", considering that sign language competence is often taken to clearly separate those who are Deaf from those who are *not Deaf enough* (Lennard 2007). Finally, the analysis of gender relations demonstrates how the Deaf Community has been deeply involved in the process by which forms of power are generated and reproduced within the Italian mainstream society.

References

Babini, Valeria Paola. 2009. *Liberi tutti. Manicomi e psichiatri in Italia: una storia del Novecento*. Bologna: Il Mulino.
Barpaga, Rinkoo. 2015. *Double discrimination: Made in Britain*. London Neath Films.
Baynton, Douglas C. 1996. *Forbidden signs: American culture and the campaign against sign language*. Chicago: University of Chicago Press.
Bertaux, Daniel. 2003. *Racconti di vita. La prospettiva etnosociologica*, Milano: FrancoAngeli.
Bourdieu, Pierre. 1979. *La distinction: critique sociale du jugement*. Paris: Minuit [Ital. *La distinzione. Critica sociale del gusto*. Bologna: Mulino, 2001].
Branson, Jan & Don Miller. 2002. *Damned for their difference. The cultural construction of Deaf people as disabled*. Washington, DC: Gallaudet University Press.
Burch, Susan. 2002. *Signs of resistance. American Deaf cultural history, 1900 to World War II*. New York: New York University Press.
Cardinaletti, Anna, Carlo Cecchetto & Caterina Donati (eds.) 2011. *Grammatica, lessico e dimensioni di variazione nella LIS*. Milano: Franco Angeli.
Casellato, Alessandro. 2010. Il figlio dell'eroe. Una fonte orale. In Sergio Luzzatto (ed.), *Prima lezione di metodo storico*, 163–182. Roma: Laterza.
Cretella, Chiara & Inma Mora Sànchez. 2014. *Lessico familiare. Per un dizionario ragionato della violenza contro le donne*. Cagli: Settenove.
Collu, Ida & Valentina Balit. 1999. *Segni al femminile. Primo rapporto sulla condizione sociale delle donne sorde in Italia*. Milano: FrancoAngeli.
Congresso Nazionale degli Educatori dei Sordomuti. 1893. *Atti del secondo Congresso Nazionale degli Educatori dei Sordomuti: tenuto in Genova dal 1 al 6 settembre 1892*. Genova: Tip. dell'Istituto Sordomuti.
Corazza, Serena. 1995. Storia della Lingua dei Segni nell'educazione dei sordi italiani. In Giulia Porcari Li Destri & Virginia Volterra (eds.), *Passato e presente. Uno sguardo sull'educazione dei Sordi in Italia*, 77–102. Napoli: Gnocchi Editore.
Debè, Anna. 2014. *"Fatti per arte parlanti". Don Giulio Tarra e l'educazione dei sordomuti nella seconda metà dell'Ottocento*. Milano: EDUCatt.

Des Dorides, Luca. 2010. *Scemi, derelitti e degenerati: strategie di potere e contrattazione del sapere nell'ospedale dei matti di Roma*. Roma: Sapienza Università di Roma PhD dissertation.
Direzione Generale della Statistica. 1903. *2: Censimento della popolazione del Regno d'Italia al 10 febbraio 1901: numero delle famiglie e numero degli abitanti classificati secondo la qualità della dimora, il luogo di nascita, il sesso, l'età, lo stato civile e l'istruzione; ciechi e sordomuti, stranieri, lingue parlate*. Roma: Tip. Nazionale di G. Bertero e C.
Edwards, Rebecca. 2012. *Words made flesh: nineteenth-century Deaf education and the growth of Deaf Culture*. New York: New York University Press.
ENS. 2004. *La storia dell'Ente nazionale sordomuti: il lungo cammino della comunità sorda italiana*. Roma: ENS.
Fiorino, Vinzia. 2002. *Matti, indemoniate e vagabondi: dinamiche di internamento manicomiale tra Otto e Novecento*. Venezia: Marsilio.
Fontana, Sabina. 2017. Esiste la cultura sorda?. In Francesco Calzolaio, Erika Petrocchi, Marco Valisano & Alessia Zubani (ed.), *In limine. Esplorazioni attorno all'idea di confine*, 233–251. Venezia: Edizioni Ca' Foscari.
Fontana, Sabina, Serena Corazza, Penny Boyes Braem & Virgina Volterra. 2015. Language research and language community change: Italian Sign Language 1981–2013. *International Journal of the Sociology of Language* 236. 1–30.
Forgacs, David. 2014. *Italy's margins. Social exclusion and nation formation since 1861*. Cambridge Cambridge University Press [Ital. *Margini d'Italia: l'esclusione sociale dall'unità ad oggi*. Roma: Laterza, 2015].
Foucault, Michel. 1976. *1: La volonté de savoir*. Paris: Gallimard. [Ital. *La volontà di sapere*. Milano: Feltrinelli, 1991].
Freebody, Paul & Des Power. 2001. Interviewing Deaf adults in postsecondary educational settings: stories, cultures, and life histories. *The Journal of Deaf Studies and Deaf Education* 6(2). 130–142.
Freire, Paulo. 1971. *La pedagogia degli oppressi*. Milano: Mondadori.
Friedner, Michele. 2010. Biopower, biosociality, and community formation: how biopower is constitutive of the Deaf Community. *Sign Language Studies* 10(3). 336–345.
Friedner, Michele & Annelies Kusters (eds.) 2015. *It's a small world: international Deaf spaces and encounters*. Washington, DC: Gallaudet University Press.
Goffman, Irving. 1961. *Asylums. Essays on the social situation of mental patients and other inmates*. London: Penguin Books.
Kusters, Annelies & Maartje De Meulder. 2013. Understanding Deafhood: in search of its meanings. *American Annals of the Deaf* 158(5). 428–438.
Kusters, Annelies, Maartje De Meulder & Dai O'Brien (eds.) 2017. *Innovation in Deaf studies: the role of Deaf scholars*. Oxford: Oxford University Press.
Hirsch, Karen. 1995. Culture and disability: the role of oral history. *Oral History Review* 22(1). 1–27.
Hole, Rachelle. 2007. Working between languages and cultures: issues of representation, voice, and authority intensified. *Qualitative Inquiry* 13(5). 696–710.
Jedlowski, Paolo. 2000. *Storie comuni. La narrazione nella vita quotidiana*. Milano: Mondadori.
Ladd, Paddy. 2003. *Understanding deaf culture: in search of deafhood*. Clevedon: Multilingual Matters.

Ladd, Paddy. 2015. Global Deafhood: exploring myths and realities. In Michele Friedner & Annelies Kusters (eds.), *It's a small world: International Deaf spaces and encounters*, 274–286. Washington, DC: Gallaudet University Press.

Lane, Harlan. 1992. *The mask of benevolence: disabling the deaf community*. New York: Alfred A. Knopf.

Lane, Harlan. 1995. Note sulla sordità in memoria di Massimo Facchini. In Giulia Porcari Li Destri & Virgina Volterra (eds.), *Passato e presente. Uno sguardo sull'educazione dei Sordi in Italia*, 46–75. Napoli: Guido Gnocchi Editore.

Leigh, Irene. 2010. Reflections on identity. In Mark Marschark & Patricia E. Spencer (eds.), *The Oxford handbook of Deaf studies, language and education*, 195–209. Oxford: Oxford University Press.

Lennard, Davis. 2007. Deafness and the riddle of identity. *The Chronicle of Higher Education* 53(19).

List, Günther. 1993. Life histories of the Deaf in an oralist world. In Renate Fischer & Harlan Lane (eds.), *Looking back: a reader on the history of deaf communities and their sign languages*, 503–513. Hamburg: Signum.

Lucas, Ceil, Robert Bayley & Clayton Valli. 2001. *Sociolinguistic variation in American Sign Language*. Washington, DC: Gallaudet University Press.

Macioti, Maria Immacolata (ed.) 1986. *Biografia, storia e società. L'uso delle storie di vita nelle scienze sociali*. Napoli: Liguori Editore.

Manfredi Montanini, Marta, Laura Fruggeri & Massimo Facchini. 1979. *Dal gesto al gesto: il bambino sordo tra gesto e parola*. Bologna: Cappelli.

McCleary, Leland. 2003. Technologies of language and the embodied history of the Deaf. *Sign Language Studies* 3(2). 104–124.

McIlroy, Guy & Claudine Storbeck. 2011. Development of Deaf identity: an ethnographic study. *Journal of Deaf Studies and Deaf Education* 16(4). 494–511.

Memmi, Albert. 1965. *The colonizer and the colonized*. Boston, MA: Beacon Press.

Montesperelli, Paolo. 2003. *Sociologia della memoria*. Roma-Bari: Laterza.

Morandini, Maria Cristina. 2010. *La conquista della parola. L'educazione dei sordomuti a Torino tra Otto e Novecento*. Torino: Società Editrice Internazionale.

Nikolarizi, Magda & Kika Hadjikakou. 2006. The role of educational experiences in the development of Deaf identity. *Journal of Deaf Studies and Deaf Education* 11(4). 477–492.

Passerini, Luisa. 1978. *Storia orale. Vita quotidiana e cultura materiale delle classi subalterne*. Torino: Rosenberg & Sellier.

Perlman, Janice. 1976. *The myth of marginality: urban poverty and politics in Rio the Janeiro*. Berkeley, CA; University of California Press.

Pigliacampo, Renato. 2000. *Il genio negato. Giacomo Carbonieri psicolinguista sordomuto del XIX secolo*. Siena: Cantagalli.

Pinna, Paola, Laura Rampelli, Paolo Rossini & Virginia Volterra. 1990. Written & unwritten records from a residential school for the Deaf in Rome. *Sign Language Studies* 67. 127–140.

Portelli, Alessandro. 2007. *Storie orali: racconto, immaginazione, dialogo*. Roma: Donzelli.

Quinn, Gary. 2010. Schoolization: an account of the origins of regional variation in British Sign Language. *Sign Language Studies* 10(4). 476–501.

Radutzky, Elena. 1992. *Dizionario bilingue elementare della lingua italiana dei segni*. Roma: Edizioni Kappa.

Raseri, Enrico. 1880. *Gli istituti e le scuole dei sordomuti in Italia: risultati dell'inchiesta statistica ordinata dal Comitato locale pel Congresso internazionale dei maestri dei sordomuti da tenersi in Milano nel settembre 1880*. Roma: Tipografia Elzeviriana nel Ministero delle Finanze.

Ruiz-Williams, Elena, Meredith Burke, Vee Yee Chong & Noppawan Chainarong. 2015. "My Deaf is not your Deaf": realizing intersectional realities at Gallaudet University. In Michele Friedner & Annelies Kusters (eds.), *It's a small world: international Deaf spaces and encounters*, 262–273. Washington, DC: Gallaudet University Press.

Ryan, Donna & John Schuchman (eds.) 2002. *Deaf people in Hitler's Europe*. Washington, DC: Gallaudet University Press.

Sala, Luciano & Rita Sala. 2006. Io ricordo . . . Testimonianza di Luigi Presotto. In Rocco Roselli (ed.), *Dall'associazione Padovana di mutuo soccorso fra sordomuti alla sezione patavina dell'ente nazionale sordomuti 1926–2006: da ottant'anni al servizio dei sordi*. Padova: ENS.

Sala, Rita. 2005. *L'interprete di lingua dei segni: orecchio per i sordi e voce per gli udenti*. Padova: Università degli Studi di Padova BA thesis, a.a. 2004–2005.

Sala, Rita. 2010. *Con-segnami la tua storia: problemi metodologici nelle interviste narrative con persone sorde*. Padova: Università degli Studi di Padova MA thesis, a.a. 2009–2010.

Sani, Roberto (ed.) 2008. *L'educazione dei sordomuti nell'Italia dell'800. Istituzioni, metodi, proposte formative*. Torino: Società Editrice Internazionale.

Schembri, Adam, Jordan Fenlon, Ramas Rentelis, Sally Reynolds & Kearsy Cormier. 2013. Building the British Sign Language corpus. *Language Documentation and Conservation* 7. 136–154.

Siisiäinen, Lauri. 2016. Foucault and Deaf education in Finland. *Nordic Journal of Social Research* 7. 51–64.

Stamp, Rose, Adam Schembri, Bronwen Evans & Kearsy Cormier. 2016. Regional sign language varieties in contact: investigating patterns of accommodation. *The Journal of Deaf Studies and Deaf Education* 21(1). 70–82.

Thompson, Paul. 1978. *The voice of the past: oral history*. Oxford: Oxford University Press.

Toffanin, Tania. 2014. The reproduction of patriarchal hegemony: Women in Italy between paid and unpaid work. *Viewpoint Magazine* September2014.

Valeriano, Annacarla. 2017. *Malacarne: donne e manicomio nell'Italia fascista*. Roma: Donzelli.

Volterra, Virginia. 1981. *I segni come parole: la comunicazione dei sordi*. Torino: Boringhieri.

Volterra, Virginia & Piera Massoni. 1978. *Un'esperienza di rieducazione con bambini sordi* [s.l.: s.n.].

Volterra, Virginia & William Stokoe (eds.) 1985. *SLR '83: Proceedings of the 3rd International Symposium on Sign Language Research: Rome, June 22–26, 1983*. Silver Spring, MD: Linstok Press & Istituto di psicologia CNR.

Aslı Göksel, Süleyman S. Taşçı, Buket Ela Demirel,
Elvan Tamyürek Özparlak, Burcu Saral, and Hasan Dikyuva

Deafness in Turkey 1930–2020: administrative, social, and cultural aspects

1 Introduction

This chapter is, in large part, based on the life experiences of 31 deaf participants from five of the major towns of Turkey, elicited by deaf interviewers within the 'Life stories' component of the SIGN-HUB Project ('SIGN-HUB: Preserving, researching and fostering the linguistic, historical, and cultural heritage of European Deaf signing communities with an integral resource'). These experiences cover personal encounters and reflections, as well as factual information about various aspects of deaf life and culture including administrative, educational, and communicative issues.

We begin in Section 2 by giving information about our participants, followed by a brief introduction to the state of the legislation and education concerning the deaf in Turkey in Section 3. We then turn to the sections based on the interviews, starting in Section 4 with the activist and educationalist Süleyman Gök who was in the center stage of deaf culture (İlkbaşaran & Taşçı 2012) and continuing with the conditions and educational methods in deaf schools. Next, in Sections 5 to 7, we explore the other themes that recurrently came up during the interviews, namely communication issues and social life, including the participation of Turkey in the Deaflympics and the international Deaf beauty contest. We conclude in Section 8 with avenues for future research.

2 Participants

The participants, 19 men and 12 women, were interviewed between June 2016 and October 2019. The oldest participant was born in 1930, which means that some of the recollections go back to the time before World War II.

Seven of the participants were from Ankara, five from Diyarbakır, four from İstanbul, and 14 from İzmir, and one from Bursa. Apart from four of the participants who had no formal education (three men, one woman), all went to deaf schools. The majority (21 individuals) went through the compulsory five-year elementary school education, with two of them dropping out before completion.

Five went to middle school, and one finished high school, which means that they had eight years and 11 years of formal education, respectively. The schools that provided the education for the majority of our participants were in İzmir (*İzmir Sağırlar Okulu* ('İzmir School for the Deaf'), ten participants) and in İstanbul (*Yıldız Sağırlar Okulu* ('Yıldız School for the Deaf'), nine participants; *İstanbul Sağır Dilsizler Cemiyeti* ('İstanbul Association for the Deaf and Mute'), one participant). The remaining schools that our participants went to were in Diyarbakır (*Diyarbakır Sağırlar Okulu* ('Diyarbakır School for the Deaf'), three participants), Ankara (*Ankara Sağırlar Okulu ve Yetiştirme Yurdu* ('Ankara Children's Home and School for the Deaf'), four participants), and Siirt (*Siirt Sağırlar Okulu* ('Siirt School for the Deaf'), one participant). The information about these schools can be found in Demirel et al. (forthcoming).

It is clear from the regional distribution of the participants that the interviews show an imbalance towards those who were based in western Turkey in their formative years. Only about a third of the participants are from Ankara in the central region and from the south eastern province of Diyarbakır. Nevertheless, this imbalance has not led to any discernable differences in the life experiences that may have aroused from regional differences. One reason for this is that the participants whom we were able to contact in the south eastern and central regions all live in urban areas and they show a high degree of mobility. They have traveled and still travel to the western parts and socialize in the Deaf associations there. It is very likely that we would have had a more varied spectrum of life stories had we been able to also conduct interviews with deaf people in rural areas.

For the interviews, we followed a questionnaire which is explained in the Introduction to this volume. We refer to the participants as M (male) and F (female) for anonymity (see Appendix for the demographic information about our participants). Some of the issues that arose during the interviews are discussed in Cramer & Steinbach (this volume). As for the interviewers, all three are deaf and are among the authors of this chapter.

3 Turkey 1930–2020

During the past 90 years, Turkey has witnessed significant political and social changes. The Republic of Turkey was founded in 1923 after the war of independence against the British, French, Italian, and Greek forces that occupied Turkey after World War I. The forming of the Turkish Republic after the fall of the Ottoman Empire brought with it changes in education, legislation, and social life. The effects of World War II on Turkey were minimal compared to the surrounding countries, as Turkey did not enter the war until the final stages. In February 1945, Turkey entered the war on the side of the Allies as a diplomatic move in order to be among the founding members of the United Nations. Turkey did not engage in actual battle, though the war had immense repercussions on the economy (Zürcher 2004). Some participants related the experiences of their parents and mentioned food rationing:

> My father suffered a lot. My mother used to say it was very difficult. [. . .] There were small cards, [. . .] ration cards for bread. There would be long queues for bread. We had vouchers and that's how we got bread. We had plants in the garden. We weren't hungry.
> [F20, 19.11.2016, 00:49–00:50]

Non-aggression treaties had been drawn between Turkey, Britain, and France before the war. To avoid entering the war with Germany and its allies, Turkey also had agreements with Germany, which enabled the two countries to continue their trade relations throughout the war. Before 1938, half of the trade was with Germany and its allies (Zürcher 2004). After 1939, Turkey tried to reduce this economic reliance while at the same time still aiming to remain neutral to both Germany and opposing countries such as Britain and France. Turkey was selling mainly chromite (Ranck 2008) but interestingly there was another commodity that was sold to Germany and that involved deaf students at the production end, as recounted by a female participant while describing her school days at the İzmir School for the Deaf:

> We would sew cotton coats for the soldiers in Germany so that they wouldn't be cold. We sewed many. In the evenings, we used to sew a lot and send the clothes to Germany. We used to sew by hand, and in the evenings with the sewing machine.
> [F19, 19.11.2016, 00:32–00:33]

There were several military coups and coup attempts between 1960 and 2020, and the armed conflict between the Turkish forces and Kurdish insurgents has been continuing over the last 35 years in the south eastern provinces. Our informants did not speak much, if at all, about these issues. However, one participant (M09, 69) in Diyarbakır mentioned the closure of a Deaf community center by the military after the military takeover in 1980. This was not at all an unusual measure against non-government organizations during that time.

Today, there are about 380,000–450,000 deaf people in Turkey (İlkbaşaran 2015). The access of the deaf to the private sector institutions and public services is fraught with difficulties. To give one example, of the four major hospital chains consulted in İstanbul, only one responded positively to the presence of an employee dealing with disabilities, and it was not clear whether they had any provisions for signing patients.

In the following, we briefly introduce the historical background in two areas: legislation relating to the deaf (Section 3.1) and the education of the deaf (Section 3.2).

3.1 Legislation

The interviews reflect the various administrative regulations, some of which were the following: the changes in the legislations about education in 1962 (Milli Eğitim Bakanlığı 1962), a legislation concerning working conditions in 1964,[1] facilitation of voting and notary procedures in 1972, facilitation of the parking conditions for the disabled in 1983, discouragement of discriminatory acts towards the disabled, children, and other vulnerable individuals in 1994, facilitation of accessibility in 1997, and the introduction of free or reduced rate travel cards in 2013–2014. These measures involved all groups of disabled people and not the deaf per se. 2005–2006 saw changes of a larger scale, some applying to all disability groups, and some particular to the deaf. During these years, regulatory measures were taken to facilitate the social life of the disabled. With a modification in the labor law in 2008, a 4% quota for the employment of disabled individuals was enforced on businesses with more than 50 employees.[2] Most notably, the Ministry of Education brought together deaf and hearing educationalists, teachers, and community workers and moved towards the recognition of Turkish Sign Language (TİD). This was followed by various regulations concerning deaf education in 2013 and 2016. Despite the positive efforts, there are still no special provisions for the deaf in university entrance exams, and related to this, the deaf constitute only 5% of the disabled university students. The entry rate to higher education is very low at 0.4–0.5% (Kemaloğlu et al. 2010).

3.2 Deaf education

Between the late 19th century, when the first deaf school was established in İstanbul, and the early years of the 20th century, there were three deaf schools within the geographical area that is now Turkey (cf. İlkbaşaran & Taşçı 2012; Göksel & Taşçı 2020). These were the *İstanbul Dilsiz ve Âmâ Mektebi* ('İstanbul School for the Mute and the Blind', 1889–1926), the Martha King Memorial School

---

[1] https://www.mevzuat.gov.tr/MevzuatMetin/1.5.506.pdf
[2] http://www.iskanunu.com/images/dokuman/4857-sayili-is-kanunu-guncel-tam-metin-2012.pdf

for the Deaf in Merzifon (1910–1921), and the *İzmir Dilsiz Mektebi* ('İzmir School for the Mute'). This latter was established in or soon after 1910 (see Arıkanlı (1973), Miles (2009), Tanyeri (2016) for different dates) and was later renamed *İzmir Sağırlar Okulu* ('İzmir School for the Deaf'). It was taken over by the Ministry of Public Health in the 1920s (Ergin 1939: 1170; Batır 2008: 20), and functioned under different names until today.

For the İstanbul School for the Mute and the Blind, sources mention an oral department and another manual department (Haydar 1925; Miles 2009). In the manual department, fingerspelling and probably sign language were taught. In addition to the manual department mentioned in Haydar (1925), further evidence that sign language was used as the language of instruction comes from the books of Necati Kemal (Kip) who was the director of the İzmir School for the Deaf. Kemal wrote that he found descriptions and illustrations of signs in the notebooks of the students who attended the Yıldız School for the Deaf (Kemal 1926a,b; Turgut & Taşçı 2011; see Section 4.2). It is not known whether sign language was used in the İzmir School for the Mute. However, considering that Albert Carmona, the founder of the school, graduated from a deaf school in Paris (Ergin 1939: 1172), it is probable that he used sign language for instruction. In the Martha King Memorial School for the Deaf, the educational strategy was oralism, that is, children were taught to replace signing with speech and lip-reading in the spoken heritage languages used at their homes, which were Armenian, Greek, and Turkish (The Anatolian 1911–1912;[3] see Göksel & Taşçı (2020) for further information).

The founding of the Republic of Turkey in 1923 paved the way for the establishment of a series of deaf schools, some for the deaf and the blind (Demirel et al. forthcoming). Signing as the language of instruction was used until the 1950s, but it was banned in schools in 1951, although no official evidence for this ban has been found (İlkbaşaran 2015). The use of languages other than Turkish in instruction was prohibited by the constitutional law in 1982. This law did not target sign language use in particular, since sign language was not officially recognized at the time.

Going back to the earlier days of the Republic, oralism was imported in the 1920s by Necati Kemal to the school in İzmir and this method probably prevailed even more in the 1950s (Turgut & Taşçı 2011). However, it is very likely that there were teachers who bypassed this rule by learning and using sign language, as two of our participants whose education years at the Yıldız School for

---

[3] This is a journal which, among other articles, contains two on the Martha King Memorial School for the Deaf. For sharing this publication with us, we would like to thank Armen Marsoobian, who himself is the grandson of one of the two Dildilian brothers, photographers based in Merzifon at the time. Some of the photographs taken at the time can be found in Göksel & Taşçı (2020).

the Deaf range from 1946 to 1963 mentioned [F12, 18.11.2016, 08:29–08:52; M25, 24.01.2017, 19:23–19:36]. Signing was not encouraged as the language of instruction until the Disability Law 2005 of which Article 15 ironically states:

> Turkish sign language [sic.] is created by the Turkish Language Institution in order to provide the education and communication of the hearing-impaired people. The methods and principles of the works for creating and implementing this system are determined by the regulation to be issued jointly by the Ministry of National Education, General Directorate of Social Services and Protection of Children Agency and Administration on Disabled People under the coordination of the Turkish Language Institution.[4]
>
> (Disability Law 2005 – Article 15)

Subsequently, the Ministry of Education set up programs to train teachers for giving classes in sign language, and research on teaching programs, curricula, and course materials flourished (e.g., Makaroğlu & Dikyuva 2016; Milli Eğitim Bakanlığı 2015, 2016). Although in earlier periods, the deaf and the blind were mixed in schools (see Section 4.2), this practice was abandoned in 1951. However, since the mainstreaming practice has become widespread in recent years, the number of students in Deaf schools is dwindling. Thus, the premises of Deaf schools in some areas (as the authors of this chapter saw in İstanbul and İzmir) host vocational or special education schools for hearing children as well (Demirel et al. forthcoming).

According to the most recent statistics of the Ministry of Education from 2017–2018,[5] there are 35 primary schools with 674 students, 35 secondary schools with 1193 students, and 20 special education vocational upper secondary schools with 1886 students for the Deaf in Turkey.

4 Süleyman Gök (1904–1979): His life and contribution to deaf education

The improvements in deaf education and social life owed much to the perseverance and efforts of several individuals. The most prominent of these individuals was Süleyman Gök (see İlkbaşaran & Taşçı 2012) and references therein). Dr. Hamdi Turgut, Erol Efrand, and Kerim Altınkaynak were other influential

---

[4] Translation by the United Nations Refugee Agency: www.ilo.org/dyn/natlex/docs/ELECTRONIC/77387/96369/F229909542/TUR77387%20English.pdf.
[5] sgb.meb.gov.tr/meb_iys_dosyalar/2018_09/06123056_meb_istatistikleri_orgun_egitim_2017_2018.pdf.

activists whose names came up during the interviews. We briefly return to them in Section 7.2.

4.1 Süleyman Gök

The interviews revealed some unpublished biographical and first-hand anecdotal information about Süleyman Gök, the pioneering sign language educationalist, author, and activist (see Figure 1).[6] Gök was the author of three books on deaf education (Gök 1939, 1940, 1958). Several participants note that he could sign, speak, and write equally well [M10, 19.11.2016, 03:59–04:00; M18, 19.11.2016, 01:41–01:43] and cite him as the inventor of the TİD manual alphabet.

Figure 1a and b: Left: Süleyman Gök (taken from the Facebook page of *Türkiye Sağırlar Tesanüt Derneği* ('Solidarity Association of Turkey for the Deaf')); right: name sign of Gök, signed by one of our participants. Gök was also referred to by the honorific form of address *baba* 'father' (Zeshan 2003), which highlights his role as a pioneer.

Gök was born in 1904. He was the youngest of four or five hearing brothers [F11, 18.11.2016, 00:15–00:16 and M10, 18.11.2016, 00:62–00:63], one of whom was called Erdem [M06]. Gök became deaf after an illness at six years of age

---

[6] We have been told that *Fatih Sağırlar Okulu* ('Fatih School for the Deaf', formerly 'Yıldız School for the Deaf') has an archive on Süleyman Gök, but at the time of writing this chapter, we were unable to get access to these files.

(İlkbaşaran & Taşçı 2012). Our participants note that Gök came from a wealthy family:

> *His father owned a block of flats. He used to give all [his sons] money, but especially to the youngest, to Süleyman Gök. He [Süleyman Gök] founded a school, he used his own money for the deaf. There is an early memory [of one his students] that made him do this. [This student's] early schooling was in Morocco. The deaf in the school in Morocco can sign very well but they can't write.* [M10, 18.11.2016, 01:02–01:03]

Gök talked about his years as a student at İstanbul University to one of our participants and, in particular, the civil unrest surrounding the occupation of İstanbul by British, French, Italian, and Greek forces (13 November 1918 to 16 March 1920).[7]

> *Süleyman Gök and three others [. . .] five of them, were next to each other in a protest march, supporting the government to get the British out of our land. There was shooting in the protest march. They were lucky, no one got shot. They continued marching, and when there was shooting, the soldiers stood in front of them. [. . .] Then the British ran away. [. . .] Süleyman Gök was a student then. He saw the end of the war.*
>
> Interviewer: *Did Süleyman Gök tell you this?*
>
> M10: *Yes, I heard it from him.* [M10, 18.11.2016, 06:04–07:07]

From these early days until he died, Gök devoted himself to the welfare of the deaf. His determination and dedication are legendary. He is remembered as a *"pioneer for everything novel"* [F11, 18.11.2016, 00:15–00:16], as someone who was the *"first to bring in artistic and cultural activities"* [F11 & F12, 18.11.2016, 03:20–03:21]. He was much liked, although he was a strict disciplinarian.

> *The teachers were [three unidentified name signs], and four and five other teachers. There was a strict discipline at the school. The teachers were relentless. But when the school recessed for the weekend, there was only Süleyman Gök. That's where I met him. He used to be angry with us all the time, he used to tell us that we were not well-behaved. He tried hard to make us succeed in life. Only afterwards did it all make sense.*
> [M09, 17.11.2016, 00:24–00:25]

> *If we were being lazy, he would get angry with us. He was a strict disciplinarian. He was trying to develop the education in both the alphabet and speaking. I am forever indebted to Süleyman Gök. Every morning, he himself would get each one us to drink egg yolks.*
> [M18, 19.11.2016, 01:41–01:43]

---

[7] Although our participant reports that Süleyman Gök was a university student during the occupation of İstanbul, this does not seem possible, as he would have been, at most, 16 years of age at the time. We can assume that either Süleyman Gök was a high school student, or that the anecdote relates to another demonstration during the Turkish Independence War (1919–1923).

He also seems to have been a central figure and a mentor in the personal and professional lives of his students:

> When we met, he told me that one day, I would be in the executive committee [of the Deaf association]. Much later, I became an executive committee member. Süleyman Gök's predictions were borne out. [F12, 18.11.2016, 03:06–03:07]

> I went to Süleyman Gök. He gave me a document and said 'Go apply for this job, don't lose time'. I went to Cevizli but the employer said 'We have too many deaf workers here, go to Siemens.' Then, I was the only deaf person there at Siemens. [M29, 09.11.2018, 00:31–00:32]

> After I finished school, Süleyman Gök took a look at me and knew that I had learned sign language properly. It was he who gave me my name [a sign that points to the nose]. [F11, 18.11.2016, 02:14–02:16]

This name sign can be seen in Figure 2.

Figure 2: Name sign of one of the participants, given to her by Süleyman Gök.

Gök was active both as an educationalist and as a community leader until his death. According to M10, he died in 1979 of a prostate-related illness, and was buried at the Eyüp cemetery in İstanbul.

> Süleyman Gök's illness was always recurring. The funeral was very crowded. People came from all over Turkey, [. . .] there was a convoy. [. . .] In the cemetery, up from the house in Eyüp, at the very top, you normally couldn't find a plot. But Süleyman Gök's father was buried there [making it easier to find a burial place]. [M10, 18.11.2016, 01:01–01:03]

4.2 The organizations and schools established by Süleyman Gök

Gök founded an unofficial deaf organization which functioned as a support group in the 1930s but which did not last more than a decade (see Figure 3).

Figure 3: Members of the first unofficial deaf solidarity group in the 1930s (taken from the Facebook page of the Solidarity Association of Turkey for the Deaf).

Following this, he established the Solidarity Association of Turkey for the Deaf in 1941 and from the income he secured from the association, he opened a school for the deaf and the blind under the umbrella of the association in 1943–1944.[8] In a photograph of Gök and school staff (see Figure 4), the name on the facade of the school building is *Dilsiz ve Körler Okulu* ('The School for the Mute and the Blind'), and above the name is written *Sağır Dilsiz ve Körler Tesanüt Cemiyeti* ('Solidarity Organization for the Deaf, Mute, and Blind').

---

8 According to Gök (1958), the date is 1943; according to a current member of the executive board of the association, it is 1943–1944.

Figure 4: The opening ceremony of the School for the Mute and the Blind (taken from the Facebook page of the Solidarity Association of Turkey for the Deaf).

The financial link between the association and the school came up in many interviews (see also Gök 1939, 1940, 1958).

> *First, there was the association. Then, with the earnings from there, he opened the school and he provided financial support this way. The state wasn't funding the school, it was a private enterprise.* [M17, 19.11.2016, 01:31–01:32]

> He founded a free school. Accommodation, food, everything was free. It was very nice. First at [. . .] Aksaray. He brought us students together there and taught us signs.
> [F11, 18.11.2016, 00:13–00:15]

Although privately funded, the school ran into many hardships and, possibly unjustly, this put blame on Gök [M14, 18.11.2016, 01:02–01:04]. At times, there was a shortage of food, and the living conditions were hard, as is evident from the following interview fragments:

> We used to say to Süleyman Gök, 'We're hungry'. No food, no meat, the food was bad. [. . .] He used to say, 'There is no money'.
> [M17, 19.11.2016, 01:31–01:32]

> One day Süleyman Gök [. . .] came to class and started talking to us. He said, 'There are rats here, be careful, the building is very old, very bad, be careful'. [. . .] The children [. . .] thought the teacher was just being very strict. [. . .] Then they saw the rats. They went and told Süleyman Gök. He put something on and came downstairs. He called us and gave us a lecture: 'In the event of a rat biting you, the doctors can't save you. You will have to be immersed in lime water, so that the virus doesn't spread'. [. . .] We were aghast. We didn't know if Süleyman Gök was telling the truth or was trying to scare us. There wasn't any medication at the time. If the rat bit one person, the disease would spread. They used to check the children regularly. [. . .] If the bite was deep, the kids would be immersed in lime water.
> [M10, 18.11.2016, 00:53–00:55]

These sentiments echo the conditions in deaf institutions of a decade ago. In the 1930s, the financial bottleneck forced Gök to find money (presumably for the deaf association although M10 below reports this as seeking money for the school, which could not have been the case, based on the dates). He went to Ankara, to see Atatürk, the founder and the first president of the Republic of Turkey (1923–1938). Gök's ability to speak must have facilitated his access to government offices and officials.

> Süleyman Gök [. . .] went to Atatürk's residence. The guards told him that he could not enter. It turns out that Atatürk was upstairs getting dressed. While Süleyman Gök was arguing with the guards, Atatürk heard the noise. From his voice, Atatürk understood Süleyman Gök was deaf. He looked out the window, 'What's going on?', he asked. The soldier said, 'Sir, this deaf man wants to speak to you'. Atatürk said, 'Let him in'. Süleyman Gök goes in, Atatürk comes downstairs, and they start talking. Süleyman Gök says, 'I founded a deaf school'. Atatürk says, 'Yes I heard, that's very good'. Süleyman Gök says he has financial problems. So, Atatürk presses a button. [. . .] He says that he will look into it and then gives 1000. In those days, 1000 was good money. [Today it would be] 100,000 [Turkish Lira] or so.
> [M10, 18.11.2016, 01:07–01:10]

Nevertheless, the financial hardships persisted:

> Atatürk was good. After he passed away, İnönü came to power [second president of Turkey (1938–1950); authors' note]. He was hard-of-hearing. He used a hearing aid. He wouldn't

> fund us very well, he was excessively frugal. Süleyman Gök used to go to him and ask for a budget, and İnönü would say, 'No'. Because of the effects of the war, he would try to make ends meet.
> [M10, 19.11.2016, 04:03–04:05]

During Fahrettin Kerim Gökay's term of office as governor (1949–1957), possibly in the early 1950s, the school started receiving subsidy from the Municipality of İstanbul [M17, 19.11.2016, 00:40–00:41]. One of our participants attributes the governor's decision to subsidize the school to a visit from the United States (see Figure 5):

Figure 5: Gök (circled in the photograph), his staff, and students, with the visitor from the United States (woman wearing a hat – mentioned in the interview) in front of the school building (taken from the Facebook page of the Solidarity Association of Turkey for the Deaf).

> An American visitor wanted to see Deaf schools. The state officials were embarrassed, as there were no publicly funded Deaf schools. She said, 'Ankara is the capital, and your Deaf school is in İstanbul?'. Once she visited the school, she was very impressed. The students were seated in a V or U shape, they could write down all the signs. And who taught them this? Süleyman Gök did. [. . .] Then the government started subsidizing the school.
> [M28, 09.11.2018, 01:07–01:10]

In 1951, the school moved first from Aksaray to Topkapı and then, in 1953, to Yıldız, and thereafter was known as the Yıldız School for the Deaf.

> Süleyman Gök decided to move the school to Topkapı for lack of funds. [. . .] They sent Süleyman Gök away, saying that he is deaf, and to bring someone else in to run the school.
> [M17, 19.11.2016, 00.40–00.41]

According to one of the participants, at some point before 1953, the government closed down the school that had been built under the association. Again, according to the same participant, this was because Gök was deaf [M17, 19.11.2016, 00.40–00.41]. According to another participant, the closure was the result of literacy training not being part of the curriculum [M10, 18.11.2016, 01:02–01:03], though this information is at odds with the sign-spoken bilingual education vision of Gök. The excerpt below indicates that Gök's deafness certainly played a part. To deal with the situation, Gök applied to re-open the school with a new curriculum, but his request was denied on the grounds that a deaf person would be unable to run a school that also had blind students. At the time, deaf and blind students studied in mixed schools, and the new school would have to enroll both deaf students and blind students. To open the school, Gök took an unusual step:

> He put up a fight against the government. [. . .] He found a blind woman and he married her. [. . .] When a deaf person married another deaf person, they were not granted the documents [to open a school]. So, he married a blind person and went to Ankara. He saw the officials face to face. [. . .] And he went there with his wife. He said, 'Look, I'm married to a blind woman, I'm helping her, we go everywhere together, this is who I married'. [. . .] He humiliated them. And they were left without anything to say. They couldn't object, they signed the documents, and gave them to him. In time, it became the School for the Deaf. He has a daughter from his blind wife. The daughter is old now, she lives in İzmir. That's how he got married. [M10, 18.11.2016, 01:03–01:06]

The school was opened, but it now belonged to the public sector, having been taken over by the Ministry of Education.[9] After the Ministry of Education took over the school and the students were moved from the district of Topkapı to Yıldız, the situation changed for the better. One of the participants compares the situation at the school before and after it was taken over by the Ministry of Education:

> At school and in the classes, the conditions were bad [before]. Süleyman Gök used to find food subsidy. Before moving to Yıldız, we had very little. [. . .] They [the state] helped with money, clothing, shoes. This didn't happen before. [M09, 17.11.2016, 00:24–00:26]

---

[9] The exact nature of the developments after the change is not clear, but it is known that the school opened as a Deaf school rather than a school for the deaf and the blind.

Gök remained the director of the Yıldız School for the Deaf until the end of the 1950s (Figure 6 shows a room in the dormitory of the school).[10] His contribution to the training of individuals and the improvement of educational methods are briefly covered in the next section.

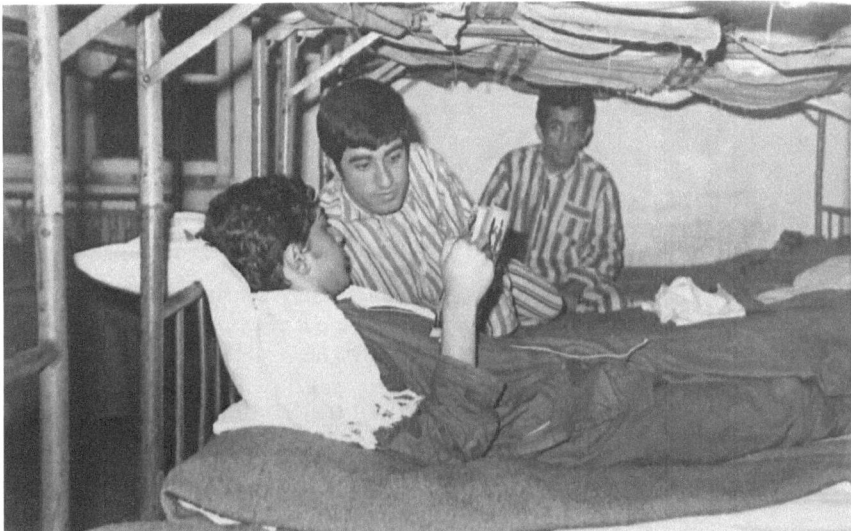

Figure 6: In the dormitory at Yıldız School for the Deaf. Private collection.

4.3 Education methods

The education in the school that Gök founded was informed by the French system of educating the deaf:

> Süleyman Gök went to France, all alone. [. . .] He learned how to educate us and came back and put it into practice. He taught the directors, directors of the associations, chairpersons, he taught them what he knew, and put a lot of effort into teaching them all [what sign language was about]. He went from one association to another and trained people.
> [M10,18.11.2016, 01:14–01:16]

The fingerspelling system at the time was an adaptation of the one-handed fingerspelling system that was used in European countries. It was adapted to the Arabic script that was in use in Turkey until 1928, the year when the script was

---

10 This school has been renamed and is the current *Mimar Sinan İşitme Engelliler Okulu* ('Mimar Sinan Secondary School for the Deaf').

replaced by the Latin alphabet as part of educational, social, and political reforms (cf. Taşçı 2012 and references therein). Gök applied a similar change to the TİD manual alphabet:

> M10: *Formerly, the old alphabet was taught. Süleyman Gök knew it very well. Then he established the TİD alphabet. He taught it to the school teachers and then it spread from there. [. . .]*
>
> Interviewer: *Did he himself decide on the signs for the letters of the alphabet? Did he make them up himself?*
>
> M10: *Yes, yes, he did it all himself.*
>
> [M10, 18.11.2016, 04:21–04:24]

Some of the participants also emphasize Gök's signing skills:

> *His signing was amazing. Anyone who saw it was amazed; you would have loved it, too. Bless him. He used to teach us sign language within a plan and a program. He was very knowledgeable, very well-read. I have great respect for him.* [F11, 18.11.2016, 02:13–02:14]

The school in Aksaray, which was situated on the floor beneath the Solidarity Organization for the Deaf, Mute, and Blind (currently the Solidarity Association of Turkey for the Deaf), had both signing and speaking lessons:

> Interviewer: *At school, was Süleyman Gök teaching how to speak (teaching the sounds, like a, b, c), or was he teaching signs?*
>
> M10: *There were instructions in signing and speaking at school. We used to have a balloon in our hand and practice with that. For example, when we made the sound p, the voice would hit the balloon. We learned through sensing.*
>
> [M10, 18.11.2016, 01:14–01:15]

One of the participants discusses his education after signing was banned at schools (see Section 2.2):

> *Speaking is difficult. We used paper. For example, the sound of p depends on the air flow. Learning it takes a long time, it is very difficult. We were looking forward to the end of class, so that we students could sign among us. The teacher banned this, too. It was very upsetting. [. . .] We didn't have an abacus, we used beans to count.*
>
> [M28, 09.11.2018, 00:29–00:31]

5 Communication issues

The interviews reveal that the communication between the participants and hearing non-signers often involved misunderstandings, discrimination, and stigmatization. The non-signers in question could be the friends or family of the deaf, their peers at school, their neighbors and fellow co-workers, or people that they came across in banks, hospitals, and various other state or private institutions. Although there were hearing individuals in the lives of our participants who learnt to sign, it emerges that most hearing non-signers expected the deaf to adapt, be it by writing when they wanted to say something, or by lip-reading when they wanted to understand what was being said by another person. Yet, speaking was discouraged, even though this was a step taken by the deaf to adapt to the communication mode of the hearing. The phrase 'X had a bad voice' came up in many contexts, and for some of the participants, the emotional repercussions of the negative experience of having a bad voice are lasting. Being sensitive about the quality of one's own voice, which stands for the quality of spoken articulation, hence a sign of 'normality', is probably an issue that deaf people are confronted with from their early childhood. Hearing people's attitudes towards the voice of the deaf may even be internalized by deaf people. One participant used the expression 'bad voice' for other deaf students. She told us that when she was at the İzmir School for the Deaf, she helped other students with their articulation:

> *My teacher was very good. Not all of the teachers were good, some deaf students had problems with learning. Everyone would ask me to help them, to educate them. [. . .] Some had good voices, and some others had bad voices.* [F21, 19.11.2016, 00:23–00:24]

The lasting effects of being told that one has a bad voice are most apparent in a male participant who shared his memory about the point at which he decided to stop speaking for good. He was 39, and the incident took place at the barbershop:

> *I tried to communicate with the barber by speech. The guy said 'Your voice isn't good. It's disturbing, I don't understand you. Don't try to talk, just write notes and give them to me. You're babbling something, and I don't understand. It sounds weird, as if you have something in your throat'. I was very upset. I thought people have always thought this way, but they never told me. How naïve I was. My family was obviously used to it, but not strangers.*
> [M01, 07.06.2016, 00:35–00:36]

The same participant was also discouraged regarding his chosen profession, acting, by a hearing actor:

> I have a neighbor who is an actor. I told him that I also wanted to be an actor. He said, 'You don't hear, you can't talk'. I said, 'I can use facial expressions and other gestures, wouldn't it work?'. He said, 'No, no way, you don't hear, you are deaf, you can't act'. This made me very sad.
> [M01, 07.06.2016, 00:41–00:43]

Another theme that came up concerns the anxiety caused by hearing people's reactions to deaf people about their life skills. In the next account, the deaf participant mentions how she was scorned by her neighbors for staying asleep while her baby was crying. The names in the quote have been changed in order to protect the anonymity of the people involved.

> I turned on the lights, put the soup on the stove. I must have fallen asleep because I was very tired. The baby was apparently screaming in my arms. One of the neighbors, luckily, heard the screaming a few minutes later. [. . .] 'The baby is crying, how am I going to wake her up', she thought, and called out to my older son: 'Ali, come quickly!', she shouted. But Ali was in the crib, he tried to get out but couldn't. In the meantime, I'm fast asleep. [. . .] And the neighbor said to Ali 'Do this, do that', and then finally, Ali could get out of the crib. The baby was on the floor. Then Ali woke me up. I took the baby in my arms. She was crying a lot. It was all very bad. I opened the door. All the neighbors were there. They were all very anxious. 'Give us the baby, she is upset and wet from crying', they said, and took the baby from my arms. 'Oh dear, what have you done?', they said. I was just this once so very tired. I am a careful, responsible person, but this exceptionally happened once.
> [F05, 15.11.2016, 01:42–01:44]

The perception of incompetence, too, can be internalized by a deaf person. A participant told us how her mother died due to being administered the wrong blood type. The striking part of her rendition is that she says that she would have sued the hospital if she wasn't deaf.

> We were going to file a suit. [. . .] My brother said, 'What good will it do? She's dead'. It was important for me, and I was angry, and said I would follow it up. My brother objected and said the whole hospital has been closed down, what more do you want? All the same, there should have been a lawsuit. If I hadn't been deaf, I would have pursued it. I built up a grudge against my brother.
> [F21, 19.11.2016, 01:00–01:02]

As a result of such experiences, some deaf individuals stated that they felt more comfortable communicating with hearing people in the presence of a close relative who could interpret:

> It was difficult to communicate with hearing people. That's why I went to work with my mother. There were a lot of customers, we were earning well. And everyone liked my work.
> [F05, 15.11.2016, 01:19–01:20]

Alongside these negative experiences, there were encounters with hearing people who were willing to adapt their rate of speech and to use more pronounced facial expressions and gestures:

> When people speak fluently and fast, I don't understand them. If a person knows that I am deaf, they don't speak fast. Sometimes, when someone speaks fast, I tell them, I am deaf. When people know I'm deaf, [. . .] they use body language with me. I don't understand long sentences. [M04, 15.11.2016, 03:13–03:15]

The perception of incompetence, just like that of 'having a bad voice', can have its roots in early childhood. Some participants report that when they were at school, instead of learning in classes, they were given chores that had nothing to do with the curriculum or education.

> They would hit our hands. There were no classes at school. We used to be given chores like sewing duvets in the dormitory. There were no classes at school. [. . .] I was zero. I wasn't taught anything. [F23, 24.01.2017, 00:31–00:33]

We lastly turn to communication with the blind. A participant who attended a school for the deaf and the blind expressed that she preferred to communicate with her blind peers through tactile signing because she was uncomfortable about her articulation:

> We would eat together [with the blind students], go do sewing, hang around together. I didn't use my voice because I thought the sounds wouldn't come out right. I felt sorry for the blind. Sometimes they [the blind students] would take my arm, but we weren't together all the time. I used to make some sounds once in a while, not all the time. We were used to the situation. When we played, they used to feel my cheeks and recognize me, they would call out my name [. . .]. They would recognize my voice. [F19, 19.11.2016, 00:35–00:37]

There is another aspect that was mentioned, this time regarding the stigmatization of the blind. One participant recounted that there were incidents of psychological and physical violence towards the blind students by some of the deaf students, and that she did her best to prevent her deaf peers from mocking the blind students.

> We were together with blind students. The deaf students would pick on them. The blind students would not know what to do. I felt for them, I would tell the deaf students to stop doing this. The blind students would recognize me from my voice and would find me. They wanted me to protect them. I would say, 'Stop doing that, stop hitting'. [. . .] They could understand the signs by touching our hands. Very difficult. [. . .] The deaf students weren't giving them any peace, they were joking, of course, but it was very unkind. I would tell them to stop it. I would keep an eye on them but it was difficult to be together. I graduated with the blind students. [F21, 19.11.2016, 01:03–01:04]

6 Military service

All of our male participants had some experience with military service, and only one of them noted that it was a valuable experience, in that he saw what the military was like, while the others recounted how much worse it was in those days. Some of the male participants had traumatic experiences during the procedures for exemption from military service. Military service is obligatory in Turkey for males over 18 years of age, and all the participants who talked about their experiences (eight in all) underwent checks for deafness around that age. The onus was on the candidates to prove that they were deaf. One participant [M26, 08.11.2018, 01:22–01:24] recalled that he had to make sure he kept silent during the tests. Another participant [M28, 09.11.2018, 01:24–01:27] mentioned that, although he showed his diploma from a deaf school, he was kept for a fortnight, as his papers were thought to be fraudulent due to his exceptionally good reading and writing skills.

Some of the tests that were administered induced pain, and there were other humiliating and traumatizing experiences during the check-ups. After checking in at the military headquarters, the informants spent from a day to a week before they were exempted. Some had their heads shaven as soon as they checked in. Despite presenting papers proving that they were deaf, the typical reaction was doubt, especially if they could speak well. In particular, officers in higher ranks were brutal. Three of the participants told us that water was spurted into their ear with some pressure, making them dizzy. One of the participants was seated on a chair which was then whirled around and this seems to have been done for no other reason than to humiliate him.

There is also reference to earlier times, when the deaf were kept in the headquarters for days, sometimes up to six months, working in the kitchens. Here are some of those experiences:

> I was sent to the tank regiment. [. . .] I am deaf, but they thought I was pretending. They wanted to see my identity card. I presented it. [The officer] thought I was lying and got angry. 'Come here', he shouted. I would have argued back but decided to keep quiet [. . .]. He said a few things in quite an aggressive manner. [. . .] 'I can't hear', I said. He was angry again and went on saying things. [. . .] He spurted something into my ear with a syringe. They did this to check if I had inserted something into my ear, so it would come out. [. . .] Nothing came out [. . .] Then they made me close my eyes and made some noises near my ear. No reaction. [. . .] They tried and tried, and nothing came of it. Then they applied electric current to my palms. They turned on the electric current. Like lighting a match, it was. I thought smoke was coming out of my head, I thought I was burning. [. . .] The commander was surprised at my resilience. I was very angry. I almost hit him. [. . .] The commander got scared. He said, 'OK, OK, do you have your identity card with you?'. When I showed it to him, he saw it was correct [that I was deaf]. He turned pale. I said, 'I told you

I am deaf'. He left the room in embarrassment. [. . .] I was angry. They said, 'Officers can beat you up if they want to, they can arrest you, but don't fight back, don't say a word'. I said to the soldier, 'You harmed me, you gave me electricity'. He said, 'What can we do, we follow orders here [. . .]'. I decided to swallow my words.

[M04, 15.11.2016, 04:04–04:06]

They put me on a chair, pressed a button, and I started whirling. The soldier asked, 'Are you on your own?' and I said, 'Yes'. 'Is that so', he said, and pressed the button again, and I started whirling again. 'Not enough?'. And it whirls again. And he keeps asking, 'Are you on your own?'. And then he sees me sticking to what I say, and then he makes me whirl again. Then they let me go. I was resilient. It was all very strange. Were the soldiers punishing me for something? I don't have a clue. I was released within a day. I passed the chair test.

[M14, 18.11.2016, 00:57–00:59]

They are terrible. They took our blood and stocked it. They closed my mouth and my face. I shouted. They spurted water into both of my ears with a syringe. They beat me up, shouted at me to see whether I heard them or not. I didn't react. Then one week later, it was over, and they sent me home. The military was awful in those days.

[M07, 16.11.2016, 01:20–01:21]

One of the participants mentions that in some provinces, deaf men were drafted and were expected to do military service:

I was 22 when I was drafted [in Sivas]. [. . .] I went through a health check-up for three days. I didn't speak during that time. [. . .] If you say even a few words, they make you serve for six months. I was told that those who cannot hear but can speak do six months' service. As for me, I did cleaning jobs for two days, three days of tests and check-ups, and then I was let go.

[M26, 08.11.2018, 01:22–01:24]

This practice may have been a remnant of the practices of earlier times, when the deaf were not only drafted but were also sent to the front, a fact related in the following anecdote:

In the time of Atatürk, there were deaf soldiers. I was in my twenties. I met a man in Taksim [Square] in his eighties, a very old man. Elderly deaf people were chatting. They were sharing their wartime experiences during the time of Atatürk. They were saying, 'I am deaf, I was finding it very difficult, I was trying to protect myself, luckily it's over'. I was overwhelmed. 'Do you have a 'Veteran's Medal?', I asked. They said 'No'. I felt so sad. There are so many hearing people with a Veteran's Medal, but when it comes to the deaf, they weren't given medals. It made me so sad to hear this.[11]   [M01, 27.06.2016, 01:51–01:53]

---

[11] The person who is reported to have been in his eighties in the 1970s was probably born in the last decade of the 19th century, which would make him somewhere between 14–24 during World War I. The reference to Atatürk, though, makes it more likely that he fought in the Turkish Independence War which took place between 1919–1923. It is known that there were deaf soldiers in the army; see the chapter 'A deaf and dumb soldier of the Turkish army' in Pye (1933).

7 Professional and social life

22 of our participants talked about their professional life. Some had more than one occupation. The majority were either tailors/dressmakers (12) or carpenters (7). The other participants had the following professions: cobbler (1), bank clerk (1), technician (1), civil servant (1), factory worker (4), ironsmith (1), domestic worker (1), and farmer (2). We also interviewed one participant who was an actor and one who owned her own hairdresser's salon (see Appendix).

The difficulty of finding jobs was a recurrent theme in the interviews. One participant [M26, 08.11.2018, 00:41–00:44] reports that he went to Ankara from his hometown to seek employment, but was turned down in a succession of job applications. In the end, a relative of his gave him a job as a technician fixing satellite dishes.

In the following subsections, we will report anecdotes from the social life of our participants.

7.1 Traveling

Despite the hardships during job searches or caused by miscommunication, many of the interviews reveal that the lack of a shared language was not in the way of traveling and the love of seeing new places was very common insofar as the external circumstances allowed it. As far as the participants related potential communication problems, these appear not to have been experienced as a hindrance. Some of these trips were made with family members, others with groups (e.g., trips organized by Deaf associations). Being more affordable, domestic trips were more common.

> We used to make cultural trips. We used to visit the historical places. In Turkey, we went and saw every part of the Black Sea Region, the Mediterranean Region, but because of terrorism, we couldn't travel to the eastern regions. [F11, 18.11.2016, 01:16–01:17]

> I went to Poland, to Syria, and on pilgrimage to Mecca. I communicated in a somewhat rude way, by waving my hands here and there, like villagers [. . .] I always traveled and wanted to learn more, tried to understand what was going on. [M28, 09.11.2018, 01:50–01:51]

One of our participants emphasizes how much she loved travelling abroad:

> It was wonderful. I went to America, I went to Germany, Russia, Kazakhstan. I never stopped. I travelled with my husband. But earlier, there was a sports group here. [. . .] X took the group and went. They stayed 20 days [. . .] I had things to do, so I couldn't join them. Our sign language was different from the people in places we travelled to. Our communication was patchy. During these trips, we didn't talk much. When they talked in their own sign

language, I would understand them but I couldn't speak their [sign] language. X communicated with them better . . . all the travelling was excellent. I also went to Dubai, two years ago, in the summer. Dubai was beautiful. [F23, 24.01.2017, 00:52–00:55]

Below, there is an anecdote about one of the participants' first meeting with his wife during such a trip.

In the past, hanging out with girls or holding their hands wasn't welcomed. I had girlfriends in Ankara, I used to pay a visit to them, and we used to chat and flirt, but we couldn't hang out. One day, two of my friends and I went to our friends in İstanbul. That was the first time that I saw her [his wife; authors' note]. *She was so sweet and naïve. I was constantly joking, and she was being shy. I didn't look at the other girls. Then, I came back to school. In the winter break, they came to Ankara, and we came across each other. We got along and started flirting. [. . .] Afterwards, I went to Sivas* [her hometown; authors' note], *and she was happy to see me.* [M04 15.11.2016, 00:25–00:29]

In one case, traveling lead to a change of domicile. Below, there is an anecdote shared by a deaf participant who settled in France.

I went to France in 1981 for travelling purposes. At that time, I had a close friend there who invited us. Then, I thought I should take a trip. [. . .] I was with my deaf friends. We liked France very much. My three-month term was over, and then I extended my stay. After that, I decided to live in France. [M01, 07.06.2016, 01:07–01:08]

As a final point highlighting our participants' desire to travel and the feeling of freedom that comes with it, we report an anecdote that reveals, yet again, the ignorance of the state officials about deafness. This particular participant wanted to get a driver's license, but since in those days (late 1960s – early 1970s) obtaining a driver's license in Turkey was not possible for deaf people, he went to Switzerland to get it (see Figure 7).

I thought if I got a driver's license in Europe, it would be accepted here in Turkey, and it was. Süleyman Gök told me to go through a police checkpoint deliberately. I was driving through it, and the police stopped my car. The police officer asked me whether I could hear. 'If you don't hear, you cannot drive', he said. I told him I had a driver's license. He looked at my driver's license, and then, at the rear of the car, he saw the emblem with a symbol for an ear and three dots, which used to be the sign for deaf people. He was very surprised. He didn't say anything else. [M10, 18.11.2016, 01:45–01:50]

7.2 Deaf organizations

Following up from the information mentioned in Section 4, we will provide some additional information regarding the prominent community leaders and the deaf associations that are mentioned in the interviews, *Türkiye Sağırlar*

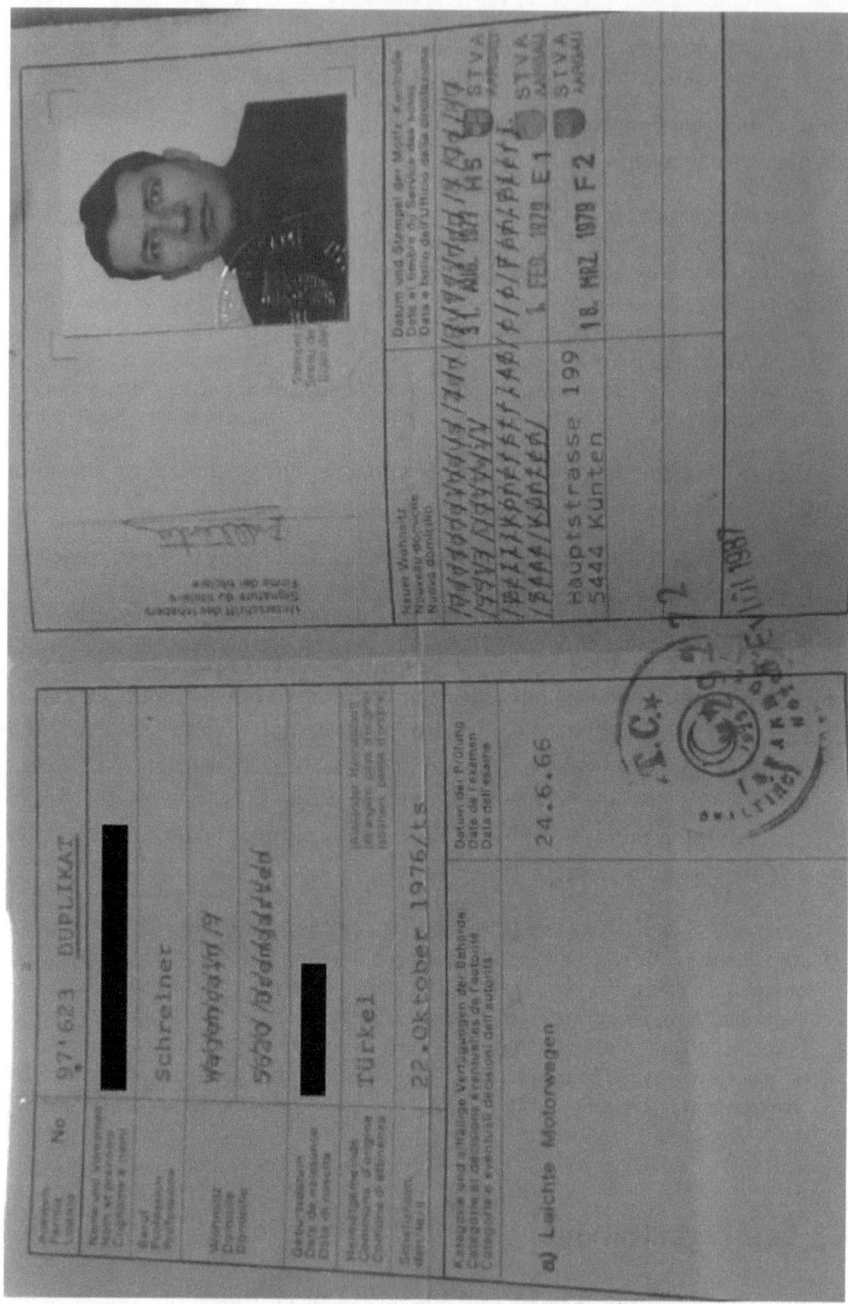

Figure 7: The driver's license of one of our participants (M10), which was issued in Switzerland and then approved in Turkey. Private collection.

Tesanüt Derneği ('Solidarity Association of Turkey for the Deaf'), *Türkiye Sağırlar Milli Federasyonu* ('Turkey National Federation of the Deaf'), and *Türkiye İşitme Engelliler Derneği* ('Turkey Association for the Deaf'). The history of these three organizations is interwoven with the personal histories of the community leaders. There are three important figures besides Süleyman Gök (see Section 4.1), who were active in the community: Dr. Hamdi Turgut, Erol Efrand,[12] and Kerim Altınkaynak.

The first of these, the Solidarity Association of Turkey for the Deaf, was founded in 1941. M04 mentions that Süleyman Gök personally founded the association.[13]

> The first person to found an association for the deaf was Süleyman Gök. A very long time ago. [. . .] He was the one who worked so very hard to get the association going, he was the one who founded it.[14] [M04, 15.11.2016, 04:22–04:23]

Kerim Altınkaynak, a hearing bank clerk [M09, 17.11.2016, 00:53–00:54], was an active member of the Solidarity Association of Turkey for the Deaf:

> Kerim was the one who really worked hard for it. Süleyman Gök, Dr. Hamdi Turgut, they all founded it together. In Aksaray and Beyoğlu. [. . .] The person who used to communicate with the public offices was Kerim. [M09, 17.11.2016, 00:53–00:54]

In 1959, Kerim Altınkaynak spearheaded a splinter group that tried to take over the executive committee from Gök's group in the elections, but then this group separated and formed what is now Turkey Association for the Deaf.[15]

Turkey National Federation of the Deaf was founded in 1962.[16] Dr. Hamdi Turgut was the president of the federation between 1962–1966 and 1977–1982 (see Figure 8 for the name sign of Dr. Hamdi Turgut, signed by one of our participants). According to M10 [18.11.2016, 01:00–01:01], he was the first person

---

12 The last name of Erol Efrand (1940–2001) appears in some sources as Efrant. Based on the inscription on his tombstone, we have used the name Efrand.
13 One of our participants, who was in the executive board in İzmir, describes the location of the İzmir branch as *"next to the mosque at the bottom of the small hill"* [M06, 16.11.2016, 00: 41–00:42].
14 One of the authors of this article, Buket Ela Demirel, was told by one of the current executive board members of the Solidarity Association of Turkey for the Deaf that the records of the association dating back to 1941 are in the possession of the brother of one of our participants (M10 from İzmir). Unfortunately, at the time of writing this article, we did not have access to these files.
15 http://www.tied.org.tr/tarihce/
16 http://tsmf.org.tr/kongre-tarihi-ve-baskanlar/

Figure 8: The name sign of Dr. Hamdi Turgut, signed by one of our participants.

to hire the premises for the Turkey National Federation of the Deaf in Fatih, a district in İstanbul. M10 remembers Dr. Hamdi Turgut:

> M10: *There used to be Doctor Hamdi, a hearing man. Süleyman Gök's [Deaf] Association was different. [. . .] I don't know if [the doctor] is still alive. He was trying to quit smoking. He would chew on a piece of wood to take his mind off cigarettes. He was a very good man. Later, Süleyman Gök still kept contact with him.*
>
> Interviewer: *Did he know how to sign?*
>
> M10: *Yes, quite well.* [M10, 18.11.2016, 01:00–01:01]

Erol Efrand, another prominent figure, was a student at the Yıldız School for the Deaf when the school was located at the district of Topkapı. M09 mentions that he himself was one year below Erol Efrand and notes, *"Erol could speak, he was 11 at the time"* [M09, 17.11.2016, 00:25–00:26].

At times, differences in personalities led to frictions or conflicts. It seems that the internal works of the deaf associations were fraught with disagreements.

> *I was, at one point, the head of the National Federation. Erol wasn't there. Süleyman Gök didn't want Erol to be there, he didn't let him in. So, Erol was the head of the National Sports Federation* [Türkiye İşitme Engelliler Milli Spor Federasyonu ('Turkey National Sports Federation for the Deaf'); authors' note], *and the chair of the association. Then in the election that took place after Süleyman Gök passed away in 1979, Erol and I talked*

about the elections and exchanged duties. He gave me the position of the head of the National Sports organization and I gave him the position of the head of the Federation. This all happened within one year. [M09, 17.11.2016, 00:53–00:55]

7.3 Deaflympics

We were fortunate enough to have among our participants some who had taken part in the Deaflympics in their youth.

The International Committee of Sports for the Deaf (ICSD) is an organization that organizes sports events that are equivalent to the Olympic Games for hearing athletes. In the Deaflympics, deaf athletes compete at an advanced level once every four years. Deaflympics is recognized by the International Olympics Committee (IOC).[17] See Yaprak Kemaloğlu (2012) for the characteristics of deaf sports communities in Turkey.

7.3.1 The history of the Deaflympics

The first competition took place in Paris in 1924 under the title 'Paris Silent Games'. After that, the name evolved to Deaflympics and was registered by the *Comité International des Sports des Sourds/CISS* ('International Committee of Sports for the Deaf/ICSD'). Except for an intermission during World War II, since 1924, the Deaflympics have been held every four years, and the number of participant athletes has been growing. Until 1949, there were only Deaflympics Summer Games, but in that year, the Deaflympics Winter Games were held for the first time, and the location was Austria.

The Deaflympics has competitions in many sports disciplines: athletics, badminton, basketball, bowling, handball, judo, karate, orienteering, and table tennis in the Deaflympics Summer Games, and curling, ice hockey, and snowboarding in the Deaflympics Winter Games.

The ICSD differs from other organizations affiliated with the IOC in terms of having deaf scrutineers and non-voting observers during the voting for the ICSD executive board. To be able to compete in the Deaflympics, the athletes must have a minimum 55 db hearing loss in their 'better ear'. To be able to

---

[17] Unlike the other competitions IOC organizes, visual tools such as flags or flash of light are used instead of referees' whistles, and audiences are expected to applaud by making a deaf clap (hands raised and wiggled).

compete at the same level, cochlear implants and hearing aids are not permitted during the warm-up and competition.[18]

Up to now, 36 towns and 21 countries hosted the Deaflympics. Among these countries, only five are outside of Europe. In total, 109 member countries, including Turkey, take part in the Deaflympics.

Turkey was the host of the 2017 Deaflympics Summer Games (see Figure 9). 3,148 athletes who came from 97 countries from six continents, came together in Samsun. The torch was lit by Ertuğrul Bursa, one of our participants, to honor his attendance at 11 Deaflympics – eight Summer Games and three Winter Games – throughout his 48 years of Deaflympics career as a football player and a technical representative.

Figure 9: Ertuğrul Bursa lighting the torch at the Deaflympics 2017, Samsun. Private collection.

7.3.2 Memories about the Deaflympics

The first Deaflympics competition that Turkey entered unofficially was held in Italy in 1957. This was a first step into the Deaflympics Games. This was yet

---

[18] https://www.deaflympics.com/pdf/AudiogramRegulations.pdf

another area in which Süleyman Gök's persistence on getting the best for the deaf had an outcome.

> *A Sports Union [İstanbul Sağırlar Gençlik Spor Kulübü Derneği ('İstanbul Sports Club Association for the Deaf Youth'); authors' note] affiliated with the Aksaray Deaf association [Solidarity Association of Turkey for the Deaf; authors' note] was established in 1955. This union was directly connected with the International Committee of Sports for the Deaf. So, as the deaf athletes in Turkey, we participated in the Olympic Games in Italy in 1957 for the first time. There were participants from all over the world. Everyone was very competent but we Turks didn't know anything. [. . .] We learned through trial and error.*
> [M10, 18.11.2016, 00:54–00:56]

According to M10, at the time of putting together the team to go to the Deaflympics in Italy, Gök asked who would want to join and composed a list of 9–10 people. In the end, the list came down to three people, chosen by the then Prime Minister Adnan Menderes (term of office 1950–1960).

> *Those who were eliminated were very disappointed. I was very disappointed. [Unidentified name sign], Erdoğan, Bülent, these were the selected ones. He [Süleyman Gök] said, 'Don't worry, when Menderes comes to İstanbul, we will go and see him together'. Menderes was at the office of the governor of İstanbul. Süleyman Gök informed me about this, and we went together. 'You can't go in together', they said. [. . .] So, Süleyman Gök went in alone. He showed Menderes the document that said I could go, too. Menderes approved and signed my papers. Süleyman Gök came and told me. I was very happy. So, I went to the Olympics.*
> [M24, 24.01.2017, 01:26–01:29]

After the first unofficial entry in 1957, in spite of the military takeover in 1960, Turkey again attended the Deaflympics held in Finland in 1961 with the help of Gök. This was the first time Turkey entered the Deaflympics officially.

> *Then, Süleyman Gök and Erol Efrand started training us. They prepared the necessary documents and submitted them to Süleyman Demirel [at the time General Director of the State Hydraulic Works, later prime minister; authors' note]. As a result, we [officially] joined the Olympics in 1961.*
> [M10, 18.11.2016, 00:54–00:56]

The governor of İstanbul, Refik Tulga, sponsored the outfits. Beyond this, no public funding was provided. The athletes faced financial difficulties, which resulted in a long and cumbersome journey. This also meant that they could not prepare well:

> *We weren't supported by public funds. The governor's office just gave us clothing. All of our remaining needs had to be met by ourselves. We found a bus company 'Varan' with the help of a person we knew. He asked for 22,000 liras [equivalent to the current amount of 150,000 Turkish Liras; authors' note], but the governor did not sponsor our transportation due to shortage of money. He gave us all the outfits with emblems.*
> [M10, 18.11.2016, 00:47–00:49]

The athletes were very tired when they arrived at the Deaflympics village. They had lost weight and were exhausted. So, Gök decided not to take part in all of the competitions and to return to Turkey before the Deaflympics were over:

> We set off. The coach was an old model, not so comfortable, the type which had iron headrests. The journey took seven days because the roads were old with bends and bumps. We finally arrived in Finland. We were all exhausted. We had no strength left. If we could have had a few days of rest after we arrived, it would have been better. But the next day, we entered a competition. My body was hurting all over. Except for two people, we all lost weight on the road. [. . .] My first competitor was an American. The Americans were not as tired as we were because they had travelled by plane. There was no knock-out but the competitor beat me with a difference in points because he pushed me out of the ring. The following day, there was one more wrestling competition but I had no strength. This time, my competitor was Russian. We had the same weight but he was very agile. He took me down in an instant. I'm surprised what I've been through. Süleyman Gök was very angry because the results were bad. [. . .] Erol Efrand and I worked a lot together, but the football team was defeated by England because, again, our team was very tired. The result was 13:1. So, as things were the way they were, Süleyman Gök decided to give up and to return to Turkey because he thought that we brought shame upon ourselves. Then, we returned to Turkey in ten days by stopping here and there. [M10, 18.11.2016, 00:48–00:53]

In Figure 10, we present two pictures from the wrestling match in 1961:

Figure 10: Two photographs from the wrestling match at the Deaflympics in Finland in 1961. Private collection.

One of our participants was the person who carried the Turkish flag at the Deaflympics held in 1961, and during the interview, he talks about his memories of the event:

> In 1961, we went to the Olympics in Finland. I was the one carrying the Turkish flag at the opening ceremony. Süleyman Gök was on my left, Erol Efrand was on my right, and I was walking in between them. Carrying a flag was a serious job, you should not sway left or

right. Süleyman Gök had also warned me by saying 'You are holding the flag of the state, be careful'. And I walked away confidently. We walked through the whole stadium like that, and then we raised the flags. [M10, 18.11.2016, 00:47–00:48]

The same participant shares his thoughts about what he saw in the Deaflympics in 1993. This further highlights how he perceived the role of carrying the flag as such an honor:

In the 1993 Olympics [Bulgaria], I saw a person carrying the Turkish flag behind his back and not in the front like I did. I got very upset. This is serious business.
[M10, 18.11.2016, 00:52–00:53]

M09, who has 48 years of experience in the Deaflympics, was a former football player, and after his career as an athlete ended, he took up a job as a technical representative in the Deaflympics. He tells the story of the establishment of the sports association, which enabled them to participate in the Deaflympics under a different official status:

In 1955, the İstanbul Sports Club [İstanbul Sports Club Association for the Deaf Youth] was established. Previously, the Sports Association was not connected to the state. Who established it? Hasan Toprak, Erol Efrand, and Kerim Altınkaynak. Kerim kept the minutes and did the bookkeeping. Together with Erol, they went to the Youth and Sports Ministry and tried to find support. At that time, there were five official clubs. Later, there were 60 clubs. Now, there are 120 clubs. In the past, there was no project, no money, only voluntary work. Costs were too much. We could not pay the ICSD, our membership was suspended. Then, the federation cleared the debt. [M09, 17.11.2016, 00:31–00:32]

In 1968, I went to Switzerland. It was so exciting. Previously, Erol did not choose me because I had cut my finger. Then, the government sent me. I was surprised about the selection because of the cut. I went to Switzerland in 1968. We were defeated 3:1.
[M09, 17.11.2016, 00:32–00:34]

The final excerpt shows that not much changed in the circumstances in later entries:

I don't remember, it was 1977 or 1978, I joined the Deaflympics in Romania. [. . .] At that time, athletes were selected from İstanbul, İzmir, and Ankara. Then we made preparations. We didn't get very good results. The conditions were not good.
[M04, 15.11.2016, 03:45–03:48]

7.4 Beauty contest

Another international event that deaf individuals participated in was the international beauty contest for the Deaf held in Yugoslavia. The winner was a

Turkish woman, Sevil Tez, a former student at the Yıldız School for the Deaf. One of our participants remembers this event:

> In 1969, we went to the Olympics in Yugoslavia. Sevil Tez was the winner of the beauty contest and became Miss Deaf World that year. [M09, 17.11.2016, 00:32–00:34]

In Figure 11, there are some pictures taken at that time and a newspaper clipping about the results of the contest:

Figure 11: Top row: Photographs of Miss Deaf World in the press; bottom left: newspaper headline which reads 'Silent beauty Sezil Tez wins'; bottom right: Miss Deaf World Sevil Tez's visit to her school (courtesy of *Mimar Sinan İşitme Engelliler Ortaokulu* ['Mimar Sinan Secondary School for the Deaf']).

8 Conclusion

In this chapter, we reported the main topics that came up during the interviews with elderly deaf signers from Turkey against the background of the political and historical changes that took place during their lives. By sharing fragments from these interviews, we hope to have shed some light on the deaf culture and deaf experiences in the second half of the last century. A few participants either refrained from expressing negative views on events or individuals or, if they did so, asked us not to report them. All of the participants were more than happy to talk to us and to share their life experiences, and for this, we are truly grateful to all of them.

Although our participants were born in diverse places and spent their lives in disparate regions, they are all from urban areas and are thus part of urban culture. Recruiting participants in villages was not possible within the scope of this project, as we had to rely on deaf individuals already known to local organizations. We hope that future work will focus on deaf individuals or groups that are not yet known to the general public, including individuals from rural areas. Expanding the scope of the pool of participants will no doubt reveal different experiences and life stories.

Acknowledgements: The research for this contribution has been possible thanks to the SIGN-HUB project, which has received funding from the European Union's Horizon 2020 research and innovation program under grant agreement No 693349, and to the Boğaziçi University Research Fund (58000212). We would like to thank *Türkiye Sağırlar Tesanüt Derneği* ('Solidarity Association of Turkey for the Deaf', İstanbul), *Türkiye İşitme Engelliler Derneği* ('Turkey Association for the Deaf', İstanbul), and *İzmir Sağırları Koruma ve Kalkındırma Derneği* ('İzmir Association for the Protection and Welfare of the Deaf') for their support, and Melihşah Aydın (İstanbul), Mehmet Nejat Tangüner (Diyarbakır), Kadir Gökgöz (İzmir), and Arzu Öztürkmen (İstanbul) for their guidance. We are also grateful to Mahmut Akay, Hakan Erdoğan, and Ayşe Pınar, the director, vice-director, and employee, respectively, of the Mimar Sinan Secondary School for the Deaf (*Mimar Sinan İşitme Engelliler Ortaokulu*) for welcoming us and making the archives accessible. Our most heartfelt thanks naturally go to our participants whose willingness and enthusiasm to share their memories made this study what it is.

References

Batır, Betül. 2008. An historical overview of development of the education of deaf, mute, and blind children in Turkey. *International Review of Turkology* 1(2). 17–24.

Cramer, Jens-Michael & Markus Steinbach. This volume. Conducting interviews with elderly Deaf people: opportunities and challenges.

Demirel, Buket Ela, Burcu Saral, Süleyman Sabri Taşçı, Elvan Tamyürek Özparlak, Aslı Göksel & Hasan Dikyuva. Forthcoming. Sağır hayatlar: dil, eğitim, iletişim [Deaf lives: language, education, communication].

Ergin, Osman. 1939. Dilsizler ve körler mektebi [School for the mute and the blind]. *Türk maarif tarihi* 3. 1165–1172. İstanbul: Osmanbey Matbaası.

Gök, Süleyman. 1939. Dilsizliğin telâfisi: Türkiye'de ve Avrupa'da dilsizler [Compensation for muteness: The Mute in Turkey and Europe]. *Dilsiz neşriyat yurdu* 1. İstanbul: Resimli Ay Matbaası.

Gök, Süleyman. 1940. Dilsizliğin telâfisi: Sağır dilsizlerin tedris usulleri ve konuşma tarzları [Compensation for muteness: Educational methods for deaf-mutes and ways of speaking]. *Dilsiz neşriyat yurdu* 2. 1–32. İstanbul: Aydınlık Basımevi.

Gök, Süleyman. 1958. Dünya'da ve Türkiye'de sağır, dilsiz okulları tarihçesi ve eğitim sistemi [The history of schools for the deaf-mute and education system in the world and in Turkey]. *Türkiye sağır, dilsiz ve körler tesanüt cemiyeti neşriyatı* 1. İstanbul: Hüsnütabiat Matbaası.

Göksel, Aslı & Süleyman Sabri Taşçı. 2020. Socio-historical background: 1. History. In Meltem Kelepir (ed.), *A grammar of Turkish Sign Language (TİD)*. 1st edn. (SIGN-HUB Sign Language Grammar Series).

Haydar, Ali. 1925. Sağırlar ve dilsizler [The deaf and the mute]. *Muallimler mecmuası* 29. 1237–1260. Available from: Hakkı Tarık Us Osmanlıca Süreli Yayınları, http://www.tufs.ac.jp/common/fs/asw/tur/htu/data/HTU1558-03/index.djvu

İlkbaşaran, Deniz. 2015. *Literacies, mobilities and agencies of deaf youth in Turkey: Constraints and opportunities in the 21st century*. San Diego, CA: University of California PhD dissertation.

İlkbaşaran, Deniz & Süleyman Sabri Taşçı. 2012. Ideology and language in the early republic: A history of deaf education in Turkey. *Proceedings of the International Symposium on Language and Communication: Research Trends and Challenges (ISLC)*. 1767–1777. Erzurum: Mega Press.

Kemal, Necati. 1926a. *Tekellüm kusurları. sağır ve dilsizlik, afazi, isteryai tutukluk, kekemelik ve tedavisi* [Articulatory disorders, deafness and muteness, aphasia, hysteria, stammering, stuttering and their treatment]. İzmir: Marifet Matbaası.

Kemal, Necati. 1926b. *Tekellüm ve tasavvutda fizyolocyai ve lahni tedkikler* [Physiological and tonal studies in articulation and phonetics]. İzmir: Marifet Matbaası.

Kemaloğlu, Yusuf Kemal, Pınar Yaprak Kemaloğlu, Cumhur Bilgin, Hasan Hüseyin Korkmaz & Mustafa İlhan. 2010. İşitme engellilerin yüksek öğrenim olanaklarının geliştirilmesinde Türk İşaret Dilinin önemi: E-işit Projesi [The significance of Turkish Sign Language in the improvement of the accessibility of the Deaf to higher education: E-İşit Project]. *II. Ulusal Engelli Bireyler için Fiziksel Aktivite Çalıştayı Bildiri Kitabı*. Available at: http://kongre.comu.edu.tr/efa2010/kitap.pdf.

Makaroğlu, Bahtiyar & Hasan Dikyuva. 2016. Yabancı dil olarak Türk İşaret Dili eğitim seti [Turkish Sign Language as a second language education package]. Ankara University. tidegitim.com.

Miles, M. 2009. *Deaf people, sign language and communication, in Ottoman and Modern Turkey: Observations and excerpts from 1300 to 2009. From sources in English, French, German, Greek, Italian, Latin and Turkish, with introduction and some annotation.* Internet publication, URL: www.independentliving.org/miles200907.html

Milli Eğitim Bakanlığı [Ministry of Education]. 1962. Özel eğitime muhtaç çocuklar yönetmeliği [The regulations for children in need of special education]. In *Milli Eğitim Bakanlığı Tebliğler Dergisi*. 164–166.

Milli Eğitim Bakanlığı [Ministry of Education]. 2015. Türk İşaret Dili dersi etkinlik kitabı (1, 2, 3. sınıflar [Turkish Sign Language Course Activity Book (1st, 2nd, and 3rd years)]. URL: http://orgm.meb.gov.tr/dosyalar/Turk_Isaret_Dili_188SFa.pdf

Milli Eğitim Bakanlığı [Ministry of Education]. 2016. Türk İşaret Dili dersi öğretim programı yürürlükte [Turkish Sign Language course education program is in operation]. URL: http://orgm.meb.gov.tr/www/turk-isaret-dili-dersi-ogretim-programiyururlukte/icerik/766

Pye, Ernest (ed.). 1933. *Charlotte R. Willard of Merzifon, her life and times* (chapter 'A deaf and dumb soldier of the Turkish army', 180–182). New York: Fleming H. Revell Company.

Ranck, Aaron. 2008. *The sinews of war: Turkey, chromite, and the second world war*. Ankara: Bilkent University MA thesis.

Tanyeri, Yücel. 2016. İzmir Sağırlar Okulu [İzmir School for the Deaf]. *Turkish Archives of Otorhinolaryngology* 54. 1–4.

Taşçı, Süleyman Sabri. 2012. *Phonological and morphological aspects of lexicalized fingerspelling in Turkish Sign Language (TİD)*. İstanbul: Boğaziçi University MA thesis.

The Anatolian. 1911–1912. Marsovan.

Turgut, Kadir & Süleyman Sabri Taşçı. 2011. *A historical perspective on first deaf schools, education methods and deafness in Turkey*. Paper presented at Conference of International Sign Language Users, Gazi University, Ankara.

Yaprak Kemaloğlu, Pınar. 2012. *Türkiye'de Sağır sporunun toplumsal analizi* [Social analysis of Deaf sports in Turkey]. İstanbul: Marmara University PhD dissertation.

Yıldırım, Nuran. 1997. İstanbul'da sağır-dilsiz ve âmâların eğitimi [The education of the deaf-mute and the blind in İstanbul]. *İstanbul Armağanı*. 305–330.

Zeshan, Ulrike. 2003. Aspects of Türk İşaret Dili (Turkish Sign Language). *Sign Language & Linguistics* 6. 43–75.

Zürcher, Erik-Jan. 2004. *Modernleşen Türkiye'nin tarihi* [Turkey, A modern history], Translated by Yasemin Saner. İstanbul: İletişim Yayınları.

Appendix

Table 1: Demographic information.

Participant	Town	Date of birth	School	Occupation/Vocation
M01	İSTANBUL	1949	Yıldız School for the Deaf	actor
M02	ANKARA	1946	Ankara Orphanage for the Deaf	tailor, civil servant
F03	ANKARA	1950	Yıldız School for the Deaf	tailor, bank clerk
M04	ANKARA	1944	Ankara Orphanage for the Deaf, Yıldız School for the Deaf	factory worker
F05	ANKARA	1946	İzmir School for the Deaf, Ankara Orphanage for the Deaf	hairdresser
M06	ANKARA	1930	İzmir School for the Deaf	carpenter
M07	ANKARA	1935	No schooling	farmer
F08	ANKARA	1938	No schooling	farmer
M09	İZMİR	1947	Yıldız School for the Deaf	carpenter, factory worker
M10	İZMİR	1936	İstanbul Association for the Deaf and Mute	carpenter
F11	İZMİR	1937	Yıldız School for the Deaf	tailor
F12	İZMİR	1946	Yıldız School for the Deaf	tailor
F13	İZMİR	1936	No information available	tailor
M14	İZMİR	1936	İzmir School for the Deaf	carpenter
F15	İZMİR	1939	İzmir School for the Deaf	no information available
M16	İZMİR	1934	No schooling	carpenter
M17	İZMİR	1935	Yıldız School for the Deaf	carpenter
M18	İZMİR	1942	Yıldız School for the Deaf	no information available
F19	İZMİR	1928	İzmir School for the Deaf	tailor
F20	İZMİR	1943	İzmir School for the Deaf	factory worker, tailor
F21	İZMİR	1932	İzmir School for the Deaf	domestic worker

Table 1 (continued)

Participant	Town	Date of birth	School	Occupation/Vocation
F22	İZMİR	1942	İzmir School for the Deaf	tailor
F23	İSTANBUL	1940	İzmir School for the Deaf	tailor
M24	İSTANBUL	1931	İzmir School for the Deaf	tailor
M25	İSTANBUL	1937	Yıldız School for the Deaf	tailor
M26	DİYARBAKIR	1950	Diyarbakır School for the Deaf	tailor, ironsmith, carpenter, technician
M27	DİYARBAKIR	1940	No schooling	cobbler
M28	DİYARBAKIR	1954	Diyarbakır School for the Deaf, Ankara Orphanage for the Deaf	tailor
M29	DİYARBAKIR	1951	Diyarbakır School for the Deaf	factory worker
M30	DİYARBAKIR	1946	Siirt School	miscellaneous jobs
M31	BURSA	1937	Yıldız School for the Deaf	no information available

Roland Pfau, Annemieke van Kampen, and Menno Harterink
Pink sign: identity challenges, choices, and changes among elderly Deaf homosexuals in the Netherlands

1 Introduction

We are all multi-faceted creatures, and no one person has but a single identity. It is thus safe to assume that in everyday situations, and on a daily basis, we are constantly juggling multiple identities. Even the proverbial middle-class white able-bodied heterosexual cisgender male will, for instance, identify at certain times foremost as a company employee, while in other contexts, he may foreground his identity as a father. In both circumstances, he will act according to the norms that society associates with the respective identity. In certain situations, it may well be that these two identities intersect or conflict with each other. To manage this, this individual will, to some extent, have the choice to put aside or suppress certain facets of his identity. Obviously, choosing or toggling between identities is much more challenging for groups that are marginalized in mainstream society and thus suffer from discrimination, especially if the identity feature linked to marginalization is visible, as is true, for instance, for gender and race. Now consider when two such features co-exist, as is the case for minorities within commonly marginalized groups, such as Black women (e.g., Sesko & Biernat 2010) or disabled Black people (e.g., Annamma et al. 2013). Clearly, in such cases, the two identities may interact or intersect in complex ways, as individuals may experience suppression and discrimination not only in mainstream society but also within their marginalized groups.

In this chapter, we are concerned with another combination of socially marginalized identities, namely Deafness and homosexuality. Note that, in contrast to gender and race, these are invisible identities. We are interested in how these social categories interact, and how individuals prioritize their identification with them, if they do at all. We add to these intersecting categories a third one, namely age, in order to scrutinize in how far self-attributions of identity may have changed over the years. To that end, we draw on interviews with elderly Deaf signers in the Netherlands, collected within the context of a European-wide project. In Section 2, we introduce the notion of intersectionality, applying it to the Deaf community and also including an overview of previous work on Deaf Queer identities. In Section 3, we outline our methodology. Section 4 sketches the history of *Roze Gebaar* ('Pink Sign'), the Dutch Association for Deaf LGBTIQ people, as this association has impacted the forming of Deaf Queer identities in the Netherlands in important ways.[1] Drawing on information from the interviews, we then discuss in Section 5 changes in the self-identification of homosexual members of the Dutch Deaf community.

Given the topic of the chapter and the type of data that our discussion relies on, we consider it appropriate to disclose some background information about ourselves: one of us is female and identifies as Deaf and heterosexual, one of us is male and identifies as Deaf and homosexual, and one of us is male and hearing and identifies as homosexual. In short, of the three authors, one identifies as female, two identify as Deaf, and two identify as gay.

2 Intersectionality – a Deaf perspective

The sociological theory of intersectionality, rooted within feminist theory, was spearheaded by legal scholar Kimberlé Crenshaw (1989). She coined the term "intersectionality" to describe how different social categories, in her case gender and race, are interwoven. Crucially, she argues, the experiences of discrimination which result from belonging to these two social categories should not be considered in isolation – a perspective that Crenshaw refers to as "single-axis framework". Rather, the focus should be on the interaction between these categories and the emergence of specific novel experiences of discrimination. Scrutinizing such interactions lies at the heart of intersectionality theory. In her groundbreaking article, Crenshaw employs the term "intersectionality" as a way to help explain the oppression of Black women.[2] She suggests

> that this single-axis framework erases Black women in the conceptualization, identification and remediation of race and sex discrimination by limiting inquiry to the experiences

---

[1] Menno Harterink, co-author of the present chapter, works as freelancer for *Stichting Welzijn Doven Amsterdam* (SWDA, 'Foundation for the Well-being of the Deaf in Amsterdam'), in particular the group *Amsterdamse Doven Historie* (ADH, 'Amsterdam Deaf History'), and he is expert for the study of the history of *Roze Gebaar*.

[2] We follow Crenshaw, and also Moges (2017), in capitalizing the terms "Black", "Deaf", and "Queer" throughout this chapter, in order to highlight affiliation with a group or community that is characterized by distinct experiences and cultural values, or, as Moges (2017: 215) aptly puts it, "to center the self-identified members of social groups that have been long marginalized in mainstream society and treated as having presumably distinct identities without any intersections". In quotes from the literature, we maintain the convention used in the original source.

of otherwise-privileged members of the group. In other words, in race discrimination cases, discrimination tends to be viewed in terms of sex- or class-privileged Blacks; in sex discrimination cases, the focus is on race- and class-privileged women.

(Crenshaw 1989: 140)

In the meantime, however, intersectional approaches have expanded to include many more aspects of social identity, such as disability, sexual orientation, religion, age, and socioeconomic class (cf. Cho et al. 2013; Romero 2018). "Attending to how such identities or memberships intersect, intersectionality theory provides the foundation to analyze multiple identities of minority groups" (Moges 2017: 218). In the present chapter, we explore aspects of the intersectionality of Deaf Queer people, highlighting the experiences of elderly Deaf signers as well as identity shifts that have occurred within the community. Before addressing previous work on Deaf Queer identities in Section 2.2, we provide an overview of other types of intersectionalities that exist within the Deaf community in Section 2.1 (see Figure 1 for the sign INTERSECTIONALITY in Sign Language of the Netherlands (*Nederlandse Gebarentaal*, NGT)).

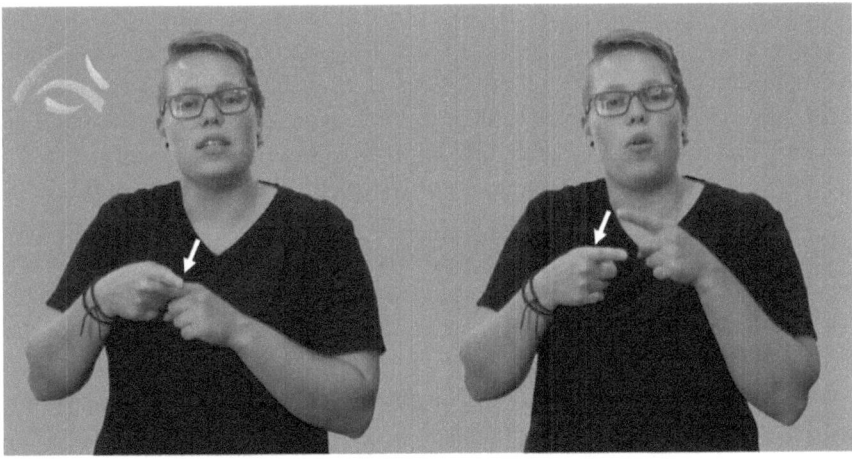

Figure 1: NGT sign INTERSECTIONALITY: index finger of the right hand first contacts index finger of the left hand (left still), then index finger of the left hand contacts index finger of the right hand (right still) (© *Nederlands Gebarencentrum*; reprinted with permission).

2.1 Intersectionalities within the Deaf community

Despite having been coined in 1989, the term "intersectionality" was not adopted widely until the 2000s. Consequently, earlier studies dealing with marginalized groups within the Deaf community use other terms such as, for instance, "multiple minorities" (e.g., Doe 1994). However, this term falls short of explaining the complex ways in which different identities are interwoven and shape each other; rather, it tends to simply inventory the respective categories.

> Being deaf and also being black, or gay, or female, or Hispanic, or Asian, or having other disabilities, or being "different" puts an individual in a multiple minority category. [. . .] Deaf people who are perceived as being different (i.e., as having more than deafness as an identifying characteristic) are often placed in this category by the deaf community itself. (Doe 1994: 464)

Doe further notes that "[t]he issues that affect multiple minorities are not valued or given high priority by the deaf community, which has its own agenda" (Doe 1994: 468). Beyond the marginalization of community-internal minorities, the Deaf community is also not immune to discrimination, of course. In fact, "[t]he deaf community treats multiple minorities in much the same way as deaf people are treated by the hearing majority – by discriminating against them" (Doe 1994: 467). Fortunately, in the 25 years since Doe's article appeared, the Deaf community has become more open to dialogue and thus practiced greater social and cultural inclusivity. For one, the impact of limited access to information (as also noted by Doe) has been mitigated thanks to the advent of the internet and visual communication devices. Moreover, various types of intersectionality within the Deaf community have been put on the research agenda in recent years, often by scholars who have intersectional identities themselves.

A group that has been comparably well-studied are Black Deaf Americans. In 1965, Carl Croneberg, in one of the appendices to the *Dictionary of American Sign Language*, addressed differences between Black and white signing that resulted from the segregation of Deaf schools in the South. Subsequent sociolinguistic studies revealed further instances of systematic phonological and lexical variation (e.g., Woodward 1976; Woodward & DeSantis 1977; Lucas et al. 2001) but, for the most part, did not include considerations regarding the identity of Black Deaf people (for an overview of the socio-historical foundation of Black American Sign Language (ASL) and different types of variation, see McCaskill et al. (2011)). One of the earlier studies that does address identity issues of the Black Deaf community is Aramburo (1989). The author contends

> that there does indeed exist a black deaf community, that it shares the characteristics and values of both the black community and the deaf community. In addition, it has some characteristics and values that are unique. (Aramburo 1989: 104)

Given that Black Deaf individuals are embedded within both Black and Deaf cultures, Aramburo further asks "Black or Deaf?", that is, whether a Black Deaf individual would identify primarily with the Black community or the Deaf community. Informal interviews with sixty members of the Black Deaf community in the Washington, DC, area revealed that 87% of the participants identified themselves as Black first. Many respondents from this group indicated "that they see their color as more visible than their deafness and that they want respect for their ethnicity before their deafness" (Aramburo 1989: 110).[3] Clark (2007) also discusses how individuals who are both Black and Deaf navigate their multiple identities. Her study is based on interviews conducted in Seattle with three women who identify as Black and Deaf. All three women report "that the Deaf community is basically a white community in which they do not feel comfortable being themselves" (Clark 2007: 118).

While these studies offer important insights regarding the identity of Black Deaf people in the United States,[4] they fall into the "multiple minority" trap discussed above in that they do not address identity issues from the perspective of intersectionality, but rather tend to bifurcate the two identities. In fact, studies that take an intersectional perspective appear to be scarce, as is also noted by Moges (2017). In her article, Rezenet Moges, a self-identified Intersectional Deaf Lesbian of Color, focuses on Deaf Queer ontologies (see next section), but emphasizes that she employs the term "Intersectional Deaf people" in a broader sense "for all Deaf and/or any Queer/Gender/Person of Color communities" (Moges 2017: 217). Moges recalls how, during "a significant and unforgettable meeting" with older Black Deaf lesbians, she came to realize that "it was our way of life, experiencing a multiplicity of involuntary struggles of loneliness and unfair treatment for being female, Black, Deaf, and Queer."

A relevant, recent addition to the field is the study by Chapple (2019), which considers ways in which intersectionality can be employed to provide insight into the lived experiences of Black Deaf women – according to her, a group that is almost invisible in all areas of scholarship. In discussing the social construction of Black Deaf women, Chapple reviews studies on Black women and Deaf women, as well as theories that are appropriate for considering one or two of the intersectional identities of Black Deaf women (e.g., feminist disability theory and critical race disability studies). However, in the spirit of intersectionality theory, she "seeks to understand how the embodiment of each identity collectively shapes the individual" (Chapple 2019: 187).

---

3 Aramburo notes that the majority of the remaining respondents, who identified as Deaf first, had Deaf parents and attended residential schools for the Deaf.
4 James & Woll (2004) ask the same question ("Black deaf or deaf black?") related to the situation in Great Britain. See Fisher et al. (this volume) for characteristics of the Black Deaf community in Philadelphia.

To that end, she introduces the theory of Black Deaf feminism (BDF), which aims at highlighting the lived experiences of Black deaf women. One of the tenets of BDF is that it

> recognizes the compounding effects of interacting identities while also recognizing the positionality that one aspect of identity may be more central than others at any moment in space, place, and time. (Chapple 2019: 194)

Another type of intersectionality, the intersectionality of Deafness and religion is the topic of Zaurov (2003). This study addresses the living environment and the experiences of Deaf Jews, based on interviews with ten participants (one woman, nine men) from Russia, Germany, and the United States.[5] It is sometimes pointed out that Deaf culture resembles Jewish culture in that cultural affiliation transcends nationalities; crucially, however, Deaf cultural values, unlike Jewish cultural values, are generally not transmitted within the family (for Deaf culture, see Ladd (2003) and Padden & Humphries (2005), among others). Zaurov reflects on the intersectional experiences of Deaf Jews as a double cultural minority and reports that they experience discrimination in both minority communities: "The Deaf thus take over the historically motivated 'religious-racial' views, while the Jews, just like the hearing society, ignore the language of the Deaf Jews" (Zaurov 2003: 100; our translation). In line with Zaurov's observations, Stein (2009), who offers a historical perspective on Deaf American Jewish culture, notes that

> [f]or these individuals, the larger Jewish and deaf communities had failed to address their dual needs as both Jews and deaf men and women. Indeed, these communities were each in their own way oblivious to the fact that deaf Jews might have ambitions or concerns of their own. (Stein 2009: 277)

Zaurov (2003: 99) problematizes that, as a consequence, Deaf Jews often saw themselves forced to leave the Jewish community and to associate with only the Deaf community, where they could communicate without problems; within the latter community, however, they did not always dare to live out their Jewish identity openly or even kept it a secret. Still, based on his interviews, he concludes that a Deaf Jewish culture exists, which thrives whenever Deaf Jews gather. Stein (2009: 305) concludes that "[f]urther scrutiny of deaf American Jewish culture promises to diversify the study both of Jewish culture and deaf culture, and to highlight their many fascinating intersections".[6]

---

5 Zaurov further mentions that two of his interview partners are homosexual.
6 For the living environment of young Deaf Muslims (in Germany), see Karar (2008). For further studies on Deaf intersectionalities, the interested reader is referred to Ahmad et al. (2002),

2.2 On Deaf Queer identities

An article published in the *New York Times Magazine* in 1994 set to point out a number of similarities between the Deaf community and the gay and lesbian community (Solomon 1994). The author notes, for instance, that within both communities, identification processes typically take place horizontally, i.e., among peers, rather than vertically, i.e., between generations.[7] This comparison was met with discomfort and rejection in part of the Deaf community. Such critical voices notwithstanding, Bienvenu (2008) provides an interesting overview of "Queer/Deaf similarities". She highlights, for instance, that "[m]embers of both communities, Deaf and Gay, are stigmatized – and Deaf Gays are stigmatized within the Deaf community" (Bienvenu 2008: 267). According to her, comparing Queer to Deaf culture "is one step toward coming out for Deaf Lesbians and Gay men, and one way to fight homophobia in the Deaf community is getting out of the closet" (Bienvenu 2008: 267).[8] That is, for her, taking the commonalities between the two communities seriously is a first step towards appreciating intersectional identities within the Deaf community. Other community members, however, might be skeptical of such an approach, as they fear "that a politically unified deaf community might be fracturing because of the intrusion of other identitarian questions that do not directly speak to the deaf community at large" (Feenstra & van Kessel 2020: 109).

Bienvenu (2008: 270) laments the fact that "[t]here are minimal formal studies, if any, on the Deaf L/G [lesbian/gay; authors' note] community" and mentions as notable exception the volume *Eyes of Desire: A Deaf Gay and Lesbian Reader*, compiled by Raymond Luczak in 1993.[9] Moges (2017: 217) shares Bienvenu's sentiment when stating "that Deaf Queer people are largely invisible in academia", and she further notes that, beyond studies on Deaf Queer identities,

> the need for more work by Queer authors experiencing multiple intersections (such as People of Color, transgender, Deaf-Blind, Deaf-Disabled) is clear – both on the theme of

---

who discuss how young Asian Deaf people negotiate identities, Foster & Kinuthia (2003), who address the identity of Deaf people of Asian American, Hispanic American, and African American backgrounds, and Leigh (2009, 2012) and Ruiz-Williams et al. (2015), who offer broader perspectives on Deaf intersectionalities.

7 Cf. Solvang & Haualand (2014: 12), who highlight that most Deaf individuals, just like gays and lesbians, are born into "a family of others".
8 Furthermore, with respect to hierarchies within minorized communities, Kane (1994) compares bisexual to hard-of-hearing individuals. We mention this comparison because we think it is thought-provoking, not necessarily because we consider it appropriate.
9 In his foreword, Luczak addresses historical parallels between the Deaf and gay/lesbian communities and points out, for instance, that "[p]ride became the password for both deaf and gay people in the 1970s" (Luczak 1993: 12).

> intersectional identities, and in the general Deaf Studies literature where more diverse insights are needed. (Moges 2017: 222)

Interestingly, one of the works she selects for in-depth study is the volume edited by Luczak. She concludes that "[u]ltimately, the Deaf Queer authors and poets' ontological experiences [. . .] build a stronger sense of belonging for Deaf Queer readers in their communities" (Moges 2017: 236), thus making a strong point for the importance of studies on Deaf Queer (and other intersectional) identities.

While it is certainly true that the number of relevant publications is still rather limited, it is encouraging to see that scholarly work on the topic has increased in recent years, broadening the perspective also to the situation and experiences of Deaf Queer people outside of the United States (see, e.g., Sheridan (2008) for Ireland; Sinecka (2008) for the Czech Republic; Michaels (2015) for Great Britain; Cappotto & Rinaldi (2016) for Sicily (Italy); Metzner (2018a,b) for Germany; Littel (2019) for Great Britain and the Netherlands; Feenstra & van Kessel (2020) for the Netherlands). The focus of these works is varied, but taken together, they offer a multi-faceted picture of issues related to Deaf Queer identities and history.

Among the earliest works on Deaf culture and (homo)sexuality are Robinson (1979) and Zakarewsky (1979), the former focusing on the sexuality of Deaf people in general, the latter on patterns of support among gay and lesbian Deaf people. Both studies emphasize the impact of communicative problems and the lack of access to information (as Luczak (1993: 13) puts it: "Deafness is *not* a handicap, but limited access to information is"). Robinson, for instance, reports a general lack of correct sexual information within the Deaf culture, for the simple reason that important information sources (such as, for instance, formal sex education) were not accessible for Deaf adolescents at the time. Based on a small-scale survey, he concludes

> that deaf people have the same type of sexual behaviors and problems which hearing people have. The problem, however, is that few competent services are available to help deaf people deal adequately with these problems. (Robinson 1979: 167)

Focusing specifically on gay and lesbian Deaf people, Zakarewsky (1979: 182) adds that "the communication problem of deaf people makes homosexuality a greater problem for them than for most other minority groups" (cf. Phaneuf 1987). When it comes to the identity of members of this group, Zakarewsky further argues that being Deaf and homosexual creates a "double jeopardy". Since gay and lesbian Deaf people are "unable to communicate with hearing gay/lesbian persons they are further discouraged from openly admitting their gayness because of what the rest of the deaf world might think of them"

(Zakarewsky 1979: 179; see also Section 5.1). After all, as already mentioned in Section 2.1, discrimination is also a reality within the Deaf community.

While not being concerned with identity issues per se, Zakarewsky (1979: 182) points out that "gay deaf men and lesbian deaf women are an invisible minority somewhere between the homosexual hearing community and the heterosexual deaf community". He further reports that the gay and lesbian Deaf people he interviewed (at the second national convention of gay/lesbian Deaf organizations in New York) preferred contact with other Deaf homosexuals.[10] At the time, many of them complained that the hearing homosexual community was "not yet sufficiently sensitized to the problems of deafness to provide a network of support" (Zakarewsky 1979: 189). Still, given the lack of acceptance within the broader Deaf community, they also indicated that their second choice would be identifying with hearing homosexuals. 15 years later, Kane (1994), focusing on the culture of Deaf gay men, reports that his informants, when asked to pick which aspect of their identity was more important to them – deafness or gayness – unanimously chose deafness (see LeBlanc & Tully (2001) for a more recent perspective based on nationwide interviews with 43 lesbians and gay men with hearing impairments of varying degrees).[11] In Section 5.1, we will see that our elderly interviewees, at least during a period of their life, gave more importance to their gay/lesbian identity, thereby distancing themselves from the Deaf community.

But why would an individual be forced to choose in the first place? Under the article heading "Identity: WHAT?", Bienvenu (2008: 264) shares that she has often been asked whether she feels more Deaf or more lesbian, and she puts forward the question "Does one identity preclude the other?" According to her, at least historically, it has indeed been the case that one had to choose to be either Deaf or lesbian. Yet, more recently, "the concept of Deaf L/G [lesbian/gay; authors' note] is beginning to emerge in the Deaf community". It should be clear that from the perspective of intersectionality theory, a question like

---

[10] Contact among Deaf homosexuals was facilitated by the *Rainbow Alliance of the Deaf*, which had been founded in 1977 and which, according to Leduc (2016), now has 15 local chapters in the United States and Canada.

[11] Discussing differences between Deaf gays and members of the Deaf community in general, Kane (1994: 483) observes that the former interact with hearing gays more commonly than straight Deaf people interact with straight hearing people. Furthermore, according to him, "[m]embers of the hearing gay community are also more aware and sensitive to the needs of deaf people than are people in the straight world" (Kane 1994: 484).

"Are you more *x* or *y*?" is generally misguided (cf. the question "Black or Deaf?" in Section 2.1). This point is made in crystal-clear terms by Moges (2017), when she writes:

> After experiencing sexual awakening and learning about their sign-language rights [. . .], Deaf Queer people come out twice and act politically in defiance of normativity, assimilation, and marginalization by resisting homophobia, discrimination, oralism, and audism. [. . .] Intersectional Deaf Queer people embody and enact their intersecting political identities [. . .] dynamically and inclusively, instead of having to pick one or another.
>
> (Moges 2017: 220)

It thus appears that the past four decades have seen important changes in the self-identification of Deaf Queer people. Adopting the above line of argumentation, it is clear that one should no longer ask "Are you Deaf *or* Queer?" But not only that, one should also no longer speak of individuals who are 'Deaf and Queer', but rather of 'Deaf Queer' individuals. After all, as pointed out by Moges (2017: 236), "[w]hen we further marginalize an identity of a group, we miss out on learning opportunities based on these groups' own perspectives, which are shaped by their unique life experiences".[12]

In order to get a better understanding of the changes that have taken place, these "unique life experiences" need to be documented before they are lost. Moges mentions the efforts of Bridget Klein, a Deaf Queer woman, who is collecting life stories from the older generation of a Deaf lesbian community in New York City, and of Dragonsani Renteria, a Deaf Latino transman, who has spent many years on compiling an archive of documents related to Deaf Queer history. Renteria, as cited in Moges (2017: 237) remarks: "After realizing that both Deaf history books and LGBTQ history books were not documenting our history, I made a commitment to begin doing so." The goal of the present

---

12 See Feenstra & van Kessel (2020) for an insightful discussion of "role models at the intersection of queer and deaf representation" (title of their article). The authors present as an illustrative example 'Deafies in Drag', two Latinx drag queens, who have posted weekly sketch videos on Youtube since 2015. "Their videos are a form of intersectional activism which does not give primacy to one identification over the other, but instead highlights the value of thinking about what happens when deaf and LGBTQ+ identifications overlap" (Feenstra & van Kessel 2020: 109). A popular culture perspective is also offered by Moreman & Briones (2018), who discuss the impact of Nyle DiMarco, a Deaf Queer celebrity (who has won both *America's Next Top Model* and *Dancing with the Stars*), on what they call "Deaf Queer world-making". They argue that "the process and politics of analyzing and theorizing DiMarco's celebrity adds to understandings and conceptions of the Deaf Queer" (Moreman & Briones 2018: 220). For the importance of Deaf role models, see Cawthon et al. (2016).

chapter is similar in spirit, with the difference that most of the interviews from which we draw information have not been conducted with the specific purpose of documenting Deaf Queer history.

3 Methodology

Just like some other contributions to this volume, the present chapter is based in part on interviews with elderly Deaf people conducted within the SIGN-HUB project. For further information about the SIGN-HUB project and the interviews, see the introduction to this volume and Cramer & Steinbach (this volume), respectively.

In the Netherlands, Annemieke van Kampen conducted a total of 24 interviews with 26 interviewees (14 female, 12 male) between 69 and 91 years of age. We were lucky to have among our interview partners two, one woman and one man, who identify as homosexual, and one man, who identifies as bisexual. The experiences they shared during the interviews constitute an important source of information for this chapter. Besides the three interviews conducted in the context of the project, we had access to an additional interview with the same female participant, conducted by Hendrik de Jong and Bram Schoemaker – coincidentally just one day before the SIGN-HUB interview with her. While the SIGN-HUB interviews tackle various topics (e.g., family, school, work, historical events), this third interview is specifically about the history of *Roze Gebaar* ('Pink Sign'), the Dutch Association for Deaf LGBTIQ people (see Section 4). Sadly, the female interviewee passed away on April 21, 2017 – only one month after she had been interviewed.[13]

In Table 1, we provide some details regarding the interviews and the interviewees. In the text, we will refer to the male interviewees as M04 and M19, respectively, but to the female interviewee by her name, Bea Visser, as she explicitly says in the shorter interview that she is *"glad that now you all see who I am: Bea Visser"* [NGT-F05-20170312-RozeGebaar, 08:18–08:30]. In the table, we also provide the interview code; this code specifies the relevant component of the project ('Task 2.4'), the sign language used, the participant code, the camera (1 or 2), and the date. When presenting quotes from interviews in the text (as, for instance, a few lines up), we drop the 'T2.4' part but add a time code.

---

[13] All three interviewees have given informed consent to use quotes, video fragments, and screenshots from the interviews in scientific output such as articles and presentations.

Table 1: Details regarding the four interviews (and the three interviewees) from which quotes have been extracted ("Age" is age at time of the interview).

Participant code	Age	Interview date	Length (mm:ss)	Interview code (on www.sign-hub.eu)
F05	80	12 March 2017	09:58	T2.4-NGT-F05-20170312-RozeGebaar
		13 March 2017	42:23	T2.4-NGT-F05-1/2-20170313
M04	75	22 February 2017	57:48	T2.4-NGT-M04-1/2-20170222
M19	71	29 June 2017	43:06	T2.4-NGT-M19-1/2-20170629

The code will help locate the interviews on the SIGN-HUB platform (www.sign-hub.eu), where interviews from all participating countries are accessible under the tab "Life stories" – provided that the interviewee has given consent. For the Netherlands, most interviews have been split up into multiple clips for both cameras; on the platform, interview codes like the ones given in Table 1 thus carry an extension following the codes. The shorter interview with Bea Visser, which carries the extension 'RozeGebaar', is available in its entirety with English and Dutch subtitles on the platform. As for the SIGN-HUB interviews, at least one fragment from each interview has been subtitled in English and Dutch, including the fragments from F05 and M19 that were relevant to the present chapter. The Dutch subtitles have been provided by Annemieke van Kampen and Merel van Zuilen, the English translations have been prepared by Roland Pfau.

Besides extracting information from the interviews, we had the opportunity to also talk to three young(er) Deaf people: a 25-year old female, who identifies as Queer; a 42-year old male, who identifies as gay; and a 43-year old bisexual male. These were informal conversations – one in person, the other two via online messaging – in NGT, which included questions targeting identity issues, their affiliation with *Roze Gebaar*, and specific vocabulary. We will refer to these participants as F25q, M42g, and M43b, respectively.

4 History of *Roze Gebaar*

One cannot talk about homosexual Deaf identities in the Netherlands, and gradual shifts in these identities, without introducing *Roze Gebaar* ('Pink Sign'), the Dutch

Association for Deaf LGBTIQ people.[14] In this section, we therefore sketch the history of the association. Without doubt, *Roze Gebaar* has had a tremendous impact on the lives of people who identify as Deaf and LGBTIQ, and we will address this impact in Section 5.2.

The history of *Roze Gebaar* begins in May 1982, when, for the first time, a weekend for Deaf gays and lesbians was organized at the adult education center *Allardsoog* in Bakkeveen. A total of 11 people took part in that meeting, eight men and three women.[15] Discussions during the weekend revealed that there appeared to be a need for a workgroup, as some members of the Deaf community were struggling with their sexual identity and did not really know who to turn to for advice and support (see Section 5.2). Bea Visser (1936–2017), one of the founders and the first chairperson of *Roze Gebaar*, remembers:

> On May 2nd, a long time ago, we came together. All in all, there were about 25 deaf people. It was very pleasant, and we discussed a lot with each other. I told them that I would like to set up something like an association or foundation for deaf gays and lesbians. Everyone reacted positively, they thought it was a great idea. [. . .] Everyone was in favor of it. [NGT-F05-20170312-RozeGebaar, 02:38–03:38]

One month later, in June 1982, some of the weekend's participants met again in Amsterdam to take further steps. Here, it was unanimously decided to indeed set up a workgroup. In the interview, Bea says *"I'm glad that now you all see who I am: Bea Visser, founder of 'Roze Gebaar'"* [NGT-F05-20170312-RozeGebaar, 08:18–08:30], but it has to be emphasized that this description is not fully accurate. Bea may well have been a driving force, but the foundation of *Roze Gebaar* was initiated by a group of six people, three women and three men, including also Annemieke van Brandenburg, Gert-Jan de Kleer, Corinne Munne, Hans van der Ploeg, and Will Schollmeijer.[16]

---

14 On the *Roze Gebaar* website (see footnote 18), only LGBTI (in Dutch LHBTI) is used as acronym, but we added the Q for 'Queer', as this appears to be more commonly used, and also because one of our informants identifies as Queer.

15 In the interview, Bea Visser mentions that about 25 people attended this meeting [NGT-F05-20170312-RozeGebaar, 02:45; see quote], and in Essink (2009: 114), it is said that there were around 20 attendees. However, the original list of attendees still exists, and it shows that these numbers are too high: 16 people had registered for the meeting, but five of them withdrew.

16 This inaccuracy was noticed after the interview had been conducted, and the plan was to address it in a follow-up interview. However, shortly after the interview, Bea fell sick and passed away a month later, and therefore, there was no opportunity to amend the

The very first activity was to organize an Open Day, which took place in October 1982 in Utrecht. The space for this meeting was made available free of charge by *Humanistisch Verbond*, a humanitarian society. The event was a success: about 60 people showed up. At this point, contact was also sought with the COC, the Dutch organization for LGBTIQ people, for subsidies and various other facilities.[17] However, the official connection with the COC was only established in 1986, and ever since, *Roze Gebaar* has officially been part of COC Netherlands.[18]

The workgroup still needed a name, and Bea Visser recalls in the interview that a competition was held to come up with an appropriate name.

> He (Gert-Jan de Kleer) came up with the name 'Roze Gebaar' The board members thought it was a nice name. First, pink is our color, the color of lesbians and gays. And gebaar ('sign') refers to our language, the language of deaf people. How appropriate! Magnificent! [. . .] It was also a nice sign: the 'Roze Gebaar'.
>
> [NGT-F05-20170312-RozeGebaar, 03:51–04:23]

Still, initially, not everyone was fond of the name. People continued to think about alternatives, but without success. It took at least another year before the name was officially accepted. In Figure 2, the sign for the association is visualized, signed by Bea Visser herself during the interview.[19]

---

mistake. In order to represent the historical facts more accurately, and to do justice to the other team members, it has been decided to change "founder" to "(co)founder" in the subtitled interview that can be viewed on the SIGN-HUB platform (in the Dutch version *(mede)oprichter*).

17 The COC was founded in 1946 and is thus the oldest existing LGBTIQ organization in the world. COC stands for *Cultuur en Ontspanningscentrum* ('Center for Culture and Recreation'), a name that was originally intended to cover the real purpose of the organization. In the interview, Bea Visser mentions that she had contacted the COC already before the weekend in Bakkeveen [NGT-F05-20170312-RozeGebaar, 01:27–01:55], but this contact was of a personal nature: she had reached out to the COC, as she felt the need to talk with someone about her recently discovered sexual identity. Still, it seems that the idea to set up a workgroup was already mentioned during this initial contact with the COC.

18 Consequently, *Roze Gebaar* is also hosted under the website of the COC: https://rozegebaar.coc.nl/.

19 In the sign Bea Visser uses for 'pink', the ring finger makes contact with the lip. This appears to be a variant of the standard sign, in which the middle finger is selected and makes contact. Interestingly, interviewee M19 uses a form in which the index finger contacts the lip, which is actually the sign for 'red'.

Figure 2: Bea Visser showing the sign for *Roze Gebaar* ('Pink Sign'), a combination of PINK (ring finger touches lower lip repeatedly) and SIGN (two hands with all fingers extended perform an alternating circular movement) [NGT-F05-20170312-RozeGebaar, 04:21].

Once the connection with the COC had been established, a board was formed in which each board member had their specific task, some of them holding their position for many years. During the 1990s, meetings were regularly organized at the homes of some of the members, and occasional use was also made of a space made available by the Amsterdam *Doven Sport Vereniging* ('Deaf sports club') *"De Amstelstad"*. This was necessary, as *Roze Gebaar* did not have a fixed space for convening at that time. In addition, one has to keep in mind that back then, homosexuality was still more of a taboo than it is now. In fact, Bea Visser remembers that in the beginning, for exactly this reason, there had been discussions among members concerning whether the group's meetings should be open to everyone.

> Many deaf people from all over the Netherlands came by, it was fun, a real community. Yet, a few deaf people wanted to turn it into a closed private meeting. Closed, because they were afraid. They had not yet made public that they were gay or lesbian. They still kept it a secret. I had my reservations about that and discussed the issue with the board. The outcome was that we should better keep it open and accessible. Because, after all, many people are gay-friendly. [. . .] The more accessible it is, the more possibilities can develop, which is good. [NGT-F05-20170312-RozeGebaar, 05:04–05:52]

Most of the activities were organized in Amsterdam, which was inconvenient for – and actually considered somewhat unfair by – interested Deaf people who lived further away (e.g., in the regions Brabant and Limburg). They therefore decided to set up their own branch of *Roze Gebaar* at the COC in Eindhoven (120 km south of Amsterdam) and to organize their own activities.

The years 1992–2002, the second decade of its existence, can be seen as the "golden years" of *Roze Gebaar*. Numerous activities were organized, with the Europride in 1994, the first symposium in January 1996 (with the theme "Is *Roze Gebaar* still in the closet?"), and the Gay Games in 1998 being the major events in the existence of the association. 2005 saw another highlight, when a second symposium was organized with the theme "Then and now". The Deaf American Raymond Luczak, editor of the book *Eyes of desire* (1993), which deals with the living situation of Deaf gays and lesbians in the United States, was the guest speaker at this symposium. Furthermore, the board had a record in 1999, when it consisted of no less than nine people (including regional contact persons; see Figure 3 for some of the board members from over the years). Moreover, it is worth noting that a *Roze Gebaar* newsletter was published between 1989 and 2002.

Figure 3: Some of the board members of *Roze Gebaar* from over the years (January 1996, on the occasion of the symposium "Is *Roze Gebaar* still in the closet?"); from left to right: René Fabert, Dick Kerkhoven, Martijn Kamphuis, David da Silva, Annemieke van Brandenburg, Eduard Leuw, and Alfons Kenkhuis.

From about 2005 onwards, the situation of *Roze Gebaar* became more difficult, as the impact of the association decreased. Partly due to the rise of social media, fewer and fewer activities were organized. The general assembly of the association was held until 2007, but after that, it also stopped. Many older members who have been part of the association from the beginning say that this is a pity. They hope that the moments of pleasant socializing and the attention for each other, young and old, will come back. Bea Visser also comments on this change in the interview.

> *I am happy that I have been able to contribute to the prosperity of 'Roze Gebaar'. At present, it's a bit . . . on the back burner. There are fewer activities. It should be activated again, one should breathe new life into it. The pink life, it's so important. Otherwise, it will disappear, and that would be a pity.* [NGT-F05-20170312-RozeGebaar, 07:41–08:17]

Yet, in 2014, *Roze Gebaar*, in collaboration with Kentalis and COC Netherlands, among others, managed to make something happen that was important to them: participating with their own boat in the annual Gay Pride Day, which in Amsterdam is "Canal Pride", with a parade of decorated boats cruising on the canals through the city. For the Deaf lesbians and gays this was an amazing and powerful experience of togetherness with other sign language users and LGBTIQ people – an experience that was repeated in 2016. Interviewee M19 remembers visiting the Gay Pride.

> Interviewer: *There is Gay Pride in Amsterdam, with all the boats. Would you sometimes go there?*
>
> M19: *Yes, I was there once. It was nice.*
>
> Interviewer: *On a boat?*
>
> M19: *[. . .] No, I only came to watch, but was not on a boat. Just watching. It was amazing. Most of all, I was curious to see who the famous artists were. [. . .]*
>
> Interviewer: *Did you identify with all the artists, who are also gay or lesbian?*
>
> M19: *Indeed. So nice . . . Everything may be visible!*
>
> Interviewer: *Did you also see a boat with deaf people?*
>
> M19: *Yes, I saw that boat pass by. HW was on it. I waved at him.*
> [NGT-M19-1-20170629-4, 10:59–11:51]

The cooperation between *Roze Gebaar* and COC has always been pleasant, ever since the contact has been established in the early 1980s. Yet, there were also some difficult moments. For instance, some members of *Roze Gebaar* only wanted a membership with their own association, but not with COC; that is, they didn't like the idea of a "double" membership. This, however, was required, as *Roze Gebaar* is affiliated with COC as a working group and is thus officially part of COC. Such occasional frictions notwithstanding, *Roze Gebaar* and COC supported each other whenever necessary, among other things with the candidacy for the Gay Pride and the partial financing of it.

5 On the (changing) identity of Deaf homosexuals

Having sketched the history of *Roze Gebaar*, we now turn to a discussion of changes within the Dutch LGBTIQ community, in particular changes in how members of the Deaf community who identify as homosexual/LGBTIQ[20] perceive their identity. It is important to realize that there are actually two (related) identity issues at play. First, there is the issue of coming to terms with one's lesbian or gay identity at a time when homosexuality was still a taboo in the Netherlands, and discrimination against homosexuals was common. This aspect will be addressed in Section 5.1. Second, there is the intersectionality issue, that is, the question whether belonging to two minority groups would force individuals to choose between identities, or at least to prioritize one of their identities. In Section 5.2, where we discuss this issue, we will also consider the impact of *Roze Gebaar*. In Section 5.3, we turn to recent developments, drawing also on information from interviews with younger interview partners. Finally, in Section 5.4, we complement our discussion of Deaf LGBTIQ identities with some observations regarding linguistic (i.e., lexical) changes that have occurred over the years.

5.1 Between taboo and acceptance

In the SIGN-HUB interview, Bea Visser shares a rather shocking anecdote from her time at *Christelijk Instituut Effatha* ('Christian Institute Effatha'), a boarding school for Deaf children in Voorburg (South Holland). Bea visited Effatha approximately from age 4 to age 15, but she does not specify how old she was

---

20 When referring to our elderly interviewees, we use "homosexual" rather than "LGBTIQ" because at the time when they discovered and came to terms with their sexuality, the acronym did not exist – and they also don't use it in the interviews.

when the incident happened. She remembers that at the time, approximately 50 girls shared a dormitory.

> *There was one girl who wanted to lie next to me in bed. I approved, and she came to lie next to me. [. . .] When mother S. walked past, she saw me and that girl lying together in bed. She pulled back the blankets and yelled: "That's not allowed!" [. . .] She took us to the back (of the room). There she pulled out a toilet brush. [. . .] With that she hit us ten times on the hand. I had to stretch out my hand, and if I had pulled back, the number of hits would have been doubled. So, I stretched out my hand, closed my eyes, and received my hits. [. . .] The other girl also got here share of hits on her hand. When it was over, we were allowed to go back to bed. There I felt something wet on my hand. It turned out to be blood. My hand was bleeding, and it was staining the sheet. I saw everything get red and wet from the blood.*
> [NGT-F05-1-20170313-2, 10:03–11:32]

The anecdote is revealing as it gives us an impression of the repressive atmosphere in which some of our interviewees grew up, in particular those who were schooled at a Christian institute.[21] Clearly, what triggered the punishment was harmless, but the extreme reaction of the warden will likely have made a lasting impression on the girls, causing them to assume that sharing the bed with another girl is fundamentally wrong. It is interesting to note that a little bit later during the same interview, Bea Visser comments on the incident by saying: *"Tough, right? Well . . . it was my own fault, but anyway . . . They were strict."* [NGT-F05-1-20170313-2, 12:12–12:20]. This is quite striking, as it suggests that even in retrospect, and after having fought for equality (for LGBTIQ and Deaf people) for a good part of her life, she felt that, in this particular situation, she had been the one to blame.

In her life story, which has been documented by Essink (2009), Bea recalls that in the 1970s, there were a few gay couples in her circle of friends; however, none of them were open about their homosexuality. She further mentions that she knew the word *homo* ('gay'), but that she had always assumed that homosexuality was something that only concerned men.

> *[. . .] this were mostly men who behaved in a somewhat effeminate manner and had an effeminate way of moving. The hairdresser in Akkerwoude also had this way of moving [. . .]. I had asked my mother once whether the hairdresser was 'homo'. She said that 'homo' was a dirty word and that I should not talk about that. Women who loved each other in this way – this I had never heard about. It was unimaginable. I found it embarrassing.*
> (Bea Visser; Essink 2009: 105f; our translation)

---

[21] There are more interviewees who report that punishments were common at the school they attended, but none of them remembers physical punishment as severe as the one reported by Bea Visser. And, to be fair, many of the interviewees also share positive recollections of their school days.

These thoughts came up in Bea after a Deaf woman had told her that she was in love with her. Bea recalls that she first got angry about this unexpected confession and then more and more confused. It took her a while to admit to herself that she was lesbian, and that she actually shared the other woman's feelings. In the interview, she comments on her coming-out.

> When I was about 40, 42 years, I realized that I am not straight but lesbian. Now you may think 'That's quite late.' Well, it was an old-fashioned time. Back then, it all happened in the underground. [NGT-F05-201706-RozeGebaar, 00:12–00:47]

In her published life story, Bea shares further details about the challenges she faced in her personal environment when trying to come to terms with her sexual identity:

> Neither in my family nor among my Deaf friends, I dared to be open about my new feelings and my new situation. Most Deaf people had, just like myself, never heard of the word 'lesbian'. My family was also not open to it – to say the least.
> (Bea Visser; Essink 2009: 111; our translation)

In fact, one of her sisters advised her to go see a doctor, pointing out that there were medicines to treat her condition and make it go away, and the other one told her to act normal and look for a husband. They further warned her that if she told their mother, it would surely kill her, and that would then be her fault. "I was so shocked by the reaction of my sisters that I decided the same moment never to talk about it again in my family." (Essink 2009: 112; our translation). The decisions taken as a result of her negative experiences and her fears had far-reaching consequences for Bea.

> The Deaf and my family were such a huge part of my identity that, even though there did not appear to be any problem at work, I no longer dared to show myself among the Deaf. I was afraid of their judgements and reactions, but actually I had not yet accepted myself in my new identity. (Bea Visser; Essink 2009: 113; our translation)

In the interview, Bea mentions that she left the Deaf world for three years, thereby temporarily disconnecting from an important part of her identity. As mentioned in passing in the above quote, reactions at work were positive. When she came out to her boss, who had noticed that something was going on, he – much to her surprise – congratulated her and told her that she was a lesbian – to which Bea reacted "Le . . . what? Would you write it down?" (Essink 2009: 108; our translation). He brought her in contact with two colleagues who were also lesbian and provided her with further information.

> The next day I received a stack of information booklets and folders from my boss, which were, just like the conversation with my colleagues, a celebration of recognition. A great weight was

lifted from my shoulders. Ok, so I was lesbian. I was also deaf. I was a deaf lesbian. I was a deaf lesbian in love, in love with a deaf woman. That was clear. That was nice.

(Bea Visser; Essink 2009: 109f; our translation)

As mentioned above, Bea was afraid of negative reactions from inside the Deaf community (see also Section 2.2). She estimates that approximately fifty percent of her acquaintances disapproved of her homosexuality, and that she wanted to avoid being confronted with this disapproval. She remembers, for instance, that some people were afraid that her condition might be contagious and no longer wanted to kiss her (Essink 2009: 112f). Interviewee M19 also talks about his coming-out and some difficult and emotionally challenging situations he was faced with. He reports an incident that took place during a trip with a group of Deaf people to the Deaflympics (since he mentions Yugoslavia, this must have been the games in Belgrade in August 1969).

> Before 'Roze Gebaar' was founded, there were the Olympic Games for Deaf people in Yugoslavia. We went there by bus, with the group. During the bus trip, a boy fell in love with me. [. . .] We got intimate in the restrooms. The next day, I felt that something was wrong. The atmosphere was different. Everyone was silent. I already suspected that someone had watched us in the restrooms. [. . .] There were rumors: 'Look, they are gays.' The next day, I fell apart. [NGT-M19-1-20170629-4, 06:03–07:07]

The last sentence suggests that the negative reaction from within the group that he identified with, in combination with shame and insecurity, caused a serious psychological crisis. In reaction to the interviewer's question whether he thinks that the situation is different nowadays from how it used to be in the 1970s, he explicitly mentions the term 'taboo' and further highlights his doubts and the sense of isolation that he experienced.

> Oh yes, it is different. For younger people nowadays, it is easier to come out of the closet. It was a taboo when we were younger. A gradual coming-out, which was really difficult for me. No-one around me was gay, but I always had doubts about some Deaf people who might be gay. All these doubts . . . Somewhat later, after my time at school, I discovered someone, who was gay. Suddenly, others came out of the closet. Why not earlier? Before, everyone had been too scared to come out. These days, coming out is much easier. It's so different from how it used to be.
> [NGT-M19-1-20170629-4, 03:18–03:56]

Although the above experiences come from only two informants, it seems safe to assume that they are representative of the challenges that Deaf homosexuals were faced with – be it within their family or within the Deaf community. It is interesting that both explicitly mention (their fear of) the reactions of members of the Deaf community, the group they identified with. The Dutch Deaf community is a rather small community, where people know each other, and it transpires from the interviews that fear of gossip played an important role.[22] For sure, not feeling at ease within that community must have had an enormous impact on the lives of our interviewees. Interestingly, in Julien & Schol (2004), which contains interviews about sexuality issues with Deaf women of various ages, a much younger bisexual woman (Tanya, around 35 at the time) makes a similar comment: *"From the moment that I started going out with women, I no longer dared attending parties and meetings at the Deaf clubs"* (Julien & Schol 2004: 69; our translation).

In conclusion of this section, it is interesting to note that M04, the interview partner who identifies as bisexual, reports much more positive experiences. In the below quote, he talks about the reaction of his family, but elsewhere during the interview, he mentions that he was also accepted in the Deaf world.

> Interviewer: *The 1980s were a difficult time for gays and lesbians. For you, too?*
>
> M04: *Yes, indeed. But fortunately, my parents accepted me. I thought 'Oh, oh'. But fortunately, they were ok with it. My brothers and sisters accepted me, too, and also my son.*
> [NGT-M04-2-20170222-2, 32:24–32:46]

5.2 The impact of *Roze Gebaar*

To be sure, in the period we were concerned with in the previous section (i.e., the late 1960s to 1980s), hearing homosexuals were faced with challenges very similar to those reported above. Homosexuality was, for the most part, a societal taboo faced with discrimination. Yet, for Deaf homosexuals, the situation was complicated by the additional communicative barrier (cf. the discussion in Section 2.2). The fact that Bea was not familiar with the term 'lesbian', for instance, is revealing. For the Deaf, it was simply much more challenging to get access to information. As they could not easily communicate about personal issues, it was difficult for them to interpret their feelings and to understand that

---

[22] As Bea remarks: *"The Deaf world functions like a small village. Everyone knows each other, and news goes around quickly."* (Essink 2009: 112). Similarly, Zakarewsky (1979: 181) describes for the situation in the United States that "problems are magnified for gay/lesbian deaf persons by virtue of the fact that the network systems in the deaf subculture are so enmeshed that an individual's most private acts may become facts for public inspection".

what they experienced was not an isolated case. Bea remembers that these problems motivated her to reach out to the COC.

> *I realized that there were quite a few problems. One lesbian woman was married but wanted to get a divorce, but how? She did not know. Such stories piled up around me and made me think. I then contacted the COC [Dutch LGBTIQ Association; authors' note]. We started to discuss the matter. I told them that there were lots of problems in the deaf world, that the deaf did not get enough information. Together with the COC, I wanted to investigate what we could do about it. I said that I would like to set up a working group. So, that happened.* [NGT-F05-201706-RozeGebaar, 01:12–01:57]

In an interview conducted by Littel (2019), Annemieke van Brandenburg, another important personage in the foundation and history of *Roze Gebaar* (see Figure 3), addresses a different type of communicative problem, resulting from the fact that a system of sign language interpreters was not yet in place in the 1970s and 1980s. She shares that it had taken her some courage to join a women's discussion group to talk about her lesbian identity, but soon she realized that she did not fit well in the group, in particular because of the obstacles she experienced in communicating with the other members (Littel 2019: 50).

With the foundation of *Roze Gebaar*, it became possible to meet likeminded Deaf people who struggled with similar issues, to converse about these issues in NGT, and thus to create awareness that there actually was a community of Deaf LGBTIQ people in the Netherlands. The positive impact of this development cannot be overestimated, as also becomes clear from the following quote.

> *I was present when 'Roze Gebaar' was founded. [. . .] I made contact with a number of Deaf people, thanks to 'Roze Gebaar'. Bea Visser was one of the founders. [. . .] I was very happy. So many deaf people had come. We recognized each other's identity, as everyone was gay, too. Why not earlier? Many of the Deaf kept silent. They went to the hearing clubs for gays and lesbians. They were scared that there would be gossip within the Deaf world.* [NGT-M19-1-20170629-4, 04:18–05:25]

The quote also suggests a crucial transition: from the hearing world to the Deaf world. M19 explains in the interview that he himself also used to frequent clubs for hearing homosexuals, where he would communicate with paper and pen, in particular when there was loud music. The experience of a Deaf man visiting a hearing gay bar is illustrated in the (fragment of a) cartoon in Figure 4. Obviously, the cartoon is meant to offer a humorous perspective, but still it neatly illustrates the frustration resulting from the omnipresent communicative barrier and the difficulties in making contact.

Figure 4: Experience of a Deaf gay man in a hearing gay club. (i) Banner at bottom "Music starts"; hearing man (H, on left) asks "Do I know you from somewhere?"; Deaf man (D) thinks "Oops! He wants to talk to me. Should I tell him that I'm deaf?". (ii) Banner at bottom: "Music gets louder"; D says: "Sorry, I'm deaf. Would you please speak slowly?"; H replies: "What do you say?". (iii) Banner at bottom: "Loud music still playing"; D thinks: "Damn, he still cannot understand me because of the music. So, one more time."; D says: "I said: I am deaf!". (iv) Banner at bottom: "Music stops"; D screams: "I am deaf!"; (v) H thinks: "He's crazy. I'm out of here!"; D thinks: "Sigh! Once again, the same old story."; text at bottom: ". . . that's just one of the experiences of a deaf homo . . ." (from *Informatie Bulletin Roze Gebaar*, May 1984; drawing Gert-Jan de Kleer).

The transition implied in the previous quote brings us back to the issue of identity, specifically the issue of intersectionality and choosing identity, discussed in Section 2.2. When being presented with two options by the interviewer, M19 makes clear that for him, his gay identity came in the first place.

> Interviewer: *I'm curious about your identity. So, here's a 'trick question'. Imagine there are two groups: a group of deaf people, with no gays, but with sign language, and another group of hearing people which includes some gay people. Which group would you then preferably identify with?*
>
> M19: *The hearing group. At first, I constantly associated with the hearing gays. I didn't know anyone among the deaf. So, I always went to the hearing until I discovered some deaf gays. After the foundation of 'Roze Gebaar', I moved towards the deaf side, and let go of the hearing side.*
>
> Interviewer: *So, for you, being gay came in the first place, and deafness was secondary?*
>
> M19: *Yes!* [NGT-M19-1-20170629-4, 08:42–09:36]

The choice expressed in the quote notwithstanding, it is clear that M19 was torn between the two worlds, and thus his two identities. He describes his experience as *"a double life. It was like constantly participating in two worlds, deaf and hearing. That was tough on me"* [NGT-M19-1-20170629-4, 08:28–08:34]. Right afterwards, he illustrates his inner conflict by means of the metaphor shown in Figure 5, in which his being torn is visualized by an imaginary rope around his neck being pulled to opposite sides. Obviously, with the establishment of *Roze Gebaar*, this inner conflict was mitigated, as the choice was now between hearing gay world and Deaf gay world, and M19 clearly expresses his preference for the latter because *"[i]t's easy to sign; with the hearing, it's cumbersome"* [NGT-M19-1-20170629-4, 08:18].

Figure 5: Interviewee M19 expressing that he was torn between the hearing and the Deaf world (which had previously been localized to the right and the left, respectively) by pulling an imaginary rope around his neck, first to his left (hearing world), then to his right (Deaf world) [NGT-M19-1-20170629-4, 08:35].

Interestingly, Tanya, who is approximately 20 years younger than M19, made a similar journey from the Deaf to the hearing world because of her homosexuality. She emphasizes, however, that at present, she is comfortable in both worlds. Yet, on the hearing side, her lesbian identity appears to be more important.

> Back then, there were not many Deaf women who had had their coming-out. I felt really alone in the Deaf world. I only went out in the world of hearing lesbians. But after two years, I began to miss the Deaf world. So, I returned and realized that Deaf people were behaving normally towards me. At that point, I finally dared to be open. Nowadays, I go out in both worlds, the hearing lesbian world and the Deaf world, and I really like it.
>
> (Tanya; Julien & Schol 2004: 69; our translation)

5.3 Recent developments: beyond *Roze Gebaar*

The statements presented in the previous section strongly suggest that, in the period covered, Deaf LGBTIQ people in the Netherlands were struggling with identity issues, and that this struggle was aggravated by the limited access to information at the time. While being part of the Deaf community was without doubt of importance to them, both our interview partners report that, after discovering their sexual identity, they no longer felt at ease within the Deaf community because they were afraid of gossip. Moreover, both M19 and the younger Tanya mention that they did not know any Deaf gays or lesbians, and that they therefore choose to socialize in the hearing homosexual scene. Regarding her search for a partner, Tanya adds that *"[t]here wasn't a lot of choice in the Deaf world, and that's why I explored the hearing world. There it was easier to find a girlfriend."* (Julien & Schol 2004: 70; our translation).[23] For M19 in particular, the foundation of *Roze Gebaar* was crucial, as it allowed him to transition back into the Deaf world. He no longer needed the hearing world to embrace his gay identity. However, as already alluded to in Section 4, from about 2005 onwards, the impact of *Roze Gebaar* has decreased. Actually, M19 himself points out:

> *Every two months, a meeting is organized. [. . .] But at each meeting, there are always the same conversations. My drive to go there has slowly been decreasing. 'Roze Gebaar' still exists, but I don't go there anymore.* [NGT-M19-1-20170629-4, 10:30–10:58]

Lulu, a Deaf lesbian who was around 40 years of age when she shared her experiences (Julien & Schol 2004), says that she visits the meetings of *Roze Gebaar* because she enjoys the intimate and friendly atmosphere. At this point in time (i.e., the early 2000s), she still felt that *Roze Gebaar* could play an important role in the coming-out of younger Deaf people.

> *I see more and more young Deaf people being open about the fact that they are gay or lesbian, and I think that's a good development. I find it important that Deaf youngsters can have their coming-out with the help of 'Roze Gebaar'.*
>
> (Lulu; Julien & Schol 2004: 38; our translation)

---

23 Both Zakarewsky (1979: 184) and Doe (1994: 466) address the challenge of finding partners. Zakarewsky, for instance, notes that it "becomes difficult for a given member of the group to find a suitable person for a lasting relationship without going outside of the subgroup". In this respect, the move to online dating might be considered a form of progress. Feenstra & van Kessel (2020), however, point out that online communication comes with its own disadvantages for Deaf persons, and that "the move to online dating privileges mostly white cis-male members of the LGBTQ+ community" (Feenstra & van Kessel 2020: 113).

She mentions, for instance, that members of *Roze Gebaar* used to go to Deaf schools to provide information about LGBTIQ issues, and she expresses that this is something that should be re-established. However, she also contributes the following observation:

> There are 25.000 Deaf people in the Netherlands, and 15% of them are homosexual. So, this amounts to 3.750 Deaf homosexuals. Still, 'Roze Gebaar' has only seventy members. I know that there are lots of Deaf homosexuals in the Netherlands who don't want to have contact with 'Roze Gebaar'. There are also older homosexual Deaf people who don't want to register because they experienced the Second World War and are afraid of having their personal data put on record. (Lulu; Julien & Schol 2004: 38; our translation)

In a small-scale study on cultural and linguistic aspects of the Deaf LGBTIQ community in the Netherlands, for which she interviewed five Deaf participants (age range 33–46, two lesbian women, two gay men, and one straight man), Van der Zwaag (2007) reports that her homosexual interview partners agree that the existence of *Roze Gebaar* was important at a time when homosexuality was a taboo. However, given societal changes regarding the acceptance of homosexuality, and of alternative lifestyles in general, the younger generation now tends to be more open about their sexuality, and the boundaries are less strict. Consequently, as the interviewees point out, there is less need for a dedicated organization to represent the interests of Deaf homosexuals. In this context, it is also interesting to note that all of Van der Zwaag's homosexual participants emphasize that, when it comes to their identity, their deafness weighs heavier than their sexuality (similar to what Kane (1994) described for the Deaf gay community in the United States; see Section 2.2). This is in contrast to what M19 reported, for whom it was clear that his gay identity came in the first place. This shift in perspective on one's own identity is likely due the before-mentioned change in attitude towards homosexuality. The negative experiences resulting from discrimination may have diminished, but the communicative barriers resulting from deafness remain – and consequently, for younger Deaf people, their Deaf identity, shaped by Deaf culture and the use of sign language, now tends to come in the first place. This preference notwithstanding, all remark that they feel a strong connection with the LGBTIQ community in the Netherlands.

Our informant M42g, for instance, reports that he never experienced discrimination because of his homosexuality; also, for him, there was no sense of taboo. Yet, he does occasionally experience the barriers resulting from his deafness (e.g., because of a lack of interpreters). He emphasizes that he is proud of who he is, and that he neither considers himself a gay Deaf person nor a Deaf gay person – it simply doesn't matter. He also notes the important role of the internet, which allowed him to chat with other gay people – be they Deaf or hearing –, to share experiences, and to access information. Consequently, he also does not think that the Deaf community would lack any information nowadays. He does not feel any connection with *Roze Gebaar*; in fact, he remarks that he considers *Roze Gebaar* too "extreme".

The experiences shared by F25q are very much in line with those of M42g. Just like him, she was never confronted with problems because of her Queer identity. In fact, she never had to "officially" announce this aspect of her identity to her Deaf friends. It just happened by itself within her circle of friends, as they know each other very well. Her parents also accepted her. Her deafness, however, does create barriers, in particular communicative obstacles. In contrast to M42g, but in line with Van der Zwaag's informants, she makes clear that for her, her Deaf identity always comes first. Another point where her opinion diverges from that of M42g concerns access to information: according to her, the Deaf Queer community is disadvantaged, as much useful information on the internet is available in the form of videos (e.g., Youtube), and these are not commonly subtitled. Consequently, the Deaf are still deprived of information. Finally, she mentions that she never got involved with *Roze Gebaar*. On the one hand, there was simply no need to seek support in coming to terms with her Queer identity; on the other hand, she also points out that she feels that the association is geared more towards older people.[24]

From the opinions collected in this section, we can infer – albeit with due caution – that there has indeed been an identity shift in at least a part of the Deaf LGBTIQ community in the Netherlands. While the older signers report that they temporarily distanced themselves from the Deaf community in order to be able to embrace their lesbian/gay identity, which for them was more important than their Deaf identity, the younger signers tend to give more importance to their Deaf identity. However, all of them agree that their Deafness creates communicative barriers. In this context, it is interesting to note that, despite this barrier, the two gay men interviewed by Van der Zwaag (2007) claim that there is more contact between Deaf and hearing homosexuals than between Deaf and hearing heterosexuals (cf. Kane 1994). Obviously, it would be interesting to reassess this claim, especially in light of recent technical developments with respect to mobile communication devices.

We conclude this section with a quote from the interview with M04, our interview partner who identifies as bisexual. M04 lives at *De Gelderhorst*, an apartment complex for elderly Deaf people (see the chapters by Reiff-de Groen & van Veen

---

[24] Our third informant M43b also mentions that he does not identify with *Roze Gebaar*. In contrast to F25q and M42g, however, he also says that he does not really identify with other homosexual or bisexual people. It is noteworthy that he composed a poem in NGT in which he expresses his bisexual identity.

and Hiddinga et al., this volume).²⁵ The heart-warming experience that he shares in this quote suggests that even among the elderly Deaf, at least those that he interacts with on a daily basis, there is now general acceptance of homosexuality.

> M04: *At present, things are better than they used to be.*
>
> Interviewer: *In how far is it better?*
>
> M04: *People are more ready to accept. It is more relaxed now. Before, everyone was closed. [. . .] One evening here at* De Gelderhorst, *I organized an event to provide information about Deaf culture and homosexuality. I got a lot of applause from the audience. They found it interesting. [. . .]*
>
> Interviewer: *What did you tell them?*
>
> M04: *That it's not just men who are homosexual but also women. [. . .] I was surprised about how many people showed up, even staff members. They applauded me and also showed their respect. I was proud.*
>
> [NGT-M04-2-20170222-2, 32:54–34:09]

It is worth noting that Sánchez-Amat et al. (this volume) report a similar observation based on the interviews they conducted in Spain: "almost all respondents who talked about homosexuality rejected discrimination against gays and lesbians, thus showing a liberal mindset".²⁶

5.4 Notes on Queer terminology

We conclude our discussion of changes in the Dutch Deaf LGBTIQ community with some observations regarding the use of Queer terminology.²⁷ Besides the signs used by our interviewees, and the opinions they express about them, we

---

25 In fact, 12 out of the 24 interviews we conducted in the context of the SIGN-HUB project involved elderly Deaf people who live at the Gelderhorst.
26 Yet, the same interview partners criticized the fact that divorces are currently so common, thus adhering to more conservative values in this respect.
27 For Queer ASL vocabulary, see Rudner & Butowsky (1981) and Kleinfeld & Warner (1996). Schmitz (2020) discusses properties of Queer German Sign Language, including implications for sign language interpreting. Beyond addressing Queer vocabulary, he also considers in-group language and humor. Michaels (2015) provides an overview of gay sign variation in British Sign Language. Interestingly, he also comments on signing style (e.g., body movements, exaggerated use of facial expressions). As for ASL, Blau (2017) proposes that some Deaf gay men employ a signing style which includes frequent use of distal joints in sign articulation.

also draw information from the conversations with the younger participants and from Van der Zwaag (2007).[28]

When first talking about his own homosexuality, interviewee M19 uses the NGT H-handshape (index and middle finger extended, slight up-and-down movement), accompanied by the mouthing 'homo'. Immediately afterwards, he uses the sign depicted in Figure 6a. The interviewer then draws his attention to the fact that this sign is commonly considered politically incorrect, as it expresses the meaning 'faggot' (Dutch *flikker*). According to her, the neutral, politically correct NGT sign for 'gay' is the one in Figure 6b, where the index finger touches the neck. M19, however, when repeating this sign, makes clear that he does not know it and says that *"the sign has always been like this"* [NGT-M19-1-20170629-4,

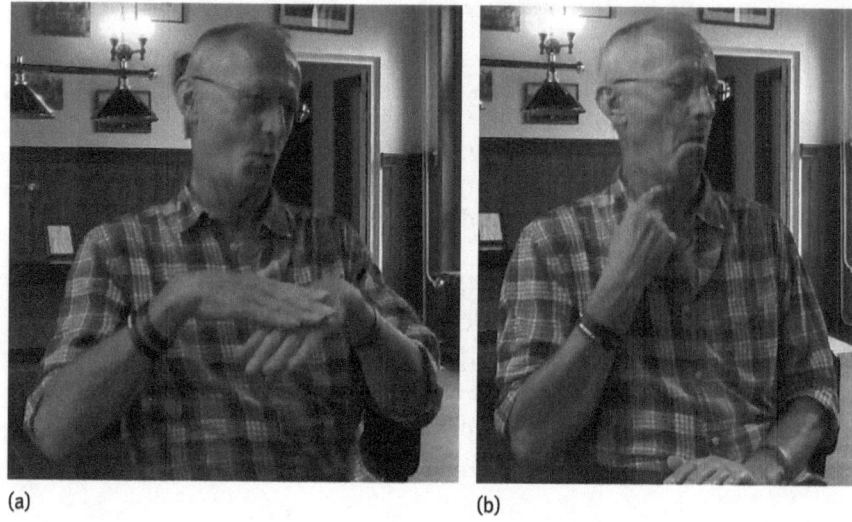

(a) (b)

Figure 6: (a) Interviewee M19 articulating a sign for 'gay', which, according to the interviewer, has a negative connotation, meaning something like 'faggot' (Dutch *flikker*) [NGT-M19-1-20170629-4, 00:43]; (b) Interviewee M19 expressing that he does not know the sign for 'gay' that is articulated with an index finger at the neck [NGT-M19-1-20170629-4, 01:28] – after articulating the sign, he shakes his head.

---

28 For a "Queer Sign Glossary" of NGT signs, see https://vanabbemuseum.nl/en/collection/queering/queer-sign-glossary/. This glossary, which contains signs like INTERSECTIONALITY (see Figure 1), CISGENDER, and QUEER (see Figure 9), together with explanations of these terms in NGT, is the result of a collaboration between the Queer Deaf community, the Dutch Sign Center (*Nederlands Gebarencentrum*), the Institute of Signs, Language, and Deaf Studies at the University of Applied Sciences in Utrecht, and the Van Abbemuseum in Eindhoven. For Queer ASL, see www.queerasl.com (for discussion, see Feenstra & van Kessel 2020).

01:22]; that is, for him the sign in Figure 6a has no negative connotation. Yet, he adds that he would generally simply use the sign with the H-handshape.

Interestingly, Bea Visser also talks about exactly these two signs in the *Roze Gebaar* interview, and her view on their use is in line with the opinion expressed by our interviewer. In fact, she explains that the *Roze Gebaar* board felt uncomfortable with the original sign (depicted in Figure 6a) and thus came up with the sign articulated on the neck. She also explains the etymology of the newly coined sign: fiddling with the ear, as she demonstrates in Figure 7a, used to be a secret code for flirting with someone of the same sex (see also Van der Zwaag 2007: 20).

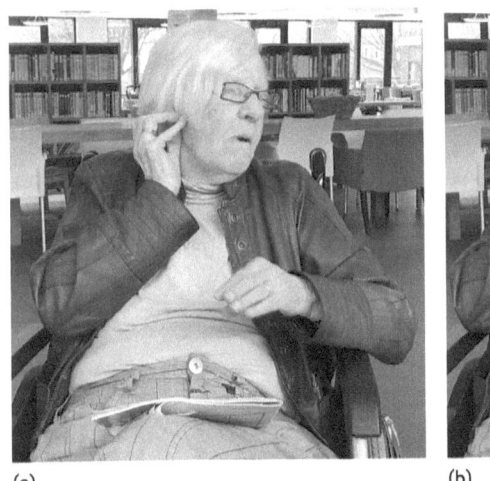

(a) (b)

Figure 7: (a) Bea Visser showing the gesture of fiddling with one's ear, which motivated the form of the NGT sign GAY [NGT-F05-20170312-RozeGebaar, 09:04]; (b) Bea Visser showing the NGT sign LESBIAN [NGT-F05-20170312-RozeGebaar, 09:09].

> *In the old days, people used this sign for 'gay'* [the one in Figure 6a; authors' note]. *But this is actually the sign for 'faggot', a swearword. I was appalled by it. Others did not like it either. We did not like it. That's why we, as a board, came up with this sign for 'gay'* [the one in Figure 6b; authors' note]. *Because of fiddling with the ear. That's why it now is this sign, near the ear. The sign for 'lesbian' is like that* [see Figure 7b; authors' note]. *Yes, this sign is logical.* [NGT-F05-201706-RozeGebaar, 08:40–09:08]

In Figure 7b, Bea shows the NGT sign LESBIAN. This is likely a loan sign from ASL, as the same form is listed in Woodward (1979) and Rudner & Butowsky (1981). However, 15 years later, Kleinfeld & Warner (1996) report four ASL variants of this sign, which differ from each other in movement (single vs. repeated) and point of contact. According to them, the variant depicted in Figure 7b is considered derogatory by those of their informants who identify as members of the LGBTIQ community, especially when signed by an outsider, as "[t]here is a strong tendency to associate this sign's meaning with that of oral sex" (Kleinfeld & Warner 1996: 25). The variant that is considered the most appropriate and most politically correct one by all their informants is the variant in which the fingertip of the index finger makes contact with the chin (cf. also Bienvenu (2008: 268), who argues that point of contact signals "a person's attitude toward Lesbian"). Among the signs she collected from her five informants, Van der Zwaag (2007) lists the form in Figure 7b, rather than the one with fingertip contact, and marks it as a loan from ASL – it thus seems that in NGT, this sign does not have the negative connotation reported for ASL. However, Van der Zwaag includes another form for 'lesbian', which she considers a native NGT sign; this sign has the same handshape as the one in Figure 7b (i.e., L-handshape with thumb and index finger extended) but the index finger makes contact next to the corner of the mouth, and the palm is oriented outward.

Another interesting finding emerging from Van der Zwaag's study is that none of her informants mentions the sign GAY depicted in Figure 6b (remember that M19 also did not know this sign), but all of them – including the straight informant – know and use the sign shown in Figure 6a. The same is true for our participant M42g, who confirms that this is the sign generally used in the Deaf community, not just in the Deaf LGBTIQ community, and who is not aware of any negative meaning associated with it. It thus seems that the newer sign, coined by members of *Roze Gebaar* in the 1980s in order to get rid of a sign that was considered politically incorrect at the time, has not been widely accepted in the Deaf LGBTIQ community. Of course, it is also possible that the negative meaning originally associated with this sign has eroded over the years. After all, it is not uncommon for a minority group to make a term its own which has originally been used as a swearword or insult – a phenomenon that is sometimes referred to as "stigma reversal" (e.g., Hoffmann 2003). This type of "positive reappropriation of negative expressions" also holds for the term 'queer', originally an insult, but now used "to affirm pride instead of shame" (Leduc 2016; also cf. the change in the connotation of German *schwul* 'gay').[29]

While Van der Zwaag's informants did not mention the sign in Figure 6b, one of her lesbian informants and both gay informants contributed another sign, which is actually closer in form to the gesture produced by Bea in Figure 7a. In this sign, which we gloss as HOMOSEXUAL, as it can refer to lesbian and gay

---

[29] In addition, we cannot exclude the possibility of dialectal variation, as NGT is known to display considerable regional variation in its lexicon (Schermer 2004).

identity, the thumb and index finger make contact with the ear lobe. The two gay informants consider this is an old-fashioned sign, which is not used much anymore. Van der Zwaag lists this sign as a native NGT sign, but Rudner & Butowksy (1981: 40) present a similar form, which they gloss as GAY(ear pinch), and for which they point out that it "is considered a secret sign" (also see Bienvenu (2008: 269), who refers to it as "closeted sign for GAY"[30]). Indeed, while basically all of their homosexual respondents knew the sign (and rated it as highly positive), only 45% of the heterosexual respondents recognized the sign.

Finally, Van der Zwaag (2007) also presents two signs that can be considered borrowings from spoken Dutch. In Dutch, the word *pot*, which means 'pot, jar', can be used to refer in a rather derogatory way to a lesbian who is perceived as masculine (comparable to English *dyke*), while the word *nicht* ('niece, female cousin') is used to refer, again in a negative way, to gay individuals, in particular when their behavior is perceived as effeminate (cf. English *sissy*, which is derived from *sister*). When asked about signs related to homosexuality, Van der Zwaag's two gay informants contributed the signs in Figure 8 – the NGT signs POT and NICHT, respectively. They point out that these signs are politically incorrect, but that it would be ok for both homosexuals and heterosexuals to use them in a

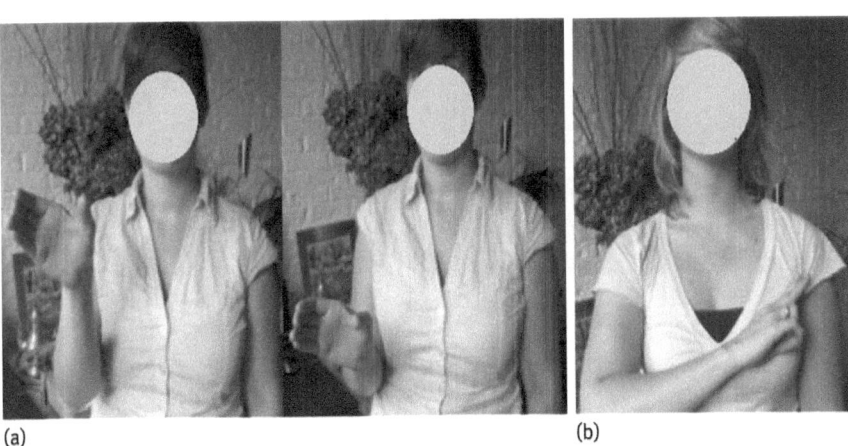

(a)   (b)

Figure 8: Two NGT signs, borrowed from spoken Dutch, which may be used to refer to homosexual individuals in a derogatory (or sometimes humorous) way: (a) POT (standard meaning 'pot, jar'), which may refer to a lesbian individual; (b) NICHT (standard meaning 'niece, female cousin'), which may refer to a gay individual (Van der Zwaag 2007: 19).

---

30 Another ASL secret code expression mentioned in both Kane (1994) and Bienvenu (2008) is the phrase GREEN AND YELLOW, based on the initial letters 'g-a-y' of the English equivalent.

humorous way. Clearly, the fact that these signs can be used in this way in NGT is motivated by the use of the corresponding words in spoken Dutch.

For the sake of completeness, we add here another sign, which is not mentioned in Van der Zwaag's (2007) study, probably because it has entered the NGT lexicon more recently: the sign QUEER shown in Figure 9. Remember that our informant F25q identifies as Queer, and this is the sign she uses to refer to her identity. The sign is likely a loan sign from ASL, although it seems that in ASL, it is more commonly signed with four fingers extended on both hands; this handshape in combination with the arc-shaped movement refers to a rainbow. The fact that QUEER is not included in the studies by Rudner & Butowsky (1981) and Kleinfeld & Warner (1996) is not surprising, as only from the turn of the millennium onward, the English term *queer* was more and more commonly used to refer to a variety of non-normative sexual and gender identities.

Figure 9: NGT sign QUEER (© *Nederlands Gebarencentrum*; reprinted with permission).

6 Conclusion

Deaf communities are multifaceted communities, pretty much like the mainstream hearing communities within which they exist. However, Deaf communities are generally marginalized, and thus some of these facets, or identity features, such as race or sexual identity, may make that a Deaf individual belongs to a doubly marginalized sub-group, faced with discrimination both within the Deaf and hearing communities. In the present chapter, we addressed the experiences of Deaf individuals who also identify as homosexual/Queer, as well as the specific challenges they are faced with when it comes to navigating their identities, from the perspective of intersectionality theory. An intersectional analysis does not merely add up individual identity traits (and the discrimination associated with them) but rather seeks to understand how these identities collectively shape the individual.

From the interviews and conversations with elderly (i.e., 65 years or older) and younger members of the Dutch Deaf community, who identify as homosexual, bisexual, or Queer, it becomes clear that significant identity shifts have taken place. The elderly interviewees report that they distanced themselves for a period of time from the Deaf community, in order to be able to explore and live their homosexual identity – a move that was also motivated by the fact that the Deaf community is a small and tight-knit community. In other words, given societal pressure, they saw no space for developing their intersectional identity within that community. It further transpires from the literature and the interviews we conducted that communicative barriers and lack of access to information were experienced as further obstacles on the bumpy path towards coming to terms with one's double identity.

We acknowledge that, at present, this path may not be entirely free of obstacles. After all, marginalization and discrimination are still a reality. Yet, it is clear that it is easier nowadays for younger Deaf people who identify as LGBTIQ to embrace their intersectional identity, instead of toggling between identities or even suppressing one of them. As we demonstrated, in the Netherlands, this positive change was induced not least thanks to the foundation of *Roze Gebaar*, an association for Deaf LGBTIQ people. It is the irony of history that now that important goals have been achieved, the importance of *Roze Gebaar* is on the wane.

In conclusion, it is safe to say that the life stories shared by the elderly Deaf signers are a true treasure, as they contribute in significant ways to our understanding of the dynamics within Deaf communities, not just regarding intersectional identities – the topic of the present investigation – but also with respect to, for instance, educational experiences, communication patterns, and social dynamics within families as well as within and outside the community. It is of utmost importance that these life stories are documented before they are lost – and this was indeed one of the goals of the SIGN-HUB project.

Acknowledgements: Work on this chapter has been possible thanks to the SIGN-HUB project, which has received funding from the European Union's Horizon 2020 research and innovation program under grant agreement No. 693349.

We are very grateful to Merel van Zuilen for her contribution to the project, in particular her excellent subtitling work, and to Judith Reiff-de Groen and Livienke Vogelaar from *De Gelderhorst* for facilitating our interviews with elderly Deaf people. Moreover, we thank Nynke Feenstra, Anja Hiddinga, Karina Hof, Mieneke van der Jagt, Hendrik de Jong, Looi van Kessel, Nathalie Muller, the *Nederlands Gebarencentrum* (Dutch Sign Center), Pamela Perniss, Markus Steinbach, and Karin Wempe for supplying helpful information and/or materials.

References

Ahmad, Waqar, Karl Atkin & Lesley Jones. 2002. Being deaf and being other things: young Asian people negotiating identities. *Social Science & Medicine* 55(10). 1757–1769.

Annamma, Subini A., David Connor & Beth Ferri. 2013. Dis/ability critical race studies (DisCrit): theorizing at the intersections of race and dis/ability. *Race Ethnicity and Education* 16. 1–31.

Aramburo, Anthony J. 1989. Sociolinguistic aspects of the black deaf community. In Ceil Lucas (ed.), *The sociolinguistics of the deaf community*, 103–119. San Diego: Academic.

Bienvenu, MJ. 2008. Queer as deaf: Intersections. In H.-Dirksen L. Bauman (ed.), *Open your eyes: Deaf studies talking*, 264–273. Minneapolis: University of Minnesota Press.

Blau, Shane. 2017. Indexing gay identities in American Sign Language. *Sign Language Studies* 18(1). 5–40.

Cappotto, Claudio & Cirus Rinaldi. 2016. Intersectionalities, dis/abilities and subjectification in deaf LGBT people: An exploratory study in Sicily. *Interalia: a Journal of Queer Studies* 11a. 68–87.

Cawthon, Stephanie W., Paige M. Johnson, Carrie Lou Garberoglio & Sarah J. Schoffstall. 2016. Role models as facilitators of social capital for Deaf individuals: A research synthesis. *American Annals of the Deaf* 161(2),115–127.

Chapple, Reshawna L. 2019. Toward a theory of black deaf feminism: the quiet invisibility of a population. *Affilia: Journal of Women and Social Work* 34(2). 186–198.

Cho, Sumi, Kimberlé W. Crenshaw & Leslie McCall. 2013. Toward a field of intersectionality studies: Theory, applications, and praxis. *Signs: Journal of Women in Culture and Society* 38. 785–810.

Clark, Heather D. 2007. Signing and signifyin': Negotiating Deaf and African American identities. *Ethnic Studies Review* 30. 115–124.

Crenshaw, Kimberlé. 1989. Demarginalizing the intersection of race and sex. A Black feminist critique of antidiscrimination doctrine, feminist theory and antiracist politics. *University of Chicago Legal Forum* 1 (Article 8). 139–167.

Croneberg, Carl. 1965. Sign language dialects. Appendix D in William C. Stokoe, Jr., Dorothy C. Casterline & Carl G. Croneberg (eds.), *A dictionary of American Sign Language on linguistic principles*, 313–319. Washington, DC: Gallaudet Press.

Doe, Tanis. 1994. Multiple minorities: Communities within the Deaf community. In Carol L. Erting, Robert C. Johnson, Dorothy L. Smith & Bruce D. Snyder (eds.), *The Deaf way: Perspectives from the International Conference on Deaf Culture*, 464–469. Washington, DC: Gallaudet University Press.

Essink, Petra. 2009. *Bea Visser, dove prinses. Het levensverhaal van Bea Visser, opgetekend door Petra Essink* [Bea Visser, deaf princess. The life story of Bea Visser, recorded by Petra Essink]. Zwolle: Petrapen.

Feenstra, Nynke & Looi van Kessel. 2020. Deafies in drag: Role models at the intersection of queer and Deaf representation. In Sophia Hendrikx, Merel Oudshoorn, Lieke Smits & Tim Vergeer (eds.), *Arts in society: Academic rhapsodies*, 107–123. Leiden: Leiden University Centre for the Arts in Society.
Foster, Susan & Waithera Kinuthia. 2003. Deaf persons of Asian American, Hispanic American, and African American backgrounds: a study of intraindividual diversity and identity. *Journal of Deaf Studies and Deaf Education* 8(3). 271–290.
Hoffmann, Rainer. 2003. Vor der Stigma-Umkehr? Performativität der Publikumswahrnehmung auf das Ereignis der Gay-Paraden. In Erika Fischer-Lichte, Christian Horn, Sandra Umathum & Matthias Warstat (eds.), *Performativität und Ereignis*, 301–318. Tübingen: Francke.
James, Melissa & Bencie Woll. 2004. Black deaf or deaf black? Being black and deaf in Britain. In Aneta Pavlenko & Adrian Blackledge (eds.), *Negotiation of identities in multilingual contexts*, 125–160. Clevedon: Multilingual Matters.
Julien, Mieke & Perwin Schol. 2004. *Vagina verhalen – van dove vrouwen* [Vagina stories – by deaf women]. Amsterdam: Handtheater. Available at: http://www.handtheater.nl/theater/vagina-verhalen/355.
Kane, Thomas P. 1994. Deaf gay men's culture. In Carol L. Erting, Robert C. Johnson, Dorothy L. Smith & Bruce D. Snyder (eds.), *The Deaf way: Perspectives from the International Conference on Deaf Culture*, 483–485. Washington, DC: Gallaudet University Press.
Karar, Ege. 2008. *Islamische gehörlose Jugendliche in Deutschland: Einblick in ihre Lebenswelt und Konzept zur Bildungsarbeit* [Islamic deaf youth in Germany: Insights into their living environment and concept for educational work]. Saarbrücken: VDM Verlag Dr. Müller.
Kleinfeld, Mala S. & Noni Warner. 1996. Variation in the Deaf community: Gay, lesbian, and bisexual signs. In Ceil Lucas (ed.), *Multicultural aspects of sociolinguistics in Deaf communities*, 3–35. Washington, DC: Gallaudet University Press.
Ladd, Paddy. 2003. *Understanding Deaf culture. In search of Deafhood*. Clevedon: Multilingual Matters Ltd.
LeBlanc, Jeanne M. & Carol T. Tully. 2001. Deaf and hearing-impaired lesbians and gay males. *Journal of Gay & Lesbian Social Services* 13(3). 57–84.
Leduc, Véro. 2016. Diversity: LGBTQI. In Genie Gertz & Patrick Boudreault (eds.), *The SAGE Deaf studies encyclopedia*, 315–319. Thousand Oaks: SAGE Publications.
Leigh, Irene W. 2009. *A lens on Deaf identities*. Oxford: Oxford University Press.
Leigh, Irene W. 2012. Not just deaf: Multiple intersections. In Reginald Nettles & Rochelle Balter (eds.), *Multiple minority identities: Applications for practice, research and training*, 59–80. New York, NY: Springer.
Littel, Nina. 2019. *'Minority consciousness gone mad?' Exclusion, inclusion and self-organisation of disabled LGBTI people in the Dutch and British LGBT+ and disability movements, in the late twentieth century*. Leiden: Leiden University MA thesis.
Lucas, Ceil, Robert Bayley, Ruth Reed & Alyssa Wulf. 2001. Lexical variation in African American and white signing. *American Speech* 76(4). 339–360.
Luczak, Raymond. (ed.) 1993. *Eyes of desire. A Deaf gay & lesbian reader*. Boston, MA: Alyson Publishers.
McCaskill, Carolyn, Ceil Lucas, Robert Bayley & Joseph Hill. 2011. *The hidden treasure of black ASL – its history and structure*. Washington, DC: Gallaudet University Press.

Metzner, Alex. 2018a. Inklusive Communities gestalten – Erfahrungen Tauber Schwuler in der schwulen Community (Teil I) [Designing inclusive communities – experiences of Deaf gays in the gay community (Part I)]. *Das Zeichen* 108. 40–53.
Metzner, Alex. 2018b. Inklusive Communities gestalten – Erfahrungen Tauber Schwuler in der schwulen Community (Teil II) [Designing inclusive communities – experiences of Deaf gays in the gay community (Part II)]. *Das Zeichen* 109. 220–231.
Michaels, Paul A. 2015. *A study of the identity, culture and language of a sample of the Deaf gay male community in Britain*. Durham: Durham University MA thesis [http://etheses.dur.ac.uk/11014/].
Moges, Rezenet. 2017. Cripping Deaf studies and Deaf literature: Deaf Queer ontologies and intersectionality. In Annelies Kusters, Maartje De Meulder & Dai O'Brien (eds.), *Innovations in Deaf studies. The role of Deaf scholars*, 215–239. Oxford: Oxford University Press.
Moreman, Shane T. & Stephanie R. Briones. 2018. Deaf Queer world-making: A thick intersectional analysis of the mediated cultural body. *Journal of International and Intercultural Communication* 11(3). 216–232.
Padden, Carol & Tom Humphries. 2005. *Inside Deaf culture*. Cambridge, MA: Harvard University Press.
Phaneuf, Jean. 1987. Considerations on deafness and homosexuality. *American Annals of the Deaf* 132(1). 52–55.
Robinson, Luther D. 1979. Sexuality and the deaf culture. *Sexuality and Disability* 2(3). 161–168.
Romero, Mary. 2018. *Introducing intersectionality*. Medford, MA: Polity Press.
Rudner, William A. & Rochelle Butowsky. 1981. Signs used in the deaf gay community. *Sign Language Studies* 30. 36–48.
Ruiz-Williams, Elena, Meredith Burke, Vee Yee Chong & Noppawan Chainarong. 2015. "My Deaf is not your Deaf": Realizing intersectional realities at Gallaudet University. In Annelies Kusters & Michele Friedner (eds.), *It's a small world: Deaf world international studies*, 262–273. Washington, DC: Gallaudet University Press.
Schermer, Trude. 2004. Lexical variation in Sign Language of the Netherlands. In Mieke Van Herreweghe & Myriam Vermeerbergen (eds.), *To the lexicon and beyond. Sociolinguistics in European Deaf communities*, 91–110. Washington, DC: Gallaudet University Press.
Schmitz, Jona. 2020. Queere DGS – Was kennzeichnet die Sprache taub-queerer Menschen? [Queer German Sign Language – What characterizes the language of deaf-queer people?]. *Das Zeichen* 115. 270–287.
Sesko, Amanda K. & Monica Biernat. 2010. Prototypes of race and gender: The invisibility of black women. *Journal of Experimental Social Psychology* 46. 356–360.
Sheridan, Sarah. 2008. *A minority within a minority: Deaf gay and lesbian people on their experiences within different communities*. Dublin: Dublin City University MA dissertation.
Sinecka, Jitka. 2008. 'I am bodied'. 'I am sexual'. 'I am human'. Experiencing deafness and gayness: a story of a young man. *Disability and Society* 23(5). 475–484.
Solomon, Andrew. 1994. Defiantly Deaf. *The New York Times Magazine*. 28 August 1994.
Solvang, Per Koren & Hilde Haualand. 2014. Accessibility and diversity: Deaf space in action. *Scandinavian Journal of Disability Research* 16(1). 1–13.
Stein, Sarah A. 2009. Deaf American Jewish culture in historical perspective. *American Jewish History* 95(3). 277–305.

Van der Zwaag, Marloes. 2007. *Doofheid & homoseksualiteit. Culturele en linguïstische aspecten* [Deafness & homosexuality. Cultural and linguistic aspects]. Amsterdam: University of Amsterdam, BA thesis.
Woodward, James C. 1976. Black southern signing. *Language in Society* 5. 211–218.
Woodward, James C. 1979. *Signs of sexual behavior: an introduction to some sex-related vocabulary in Americna Sign Language*. Silver Spring, MD: TJ Publishers.
Woodward, James C. & Susan DeSantis. 1977. Two to one it happens: Dynamic phonology in two sign languages. *Sign Language Studies* 17. 329–346.
Zakarewsky, George T. 1979. Patterns of support among gay lesbian deaf persons. *Sexuality and Disability* 2(3). 178–191.
Zaurov, Mark. 2003. *Gehörlose Juden. Eine doppelte kulturelle Minderheit* [Deaf jews. A double cultural minority]. Frankfurt am Main: Peter Lang.

Part III: **"Apparently, one could hear airplanes, but we knew nothing": Deaf lives in times of conflict and oppression**

Annika Mittelstädt and Jana Hosemann

Impairment vs. *disability*: The paradoxical situation of deaf people during the German Nazi Regime

1 Introduction

The time of National Socialism, that is, the time between 1933 and 1945, is a crucial period in German history. Many minorities have suffered immensely during the Nazi Regime, have been discriminated, harassed, persecuted, deported, imprisoned, and killed – and this is also true for deaf people.[1] The National Socialists had the ideology of a superior Aryan master race: Healthy strong people with a pure German ancestry and a Germanic physiology were seen to be the superior 'race'. Hence, people of different race, of different political or religious beliefs than the Nazis, and people with physical or mental impairments were considered inferior and a threat to the Nazis' idea of a healthy national "People's Community" (*Volksgemeinschaft*). With the goal to "northern up" (*aufnorden*) the People's Community, various groups like Sinti and Roma, communists, Jehova's witnesses, people with divergent political beliefs, homosexuals, people declared as impaired, and, as is most commonly known, Jews were persecuted and murdered.

Deaf people were also one of the groups that suffered massively from the National Socialists' ideology. As deafness was categorized as an alleged genetic disorder, deaf people fell under the category of "hereditarily diseased" and were legally sterilized under the "Law for the Prevention of Offspring with Hereditary Diseases" (*Gesetz zur Verhütung erbkranken Nachwuchses*). Interestingly, and very strikingly, in retrospective, deaf people nowadays hold contradictory opinions about the Nazi Regime, as is evident from the interview fragments in (1) and (2).

(1) A negative report about the Nazi Regime:
There were two women, who were also members of the club for senior citizens. Both of them were more than 90 years old. One woman had two hearing sons. When she had to be sterilized, she took them with her to the responsible office. She wanted to show that she had

---

1 We are aware of the conventionalized distinction between "deaf" and "Deaf", in which "deaf" refers to the physiological condition of not being able to hear, whereas "Deaf" refers to the cultural identity. Since the Deaf pride movement started only in the late 1960s and 1970s in the United States, and did not reach Germany until the late 1980s and 1990s, we use the word "deaf" as an adjective throughout, thereby referring to people who lived and grew up under the Nazi Regime and had a medium or severe hearing loss.

given birth to two hearing sons. So, why would she have to be sterilized? Regardless, she was sterilized. The other woman was five months pregnant. The baby was aborted by force, and she was sterilized. She mourned for her unborn son until the end.

[W02, 06.02.2017, 00:59–1:01; translation by the authors]

(2) A positive report about the Nazi Regime:

Deaf informant: *He [Adolf Hitler] made Germany strong. Under Hitler, there was order, work, and no hunger. Every year, we attended a huge youth camp. We were able to do military exercises, enjoy a nice camp life under open skies, evenings around a romantic campfire, and very good organization. I became familiar with discipline there and learned how to darn socks. All that was useful, and I'm thankful for it. It was nice!*

JM: *But what do you think about forced sterilization and the war?*

Deaf informant: *Yes, but that wasn't so bad.*

JM: *And the Jews?*

Deaf informant: *Well, we didn't know about that. No one told me that – not even the church. We were told they were in the East and had to work in the countryside.*

(Interview by Jochen Muhs; Muhs 2002: 79f.)

This seems to be puzzling: How can members of a group who, on the one hand, were declared defective, who were discriminated against and persecuted, and who were targeted to be eliminated, on the other hand, come to a positive interpretation of this time? Many deaf contemporary witnesses remember the "Third Reich" not exclusively as a time of terror, but also describe the positive feelings of having been included and of being part of the German community. It is this puzzle that the present chapter addresses.

The aim of our study is to find an explanation for the deaf people's ambivalent interpretation of the Nazi Era. We will argue that deafness is an invisible impairment, which allowed the Nazis to have two different views on deaf people: on the one hand, deafness as an inherited unrepairable impairment, which was to be eliminated; and on the other hand, people with (often acquired) deafness, who – in principle – would fit into the picture of the healthy, strong, laboring Aryan, and who could contribute to the People's Community. This two-fold interpretation of deafness led to opposing political strategies of how the Nazi Party, the National Socialist German Workers' Party (*Nationalsozialistische Deutsche Arbeiterpartei*, NSDAP), treated deaf people: At the same time as deaf people were prevented from marrying each other, were sterilized, and underwent enforced abortions, the Nazi Party also included deaf people in their political youth organization "Hitler youth" (*Hitlerjugend*) and educated them in designated "institutes for the deaf-mute" (*Taubstummen-Anstalten*). Interestingly, the modern differentiation between *impairment* and *disability*, a key distinction in Disability Studies, which evolved within the past 40 years, can provide us with an explanatory approach to this dichotomy. The distinction between impairment and disability allows for a better understanding why deaf people were treated ambivalently in Nazi Germany. First, in Section 2, we present a detailed description of the ambiguous situation of deaf people in the 1930s and the first half of the 1940s, including both the eugenic approach and the conjectural integration of deaf people. In Section 3, we then outline the modern concept of distinguishing between impairment and disability in order to analyze this ambivalence. Finally, in Section 4, this distinction will be exemplified by a discussion held in the 1930s among educators, teachers, and physicians about whether "institutes for the deaf-mute" should be closed or not. This discussion was publicized in the journal "The German Special School" (*Die deutsche Sonderschule*) during the years of the Nazi regime.

2 The ambiguous situation of deaf people during the Nazi Regime

One of the main doctrines of the Nazi Party was to improve the genetic quality of the Aryan German population by excluding and eliminating individuals who were judged to be weak, sick, and inferior. The idea of eugenics became popular in the late 19th and early 20th century and was closely linked to Social Darwinism. In the middle of the 19th century, Charles Darwin developed his scientific theory on evolutionary biology in his book "On the Origin of Species by means of Natural Selection" (Darwin 1859). His main claim for all species was that during a struggle for survival, only the "fittest" individuals will survive, which leads to natural selection of the strongest and most robust individuals in the next generations. This theory was applied to humans by leading scientists at the time, like, for instance, Ernst Haeckel, who advocated a hierarchy of races: "In the same way [as all organisms] the value of the various races and nations is very unequal in human history." (Haeckel 1904: 406f). This perspective on human beings and their genetic material resulted in the development of the pseudo-science "eugenics", which became very popular around World War I. It changed the societal attitudes towards racism and found its way into the state's legislation with the political rise of the National Socialist German Workers' Party (*Nationalsozialistische Deutsche Arbeiterpartei*). Social Darwinism and eugenics were taken to justify an aggressive militarism against individuals who were declared as physically and mentally inferior (Biesold 1988; Büttner 2005). The idea of a genetically superior human species, which should be achieved by improving the strength and robustness of individuals throughout the next generations, led to a classification of people according to their economic and social value, and how much they would contribute to the well-being of the whole society. Since the value of an individual was measured based on his/her physical or mental contribution to the productiveness and economy of the society, impaired people were seen as almost worthless. By this definition, the impaired person had turned into a problem for the German society (cf. Davis 1995: 74).[2]

In Nazi ideology, the German nation was understood as an overall body, comprising racially desirable Germanic people – the so-called *Volkskörper* (national body). The ultimate goal was to strengthen the *Volkskörper* by building a community without any weak, that is, economically worthless or inferior, members. In order to increase the genetic quality of the German people, eugenicists demanded that the gene pool of the *Volkskörper* should be controlled. By this, the persistence and strength of the German nation would improve (Poore 2010: 67). As a consequence, the Nazi Party claimed it to be the state's responsibility to counteract the weakening of the population's quality. This was operated, on the one hand, by "positive eugenics" through supporting marriage and childbirth in genetically accepted people. On the other hand, the party practiced "negative eugenics" by preventing any inferior-judged individuals from reproducing, in order to stop the transmission of "bad" genes. Among many other groups, this affected the lives of thousands of deaf people (Friedlander 2002: 17–19).

2.1 The one perspective: Deaf people have a hereditary disease

One side of the ambiguous situation of deaf people during the Nazi Regime was that they fell under the category of suffering from a "hereditary disease" (*erbkrank*). Being lumped together with other groups of hereditarily sick people, deaf people were subject to a specific political program that regulated the treatment of people, who the Nazi Party considered (hereditarily) impaired. Shortly after

---

[2] The claim that Nazi ideology was induced by Darwinism is controversial (see Arendt 1951; Weikart 2004; Richards 2013). The factors that led to the Holocaust are far more complex than what can be reported here. Hence, at best, we can describe a fraction of the circumstances.

Adolf Hitler had been named Reich Chancellor in January 1933, on July 14th 1933, the Nazi Party passed the "Law for the Prevention of Offspring with Hereditary Diseases" (*Gesetz zur Verhütung erbkranken Nachwuchses*, abbreviated as LPOHD). This law declared that "[a]nyone suffering from a hereditary disease can be sterilized by a surgical operation if, according to the experience of medical science, there is a high probability that his offspring will suffer from serious physical or mental defects of a hereditary nature." (LPOHD 1933). The law defined the following groups as "hereditarily diseased":

> Anyone suffering from any of the following diseases is considered hereditarily diseased under this law: 1. Congenital mental deficiency, 2. Schizophrenia, 3. Manic-depression, 4. Hereditary epilepsy, 5. Hereditary St. Vitus' Dance (Huntington's Chorea), 6. Hereditary blindness, **7. Hereditary deafness**, 8. Serious hereditary physical deformity. Furthermore, anyone suffering from chronic alcoholism can be sterilized.
> (LPOHD 1933: §1; emphasis by the authors)

By this law, it was legal to sterilize a person in favor of the quality of the population's gene pool. The decision, whether the person was going to be sterilized or not was based on "the experience of medical science", executed by a so-called hereditary health court or "Eugenic court" (*Erbgesundheitsgericht*), which "consists of a district court judge acting as chairman, a state physician, and another physician certified by the German Reich and particularly well trained in eugenics." (LPOHD 1933: §6). By this law, the principle of manipulating the gene pool of the German population could directly enter into force. Since "forced sterilization" of certain groups of people was legalized, the medical intervention could be executed against the will of the patient (Klee 1997: 36; see also Schmidt 2016 and Brockmann & Kozelka, this volume).

In the following years, the legal situation for people with hereditary diseases, including deaf people, worsened: In June 1935, a first change to the LPOHD was released,[3] according to which women, who were pregnant at the time of their planned sterilization, could have an abortion until the 6th month of their pregnancy. Although, according to this law, the mother-to-be had to agree to the abortion, practice showed that doctors did not follow this regulation. In the 1980s, Horst Biesold was one of the first researchers to scrutinize the societal trauma of deaf people during the Nazi Regime. In a questionnaire-based survey, he asked deaf women who had undergone forced sterilization about an additional abortion. None of the women, on whom an abortion had

---

[3] Law for change in the Law for the Prevention of Offspring with Hereditary Diseases, 26th of June 1935 (*Gesetz zur Änderung des Gesetzes zur Verhütung erbkranken Nachwuchses vom 26. Juni 1935*).

been performed, had agreed with it (cf. Biesold 1988: 43). Thus, since June 1935, abortions were legalized for married couples, in which one of the parents was deaf. This legislation appears especially extreme in light of the fact that in general, abortions were illegal for married couples, in which both parents were considered to be healthy and to have good genetic material (cf. Friedlander 2002: 22).

Only a month later, in July 1935, a decree on the execution of the LPOHD announced that sterilization and abortion should be executed at the same time. Also, ending a pregnancy was considered to be the same as taking the life of an infant during birth.[4] Thus, just after it had been legalized to prevent the birth of children who were seen as unworthy of life, it was now legitimate to kill them prematurely.

In October of the same year, 1935, the "Marriage Health Law" (*Ehegesundheitsgesetz*) was released. According to this law, a couple was not allowed to marry if one or both of the partners suffered from a hereditary disease listed in the LPOHD, unless he or she was sterilized.[5] In order to actually get married, people needed to get a certificate from the health office, attesting their suitability for marriage (*Ehetauglichkeitszeugnis*).

After another four months, in February 1936, the LPOHD was adapted a second time, now allowing to use methods for sterilizations and abortions other than surgical operation. This change was achieved by deleting the words "by a surgical operation" in the very first sentence of the original law: "Anyone suffering from a hereditary disease can be sterilized by a surgical operation if, [. . .]".[6] Although the change in the law was very subtle, it marks the beginning of a possible variety of legally and illegally extreme measures that were used to perform sterilizations and abortions, which ultimately even led to killings of young infants. Among other methods, this was executed by poisonous injections, as has been described by a contemporary witness, who survived a poisonous injection as a four-year-old child (Brockmann 2016: 15–21).

---

[4] Fourth decree on the execution of the Law for the Prevention of Offspring with Hereditary Diseases, 25th of July 1935 (*Vierte Verordnung zur Ausführung des Gesetzes zur Verhütung erbkranken Nachwuchses vom 25. Juli 1935*).

[5] Law for the Protection of the Hereditary Health of the German People, 18th of October 1935 (*Gesetz zum Schutze der Erbgesundheit des deutschen Volkes (Ehegesundheitsgesetz) vom 18. Oktober 1935*).

[6] Second change in the Law for the Prevention of Offspring with Hereditary Diseases, 4th of February 1936 (*Zweites Gesetz zur Änderung des Gesetzes zur Verhütung erbkranken Nachwuchses vom 4. Februar 1936*).

All of these laws were part of the political management of disabled people under the Nazi Regime. With the beginning of World War II in September 1939, the treatment of impaired people became, once again, more radical. Under the name "Action T4" (*Aktion T4*, because it was planned in a house in Tiergartenstraße 4, Berlin), the Nazi Party planned an euthanasia program, to eliminate "life not worth living". A signed letter by Adolf Hitler, backdated to September 1st, 1939, authorized the Reichs' leader Philipp Bouhler and the medical doctor Dr. Karl Brandt to perform targeted killings:

> Reichsleiter Bouhler and Dr. Brandt, M.D., are charged with the responsibility of enlarging the authority of certain physicians to be designated by name in such a manner that persons who, according to human judgment, are incurable can, upon a most careful diagnosis of their condition of sickness, be accorded a mercy death. (signed) A. Hitler
> (Hitler, 1939)

Based on this authorization, 70,000 people with incurable hereditary diseases – mainly mentally and physically impaired patients, who lived in institutions – had to be identified for extermination. Within two years, six mental institutions changed into (secretive) mass execution institutions, in which people were gassed. Although Action T4 officially ended in August 1941, the killings did not stop but were executed locally and in secret, by poisoning and starving people. Over the course of Action T4, about 100,000 impaired persons were killed, 1,600 of them being deaf (cf. Aly 1989; Büttner 2005: 23). Additionally, deaf Jews suffered immensely and were killed under the Nazi Regime, as they were a cultural minority in two senses (Zaurov 2003). The overall political program of genetic "enhancement" of the Germanic race, and the related elimination of people with hereditary diseases, led to the sterilization of about 400,000 people in Germany, of which approximately more than 15,000 individuals were deaf (Biesold 1988: 27).

2.2 The other perspective: Deaf people as part of the *Volkskörper*

Under the conditions described above, deaf people in Nazi Germany were treated as hereditarily impaired people, who constituted an economic burden to the state and were considered as not being worth of life or reproduction. Strikingly, however, there is another side to the treatment of deaf people during the Nazi Regime. At the same time as the racial hygiene program was pushed forward, there were also attempts to integrate deaf people into the *Volksgemeinschaft*.

From 1933 until 1945, the Hitler Youth was the only officially approved youth organization of the Nazi Party. With its paramilitary structure, it was composed of two sub-organizations, one for boys and one for girls: the initial Hitler Youth for male youngsters aged 14 to 18 (*Hitlerjugend*, HJ), and the League of German Girls for girls of the same age (*Bund Deutscher Mädel*, BDM). Both organizations were supplemented with sections for younger boys and girls aged 10 to 14 – the German Youngsters for younger boys (*Deutsches Jungvolk*) and the Young Girls' League (*Jungmädelbund*) – so that already young children could be indoctrinated with Nazi ideology. In April 1934, the foundation of a separate subgroup for deaf children in the HJ was granted. It was locally initiated by teachers of deaf schools and was called *Bann G*, meaning 'group G', where the G stands for 'hearing-impaired' (*Gehörgeschädigte*). Deaf children had to wear the letter G on their uniform. Heinrich Eisermann, director of the institute for deaf-mutes in Tilsit (*Taubstummenanstalt Tilsit*), became leader of the Bann G. All four HJ organizations for young and older boys and girls had a section for hearing-impaired children. Since December 1936, it was mandatory by law for any 'Aryan' adolescent to become a member of the Hitler Youth or the League of German Girls. This political pressure extended to deaf people, so that by 1939, the Bann G had approximately 4,000 deaf and hearing-impaired members, divided into the sub-groups North, East, West, Central, and South. Bann G was financially independent and had its own monthly journal called *Die Quelle* ('The Well', Büttner 2005: 9).

The political motivation to open the HJ to deaf children, was – besides economic reasons – to teach them 'German values', such as comradeship, loyalty, discipline, etc. Initiated by Bann leader Heinrich Eisermann, an education and training course for the hearing sub-group leaders of Bann G was organized in October 1936, in order to teach them the same ideological, national socialist practice. Hearing group leaders reported a positive effect of Bann G, namely that by letting their protégés work side by side with deaf children, it was possible to resolve prejudices against deaf people (cf. Brill 2011: 161–174). At the same time, being a member of Bann G was a social improvement for deaf children. They enjoyed camp life, did sports, were allowed to wear the same uniform as the hearing HJ (with a special bandage marking them as hearing-impaired), and were trained to be part of the *Volksgemeinschaft*. Many enjoyed the discipline, the good organization of the group, and simply being able to come together with other deaf children. Such a program, specifically arranged for deaf children and young people, had not existed before in the Weimar Republic (Muhs 1996: 197–199).

> *I liked the League of German Girls and the Hitler Youth. I was proud of the uniform. The spare time was great: doing sports, going for a walk, collecting bird food, doing handicrafts for the soldiers, and playing dodgeball.*
> [W02, 06.02.2017, 00:16–00:17; translation by the authors]

> *Yes, I was a member of the Hitler Youth. We all were. That's what it was like under Hitler.*
> [M05, 12.05.2017, 00:19; translation by the authors]

The organization of a special Bann for deaf youngsters in the HJ was clearly politically motivated by the Nazi Party. In training camps, especially designed for this purpose, the youngsters could be taught in military discipline. They had to march in troops, held flag parades, and were educated in Nazi ideology. Although Bann G was used to indoctrinate deaf children politically as young national socialists, many deaf people remembered their time in the Hitler Youth positively.

Another way to structurally integrate deaf people into the Nazi system was through the establishment of the first association for deaf people. Already in 1927, a group of deaf people founded the first association representing the rights of deaf people in Germany: The Reichs' Union of the German Deaf (*Reichsverband der Gehörlosen Deutschlands e.V.*, ReGeDe). Their main goal was to connect deaf people with each other and to protest against the emerging practice of eugenics. However, their original purpose was indoctrinated by the Nazi Party, the NSDAP. In 1933, with the beginning of the Nazi Regime, all smaller associations and clubs of deaf people were subsumed under the ReGeDe. One of the founders of this deaf association, Fritz Albreghs, became its leader (*Reichsfachschaftsleiter*) in 1933 because he was already a devoted member of the Nazi Party. He had proven his political loyalty by additionally leading a group of deaf people in the paramilitary organization *Sturmabteilung* (SA). Albreghs facilitated the connection of the ReGeDe to the social welfare organization of the Nazi Party, the National Socialist People's Welfare (*Nationalsozialistische Volkswohlfahrt*, NSV). As a consequence, all members of the ReGeDe became members of the Nazi Party. Through this close connection to the Socialist People's Welfare, the Nazi ideology found its way to deaf people. For example, the ReGeDe regularly received information and propaganda-material directly from the NSDAP. Thus, the Nazi Party had a channel to propagandize racial hygiene and self-announced sterilizations directly among deaf people (Vogel: "Organisation in der Nazizeit").

The aim of deaf people, that is, to be accepted by the National Socialists as strong and fully equivalent members of the society, who can communicate and work, has been expressed in the very first movie about deaf people: "Misjudged People" (*Verkannte Menschen*, 1932). This documentary movie was produced by the ReGeDe as an educational film about the capabilities of deaf people. Against all prejudices of the time, deaf people are presented as healthy, vigorous, athletic humans, who can work hard, who are educated at the schools for deaf-mutes, and who can therefore support the social system. This film clearly aimed at counteracting the threat of being sterilized. However, under the new ReGeDe leader, national socialist Fritz Albreghs, the film was forbidden and all copies (but one) were destroyed. At that time, the beginning of the 1930s, about 80% of deaf people were unemployed. They hoped that by joining and supporting the NSDAP, they would prove their devotion to the regime, would get employed, and thus escape sterilization (Anonymous 2007). Figure 1 shows a poster advertising the movie.

Figure 1: A poster advertising the movie "Misjudged People" (*Verkannte Menschen*) produced by the ReGeDe 1932.

Taken together, despite the eugenics program, the stigmatization, and the many sterilizations and killings of deaf people on the one hand, they were, on the other hand, under certain conditions considered worthy members of the community, who could contribute to the welfare of the German society. And some of them would later report positive aspects of the Nazi Regime. These positions seem to be inconsistent and contradictory. How is it possible that both behaviors towards deaf people could exist simultaneously within the same society and under the same political regime?

3 The modern differentiation between *impairment* and *disability*

The young scientific discipline *Disability Studies* established a perspective shift in differentiating between the *impairment* of an individual's mind or body and *disability* as a social construct. This distinction offers an analytic instrument which helps to shed light on the dichotomy in the perspective on deaf people during the Nazi Regime.

The first initiatives that gave rise to the discipline Disability Studies began in the 1970s, when disabled people in Great Britain and the United States of America demonstrated against exclusionary conditions on the job market. The majority of problems disabled people were faced with in everyday life originated in societal barriers, not in their bodily differentness (cf. Davis 1995: 85; Dederich 2007: 22). This new understanding of disability led to the following definition, published in 1976 by the *Union of the Physically Impaired Against Segregation*:

> [Disability is] the disadvantage or restriction of activity caused by a contemporary social organization which takes no or little account of people who have [. . .] impairments and thus excludes them from the mainstream of social activities.   (Thomas 2002: 39)

Disabilities were thus no longer seen as deficits of the human body, but as a form of social oppression (cf. Dederich 2007: 23). As an example, picture a person in a wheelchair, who would like to use a public transportation system. In order to enter the subway station, the person needs to pass a turnstile, but unfortunately, the wheelchair is too wide for it. This situation offers two interpretational perspectives. On the one hand, one can argue that it is the person's physical condition that is the reason for the barrier: if the person could walk, the person could pass the turnstile. On the other hand, in the sense of Disability Studies, one can argue that the society failed to take into consideration the needs of all of its members when the turnstile was installed. Hence, the flawed planning and construction of the turnstile are the reasons for the barrier: if turnstiles were wider, everyone could pass through them.

Since the 1980s, the discipline of Disability Studies has argued for a perspective shift from the *medical model of disability* towards the *social model of disability*. The medical model of disability presumes a healthy norm of the human body. Any physical aspect that differs from this norm is believed to be an impairment and thus the cause of inabilities and limitations for the individual (cf. Waldschmidt 2010: 14). The physical 'abnormality' leads to barriers in everyday life, and in order to overcome these barriers, the impairment needs to be overcome. The focus on the deficiency of the impaired body in the medical model implies that barriers can be removed by eliminating or reducing the impairment. For example, having a hearing-impairment is a deviation from the hearing norm, which can be overcome by means of a hearing aid or cochlear implant, so that oral communication with hearing people is possible.

In contrast, the social model of disability argues that a particular physical condition cannot be a constant norm, because the definition of physical health and beauty depends on cultural and social values. Hence, what is understood as the norm of a healthy body in a particular culture is not defined by the body itself, but is rather defined within a specific set of cultural ethics and moral principles. Consequently, what is described as a deviation from the respective norm also depends on the same social, historical, and cultural context. These moral principles come into being, and can change, via political acts, discourses, the creation of specific institutions or regulations, and other direct and indirect measures (cf. Waldschmidt 2010: 17). The social model of disability differentiates between the two concepts *impairment* and *disability*. Impairment refers to the physical divergence from what is thought to be the norm of a healthy human body. In contrast, disability refers to the social divergence impaired people experience within the existing social, cultural, and political conditions in the respective society. This differentiation does not presuppose that all barriers are caused by society. Instead, disability arises in situations in which social and cultural structures and practices result in an exclusion of people with a physical or mental difference (cf. Thomas 2002: 43). Within the social model of disability, it is assumed that barriers can be overcome by an adaptation of the societal and cultural structures. For example, having a hearing-impairment causes difficulties in oral communication, which can be overcome if hearing-impaired as well as hearing people are capable in communicating visually in a sign language. That is, instead of changing the physical state of the impaired person, the social system is changed to address everybody's needs.

To sum up, according to Disability Studies, the concept of disability (in a broad sense) is a social construct. Describing a person as healthy and 'intact' is based on an image of a norm. However, this norm was constructed directly or indirectly under the influence of cultural, social, and historical aspects of the respective society. In a similar vein, describing a person as being impaired is based on the same societal aspects. Additionally, disability describes the barriers constructed by society, which commonly exclude impaired people. The objective of Disability Studies is to examine why certain groups of people are labeled as being impaired within a society. The principles thus discovered allow for drawing further conclusions about the majority of the society itself. Therefore, the concept disability can be used as an analytical tool (cf. Dederich 2007: 29; Bösl 2010: 29).

4 Shedding light on the ambiguous situation of deaf people during the Nazi Regime

In Germany, the implementation of Disability Studies into the scientific curriculum was strongly motivated by the goal to scrutinize the euthanasia crimes during the Nazi Regime (cf. Klein 2010: 52). This section pursues a similar goal: In this first attempt, we will examine the ambivalent situation of deaf people during the Nazi Regime – in which they were both included as well as excluded, stigmatized, and even killed – with the analytical tools provided by Disability Studies. Guiding questions are: What was considered as the human physical norm at that time? What underlying values did humans have according to the Nazi ideology? What made deafness an impairment divergent from the other "diseases" listed in the LPOHD?

We do not assume that the National Socialists differentiated between impairment and disability. After all, this is a modern distinction, and in Nazi terminology, a physical condition other than the norm was undoubtedly characterized as an impairment, as a physical or mental dysfunction and abnormality. The concept of disability as a social construct was never a prospect of National Socialists. However, we will use the distinction between impairment and disability for their consequential measures. *Impairment* describes a dysfunction in the human body or mind that should be resolved, either by eliminating or minimizing the condition (mild measures), or by eliminating the carriers of the condition themselves (extreme measures). In contrast, *disability* describes the barriers that an impaired person faces in society, which should be removed by an adaptation of the societal structure.

4.1 The physical norm and the value of humans

The conceptual meaning of the term "impairment", as understood in the Nazi era, differs from our understanding nowadays. Being classified as "impaired" in Nazi Germany had far-reaching consequences. Individuals were not only seen as having physical or mental limitations, but being impaired could also lead to execution. The term thus marks a separation of two different human classes: healthy humans, worthy of living, and impaired humans, unworthy of living or reproduction. The medical body norm of the National Socialists was a physically strong person, with an Aryan appearance (i.e., tall, blond, pale skin). With the goal of creating an Aryan superior race, society's members were measured against how much they could contribute to the welfare of the whole society, in genetic terms as well as in economic terms. Hence, a person was declared defective or impaired by the same two measures. First, by its genetic value: If a person was physically deformed, mentally limited, or had a condition listed in the LPOHD, this person was identified as impaired. Second, by its economic value: If a person was not able to contribute the same amount of labor as the others, this person was also identified as abnormal.[7] That the economic value of impaired people was crucial to the National Socialists can be seen in the selection process during Action T4. Throughout the course of this euthanasia program, around 70,000 people, who had been declared as impaired and lived in mental health facilities, had been gassed. In order to determine who was going to be killed and who was going to live, hospitals, nursing homes, and sanatoria had to report all eligible patients to the T4 center. T4 assessors then categorized the reports by marking them with a "+" for death, a "–" for life, and occasionally a "?" for a later decision. Three criteria were crucial for their decision: (i) Can this person work and if so, how hard? (ii) How long has he/she been in the institution? (in other words, how much had this person already cost the state?) (iii) How often does he/she get visited? (cf. Klee 1985: 95ff). Hence, the value of a person was measured crucially by economic rationale, a fact that was also disseminated via propaganda posters to the People's Community (see Figure 2).

These two fundamental criteria – an individual's genetic and economic value to the People's Community – were also applied in the decisions about how to deal with deaf people.

---

[7] This is only a fragment of the Nationals Socialists' value system. We are aware that people of different 'race' or political belief (among many others) were also seen as unworthy of life. In the present context, we focus on the group of impaired people.

Figure 2: A poster advertising the monthly journal "New People" (*Neues Volk*) by the Office of Racial Policy of the NSDAP. The text on the poster reads: "60,000 Reichsmark is what this person suffering from a hereditary disease costs the People's Community during his lifetime. Fellow citizen, that is your money, too." (*Neues Volk*, 1938).

Even though the list of hereditary diseases in the LPOHD was not ranked in any specific order, teachers of "special schools" argued for a hierarchy in the value of people with one of these conditions. Here, the value of the people was once again determined by economic considerations. In contrast to people with one of the other listed impairments (e.g., mental deficiency, schizophrenia, epilepsy, or physical deformity), deaf people were considered to be of a higher value. This had two main reasons. First, deafness is an invisible impairment, that is, just by looking at a deaf person, the impairment is not noticeable. Hence, within the Nazi ideology, deaf people could in principle comply with the Aryan ideal, since body and mind are "intact", with the only exception of not being able to hear. Second, deafness may or may not have a hereditary origin. So, in principle, only hereditary deafness was considered a threat for the next generation of the *Volksgemeinschaft*.

Based on these two criteria – deafness being an invisible impairment and potentially being acquired rather than inherited – deaf people were treated in contradicting ways under the Nazi Regime: On the one hand, they were treated as defective people whose impairment should be overcome by eliminating the condition, or even by eliminating the people themselves. On the other hand, their (economic) potential was realized, and they were thus seen as people who could be integrated by adapting the societal structure.

4.2 Eliminate or integrate – keeping or closing schools for the deaf

We now turn to a demonstration of the ambivalent management of deaf people under the Nazi Regime based on a discussion of the importance of deaf schools. The discourse presented here comes from the German periodical "The German Special School" (*Die Deutsche Sonderschule*, DDS), a press medium that still exists and that was first published in 1908/1909. During the process of Nazification of state and society (*Gleichschaltung*), in the course of which the Nazi Party initiated a system of totalitarian control and coordination over different aspects of German society, all associations and organizations of teachers had been merged into one grand organization called "National Socialist Teachers League" (*Nationalsozialistischer Lehrerbund*). One subdivision of the league was the section for special schools (*Reichsfachschaft V / Sonderschulen*), for which the journal DDS was the quarterly print medium (cf. Schwerkolt 1990: 146; Büttner 2005: 58–63). Here, teachers and pedagogic educators, as well as doctors, published articles about the didactics, schooling, and eugenic matters related to impaired children in special schools. Since deaf children and deaf adults had substantial difficulties in articulating themselves in spoken German, the predominant opinion in society at that time was that deaf people are dumb. This preconception was based on the idea that without being able to hear, one could not process thoughts and therefore had to remain uneducated (cf. McBurney 2012: 912–914). Therefore, in the DDS, the question was raised whether it was worthwhile at all to teach deaf children in special schools, or whether the schools for the deaf should rather be closed. Four different arguments had been particularly influential in this discussion: (i) the importance of acquiring spoken German; (ii) the relevance of the schools for eugenic matters; (iii) the financial benefits of educating deaf children; and (iv) the ambivalence of heterogeneous genetic material. In the following sections, we will present these arguments in light of an impairment-perspective, according to which the condition of being deaf should be eliminated, versus a dissenting disability-perspective, under which deaf children should be integrated in the system.

4.2.1 The importance of acquiring spoken German

The main argument for keeping schools for the deaf was not to educate the children in general, but primarily to teach them spoken German (cf. Kunze 1935: 173; Rowak 1934: 446f). According to these authors, learning to speak German was of utmost importance for deaf children, so that they could be cultivated according to the Nazi ideology in the first place – and would thus no longer be dumb. It was argued that only by learning to speak the German language, deaf children would be able to understand German culture and values. Crucially, in National Socialism, the German language was not only understood as a medium to transmit information, but also as a fundamental carrier of German values. German values were seen to be inherent to the German language. Hence, the ability to speak German was considered an essential precondition for a sense of national and social affiliation to the German society (cf. Kroh 1934: 605; Kulemeyer 1934: 32).

> [The language] reflects national manner, national history and culture, and creates the awareness of a super-personal connection between all members of the nation, [. . .] it is indeed required for a vital *Volksgemeinschaft*. The functions of language [. . .] reach far beyond the original expressive function of language. It is them that make humans truly human.[8]   (Kroh 1934: 609; translation by the authors)

The first motivation for keeping deaf schools was to educate deaf children from a young age in the context of National Socialist beliefs and ideals. The effort to integrate deaf children into the German society by minimizing communication barriers was, once again, economically motivated. Facilitating the contact with the hearing majority of the society would allow deaf people to obtain more jobs. The better deaf youngsters could speak German, the easier it would be for them to get a vocational qualification and find an occupation – predominantly

---

8 "[Die Sprache] spiegelt in sich völkische Art, völkische Geschichte und Kultur und schafft das Bewußtsein des überpersönlichen Zusammenhangs aller Volksgenossen, ja sie macht [. . .] selbst erst lebendige Volksgemeinschaft möglich. Die Funktionen der Sprache [. . .] erheben sich weit über die ursprüngliche Ausdrucksfunktion der Sprache. Sie machen den Menschen erst zum Menschen."

handicraft jobs, such as tailor, shoemaker, weaver, or blacksmith, which contributed to the state's economy.

Clearly, this line of reasoning is based on an impairment-perspective. Deafness – especially acquired and not inherited deafness – is seen as a defect that stands in the way of educating the intellect, of learning the cultural values, and of devoting oneself to the nation. Hence, uneducated deaf people were a financial burden for the state (see argument (iii), Section 4.2.3). Teaching deaf children the oral articulation of spoken German was a mild measure taken to minimize these barriers by fully adapting the deaf person to the ideal (hearing) human norm. In contrast to the extreme measure of euthanasia, this line of argumentation shows a tendency to include deaf people by providing a societal structure for them.

4.2.2 The relevance of the schools for eugenic matters

The second argument for keeping special schools for the deaf was that they simplified the procedure of sterilizing deaf children. In order to identify those children who were likely candidates for sterilization, the teachers were an important source of information to evaluate whether a particular deaf child would either grow up to be a valuable member of society or – in extreme terms – be a waste of resources. Therefore, teachers were encouraged by hereditary health courts and doctors to investigate their pupils' ancestry for deaf relatives, so that they could determine whether the child was hereditarily impaired or not. A child with deaf relatives was designated as hereditarily deaf and thus had to be sterilized. Gathering this information about deaf individuals was much easier in a special school than outside of school (cf. Gastpar 1934: 568f; Singer 1934: 576). In fact, it was said to be one of "the most noble functions of special schools" to assist the execution of the LPOHD (*eine "der vornehmsten Aufgaben der Sonderschule"*; Sunderbrink 1936: 742).

Additionally, the authors of the periodical "The German Special School" (*Die Deutsche Sonderschule*, DDS) argued that it was the teachers' task to promote sterilization as an honorable service to the nation, which should be approved by the parents and the children themselves. The goal was to make them understand why sterilizations were needed for the advancement of society, such that parents would give their permission to let their own children be operated on (cf. Singer 1934: 574). It was also considered important that the children comprehended that "a healthy nation would never ever be able to care for something hereditarily ill at the cost of the hereditarily healthy"[9] (Wiedner 1935: 171; translation by the authors).

Hence, as for eugenic matters, special schools had two important functions regarding the execution of sterilization laws. For one thing, they simplified the identification of those children that should be sterilized, as the teachers could easily gather background information about their pupils' family history. For another thing, teachers were able to manipulate parents and children towards supporting and even registering themselves for sterilization. Both tasks were much easier accomplished when deaf children were brought together in one school. Group leaders in the Hitler Youth proceeded similarly. Even within the Bann G for hearing-impaired youngsters in the HJ, the propaganda and actions taken in favor of eugenics were promoted. Children had to draw their family tree, so that the group leaders could identify which of them were hereditarily deaf and therefore needed to be sterilized or – even worse – be executed (Muhs 1996: 199).

In the discussion in the DDS, the authors explicitly differentiate between hereditarily deaf children and children with acquired deafness (be it by an accident or illness) and argue that all of the proposals concerning sterilization should apply only to the former, but not to the latter group of children (see discussion in Section 4.2.4). This shows that deafness was seen as a deficiency that needed to be eliminated. Hence, we interpret this second argument also from an impairment-perspective. In contrast to the first argument, extreme measures were proposed to overcome the deficiency: stopping the propagation of deafness by sterilizing the genetic carrier. The severe measure of sterilization was even exceeded by the euthanasia program T4 – the most extreme form of eliminating a (determined) dysfunction.

4.2.3 The financial benefits of educating deaf children

One of the most cited arguments for closing special schools for the deaf had to do with the financial expenses for the schools. Educating deaf children was supposed to cost the state too much money. However, this accusation was rejected by many authors of the DDS. Dr. Hermann Maeße, the leader of the Reich's league subdivision for special schools (*Reichsfachgruppenleiter*), for instance, calculated how much a deaf person costs the state. He compared the

---

9 "[weil] ein gesundes Volk nie und nimmer Erbkrankes auf Kosten und zu bitteren Lasten des Erbgesunden zu pflegen vermag".

expenses for the education of a deaf child to the expenses for a lifelong institutional placement of an uneducated individual and came to the conclusion that educating deaf children would lead to a long-term financial benefit for the state.

> Through education, averagely gifted deaf people become fully employable. Thus, their schooling and education is economically justified; as these people will even become taxpayers for the state. After all, if one would not educate them, most of the deaf-mutes would be a burden to the general public for most of their lives. This, however, would cost much more than the schooling and education.[10] (Maeße 1934: 25)

While Maeße differentiated between averagely gifted and dumb deaf children, two groups that were supposed to cause different financial burdens for the state, other teachers even suggested that less sophisticated deaf children could also become "useful members of the Peoples' Community" ("*brauchbare Glieder der Volksgemeinschaft*"; Rowak 1934: 446), as they could be instructed to carry out physical labor.

This line of argumentation is purely economically motivated. Here, the motive to maintain special schools for the deaf is not based on empathy, tolerance, or kindness, but rather on a financial advantage. Nevertheless, we argue that, although deafness is understood to be an impairment, the strategy that is suggested for the integration of deaf people into the community involves adapting the system according to their needs (at a minimal level). By schooling deaf children and giving them a job perspective, these children could be partly included in the *Volksgemeinschaft*. Hence, it can be seen as an act of adjusting the educational system to create a place for deaf people.

4.2.4 The ambivalence of heterogeneous genetic material

The last argument for maintaining special schools for deaf children reflects the ambivalent assessment of deaf people during the Nazi Regime. This can be seen in the different, and sometimes even contradictory, argumentations by the authors who published in the DDS. Their main claim is that special schools for the deaf are needed because some deaf children 'cannot be blamed' for their

---

[10] "Durch Beschulung werden normalbegabte Taubstumme vollerwerbstätig. Damit ist ihre Beschulung und Ausbildung wirtschaftlich gerechtfertigt; denn diese Menschen werden dadurch für den Staat sogar Steuerzahler. Wenn man sie nämlich nicht beschulen würde, müßte der größte Teil der Taubstummen die längste Zeit seines Lebens der Allgemeinheit zur Last fallen. Das würde aber weit mehr kosten als die Beschulung und Berufsausbildung."

condition (as their deafness was not inherited), and they should therefore be integrated in the *Volksgemeinschaft*. In all articles, the view is taken that only hereditarily deaf people should be sterilized, while those with acquired deafness need not be. The disagreement between the authors was on how these two groups should be defined, and what the best way would be to deal with them.

One line of argumentation declared deaf people as abnormal, irrespective of the origin of their deafness. Yet, deaf people were clearly distinguished from other "abnormal" people, such as the mentally impaired. In contrast to people with schizophrenia or "idiocy" (*Schwachsinn*), deaf people were not dumb and could work regardless of their impairment. Due to this fact, they were seen as more valuable than mentally disabled people, which manifests itself in the requirement for special schools for deaf children (Kulemeyer 1934: 31; Glau 1936: 104).

However, the progress of the schools for the deaf was controversially discussed. Even though all authors considered forced sterilizations a necessary measure (e.g., Kulemeyer 1934: 33), the abolition of special schools for the deaf was foreseen as impossible. Most of the pupils were not hereditarily deaf and should therefore continue to be educated. Although in one article, Kulemeyer mentions the goal to reduce the number of schools, a few pages later, he opposes his own words by declaring that it is required to expand this institution (Kulemeyer 1935: 56–59). Furthermore, even if a (hereditary) deaf child had shown talent and was to become a valuable member of the society, sterilization should be executed:

> Even though, from the perspective of humanity, it may be hard for us to see some of our best deaf individuals condemned to childlessness, the greater good demands this sacrifice.[11] (Singer 1934: 577; translation by the authors)

These assertions focus on the impairment-perspective on deafness and refer mainly to people with (assumed) hereditary deafness.

Another line of argumentation, addressing primarily those people with acquired deafness, demanded that deaf people be integrated in the society. In everyday life, the majority of the German Nazi society looked down on deaf people. However, Wiedner criticizes this view in his article, pointing out that people with acquired deafness do not have defective genes. Therefore, he writes, they are part of the German People's Community just like other Aryan Germans (Wiedner 1935: 172). The invisibility of deafness made it impossible to

---

11 "Mag es uns menschlich schwer fallen, auch manchen unserer besten Gehörlosen zur Kinderlosigkeit verurteilt zu sehen, das Gemeinwohl fordert dieses Opfer."

distinguish between those with acquired deafness from those being born with it. Illogical as it seems, it was claimed that one group could be part of the German community while the other could not, although both groups were treated equally by the surrounding society.

In favor of integrating deaf people into society, Kroh argues that by learning spoken language, a deaf person could become a "supportive and almost full-fledged member"[12] of the German community (Kroh 1934: 613). Scherzer even declares the society to be the biggest obstacle for deaf people's social life. He demands "their liberation from involuntary isolation by means of education and instruction, and their integration into the nation's working community",[13] regardless of the cause of the individual's deafness (Scherzer 1936: 183). Hence, there were also authors who held the opinion that even individuals with hereditary deafness could be part of the *Volksgemeinschaft*.

One article even points out advantages of being deaf. Scherzer – like all the other authors – acknowledges the importance of sterilization and states that deafness should be cured. However, he also highlights positive aspects of being deaf and reports that in specific situations, the deaf trainees were superior to the hearing ones:

> It makes sense to everyone that, given the noise in the factory's workshop, even the ears of a hearing person are switched off and often fail, whereas the refined sense for vibration offers the deaf person reliable protection and support.[14]
>
> (Scherzer 1936: 176; translation by the authors)
>
> Our male and female apprentices were not only equivalent but, most of the time, superior to their hearing workmates.[15]
>
> (Scherzer 1936: 173; translation by the authors)

In summary, the many-facetted discussion on the approaches to special schools for the deaf, published in the DDS, reflects the general ambivalent perspective on deafness during the Nazi Regime. The main disagreement concerned the status of deaf people and whether they belonged to the *Volksgemeinschaft* or not. Some authors emphasized the defectiveness of deaf people's genetic material, and therefore concluded that they should not be part of the People's Community.

---

12 "förderliche[s] und nahezu vollwertige[s] Glied".
13 "ihre Befreiung aus unverschuldeter Isoliertheit durch Erziehung und Unterricht und ihre Eingliederung in die Arbeitsgemeinschaft des Volkes"
14 "Es leuchtet ja jedem ein, daß bei dem Lärm in der Fabrikwerkstätte auch das Ohr des Hörenden ausgeschaltet ist und oft versagt, während der verfeinerte Vibrationssinn [. . .] dem Gehörlosen zuverlässigen Schutz und Hilfe bietet."
15 "Unsere Lehrmädchen und Lehrlinge waren ihren hörenden Arbeitskameraden nicht nur gleichwertig, sondern meist überlegen."

In contrast, others foregrounded the invisibility of deafness, when arguing that deaf people were healthy otherwise and could be of profit for the state's economy. Although all authors agreed that deafness should be eliminated by means of sterilization, they also showed attempts to adapt the system to facilitate the integration of deaf people. By their ambiguous lines of argumentation, they mirrored and actually contributed to the paradoxical situation of deaf people during the Nazi Regime.

5 Conclusion

During the time of the Nazi Regime in Germany, deaf people were a special minority. Crucially, deafness was understood as a physical defect, separating deaf people from the ideal picture of a human being. By using the modern conceptual difference between the terms *impairment* and *disability*, we were able to analytically shed light on the ambivalent situation that deaf people were exposed to during the Nazi Regime. In the sense of present-day Disability Studies, the concept *impairment* refers to a dysfunction in the human body or mind that should be resolved, either by eliminating or minimizing the condition (mild measures), or by eliminating the carriers of the condition themselves (extreme measures). In this sense of impairment, the National Socialists declared deafness as a defect that was supposed to be eliminated by mild and by extreme measures. The "Law for the Prevention of Offspring with Hereditary Diseases" provided the legal basis to do so. Under the eugenics program, which aimed at eliminating all inferior genetic material, deaf people had to be sterilized. Under the extreme measure for eliminating the defect, deaf people were persecuted and even executed.

Yet, at the same time, National Socialists treated deaf people differently from other people with impairments, which is likely due to the fact that deafness can be understood as an invisible impairment. For example, they established a separate subgroup for deaf children in the Hitler Youth. In the modern understanding of Disability Studies, the term *disability* describes the barriers that an impaired person faces in society, and which should be removed by an adaptation of the societal structure. National Socialists acknowledged to some extent that deafness is not always inherited, which allowed for a different perspective on deaf people: people who lived in undeserved isolation, who could be educated, and who could contribute to the state's economy. This economic consideration led to a perception under which educating deaf children was more profitable to the state than not educating them. These measures – although clearly economically motivated – led to a perspective in which deaf people were partly integrated into the German Nazi society by means of adapting certain aspects of the societal structure.

Acknowledgements: This contribution has been possible thanks to the SIGN-HUB project, which has received funding from the European Union's Horizon 2020 research and innovation program under grant agreement No 693349.

Historical sources

Brockmann, Elisabeth. 2016. *"Euthanasie" und Zwangssterilisation zwischen 1933 und 1945: Gehörlose Opfer und Zeugen berichten*. Norderstedt: Books on Demand.
Darwin, Charles. 1859. *On the origin of species by means of natural selection*. London: John Murray.
Gastpar, Alfred. 1934. Die Aufgabe der Sonderschulen im nationalsozialistischen Staate vom rassehygienischen Standpunkt aus. *Die Deutsche Sonderschule* 8. 566–571.
Glau, Walter. 1936. Schwerhörig-schwachsinnige Schüler. *Die Deutsche Sonderschule* 2. 104–109.
Haeckel, Ernst. 1904. *The wonders of life*. (Translated by Joseph McCabe). London: Watts & Co.
Hitler, Adolf. 1939. Source of English translation: Signed letter by Hitler authorizing euthanasia killings (backdated to September 1, 1939). In United States Chief Counsel for the prosecution of axis criminality, *Nazi conspiracy and aggression*, Volume 3. Washington, DC: United States Government Printing Office, 1946, Document 630-PS, p. 451.
Kroh, O. 1934. Die Bildungsfunktion der Sprache mit besonderer Berücksichtigung des Sprachunterrichts beim Taubstummen. *Die Deutsche Sonderschule* 8. 599–618.
Kulemeyer, Walter. 1934. Die Beschulung schwerhöriger Kinder im neuen Staat. *Die Deutsche Sonderschule* 1. 31–35.
Kulemeyer, Walter. 1935. Das Schülermaterial der Schwerhörigenschulen. Ergebnisse einer Statistik. *Die Deutsche Sonderschule* 1. 56–59.
Kunze, Paul. 1935. Wie ist der Schulbetrieb in der Taubstummenanstalt zu gestalten, um den Forderungen des nationalsozialistischen Staates gerecht zu werden? *Die Deutsche Sonderschule* 2/3. 173–175.
LPOHD 1933. Source of English translation: Law for the prevention of offspring with hereditary diseases (July 14, 1933). In US Chief Counsel for the prosecution of axis criminality, Nazi conspiracy and aggression. Volume 5, Washington, DC: United States Government Printing Office, 1946, Document 3067-PS, 880–883.
Maeße, Hermann. 1934. Taubstummenbildung und -fürsorge im nationalsozialistischen Staat. *Die Deutsche Sonderschule* 1. 21–31.
Neues Volk. 1938. Offsetdruck, 56 x 42 cm, Deutsches Historisches Museum, Berlin. Inv.-Nr.: 1988/1284. Lebendiges Museum Online, https://www.dhm.de/lemo/bestand/objekt/plakat-zu-eugenik-und-euthanasie-um-1938.html; retrieved 11 July 2019.
Rowak, Georg. 1934. Ein Beitrag zur Neugestaltung der Unterrichts- und Erziehungsarbeit in der Taubstummenschule. *Die Deutsche Sonderschule* 6. 444–457.

Scherzer, Leo. 1936. Gebt den Gehörlosen eine gute Berufsausbildung! *Die Deutsche Sonderschule* 3. 172–183.
Singer, Edwin. 1934. Das Gesetz zur Verhütung erbkranken Nachwuchses und die Taubstummenanstalten. *Die Deutsche Sonderschule* 8. 571–578.
Sunderbrink, Otto. 1936. Beitrag zur Zusammenarbeit zwischen Sonderschule und Gesundheitsamt im Dienste der Erbgesundheitspflege. *Die Deutsche Sonderschule* 10. 742–754.
Wiedner, Otto. 1935. Nationalsozialistische Erziehung in der Taubstummenanstalt. *Die Deutsche Sonderschule* 2/3. 166–173.

References

Aly, Götz (ed.) 1989. *Aktion T4 1939–1945: Die „Euthanasie"-Zentrale in der Tiergartenstraße 4*. Berlin: Edition Hentrich.
Anonymous. 2007. Gehörlose im Dritten Reich. *Deutsche Gehörlosen Zeitung* 4/07. 99–104.
Arendt, Hannah. 1951. *Elements of totalitarianism*. New York: Harcourt Brace Jovanovich.
Biesold, Horst. 1988. *Klagende Hände: Betroffenheit und Spätfolgen in bezug auf das Gesetz zur Verhütung erbkranken Nachwuchses, dargestellt am Beispiel der "Taubstummen"*. Oberbiel: Solms-Oberbiel. [English edition: Biesold, Horst. 1999. *Crying hands. Eugenics and deaf people in Nazi Germany*. Washington, DC: Gallaudet University Press.]
Bösl, Elsbeth. 2010. Was ist Disability History? Zur Geschichte und Historiografie von Behinderung. In Elsbeth Bösl, Anne Klein & Anne Waldschmidt (eds.), *Disability History: Konstruktionen von Behinderung in der Geschichte. Eine Einführung*, 29–43. Bielefeld: transcript.
Brill, Werner. 2011. *Pädagogik der Abgrenzung. Die Implementierung der Rassenhygiene im Nationalsozialismus durch die Sonderpädagogik*. Bad Heilbrunn: Klinkhardt.
Büttner, Malin. 2005. *Nicht minderwertig, sondern mindersinnig . . . Der Bann G für Gehörgeschädigte in der Hitler-Jugend*. Frankfurt am Main: Peter Lang.
Davis, Lennard J. 1995. *Enforcing normalcy: Disability, deafness, and the body*. London/ New York: Verso.
Dederich, Markus. 2007. *Körper, Kultur und Behinderung: Eine Einführung in die Disability Studies*. Bielefeld: transcript.
Friedlander, Henry. 2002. Holocaust studies and the Deaf community. In Donna F. Ryan & John S. Schuchman (eds.), *Deaf people in Hitler's Europe*, 15–31. Washington, DC: Gallaudet University Press.
Klee, Ernst. 1997. *"Euthanasie" im NS-Staat: Die "Vernichtung lebensunwerten Lebens"*. Frankfurt am Main: Fischer.
Klee, Ernst. 1985. *Dokumente zur "Euthanasie"*. Frankfurt am Main: Fischer.
Klein, Anne. 2010. Wie betreibt man Disability History? Methoden in Bewegung. In Elsbeth Bösl, Anne Klein & Anne Waldschmidt (eds.), *Disability History: Konstruktionen von Behinderung in der Geschichte. Eine Einführung*, 45–63. Bielefeld: transcript.
McBurney, Susan. 2012. History of sign languages and sign language linguistics. In Roland Pfau, Markus Steinbach & Bencie Woll (eds.), *Sign language: An international handbook*, 909–948. Berlin: De Gruyter Mouton.

Muhs, Jochen. 1996. Followers and outcasts. Berlin's Deaf community under National Socialism (1933–1945). In Renate Fischer & Thomas Vollhaber (eds.), *Collage. Works on international Deaf history*, 195–204. Hamburg: Signum.

Muhs, Jochen. 2002. Deaf people as eyewitnesses of National Socialism. (Translated by Robert Harmon). In Donna F. Ryan & John S. Schuchman (eds.), *Deaf people in Hitler's Europe*, 78–97. Washington, DC: Gallaudet University Press.

Poore, Carol. 2010. *Disability in twentieth-century German culture*. Ann Arbor: University of Michigan Press.

Richards, Robert John. 2013. *Was Hitler a Darwinian? Disputed questions in the history of evolutionary theory*. Chicago: The University of Chicago Press.

Schmidt, Marion. 2016. Normalization and abnormal genes. Heredity research at the Clarke School for the Deaf, 1930–1950. In Brian Greenwald & Joseph J. Murray (eds.), *In our own hands. Essays in deaf history 1780–1970*. Washington, DC: Gallaudet University Press.

Schwerkolt, Andreas. 1990. Die Schwerhörigenpädagogik im Nationalsozialismus (1933–1945). In Martin Rudnick (ed.), *Aussondern – Sterilisieren – Liquidieren: Die Verfolgung Behinderter im Nationalsozialismus*, 145–169. Berlin: Spiess.

Thomas, Carol. 2002. Disability theory: Key ideas, issues, and thinkers. In Colin Barnes, Mike Oliver & Len Barton (eds.), *Disability studies today*, 38–57. Cambridge: Polity.

Vogel, Helmut. N.d. Organisation in der Nazizeit. Taubwissen – Geschichte – Gehörlose in der Zeit des Nationalsozialismus. https://www.taubwissen.de/content/index.php/geschichte/gehoerlose-in-der-zeit-des-nationalsozialismus/organisation/583-naziorganisation.html. Accessed 3 June 2019.

Waldschmidt, Anne. 2010. Warum und wozu brauchen die Disability Studies die Disability History? Programmatische Überlegungen. In Elsbeth Bösl, Anne Klein & Anne Waldschmidt (eds.), *Disability History: Konstruktionen von Behinderung in der Geschichte. Eine Einführung*, 13–27. Bielefeld: transcript.

Weikart, Richard. 2004. *From Darwin to Hitler: Evolutionary ethics, eugenics, and racism in Germany*. New York: Palgrave.

Zaurov, Mark. 2003. *Gehörlose Juden. Eine doppelte kulturelle Minderheit*. Frankfurt am Main: Peter Lang.

Elisabeth Brockmann and Elena Kozelka
Forced sterilization of deaf people during the German Nazi Regime – a trauma and its compensations after 1945

1 Introduction

In 1933, the *National Association of Evangelic Chaplains for the Deaf* in Germany published a pamphlet containing the following appeal to deaf people:

> Today we want to address evangelic deaf people, who suffer from a hereditary disease.
> The government addresses the people in question: Everybody who is concerned by being deaf should not have children themselves. Our Fatherland needs healthy and capable people.
> There are quite a lot of people suffering from a severe illness right from birth. Some by impairment of their hands, arms or feet, others by being mentally weak, so that they were not even able to go to school. And then, there are those blind people. – And you, my dear friend, are suffering from deafness. What an affliction! Very often you feel sad. You may have asked yourself a hundred times: "Why me?" And how sad your parents must have been when they noticed that you cannot hear!
> There are deaf children whose parents are also deaf. Additionally, there are also deaf people whose grandparents were deaf, simply by **inheritance**.
> To those people the authority says: **You shall not pass on your disease to further generations**; you shall remain childless.
> If you suffer from inherited deafness, you will get a letter from the Hereditary Health Court. They want to find out if you should ever have children or not. Above all, you should promise to tell the **truth. And that is what pleases our Lord!** You will be honest, even though this upsets you.
> The Court will decide: You will be made infertile through an operation. This makes you sad. You think: "I do not want that. I want to get married and have children. I love children." Well, think it over: Do you really want to be responsible for deafness to be passed on? And would you not be sad to see your children or grandchildren also being deaf? Would you not feel guilty? No, you would not want that. **The responsibility is just too big**.
> Can you not see that the authorities want to help you? They want to protect you from passing on your defects to another generation.
> You may think: The whole thing is quite disagreeable because people will gossip after I have become infertile. They will despise me. But no, you should not think like that. The authorities say: **Nobody must speak about sterilization**. And you must not speak about it either. Take care: Never tell anybody about your situation, not even your family and relatives. And even the doctors and the lawyers, they all have to keep silent!
> Be obedient to authorities! You must obey your superiors even if you find it hard to do so! Always bear in mind the future of your nation, and make this sacrifice for the nation's

sake as demanded from you. Trust in our Lord and never forget the words of the Bible: **"We are conscious that all things are working together for the good of those who have love for God."**
(Voss 2018: 78f.)[1]

The content of this pamphlet reveals the underlying spirit, that is, the ideas and beliefs of the time that were disseminated among people who were declared to have a "hereditary disease". The main points were: You have an awful disease. Hence, you need to be sterilized, in order to protect the next generation of the society from your disease. Do not speak about sterilization.

In this chapter, we investigate in more detail the underlying laws, the consequences for deaf people, and the monetary compensations after 1945 for these crimes.

2 The Sterilization Law and its scope

Just six months after the National Socialists came to power, on July 14th, 1933, the Cabinet passed the *Gesetz zur Verhütung erbkranken Nachwuchses (GzVeN)*, i.e., the *Law for the Prevention of Offspring with Hereditary Diseases*.[2] This law came into force on January 1st, 1934. The purpose of this law was to expand and manifest the idea of 'racial hygiene' by legalizing the sterilization of people with a potential hereditary disease. The overall objective of the Nazi Party was to gradually clean the German *Volkskörper* (the German 'national body') from unwanted influences of illness or disabilities. Thus, everyone degraded by the Nazis by reason of having 'minor value' or deemed 'not worth living' was to be denied reproduction. This ultimate plan of 'cleaning the national body' has been masked, however, by laws for 'hereditary health' and 'racial hygiene'. That is why the Sterilization Law was also often defined as *Hereditary Illness Law* or *Hereditary Health Law* (cf. Bock 1986: 7).

Here, we will provide a closer look at the circumstances that led to the forced sterilization of deaf people during the time of German National Socialism, 1933–1945. Furthermore, we will present individual tragedies of deaf contemporary witnesses, which exemplify how traumatic these sterilization experiences were and how they affected the victims, even until today. We also discuss how these traumas and their long-term effects have been considered and debated in the time between 1945 until today, and we will address the fact that the victims

---

1 All quotations in this article were translated by Elena Kozelka. Emphasis marked in bold letters also by Elena Kozelka.
2 In the following, this law will be referred to as *Sterilization Law*.

have been refused offers for monetary compensation. With this article, we want to point out that the treatment the deaf victims had to endure after the end of World War II in 1945 is not commensurate to their immeasurable suffering under the Nazi Regime. A central aspect of the discrepancy between the consequences of forced sterilization on the one hand and a minor monetary compensation on the other hand, is the fact that the sterilization procedures were administered under apparent legitimacy. This is why sterilization has also been accepted by a large number of the victims. The final consequence was that after 1945, the compensations offered were much too low.

The Sterilization Law was based on a concept which had already been laid out in 1932 by the Prussian Health Office in the Weimar Republic. In contrast to the previous draft of the law, which included sterilization by choice, the Sterilization Law adopted by the Nazi Party was more rigid in several respects (see the Appendix for the main paragraphs of the Sterilization Law): This law imposed forced sterilization, so that the people in question could be sterilized against their will. Furthermore, the law directly listed the so-called 'hereditary diseases'. Hence, people who were thought to carry one of these diseases could be legally banned from reproduction. This list contained several mental diseases, such as schizophrenia, manic-depression, and epilepsy, but also physical deformity, inherited blindness, and inherited deafness. At the same time, this list also functioned as the foundation for the legal practice of the so-called *Erbgesundheitsgerichte* ('Hereditary Health Courts'). These courts comprised one lawyer and two medical doctors, who decided whether forced sterilization was going to be carried out. In most cases, however, the decision was only based on the existing medical and psychiatric reports. At the time, there was no substantial medical understanding of hereditary diseases and how they were inherited. For the listed condition of deafness, racial hygienists merely based their decisions on the rate of deafness within the family. The simple assumption was that deaf people would have deaf children, and this is what should be prevented. Racial hygienists basically claimed that deafness in general was hereditary; therefore, deaf people in question had to prove that they did not have hereditary deafness. Hence, forced sterilization could only be avoided by providing evidence that the particular case of deafness was acquired after birth, and that there were no signs for inherited deafness within any members of the family. However, producing this evidence was difficult, if not impossible, in most cases (cf. Vogel n.d. a; Bock 1986; Schmuhl 2005).

The politics behind sterilization procedures were not so much based on economic benefits, but more on current ideologies of a healthy 'Aryan race'. This explains why people with a strong manifestation, as well as people with a minor manifestation of their 'disease' had to be sterilized. The legalization of sterilization was justified by an unacceptable suffering of the *Volksgemeinschaft* ('People's Community'), not by a suffering of the individuals themselves (cf. Bock 1986; Schmuhl 1992).

In order to implement the sterilization procedures as soon as possible and thus to prevent further inheritance, it was the Nazi Party's priority to pass the Sterilization Law immediately. As a consequence of discord with the Vatican, the law was not made public until July 25th, 1933. The Sterilization Law was amended numerous times to cover more severe measures in sterilization procedures (see also Mittelstädt & Hosemann, this volume). From June 1935 onward, this formed the basis for legally enforcing an abortion after the parents were diagnosed with a 'hereditary disease'. A further extension of the law from October 18th, 1935, forbade the marriage between healthy and disabled people, including those being affected by a 'hereditary illness' (cf. Büttner 2005).

As a consequence, by the end of the Nazi regime in May 1945, 400,000 people had been forcibly sterilized. Among them were approximately 15,000 deaf victims. 1,600 deaf people were killed in the execution of the 'euthanasia' program. It was estimated that during the medical procedures, 6,000 women and 600 men died due to medical complications. According to Bock (1986: 379), "pneumonia, cardiac insufficiency, circulation problems [and] embolism" were the most common physical reasons for the death of the patients. To these we can add psychological strain resistance, panic disorders, and anxiety, all of which increased the risk of death during or before the enforced surgery. However, given that the government often made an effort to conceal the actual death rate, we may expect that the estimated number of unreported cases is actually much higher and cannot be traced back factually. Scientists assume that another large group of people were sterilized illegally, and thus unnoticed under the Sterilization Law bureaucracy (cf. Vogel n.d. a; Bock 1986; Biesold 1988; Büttner 2005).

A crucial aspect is that the sterilization procedures rested upon assumed objective and legal reasons. The fact that the procedures appeared to be based on juridical justification made it possible that they were tolerated by the affected people, as well as the general population. This acceptance was not only prevalent at the time of the sterilizations but lasted until the postwar period. As a consequence, it became a point of debate after 1945 whether compensation was necessary at all for forced sterilizations (cf. Ley 2003).

The whole sterilization procedure, including an official summoning for sterilization and a two weeks' period to react to that, postulated objectivity and legal correctness. This appearance was emphasized by the efficient and systematic procedures of the *Hereditary Health Courts*. But in fact, the National Socialist

(NS) dictatorship strongly pushed the social disintegration of people with "hereditary diseases", thereby depriving them in fundamental ways of their legal place in society (cf. Büttner 2005). The means of persecution ranged from intimidation to arbitrary state-run enforced measures by the NS-regime. An essential part of this totalitarian practice was the compulsory sterilization of deaf people. Most of the sterilization victims (96%) were sterilized due to mental incapacity. Yet, it was not unusual that other groups, such as deaf people, were also stigmatized as weak-minded by the racial hygienists. Social and medical diagnoses became indistinct and formed the basis for the killing of deaf people with multiple disabilities. Medical knowledge was suppressed by ideology and was misused and distorted on purpose for legitimizing the practice of sterilization (cf. Schmuhl 1992, 2005).

However, the sterilization politics of the NS-regime were only the beginning of the cruel killings of more than 300,000 mentally and physically disabled people after 1939. The systematical killing of the so-called 'unworthy lives' was practiced until the downfall of the Hitler regime.

3 The execution of forced sterilizations

From 1934 until the end of the Nazi regime in 1945, different procedures of sterilization were tested. The sterilization fanaticism aimed at sterilizing a considerable number of people "within the shortest time possible and with the least effort" (Ebbinghaus 2008: 220). Various methods of sterilization "with X-rays and medication as well as by operation" were tested experimentally on countless victims (Ebbinghaus 2008: 220).

The community of the deaf was, henceforth, strictly divided between those who were born deaf and those who had become deaf in the course of their life. This division also led to an ambiguous situation for deaf people in the Nazi German society, between persecution on the one hand and alleged integration on the other hand (for a detailed analysis, see Mittelstädt & Hosemann, this volume). However, deaf German Jews suffered from a double persecution during National Socialism: They were oppressed on the basis of their religion, as well as because of their stigmatization as people with an 'inherited disease'. Once they were placed in so-called nursing homes (*Anstalten*), they were one of the first groups to be declared as *Ballastexistenzen* ('burdensome existences') for the *Volksgemeinschaft*. Sterilization experiments were carried out on Jews, both male and female. The Nazis, with their inhumane sterilization fanaticism, used them as human "guinea pigs" (Bock 1986: 455). In the concentration camps, mass sterilizations were carried out "with threats, beatings and almost incessant forced labor" (Bock 1986: 455). The deaths of countless people were approved of in this way. There were about 600 deaf Jews among the victims of National Socialism (cf. Vogel n.d. b; Bock 1986; Krausneker & Schalber 2009; Van der Locht 2010; Schneider & Lutz 2014; Hocke 2017).

These crimes were committed "in the midst of the German society" (Schneider & Lutz 2014: 9). They were executed by offenders and were kept secret and/or accepted by the accessories to the crimes. Scientific personnel with their racial hygienic ideas provided the theoretical basis, while the media spread the propaganda. Potential victims of sterilization could be reported by doctors, as well as by neighbors, teachers, or ordinary citizens. During an *Erbgesundheitsverfahren* ('procedure to detect inherited illnesses'), medical practitioners and lawyers decided on the forced sterilizations. These procedures obviously contradicted constitutional principles of trial, yet in 94 percent of the cases, the victims were sentenced to forced sterilization. In the final stage, the doctors carried out the operations (cf. Schneider & Lutz 2014).

When, on July 25th, 1933, the sterilization of impaired people was legalized, only the Catholic bishops protested against it. In their function as moral examples, both the Catholic and the Protestant Church criticized the intention of the law. However, they did not distance themselves from the persecution of and sanctions against deaf people. In fact, they failed when their duty of care for people in need was necessary. The circumstances regarding the participation of the teachers of deaf children in the sterilization procedures was a taboo subject for a long time. It lasted throughout the first decades after the end of the war and was only addressed later (cf. Biesold 1988).

It is obvious that deaf people were deceived and manipulated on purpose during the Nazi regime. This was to cover up the actual ideology behind the forced sterilizations – the cleaning of the German 'national body'. Cover-up tactics, which involved numerous laws and decisions, were used to justify the sterilization procedures towards the deaf victims, by claiming that their sterilization would contribute positively to the *People's Community*.

4 The consequences of forced sterilization for the deaf victims during the Nazi regime

The National Socialists used the term *taubstumm* ('deaf-mute') for all the people who were deaf, hard-of-hearing, or suffered from a speech disorder. When deaf contemporary witnesses talk about their experiences with sterilization, it very often happens that they use the signs HITLER and CUT in German Sign Language (*Deutsche Gebärdensprache*, DGS), while, at the same time, mouthing "Hitlerschnitt" ('Hitler-cut'). This phenomenon makes us aware of how drastic the experiences for the deaf people during the NS-dictatorship have been, and how deeply they still touch them today. The formation and anchoring of that DGS sign shows that forced sterilization and the related traumatic experiences form a constitutive element of the self-image of that generation. The practical application of the Sterilization Law during the Nazi regime constituted a life-threatening factor for the Deaf community: The Nazis reduced the assumed hereditary deafness "to a physical and genetic defect that could have been avoided" (Kutsch 2018: 181).

Forced sterilization of deaf people is a topic which, for a long time, was neither noticed in academia nor by the public. It took about 40 years after the end of World War II to initiate a rethinking, which was mainly a consequence of the studies of the historian Dr. Gisela Bock, which appeared in 1986, as well as of the treatise of the historian Hans-Walter Schmuhl in 1987. Since the victims of the Sterilization Law have, to date, not been officially accepted as persecutees of the Nazi regime, it is almost impossible for them to get the right to submit a claim for compensation. This is difficult to understand, as the victims still suffer – both physically and mentally – from the consequences of the injustice they experienced. Forced sterilization, and the resulting enforced childlessness, are a lifelong trauma for many victims. Many of them died during the operation or from complications afterwards, or committed suicide as a result of the after-effects. 90 percent of the victims who died during the operation were women (cf. Biesold 1988; Büttner 2005).

The racial hygienic crimes of the Nazis, which were based on the Sterilization Law, are "in its complexity, radicality, and effectiveness a sterilization program beyond example" (Hocke 2017: 38). The central part of the criminal practice was "humiliation, mutilation and lifelong shame" (Hocke 2017: 39), which the victims were confronted with and suffered from for the rest of their lives. With the abolishment of the democratic system, any constitutional principles, as well as the principle of equality for all people were invalidated (cf. Nowak 1984).

Only in the 1980s did a teacher for the deaf, Horst Biesold, succeed in bringing attention to deaf victims for the first time and to make people aware of the impact of the forced sterilizations (cf. Büttner 2005). Out of shame, many deaf people had kept silent for decades. At present, there are only a few survivors who could give an account of the crimes conducted during the Nazi time.

In 2002, Henry Friedlander mentioned that "the fate of deaf people in Nazi Germany is a neglected aspect of the Holocaust" (Friedlander 2002: 15). For a long time, the traumatic experiences of the sterilized deaf victims as well as the late effects of the sterilizations had been a taboo in the society. The apparent juridical neutrality with regard to the sterilizations, together with a general social acceptance, created an atmosphere of indifference towards the crimes that had been committed. The denial of what had really happened prevented adequate compensation for the victims. Embedded in collective silence, the majority of the victims did not confront society with their personal suffering.

5 Experiences of the deaf victims

There were a few deaf victims who were ready to share their experiences with the public. During an interview, a female victim reported how, in 1940, an *SS-man* (an officer of the paramilitary organization *Schutzstaffel*) and two policemen violently forced their way into her apartment. This happened when she was just 16 years old. She was brought to a hospital against her own will and without knowing what was going on, and was forcibly sterilized (Brockmann 2016: 34). Nobody told her about the particulars of the surgery, they only said "it would not be bad". After the surgery, the girl suffered from severe pain. The use of force and the experience of helplessness and isolation left her in a state of panic. The incident lead to permanent dark memories. She reported: "[I] went entirely quiet". "For me, the whole world crashed when I was informed that I could not have children anymore" (Brockmann 2016: 36; for the interview recorded on video see Vogel 2015: 00:01:35 ff.).

These procedures affected both women and men. When searching for answers to why all that happened, a deaf victim wrote about the painful and cruel treatment, as nobody had informed him of the consequences of forced sterilization. He described the sterilization "as a killing" which "made the body unworthy" (cf. Biesold 1988: 121). He declared that he experienced his infertility and childlessness as "damage and ruin", and further referred to the 5th commandment, which states "Thou shalt not kill". He was resentful that he no longer felt as a real human, and that the Nazi party, the NSDAP, had spread "fraud and lies". His experiences of killing and sterilization were going to be punished as "mortal sins" by God. He was convinced that his life had lost much of its value "because there was no happiness in love anymore". "They lay guilt on me. They insulted me. They have sterilized, killed, and broken me, because I cannot have a child. They do not seem to have understood what a man is." (Biesold 1988: 121).

There are other victims and contemporary witnesses who report multiple forced sterilizations in connection with the imposed silence about what had happened. Furthermore, there are also reports of forced abortions, in many cases even after the sixth month of pregnancy, and this, even though the affected women had already given birth to children who could hear (cf. Biesold 1988; Vogel 2015).

These National Socialist crimes left deep physical and mental scars on the people who have survived. Affected and broken partnerships, the involuntary renouncement of parenthood and, as a consequence, loss of the possibility to pass on one's own genes to the next generation have had a tremendous impact on these people and are part of their painful experiences. Such aspects and the circumstances of the interventions, as well as lasting physical pain, often had a negative impact on the self-perception and sexuality of the victims and marred their everyday life and relationships (cf. Biesold 1988).

6 Compensations for the deaf victims after 1945

After the end of World War II and the unconditional surrender of the German Reich on May 8th, 1945, the Allies agreed on the passing of the "Berlin guideline[s] for the approval of the victims of fascism" (Doetz 2010: 218) in 1946. Next to some other persecuted groups, forcibly sterilized people were excluded from the definition of the guidelines, with the argument that sterilizations were not "done for racial, religious or political reasons" (Braun 2017: 202). In the Soviet zone of occupation, which became the German Democratic Republic (GDR), the Soviet military leadership condemned the Sterilization Law as "antidemocratic" (Weindling 2008: 249) and "tendentiously fascistic" (Doetz 2010: 215). While the Soviet zone and Bavaria completely abolished the Sterilization Law, "the other federal states, however, left open further juridical possibilities for a reactivation" of the law (Doetz 2010: 205f.). The US-American Military Administration did not regard the Sterilization Law as a "typical" National Socialist injustice, but considered it an "adequate measure of population control" (Herrmann & Braun 2010: 7). Similar eugenic measures of sterilization were also found in other countries, some of them democratically ruled (cf. Herrmann & Braun 2010).

The *Nürnberger Ärzteprozess* ('Nuremberg Doctors' Trial') in 1946–1947 introduced the first account of the past concerning the "medical war crimes" (Weindling 2008: 247). As a result of the Nuremberg Trials, the Nuremberg Code stated that the individual protection of each person was the highest legal moral value. It declared that, in the future, the overall social benefits and scientific progress should take second place, and that the central goal of medicine should always be legal protection of humans (cf. Ebbinghaus 2008).

Doctors were then "obliged never to destroy fertility without an urgent reason" (Benz 2017: 19).

The political debates for compensation distinguished between "legal" and "illegal" sterilization. This was motivated by the distinction between sterilizations that were performed on the basis of the National Socialist Sterilization Law and sterilizations that were performed on a formally invalid legal basis. Since, in general, the constitutional legality of the Sterilization Law was assumed, the distinction between "legal" and "illegal" sterilizations had a major influence on the political claims for compensation, with a tendency to describe the sterilizations as "legal". (cf. Weindling 2008; Herrmann & Braun 2010). But in fact, from a historical perspective, this distinction is absolutely redundant, because the Sterilization Law had resulted in massive human rights violations and came into force in a non-constitutional manner in a totalitarian system.

After the end of the War, the widespread mentality in the general population was to leave the past behind as quickly as possible and to move on. Moreover, the end of the War also marked the beginning of a period of material boom. Both phenomena entailed that the social recognition of the persons who had been discriminated against by the Sterilization Law and the compensatory measures were nearly forgotten. "The denied memory became another discrimination" (Benz 2017: 21f.) and cast a shadow over the German culture of remembrance (cf. Saathoff 2017).

"The public and the private denial went hand in hand" (Schneider & Lutz 2014: 196). As for the public denial, in the 1950s and 1960s, there was a considerable number of former National Socialist perpetrators and abettors among Federal German policymakers, lawyers, and administerial workers of high rank. They were opposed to the re-evaluation of the Nazi crimes and partly worked against the acknowledgement of the victims. The illegal forced sterilizations were disregarded during the measures of denazification (cf. Doetz 2010; Saathoff 2017). In 1967, Franz Josef Strauß, the chairman of the Christian Social Union (CSU) in Bavaria, spoke against the alimony for the victims of the Sterilization Law. He claimed that more than half of the compensation "had to be paid to the mentally ill, weak-minded, or severe alcoholics" (Scheulen 2017: 166).

When it comes to private denial, several victims of forced sterilization considered the crimes committed against them "as the smaller evil" (Wierling 2017: 93), as compared to the crimes committed against other groups of victims. This can be explained by the fact that a whole generation experienced mass violence during the time of National Socialism. Yet, after 1945, there were several victims who hoped for the possibility of re-fertilization. However, for this procedure to be applied, it was necessary to get a legal suspension of the official sentence for sterilization, and many doctors indeed demanded this suspension. Consequently, the wish to have a child could only be realized in the case of a few women and men (cf. Westermann 2017).

In 1956 and with a majority of representatives, the *Bundestag* ('Lower House of the German Parliament') passed the *Bundesentschädigungsgesetz* (BEG) ('Federal Law of Compensation'). This law came into force retroactively, starting from 1953. It includes a non-expandable definition of the groups that suffered from National Socialist injustice and should therefore have a right for compensation. In this law, too, forcibly sterilized people were excluded from compensation. And even today, the definition included in the BEG is still applied in juridical procedures regarding repayment claims. As a consequence, for decades, these people have been refused compensation because – in strictly legal terms – the legal basis was missing (cf. Herrmann & Braun 2010).

In the decades after World War II, the victims of the forced sterilizations fought not only for monetary compensation, but especially for "moral and juridical rehabilitation" (Herrmann & Braun 2010: 11). The central demand concerns the strict abolishment of the Sterilization Law and the acknowledgement of the sterilized people as victims of the National Socialist regime. Strikingly, however, the Sterilization Law lost its formal validity in the *Bundesrepublik Deutschland* (BRD) (West Germany) only in 1968, that is, ten years after its definition as a permanent federal right was declined (cf. Doetz 2010).

The deaf victims of the National Socialist crimes also tried to cope with their personal problems stemming from the injustice of the past. It was necessary for them to look back and reappraise the past with the help of friends and family members who had sympathy for their situation, and who joined their fight for re-evaluation and compensation. But only in 1980, Ernst Waltemathe, a politician for the Social Democratic Party of Germany (SPD), together with Horst Biesold, a teacher for the deaf, achieved that the forcibly sterilized people received a first and one-time reparation payment of 5,000 D-Mark, which is equivalent to 5,800 € nowadays. In contrast, other victim groups of the Nazi regime got a lifelong payment of approximately 1,000 € per month (cf. Bundesministerium der Finanzen 2020: 29). Thanks to the help of the *Deutsche Gehörlosenzeitung* ('German Journal for the Deaf') and the journal *Epheta* (Association of the Catholic Deaf of Germany), the deaf victims became aware that Biesold had initiated a public call and asked for support in terms of compensation. Deaf people who were affected were asked to contact him. As a result, he received many letters and was therefore able to help many of the victims. In the 1980s, there was a shift in the public discussion as well as in the debates on the consequences of the war and the moral and legal compensation of the victims – a "shift in discourse" (Herrmann & Braun 2010: 19). This shift could clearly be perceived in the speech of the federal president Richard von

Weizsäcker in 1985. In his speech, he explicitly remembered the victims of forced sterilizations and of the NS psychiatric clinics (cf. Herrmann & Braun 2010).

Another important event in the shift in discourse took place in January 1985, when the Protestant Church of the Rhineland gave a statement during their regional synod meeting.[3] This statement concerned forced sterilization, the killing of so-called "unworthy life", and the medical experiments conducted on humans during the Nazi regime. This was the first statement after the War addressing these topics during a regional synod. In their confession of guilt, the regional synod talked about the forcibly sterilized people. In contrast to most of the other regional synods, in January 1987, the Protestant Church of the Rhineland appealed to the legislature and requested to nullify the Sterilization Law from 1933.

A milestone in the evaluation of the forced sterilizations during National Socialism was the feminist-historic analysis by Gisela Bock in 1986, which constitutes a first academic confrontation. Bock provided evidence for "the excessive application of force and the involvement of non-state institutions" (Herrmann & Braun 2010: 17). In the course of historic research, Bock's work became one of the most important reference texts for political claims for financial compensation. Bock examined the Sterilization Law directly against the background of the National Socialist racial politics and classified "eugenic ideas and practices to be a constitutional element of the racist National Socialist ideology" (Herrmann & Braun 2010: 17). As a consequence, this led to the request that forcibly sterilized people should get the status of 'NS-persecuted', as defined by the *Bundesentschädigungsgesetz* (BEG, 'Federal Law of Compensation'). As the first court of the Federal Republic of Germany, the district court of Kiel came to the conclusion during a retrial that the Sterilization Law was unconstitutional. It was claimed that the Law transgressed "natural human rights" (Herrmann & Braun 2010: 21).

In order to help the NS-victims, the former victim Klara Nowak founded the *Bund der "Euthanasie"-Geschädigten und Zwangssterilisierten e.V.*, BEZ ('Association of the Victims of 'Euthanasia' and Forced Sterilization') in 1987. Nowak was one of the first to speak in public: "The non-acknowledgement of our destiny as persecutees of the Nazi regime and the many arguments we had, repeatedly without result, are the second trauma we had to endure" (Schneider & Lutz 2014: 188). The association campaigned for the rehabilitation and compensation of

---

[3] The regional synod is the head of a Protestant regional church in administration. It comprises as parliamentary representation the entirety of the church community. It also passes the laws and the economy of the regional church and elects their leading clerics.

the victims and their families. As a result, there was a change in mentality within the group of the forcibly sterilized victims: The affected people realized the chance to connect with each other and to get attention from society. For decades, the shame to talk about what had happened had been overwhelming. Also, for many years, the victims had been manipulated to keep silent and to believe that it was their own fault and fate. Thanks to the BEZ, their mindset could change, and the question of guilt could be re-evaluated. The time of "persisting humiliation" (Saathoff 2017: 9) had come to an end. However, "the late rehabilitation and the acknowledgement of the state and the society" (Saathoff 2017: 9) came too late for many of the victims.

In April 1987, the parliamentary group of the Green Party in the German Bundestag proposed the annulment of the Sterilization Law. However, the majority of the German parliament members refused this proposal "because of constitutional concerns as well as fiscal considerations" (Herrmann & Braun 2010: 23). One year later, in 1988, the parliament reached a majority for a law that condemned forced sterilization according to the Sterilization Law, but did not acknowledge the Law itself as a National Socialist injustice. This case was taken as "a change of direction in the compensation politics" (Herrmann & Braun 2010: 23f.), but did not lead to the acknowledgement of sterilization victims getting the status 'NS-persecuted', as defined by BEG.

Interestingly, while other groups of victims received financial aid from the Federal Ministry of Finance, the BEZ, as a victims' association, received financial aid from the Federal Ministry of Health. The major change leading to the official acknowledgement of sterilization victims happened in 1988, when the majority of the German Bundestag passed the *Allgemeine Kriegsfolgengesetz*, *AKG* ('General Act of War Consequences') and the associated *AKG-Härterichtlinien* ('Guidelines for Severity') (see also Bundesministerium der Finanzen 2020). On the basis of the studies of Horst Biesold and the initiative of several politicians, sterilization was then officially accepted as illegal in these guidelines. In 1988, Horst Biesold interviewed for the first time a larger number of deaf victims of National Socialism. He showed that a considerable number of the German deaf victims suffered from the late complications caused by their forced sterilization. Starting in 1990, the new legal foundations made it possible that the victims were payed a monthly pension of 100 German D-Mark. These payments were officially enforced and are still adjusted for the effects of inflation (cf. Doetz 2010; Vogel 2015; Braun 2017).

In 1996, the former Federal President Roman Herzog declared January 27th as the memorial day for the victims of National Socialism. In his speech he declared: "The remembrance should never stop and should also keep further generations alert. Therefore, it is important to find a way of remembrance that is far-reaching for the future. This remembrance is to express grief over sorrow and loss; it is devoted to the victims and shall help in not repeating what had happened." There is no 'worthy' or 'unworthy life' – nobody is to be treated as second class because of their disability. For people with an impairment, forced sterilizations and euthanasia were the worst consequences of the National Socialist ideology of a 'healthy race'.

Any resolutions of the Hereditary Health Court – that is, the institution with legal validity that decided in Nazi Germany on forced sterilizations – were suspended in 1998. But this suspension had no influence on the financial compensation of the victims. In 2007, the German Bundestag decided to condemn the Sterilization Law, but did not pass an annulment of it. This missing legal annulment of the Sterilization Law had the crucial consequence that the victims of forced sterilization did not receive legal claims for compensation according to the BEG (the 'Federal Law of Compensation'), but were only regarded under the paragraphs of the AKG (the 'Act of War Consequences'). This is the reason why sterilization victims have been refused a legal status comparable to that of other groups of National Socialist victims, which in turn has led to lower financial compensation according to the AKG (cf. Herrmann & Braun 2010; Vogel 2015).

Since 2017, applying retroactively from September 1st, 2016, the compensation payments for the victims of forced sterilization amount to 352 € per month (BEZ 2018). From January 1st, 2020, onwards, every person still alive who was forcibly sterilized receives 513 € per month. However, until the present day, there is no official acknowledgement that forcibly sterilized (deaf) people have the status of 'NS-persecuted', as defined by the BEG in 1956. A status equivalent to that of other groups of victims of National Socialism is still missing today, and the socio-political debate is yet to take place. Already in 1988, Horst Biesold described the danger of historical amnesia, from which the deaf victims of forced sterilizations had to suffer a second time. Hence, the scientific debate has to go on. But the personal suffering of the victims, physically and mentally, cannot be outweighed by material means.

7 Conclusion

The "prolongation of the injustice in the Federal Republic [disappears] in a black hole of anti-thematization" (Westermann 2017: 33). As a consequence, it did not lead to the formation of a public moral opinion about sterilizations in the National Socialist dictatorship, but rather to a rejection of the topic. The changes regarding how the topic has been addressed in historical and political memory came in very small steps, which were difficult to evaluate as a whole. On the political side, it never came to a comprehensive and coherent commitment for the victims of the Sterilization Law. The reason for that was that eugenic beliefs continued to exists after 1945 and had a strong support in the public. Those victims of National Socialists who did not fit into the picture of a healthy person have been placed on the margin of society. They never got the social acceptance they deserve (cf. Westermann 2017).

Without an investigation and evaluation of the past, it will not be possible to come to a critical approach to our current, real-life conditions and to further developments. It is the task of any community to actively preserve the possibility of self-reflection and to build upon it (cf. Kutsch 2018). The present majority of our society is aware of the crimes convicted during National Socialism. However, people may not have fully overcome deeply rooted anxieties.

When talking about disabled or impaired people, there is often a focus on the economic balance between benefit and costs for the society. This attitude ignores the fact that everybody has a natural right to live. In a survey in the 1990s, 86 percent of the interviewed pregnant women agreed that it was irresponsible to give birth to a disabled child. Still today, a number of impaired children are aborted with the diagnosis "unacceptable" by conventional medicine (cf. Oestreich 2008). Medical possibilities of intervention in human genetic material become more and more complex. The number of selection criteria increases, and the prenatal medical investigations provide a more detailed result of the child's genetic material. This medical development raises the question in how far we can or should (not) influence the genes of future generations.

The life of a deaf person is characterized by a number of aspects, of which a few have fundamentally changed within the last 70 years, while others still constitute an important challenge in the social dispute with the majority of society. The question whether deafness is an impairment or not is still a crucial issue of debate. For example, in actual social debates and medical diagnoses, we still find aspects that can be traced back to the medical ethos concerning deafness in the Sterilization Law. The scientific progress of human genetics – such as prenatal or preimplantation diagnostics – necessarily has consequences for the Deaf community. Scientists raise the question in how far eugenic concepts and their selection mechanisms are socially accepted today. Against this background, it is debatable whether the danger of "stigmatization and traumatization of a further generation" (Westermann 2017: 41) might follow.

The extreme actions during the Nazi regime have shown in a fatal way what can happen in the name of an ideology that is based on distinguishing people in terms of different classes and their 'worth' or 'worthlessness'. The systematic forced sterilization of deaf people during National Socialism formed one part of this ideology. In this context, the Sterilization Law functioned as an apparent legal base in the course of actions. This tactic of legalizing a crime not only avoided building up a conscience of injustice before and after 1945, but it also prevented the adequate compensation of the victims in the further social debate about damages. Public awareness with respect to the group of deaf victims of forced sterilization, therefore, could barely progress in the socio-political debate. What remains for the deaf victims is the obstruction of juridical and financial compensation, as well as the social rehabilitation in comparison with other victim groups of the Nazi regime. Central political participants of the new Federal Republic, and a big part of the population, did not classify the Sterilization Law as a typical National Socialist injustice. Therefore, the deaf victims did not receive political compensation claims. Debates on the financial settlement and the compensatory payment for the deaf victims of forced sterilization have so far not been conducted sufficiently. The suffering experienced by the victims is immense and could not be compensated for by any material means.

Acknowledgements: This article is based on an extensive private collection of historical documents, journal and newspaper articles, and pamphlets, as well as research conducted in the context of a bachelor of arts thesis. We thank the three reviewers for their helpful comments and corrections.

References

Arbeitsgemeinschaft Bund der "Euthanasie"-Geschädigten und Zwangssterilisierten (BEZ). 2018. Zeittafel der Entschädigungspolitik für Zwangssterilisierte und "Euthanasie"-Geschädigte. https://www.euthanasiegeschaedigte-zwangssterilisierte.de/themen/entschaedigung/zeittafel-entschaedigungspolitik-fuer-zwangssterilisierte-und-euthanasie-geschaedigte/ [accessed May 10th 2019].
Benz, Wolfgang. 2017. Verweigerte Erinnerung als zweite Diskriminierung der Opfer nationalsozialistischer Politik. Zur Einführung. In Margret Hamm (ed.), *Ausgegrenzt! Warum? Zwangssterilisierte und Geschädigte der NS-"Euthanasie" in der Bundesrepublik Deutschland*, 15–23. Berlin: Metropol Verlag.
Biesold, Horst. 1988. *Klagende Hände. Betroffenheit und Spätfolgen in Bezug auf das Gesetz zur Verhütung erbkranken Nachwuchses, dargestellt am Beispiel der "Taubstummen"*. Solms: Jarick Oberbiel.
Bock, Gisela. 1986. *Zwangssterilisation im Nationalsozialismus: Studien zur Rassenpolitik und Frauenpolitik*. Opladen: Westdeutscher Verlag.
Braun, Kathrin. 2017. "Ob es tatsächlich dazu kommt, ist nach wie vor offen und bleibt abzuwarten." Der Kampf des BEZ um die Anerkennung der "Euthanasie"-Geschädigten und Zwangssterilisierten als Verfolgte des Nationalsozialismus und die Antworten der Politik. In Margret Hamm (ed.), *Ausgegrenzt! Warum? Zwangssterilisierte und*

Geschädigte der NS-"Euthanasie" in der Bundesrepublik Deutschland, 199–223. Berlin: Metropol Verlag.

Brockmann, Elisabeth. 2016. *"Euthanasie" und Zwangssterilisation zwischen 1933 und 1945. Gehörlose Opfer und Zeitzeugen berichten*. Norderstedt: Books on Demand.

Bundesministerium der Finanzen, Referat für Öffentlichkeitsarbeit, 2020. *Entschädigung von NS-Unrecht. Regelungen zur Wiedergutmachung*. https://www.bundesfinanzministerium.de/ Content/DE/Downloads/Broschueren_Bestellservice/2018-03-05-entschaedigung-ns-unrecht.pdf?__blob=publicationFile&v=10 [accessed June 10th 2020].

Büttner, Malin. 2005. *Nicht minderwertig, sondern mindersinnig . . . . Der Bann G für Gehörgeschädigte in der Hitler-Jugend*. Frankfurt am Main: Peter Lang.

Doetz, Susanne. 2010. *Alltag und Praxis der Zwangssterilisation. Die Berliner Universitäts-frauenklinik unter Walter Stoeckel 1942–1944*. Berlin: Charité Universitätsmedizin, Universität PhD dissertation.

Ebbinghaus, Angelika. 2008. Mediziner vor Gericht. In Klaus-Dietmar Henke (ed.), *Tödliche Medizin im Nationalsozialismus. Von der Rassenhygiene zum Massenmord*, 203–225. Wien: Böhlau Verlag.

Friedlander, Henry. 2002. Holocaust studies and the Deaf community. In Donna F. Ryan & John S. Schuchman (eds.), *Deaf people in Hitler's Europe*, 15–32. Washington, DC: Gallaudet University Press.

Herrmann, Svea Luise & Kathrin Braun. 2010. Der Geist des Gesetzes: Das Gesetz zur Verhütung erbkranken Nachwuchses und der Umgang mit den Opfern in der Bundesrepublik. https://www.ipw.uni-hannover.de/fileadmin/_migrated/content_uploads/ HERRMANN_BRAUN_2010_Geist_des_GzVeN.pdf [accessed May 13th 2019].

Hocke, Michaela. 2017. Zwangssterilisation 1934–1945. In Elsbeth Andre (ed.), *"Lebensunwert"– entwürdigt und vernichtet. Zwangssterilisation und Patientenmorde im Nationalsozialismus im Spiegel der Quellen des Landeshauptarchivs Koblenz*, 37–55. Rheinland-Pfalz: Landesarchivverwaltung.

Krausneker, Verena & Katharina Schalber. 2009. *Gehörlose Österreicherinnen und Österreicher im Nationalsozialismus*. Eight short films in Austrian Sign Language (ÖGS) with German subtitles, without sound.

Kutsch, Clara. 2018. Erst Sterilisation, dann Selektion? Das "Gesetz zur Verhütung erbkranken Nachwuchses" von 1933 und seine Rezeption durch die Wiener Gehörlosengemeinschaft: eine printmediale Spurensuche (Teil I). *Das Zeichen* 109. 180–190.

Ley, Astrid. 2003. *Zwangssterilisation und Ärzteschaft. Hintergründe und Ziele ärztlichen Handelns 1934–1945*. Frankfurt: Campus Verlag.

Nowak, Kurt. 1984. *"Euthanasie" und Sterilisierung im "Dritten Reich". Die Konfrontation der evangelischen und katholischen Kirche mit dem Gesetz zur Verhütung erbkranken Nachwuchses und der "Euthanasie"-Aktion* (3rd ed.). Göttingen: Vandenhoeck & Ruprecht.

Oestreich, Heide. 2008. Allein gelassen bei Spätabreibungen. Und dann war Lea weg. http://www.taz.de/!5170949/ [accessed May 15th 2019].

Saathoff, Günter. 2017. Geleitwort. In Margret Hamm (ed.), *Ausgegrenzt! Warum? Zwangssterilisierte und Geschädigte der NS-"Euthanasie" in der Bundesrepublik Deutschland*, 7–15. Berlin: Metropol Verlag.

Scheulen, Andreas. 2017. Von der Verfolgung zur Entschädigung NS-"Euthanasie" und Zwangssterilisation in der Bundesrepublik Deutschland. In Margret Hamm (ed.),

Ausgegrenzt! Warum? Zwangssterilisierte und Geschädigte der NS-"Euthanasie" in der Bundesrepublik Deutschland, 161–177. Berlin: Metropol Verlag.

Schmuhl, Hans-Walter. 1987 [1992]. *Rassenhygiene, Nationalsozialismus, Euthanasie. Von der Verhütung zur Vernichtung "lebensunwerten Lebens", 1890–1945*. Göttingen: Vandenhoeck & Ruprecht.

Schmuhl, Hans-Walter. 2005. *Grenzüberschreitungen. Das Kaiser-Wilhelm-Institut für Anthropologie, menschliche Erblehre und Eugenik 1927–1945*. Göttingen: Wallstein Verlag.

Schneider, Frank & Petra Lutz. 2014. *Erfasst, verfolgt, vernichtet. Kranke und behinderte Menschen im Nationalsozialismus (Ausstellung der Deutschen Gesellschaft für Psychiatrie und Psychotherapie, Psychosomatik und Nervenheilkunde (DGPPN))*. Berlin: Springer Medizin.

Van der Locht, Volker. 2010. Juni 1940: Der Beginn der Ermordung jüdischer Behinderter und der Holocaust. https://www.euthanasiegeschaedigte-zwangssterilisierte.de/nl-beh/newsletter-behindertenpolitik-nr40-beginn-ermordung-juedischer-behinderter.pdf [accessed May 10th 2019].

Vogel, Helmut. 2015. *Gehörlose Opfer der Zwangssterilisation und der "Euthanasie" in der NS-Zeit*. Documentary movie in German Sign Language (DGS) and spoken German, with subtitles). https://www.euthanasiegeschaedigte-zwangssterilisierte.de/dokfilme/film-gehoerlose-opfer-zwangssterilisationen-und-euthanasie-ns-zeit/ [accessed May 13th 2019].

Vogel, Helmut. n.d. a. Sterilisation und Euthanasie. https://www.taubwissen.de/content/index.php/geschichte/gehoerlose-in-der-zeit-des-nationalsozialismus/sterilisation-und-euthanasie/591-nazisterilisationeuthanasie.html [accessed May 13th 2019].

Vogel, Helmut. n.d. b. Gehörlose Juden. https://www.taubwissen.de/content/index.php/geschichte/gehoerlose-in-der-zeit-des-nationalsozialismus/gehoerlose-juden/595-nazijuden.html [accessed May 13th 2019].

Voss, Burger. 2018. *Ausgeglaubt! Warum Atheisten für die Gesellschaft wertvoll sind*. Baden-Baden: Tectum Verlag.

Weindling, Paul. 2008. Entschädigung der Sterilisierungs- und "Euthanasie"-Opfer nach 1945? In Klaus-Dietmar Henke (ed.), *Tödliche Medizin im Nationalsozialismus. Von der Rassenhygiene zum Massenmord*, 247–259. Wien: Böhlau Verlag.

Westermann, Stefanie. 2017. "Ein Mensch, der keine Würde mehr hat, bedeutet auf dieser Welt nichts mehr." Zwangssterilisierte Menschen in der Bundesrepublik Deutschland. In Margret Hamm (ed.), *Ausgegrenzt! Warum? Zwangssterilisierte und Geschädigte der NS-"Euthanasie" in der Bundesrepublik Deutschland*, 23–41. Berlin: Metropol Verlag.

Wierling, Dorothee. 2017. Scham und Lebenswille. Zwangssterilisation und "Euthanasie" in autobiografischen Erzählungen. In Margret Hamm (ed.), *Ausgegrenzt! Warum? Zwangssterilisierte und Geschädigte der NS-"Euthanasie" in der Bundesrepublik Deutschland*, 55–141. Berlin: Metropol Verlag.

Appendix

Law for the Prevention of Offspring with Hereditary Diseases (July 14, 1933)[4]

The Reich government has passed the following law, which is hereby promulgated:

§1.
Anyone suffering from a hereditary disease can be sterilized by a surgical operation if, according to the experience of medical science, there is a high probability that his offspring will suffer from serious physical or mental defects of a hereditary nature.
Anyone suffering from any of the following diseases is considered hereditarily diseased under this law: 1. Congenital mental deficiency, 2. Schizophrenia, 3. Manic-depression, 4. Hereditary epilepsy, 5. Hereditary St. Vitus' Dance (Huntington's Chorea), 6. Hereditary blindness, 7. Hereditary deafness, 8. Serious hereditary physical deformity. Furthermore, anyone suffering from chronic alcoholism can be sterilized.

§2.
Applications for sterilization can be made by the individual to be sterilized. If this person is legally incompetent, has been certified on account of mental deficiency, or is not yet 18, a legal representative has the right to make an application on this person's behalf but needs the consent of the court of guardians to do so. In other cases of limited competency, the application needs to be approved by the legal representative. [. . .]

---

4 Source of English translation: Law for the Prevention of Offspring with Hereditary Diseases (July 14, 1933). In US Chief Counsel for the Prosecution of Axis Criminality, *Nazi Conspiracy and Aggression*, Volume 5. Washington, DC: United States Government Printing Office, 1946, Document 3067-PS, 880–883. (English translation accredited to Nuremberg staff; edited by GHI staff.)
   Source of original German text: Das Gesetz zur Verhütung erbkranken Nachwuchses (14. Juli July 1933). In *Reichsgesetzblatt*, Teil I, 1933, page 529; reprinted in Paul Meier-Benneckenstein (ed.), *Dokumente der deutschen Politik, Vol. 1: Die Nationalsozialistische Revolution 1933*, edited by Axel Friedrichs. Berlin, 1935, 194–195.
   Webpage: http://ghdi.ghi-dc.org/sub_document.cfm?document_id=1521
   [last accessed July 4th 2020]

§3.

Sterilization can also be requested by the following: 1. the state physician. 2. In the case of inmates of hospitals, nursing homes, and penal institutions, by the head thereof.

§4.

The application is to be made to the office of the Eugenics Court; it can either be made in writing or dictated to the court. The facts upon which the application is based should be supported by a medical certificate or confirmed in some other way. The office must inform the state physician of the application.

§5.

Responsibility for the decision rests with the Eugenics Court that has jurisdiction over the district in which the person to be sterilized officially resides.

§6.

The Eugenics Court is to be attached to a district court [*Amtsgericht*]. It consists of a district court judge acting as chairman, a state physician, and another physician certified by the German Reich and particularly well trained in eugenics.
[. . .]

§12.

Once the Court has decided on sterilization, the operation must be carried out even against the will of the person to be sterilized, unless that person applied for it himself. The state physician has to attend to the necessary measures with the police authorities. Where other measures are insufficient, direct force may be used.
[. . .]

This law comes into effect on January 1, 1934.
Berlin, July 14, 1933.

The Reich Chancellor Adolf Hitler
The Reich Minister of the Interior Frick
The Reich Minister of Justice Dr. Gürtner

Lisa Rombouts and Myriam Vermeerbergen
Surviving a war of silence: Deaf people in Flanders during the Second World War

1 Introduction

Our grandparents regularly tell us about how they experienced the war. They mention how a bombing ravaged their house and destroyed all their possessions. And how the coat grandmother had to wear the following winter was made out of a soldier's coat. During the war, our grandparents were teenagers. What happened from 1939 until 1945 has clearly left a lasting impression, even on those who were still young at the time, and they still often recount the war when talking about the past. Out of interest for the sign language use of elderly deaf people, in 2012, the center of expertise for Flemish Sign Language, the *Vlaams GebarentaalCentrum* ('Flemish Sign Language Centre'), recorded stories told by 21 deaf people over 70 years old. The project is generally referred to as the *Seniorenproject* ('Senior Citizens Project'). As a part of this data collection, the participants were invited to share their experiences from the past; World War II was one of the topics discussed (Van Herreweghe et al. 2015).

In the last two decades, we have observed within the Flemish Deaf community a growing interest for the past of one's own community. The volunteers of *Doof Verleden Vlaanderen* ('Deaf History Flanders'), in cooperation with *Doof Vlaanderen* ('Deaf Flanders'), the Flemish Deaf association, collect and preserve the heritage of the Flemish Deaf community and make it accessible to a wide audience (see https://archieven.doof.vlaanderen). However, scientific research is (still) scarce. The project *Ongehoord Verleden* ('Unheard Past') focused on Deaf activism at the beginning of the 20th century (Raemdonck & Scheiris 2007). In *Vive la parole. Milaan 1880 als scharniermoment in het dovenonderwijs* ('Vive la parole, Milan 1880 as a turning point in deaf education'), Beelaert et al. (2009) investigate the impact of the 1880 Milan conference on Flemish deaf education.

In this chapter, we present our own historical study.[1] The purpose of the study is to document and analyze the experiences of Flemish deaf people during the Second World War and to examine whether their deafness affected

---

[1] This chapter is mainly based on the master's thesis of Lisa Rombouts, who is the first author of this chapter (Rombouts 2016). The second author, Myriam Vermeerbergen, was the supervisor of the master's thesis.

these experiences. For this, we looked into the stories from the *Seniorenproject* mentioned above, but we mainly drew from interviews we conducted ourselves. We also browsed the archives of *Doof Vlaanderen* and of the Antwerp Deaf club, *Madosa*.

Before presenting our own findings in Section 3, we provide some general background information. Section 2 briefly lays out the Nazi regime's views on people with disabilities, subsequently focusing on deaf people's experiences in Nazi-ruled Europe, and ends with a subsection dealing specifically with the situation of Flemish deaf people.

2 Deaf people in Nazi Europe

2.1 The Nazi regime's views on 'imperfection'

The connection between the Nazi regime, World War II, and the Holocaust is generally known. It is probably also common knowledge that not only Jews, but also gypsies, homosexuals, and political dissidents fell victim to the extermination programs. However, (much) less known is the fate of people with disabilities. Already in the 1920s, disabled people were seen as an obstacle to the reconstruction of Germany (Mostert 2002). Important arguments for attitudes and politics vis-à-vis disabled people have their origins in Social Darwinism and eugenics.

Charles Robert Darwin studied the evolution of animals and plants and developed the theory of biological evolution in the second half of the 19th century. This theory posits, among other things, that individuals can acquire certain unique features that enable them to survive in unfavorable conditions, as opposed to those individuals that did not acquire those features. This implies that there are inequalities within one species. 'Superior' individuals will survive more easily and as such, pass on their features to their offspring, whereas 'weaker' individuals will eventually become extinct.

Within Social Darwinism, the principles of natural selection that Darwin described for animals and plants are applied to human society and human behavior. Although studies from the early 20th century showed that deafness rarely was hereditary, "Nazi race hygienists distorted what little evidence there was about the frequency of hereditary deafness (as well as its applicability to particular individuals) to fit their ideological goals and preconceived beliefs" (Biesold 1999: 28).

The eugenics movement that emerged at the end of the 19th century used several Social Darwinist concepts. *Eugenics* is an umbrella term for a range of beliefs and/or practices aimed at improving the gene pool of the human species through selective reproduction. Positive eugenics entails that people with 'good genes' are encouraged to reproduce, whilst negative eugenics means discouraging people with a 'defect' or who are considered to be inferior to reproduce (Proctor 2002). Social Darwinism and eugenics are the foundations of Nazi Germany's racial policies, and also of the crimes against people with disabilities (Ryan 2002). Indeed, not only biological features but any "deviation from the norm" was considered – or presented – as genetic: disabilities, but also alcoholism, homosexuality, prostitution, crime, etc. (Friedlander 2002).

Social Darwinism and eugenics were the basis and the inspiration for a policy that translated into a number of regulations and laws to protect the 'superior race' (Bergman 1999). A first law in this regard was the sterilization act (in German: *Gesetz zur Verhütung erbkranken Nachwuchses*), introduced on July 14th, 1933. This law required the compulsory sterilization of any citizen who, according to court, suffered from a genetic disorder. According to the so-called *Erbgesundheitsgericht*, people with 'feeblemindedness', schizophrenia, manic depression, or hereditary epilepsy, and even alcoholics were included (Proctor 2002). From January 1934 until the end of the war in May 1945, approximately 400,000 Germans were forcibly sterilized (Heberer 2002). If a woman with a 'hereditary disorder' was pregnant, the child was immediately aborted and the woman sterilized.

After the sterilization law, the 'Law for the Protection of the Hereditary Health of the German People' was passed in 1935 as part of the Nuremberg laws (*Nürnberger Gesetze*). This law "prohibited the marriage of 'diseased, inferior, or dangerous genetic material with those of superior material'" (Heberer 2002: 56).

In 1937 and 1938, the first disabled children were given a 'merciful death'. In the beginning, there were only a few individual cases, but in the winter of 1939–1940, the T4 program, a killing program targeting disabled Germans, institutionalized the extinction of children with a disability (Friedlander 2002). Later, also adult 'disabled people' were included in this program (Mostert 2002). When in 1941, the T4 program was (temporarily) suspended under pressure from the church, doctors, and general public opinion, the six specialized euthanasia centers were closed. However, the killing continued in regular hospitals and institutions, be it to a lesser extent and less centralized. Between 1939 and 1945, approximately 200,000 to 250,000 people with a mental or physical disability were killed (Heberer 2002). The Nazi leaders of the concentration camps relied on the logistical and administrative experience of the T4 program (Mostert 2002).

In the 1930s, several movies came out that emphasized the disadvantages of people with disabilities. Two examples are *Das Erbe* ('The heritage', 1935), which illustrated the medically, socially, and economically harmful effects of people with 'disabilities', and *Opfer der Vergangenheit* (1937), in which 'healthy' German citizens are compared to people with severe disabilities. This type of propaganda led to an increased acceptance among Germans for euthanizing people with disabilities. It even came to a point where parents themselves requested euthanasia for their disabled babies (Mostert 2002).

2.2 Nazism and deaf people in Europe

According to the German Nazi regime, deaf people belonged to the group of 'people with a disability' as well (Friedlander 2002). They were therefore also victims of the sterilization law. Biesold (1999) states that deaf men and women were not only physically harmed by sterilization, but that their mental integrity was also affected. He further mentions:

> The emphasis on the congenital nature of the disability was often disregarded, and intervention was often expanded to include persons whose disability was not severe; thus sterilization was not always confined to persons who were blind or deaf but was also applied to those with a more limited impairment in vision or hearing. (Biesold 1999: 2)

The negative attitude towards deaf people also affected deaf education:

> In 1926, there were seventy-three schools for deaf children in Germany, with 787 teachers for 6149 pupils. [. . .] Teachers of deaf children had two years of additional university training after first qualifying as public school teachers. They had a national professional association and published their own journal. When the Nazis took control of the government in 1933, they destroyed the teachers' organization, banned their professional journal, consolidated several of the schools, and provided few funds for the education of deaf children. (Schuchman 2002a: 108)

According to Biesold (2002), from 1932 on, the training of teachers in schools for the deaf also included subjects such as "Eugenics" and "Hereditary diseases", undoubtedly shaping views on deaf children and adults. It is known that teachers were actively involved in selecting deaf children for sterilization. Parents did not have a say in this matter: even if they refused, the child was taken away from school in order to perform the medical procedure.

The German Deaf community reacted upon the increasing discrimination. In 1932, the movie *Verkannte Menschen* ('Misunderstood people') was released. This movie, financed and produced by deaf people, aimed to create more understanding for deaf people's lives and for their sign language. Important topics were deaf children's education and discrimination in the workplace. Deaf people were presented as model citizens, who stop at a red light, win medals at swimming competitions, and follow political speeches with the help of an interpreter. The movie ends with the image of a blond, muscular German deaf man asking the audience not to pity deaf people, but to simply treat them equally. This view of the Deaf community did not correspond with Hitler's racial hygiene. Presenting deaf people as full citizens and highlighting the fact that 90% of deaf children have hearing parents – implying that deafness is not always hereditary – did not fit within Nazi philosophy and politics. Consequently, in 1934, the movie was banned by the German minister of propaganda Joseph Goebbels (Schuchman 2002a).

When reviewing literature for this chapter, only a few studies were found in which deaf participants themselves testify. In Biesold (1999), deaf people from Germany recount their sterilization experience. Schuchman (2002b) refers to interviews conducted in 1997 by himself and Donna Ryan with a number of Hungarian deaf people. The methodology of Pullen & Sutton-Spence (1993) is highly similar to the methodology used for our study. They interviewed elderly people from Bristol, England, about their experiences during World War II. One of the topics in the interviews is the food rationing system. The interviewees mention that the government information on rationing was not accessible to them. Whenever they had questions about the food rationing, they had to ask the missionary of the Deaf association. Moreover, news about food supplies did not reach them:

> Hearing people often heard rumours about shops which had certain foods for sale, but Deaf people missed out on that. Like everyone else, a Deaf woman might be queueing from early in the morning to get what she wanted. A rumour would be running up and down the line that another shop had just received a certain food, but the Deaf woman would not be aware of this. Suddenly the queue would melt away as all the other women dashed off to another shop, leaving the Deaf woman wondering what had happened.
>
> (Pullen & Sutton-Spence 1993: 172)

Some shop owners helped their deaf clients by writing down important information, or by helping them to fill their shopping basket. Other members of the Deaf community were of great help, too, and the Deaf club became the center for exchanging things (Pullen & Sutton-Spence 1993).

The second topic discussed by the interviewees are the air-raid sirens, explaining how deaf people in Britain were notified of the alerts. In most cases, they were warned by a hearing person in their vicinity. It was more complex for families whose members were all deaf. Sometimes they left the front door open, so someone could come and warn them. Others bought a dog or a cat. When the pet started running around nervously, they knew they had to hide from air strikes. Some deaf families gave their house keys to a hearing neighbor, so that the neighbor could also alert them at night. Still others tied a string around their toe and let it hang out of a window, so that, in the event of a bomb alert, a hearing person could pull the string at night and thus wake the deaf person (Pullen & Sutton-Spence 1993).

Pullen & Sutton-Spence report a number of personal stories. A man talks about another deaf man who became a member of 'the Blackshirts' – the British Union of Fascists – and was therefore banned from the Deaf Club in Bristol. After the war, he was welcome again, but he did not return. Another deaf man testifies about the bombing of his house:

> My wife and I were at home when an air-raid began. We took shelter under the stairs, because that was the strongest part of the house. A bomb fell on our house and destroyed it, but the stairs did not collapse and we were not hurt. We were trapped in the ruins and had to wait for help. It was completely dark, so we could not see each other signing. Instead, we felt each other's hands while we signed. I kept my hands on the stairs above me, to try and feel any vibrations from rescue-workers moving the rubble. For a long time, nobody came and we began to worry that no one would come and rescue us. We thought we might die in the ruins. Finally, we were dug out. (Pullen & Sutton-Spence 1993: 175)

The hearing rescue-workers were surprised to find survivors under the rubble, since they had already called several times and no one had responded.

2.3 Being deaf in Flanders during World War II

As far as we know, little or no research has been done in Flanders into the living conditions of deaf persons during the Second World War. However, there seems to be a lot of interest in this topic, at least within the Deaf community. On 16 February 2019, *Doof Verleden Vlaanderen*, in collaboration with *Doof Vlaanderen*, organized a seminar on the theme. Various representatives of Belgian Deaf organizations, including the *Centre Robert Dresse* and the Deaf club *Nowedo* from Bruges, argued for a well-developed archiving system within Deaf organizations, so as not to lose the information from the past and to enable historical research (personal communication Vincent Ameloot, chairman of *Doof Verleden Vlaanderen*, 15 April 2019).

Although initially not intended, given the focus and methodology of our own research, we decided to conduct a (by necessity fairly superficial) search in the archives of the Antwerp Deaf club *Madosa* and of *Doof Vlaanderen*. It seemed interesting to explore whether certain information mentioned in the interviews we analyzed (see Section 3) could be substantiated with primary source material from the archives.

The Antwerp Deaf club *Madosa* is particularly interesting because it is the only Deaf club in Flanders that was allowed to remain open during World

War II. The Deaf clubs in the other provinces were forced to close from 1940 until 1945. It is still unclear why the Antwerp club was favored by the German rulers. We have not found any official document that gave permission to *Madosa* to stay open. However, we did find correspondence from which we can – with great caution – infer that there was (at least) one *pro-German* board member, which could be a possible explanation. Clearly, further research of the archives of Deaf organizations and probably also the city archives is necessary in order to arrive at more than very cautious and preliminary assumptions.

In addition, two testimonials from deaf Jewish women appeared in the media. The first documentary, from 2008, tells the story of the Dutch woman Anna van Dam, who attended the deaf school in Antwerp when the war began (Lindwer & Linszen 2008). The second documentary was produced in 2014 by Visual Box, a Flemish deaf-led organization founded in 2011 with the aim to promote Deaf Cinema, among others by creating and distributing their own productions (www.visualbox.biz). This documentary presents an interview with Lea Huysman, who is also deaf and Jewish and attended the same school as Anna (Visual Box 2014).

The stories of these two women, as shown in the documentaries, are briefly presented below, given the limited material available. Furthermore, the deaf participants in the present study often refer to these two Jewish women and their stories. In the summaries below, we mainly focus on the experiences that relate to their being deaf.

Anna van Dam was born in Antwerp in 1927. Her parents had moved from Amsterdam to Antwerp for economic reasons. Anna was the only deaf person in her family; her parents and her younger sister were hearing. The deaf school in Antwerp, which both Anna and Lea attended, was a Catholic school, but their Jewish identity had not played any role until the war. Only when they had to wear the Star of David, were they expelled from school. According to Anna, the school board had become very frightened, and the two deaf girls had to leave as quickly as possible. Anna, 15 years old at the time, had to go into hiding with her family and was later arrested by the Nazis. At a certain moment, she asked her father what was going on, as she testifies in the 2008 documentary *Anna's stille strijd* ('Anna's silent battle') by Lindwer and Linszen:

> Then I said to daddy: – only now I begin to realize – "Why is this? Why do I have to flee? Germans are coming, but why are we fleeing? We have not done anything wrong?". And then daddy said: "Yes, but we are Jewish". "Yes, I am Jewish, but I am good, right? We have not done anything wrong". And daddy was so sorry, because I did not understand a thing. My father started crying. "No, we have not done anything wrong, but we are Jewish. Germans do not like Jewish people".   (Anna van Dam in *Anna's stille strijd*, 2008)

Anna seems to know little about the war. Whether this is due to her being deaf and/or to other factors is unclear (see also Section 4).

Anna and her family were taken to the barracks of the Kazerne Dossin, a transit camp for Jews, Roma, and Sinti in Mechelen (www.kazernedossin.eu). There she met her hearing cousin Jettie, who was a great support for her during their stay there and also later in Auschwitz. Jettie realized that Anna needed to make an effort not to stand out too much. That is why she taught her to breathe more quietly. Thanks to Jettie, Anna could pass for a 'hearing person'. However, at one point, a German soldier did notice that she was deaf, because she was signing with her cousin:

> I remember being in the sleeping room. I was signing with my cousin.[2] Then a German soldier approached. He said: "Are you using signs? Are you deaf?" We replied that we were deaf and he said: "Then I will come back later." I did not understand him. After he left, we just continued signing. Two days later, he returned with a signboard that said 'deaf-mute'. There was a string attached to tie it to your back. (Anna in *Anna's stille strijd*, 2008)

From that moment on, Anna's deafness was made clear by the signboard she had to wear at all times. When she later arrived in Auschwitz with her family, a warning from a Jewish camp guard saved her life:

> I was wearing that signboard and when I arrived, I had to get out. A prisoner, a kapo, a Jewish camp guard saw my board. He looked around and when nobody noticed, he warned me. He said: "Take off that signboard!" I said: "No, I have to keep it on, otherwise they will shoot me, because I am deaf. No, I have to wear the signboard." He said: "No, please take it off!" My deaf cousin also had a signboard. And then my cousin said: "Just take it off, that man says so." And so I did. [. . .] I actually did not know why I had to take off the signboard. Only later, I understood: I would have been killed immediately. (Anna in *Anna's stille strijd*, 2008)

Later in the camp, nobody was to find out that Anna was deaf. Here, too, her cousin Jettie came to her aid. Jettie says:

> I mimicked her voice with my mouth when they watched. She got a lot of beating because she did not hear when they shouted "Stop!" Then she would go one step further, but I was always by her side. (Jettie in *Anna's stille strijd*, 2008)

Anna and her cousin Jettie had no contact with anyone else, because she did not understand the other people, and because Anna's deafness might be discovered. They did not sign to each other either. After the liberation, the two cousins ended up in Antwerp again. Anna's hearing parents and sister were

---

2 We should point out here that this cousin is not Jettie but a different cousin, a deaf boy.

murdered in the Auschwitz concentration camp, as well as Jettie's brother and mother.

Lea Huysman was another deaf Jewish woman who went to school in Antwerp at the beginning of the Second World War. When the war started, Lea fled to France with her family, but in October 1940, she returned to Belgium. Her father believed returning was better, since he thought that abroad, Lea would struggle with foreign languages because of her deafness. However, her father was arrested in Belgium, and she never saw him again. In 1942, Lea's hiding place in Antwerp was discovered, but she and her mother were able to escape the German soldiers just in time. For two years, they lived in hiding. Lea and Anna remained best friends until Anna died in 2013 (Visual Box 2014).

It is, of course, impossible to draw general conclusions from only two testimonies, but due to the lack of historical sources and scientific research on deaf people in Flanders during the Second World War, we decided to include this information in our study. These two documentaries, together with the literature review, enabled us to ask more specific questions during the interviews conducted for our own study, which is presented in the next section.

3 The experiences of Flemish deaf people during World War II

3.1 Methodology: data collection

Two types of data were used for this study. On the one hand, we used recordings from the *Seniorenproject*, a project from the Flemish Sign Language Centre. On the other hand, we conducted six interviews ourselves.

Within the framework of the *Seniorenproject*, in 2012, Flemish Sign Language data from 21 deaf signers over 70 years old were recorded. As part of that data collection, participants were encouraged to talk about experiences from the past, and in 11 recordings, World War II experiences are rendered. These movie clips are between 6 and 40 minutes long. In most cases, two older deaf participants are interviewed together by a deaf interviewer, Diane Boonen, a well-known member of the Flemish Deaf community. In one case, a participant is interviewed alone. The interviewer asks fairly general, open questions, such as "What can you tell about the war?". In this way, the elderly deaf participants get the chance to talk freely about their memories. The recordings from the *Seniorenproject* have been integrated into the Flemish Sign Language Corpus (Van Herreweghe et al. 2015). The data collection for the latter larger Corpus took place between 2012 and 2015, and the annotation of the data is still ongoing (Vermeerbergen & Van Herreweghe 2018).

The recordings from the *Seniorenproject* related to World War II had not been transcribed at the start of our own investigation. Therefore, the data were transcribed by the first author, using ELAN (Crasborn & Sloetjes 2008). Transcribing spontaneous language use by elderly deaf persons proved to be very challenging, and therefore, assistance from native users of Flemish Sign Language was indispensable. As a result, to date, only three of the 11 recordings have been transcribed and analyzed, 44 minutes of data in total. As said, each recording involves two participants. Table 1 provides an overview of the participants' characteristics (we refer to participants by a code consisting of the letter C and a number; C refers to 'Corpus', i.e., the Flemish Sign Language Corpus).

Table 1: Participants from the *Seniorenproject* (Flemish Sign Language Corpus).

	Gender	**Age in 1940**	**Region**
Participant C1	Woman	6 years old	Flemish Brabant
Participant C2	Woman	12 years old	Flemish Brabant
Participant C3	Woman	19 years old	Antwerp
Participant C4	Man	15 years old	Antwerp
Participant C5	Man	10 years old	Antwerp
Participant C6	Woman	11 years old	Antwerp

In addition to the existing data, new data were collected. Six elderly Flemish deaf people were interviewed. They were recruited in the following way. We first contacted the large(r) Deaf organizations in Flanders. Fourteen organizations were contacted by email (in Dutch and Flemish Sign Language), asking whether they knew deaf people who had consciously experienced World War II. By asking the question in this way, rather than suggesting age limits, we hoped to appeal to the widest possible audience. The response was overwhelming: many people responded positively to the email and forwarded it to others, creating a snowball effect. In this way, and through attending an activity for deaf senior citizens, six suitable participants were found. Their characteristics are given in Table 2 (here, the letter I in the participant code refers to 'interviewee', as these participants were interviewed specifically for this study).

Table 2: Participants interviewed specifically for the present study.

	Gender	Age in 1940	Region
Participant I1	Woman (Jewish)[3]	13 years old	Antwerp
Participant I2	Woman	11 years old	West Flanders
Participant I3	Man	10 years old	Antwerp
Participant I4	Woman	11 years old	Antwerp
Participant I5	Woman	9 years old	Antwerp
Participant I6	Woman	12 years old	Antwerp

It is important to note that participants I3 and I4 are the same persons as participants C5 and C6 from the *Seniorenproject*. However, the previously recorded data of these two participants were rather limited. That is why we decided to interview them again and to give them the opportunity to tell their stories in more detail. This means that our analysis is based on 12 interviews conducted with 10 interviewees.

All six participants included in Table 2 were interviewed by the first author. The interviews were semi-structured, that is, the interviewer did not work with a predefined questionnaire, but rather with a number of fairly general themes. Examples are: the onset of the war, the food rationing, the air-raid sirens, the situation at the school for the deaf, and the liberation.

The interviews were recorded on video. Due to a technical problem there are no recordings of the interviews with participants I5 and I6, but thanks to the extensive notes taken during and after the interviews, the recollections of these two participants are still available and have been analyzed. However, it is not possible to offer quotes from these participants in the presentation of the results in Section 3.3.

3.2 Analysis

For this qualitative study, we opted for a thematic analysis using the program Kwalitan (Kwalitan 2019). This program allows the researcher to assign codes to

---

[3] This participant is Lea Huysman, the deaf Jewish woman also featuring in the documentary by Visual Box. With her permission, her name is revealed in the study, because it may be interesting to link the data from the interview to the data from the documentary.

specific text segments. These codes can then be used to extract the marked segments from the data, so that it becomes possible to compare text segments from the different interviews that are related to the same theme.

3.3 Results

Based on the analysis in Kwalitan, ten themes were selected: the onset of the war, the provision of information, the situation in the school for the deaf, the air-raid sirens, food rationing, flight from the Nazis, the arrest of Jewish people, sterilization, contact with German soldiers, and the liberation. These themes are discussed one by one below. We want to remind the reader that codes C1 to C6 refer to participants interviewed by Diane Boonen, within the context of the *Seniorenproject*, while codes I1 to I6 refer to participants who were interviewed by ourselves. Two participants receive a combined code, namely participant I3/C5 and participant I4/C6 (see also Section 3.1). When presenting quotes from one of their interviews below, we use **bold** font to identify the specific source; for instance, '**I4**/C6' implies that the quote is taken from our interviews with this participant, whereas 'I4/**C6**' means that the quote is included in the data from the *Seniorenproject*.

3.3.1 The onset of the war

Almost all participants indicate that they were in school when the war broke out in May 1940. They were all picked up by their parents that same day. Participant I6, however, remembers she was at home, because she was ill. Participant I4/C6 recounts, both in the corpus and in our interview, how she was told that the war had begun:

> *When the war began, I was in school. We were all in boarding school. One morning, we had to get up very early, we did not know why. We wanted to put on our school uniforms, but the sisters told us to put on our clothes from home. We were all very pleased that we could go home. The sisters told us that it was war, but we did not know what that meant.* (**I4**/C6)

The same participant also says that when she got up, she asked where participant I1, Lea Huysman, was. Lea had been picked up by her parents earlier, but participant I4/C6 did not know why. She later realized that it was because Lea was Jewish. Lea herself reports very little on the onset of the war, only that her father came to pick her up at six o'clock in the morning.

Participants C2 and I2 tell a similar story to that of participant I4/C6, namely that they were suddenly woken up by the sisters and had to leave and go home. Participant C1 states that she repeatedly requested more information from the sisters, but did not get it:

> It was in 1940. It was war, but I did not know. The sisters entered the dormitory and stomped the floor hard. We got up, and they shouted that we had to leave quickly. We were still in our pyjamas. [. . .] When we got op, we normally always had to kneel and pray, but the sisters told us not to do that now. We had to leave. We asked what was going on. They did not reply. They had heard some noise; I do not know what exactly. We all went to the basement. One sister said: "Airplane, airplane!", but we did not understand her. We just kept praying. Apparently, one could hear airplanes, but we knew nothing. Then it was over, and they told us to return upstairs very quietly. We asked what had happened, because we still did not know anything. We went upstairs, got dressed and prayed. (C1)

Later, the same woman mentions that an antenna on the roof of their school had fallen because the German planes had flown so low.

Participant C1 continues her recollection of the outbreak of the war:

> At school, we had to go to church every day from 6 to 7.30am. We were praying when suddenly I felt a lot of vibrations. The priest was looking around to see what was going on. He heard the sound of bombs. Not much attention was paid to it. Later we changed our clothes and went to the refectory for breakfast, but we did not start eating immediately. One sister was standing on a wooden platform, so that she had a good overview of the room. She stomped her feet on the bench in order to attract everyone's attention. She said: "I have bad news. Everyone has to go home. The older children will leave the room from the right side and the little ones from the left side." We had to change our clothes to go home, but we did not know why we had to leave. She told us that when we had put on our clothes, we had to go back to the refectory to eat. There we all got a Saint Christopher to wear around our neck, to protect us. We all went upstairs to put on our clothes and were happy that we could go home. Of course, we did not know it was war. There was a lot of chaos. Everyone was running around. [. . .] The sister said that all lessons were cancelled, and that our parents would come and pick us up. She entered the room and called out the name of the pupil whose parents arrived. It took a long time before they called my name, but eventually my mother came. She cried very hard. I did not know what was going on, as I was only six years old. I remember that. I did sense that something was not normal. (C1)

Participant I3/C5 and participant I5 cannot remember whether they were in school or at home when the war broke out. Participant I3/C5 does remember that the Germans wanted to bomb the train tracks close to his home. The bombs had fallen next to the tracks, resulting in a large dust cloud and a destroyed road.

3.3.2 The provision of information

Section 3.3.1 shows that deaf children were ill-informed at the beginning of the war. They did not know that the Germans had invaded the country, that it was war, or what "war" meant at all. Whether this is due to the fact that they were deaf or rather due to their relatively young age is not clear. We will return to this point in the discussion in Section 4.

However, it is clear that the participants, due to their deafness and/or their limited knowledge of Dutch, lacked information compared to their hearing peers. For example, they did not have access to radio news, as participant I4/C6 recalls:

> *My mother could not sign. Nobody at home could. But they did listen to the radio all day, pfff... In the morning, when they got up, they immediately turned it on.* (I4/C6)

Participant I2 also talks about the radio that was often switched-on at home.

> *Yes, we had a radio at home to listen to the news, but I did not hear that, you know. The others listened to it.* (I2)

When asked whether they read newspapers to stay informed, they both answered negatively. Presumably, they did not have access to newspapers, or their knowledge of written Dutch was not good enough to be able to read fluently.

Participant I3/C5 says that many deaf youngsters quickly lost interest due to the lack of accessible information:

> *I was often at a loss at school. The teachers talked a lot. A hearing and a hearing-impaired teacher talked about bread, the food rationing, the stamps, etc. The hearing teacher was called [name sign]. He talked about food and about going into hiding. But the deaf pupils did not understand much. They barely cared.* (I3/C5)

The war came completely unexpected for all participants. Several participants stated that they did not know that war was imminent. Just as suddenly as the news came that the war had started, they learned that the war was over again. During the war, they were also unaware of the political wrangling. Perhaps because of that, they were more receptive to the untruths that were being told. Participant C2 says:

> *German soldiers in green uniforms came. We looked surprised; we did not know who they were. The sisters told us they were doctors. They were wearing green clothes. Only later did I learn that they were Germans. At the moment, we did not know. Nobody told us. [. . .] The sisters were afraid of them. The Germans always brought us bread.* (C2)

Here, too, it is possible that the sisters acted in this way because they thought the deaf pupils were too young to be properly informed. In any case, it is clear that all participants in this study had very little access to information about the war.

3.3.3 The school for the deaf

Most participants remember that their time in school was as good as normal during the war, except for the frequent air-raid sirens (see Section 3.3.4). See Figure 1 for an impression from a Deaf classroom in Belgium in the 1930s.

Figure 1: A typical classroom in a school for Deaf girls in Ghent, Belgium, during the 1930s (Source: Erfgoedhuis | Zusters van Liefde).

Participant I4/C6 mentions that the pupils even benefited a little from the slightly changed conditions at school:

> In those days, we had to go to church every day, to the Saint Laurentius church. We always went on foot. The church was close to the boys' school, but normally, we never met. First, they went to mass, and then we went. But that did not work during the war. During this period, the mass was held in the basement of the church. In the middle was the altar. The girls were sitting in front of the altar and the boys behind. We always peeked at each other and waved. But that was actually not allowed. We were not allowed to look at the boys. (I4/C6)

Participant I3/C5 recalls:

> We had mass at seven o'clock and they at half past seven. So, we always lingered a bit . . . Or we pretended to be reading our missals, but actually we were peeking over at the girls. The teachers behind us always told us to be quiet. (I3/C5)

When asked about negative experiences, participant I2 mentions that the sisters took the apples she brought from her parents to the boarding school. Participant

I3/C5 states that things, such as the heating system, were regularly broken at school, but it is not clear whether this is related to the war.

3.3.4 The air-raid alerts

It is natural that deaf people perceive an air-raid alert in a different way than hearing people. Participant C4 states that he could hear the V1 bombers, whereas he could not hear the V2 bombers (see Figure 2).[4] Participants I6 and C2 could feel the aircrafts' vibrations. Participant I6 could even figure out the type of aircraft based on the rhythm of the vibrations.

Figure 2: Exposition of V2 artillery in Antwerp, Belgium, 1945 (Source: FelixArchief, Antwerp city archive, 857#3).

---

4 V-weapons were a particular set of long-range artillery weapons designed for strategic bombing, particularly terror bombing and/or bombing of cities (Collier 1976). They comprised the V-1, a pulsejet-powered cruise missile, the V-2, a liquid-fueled ballistic missile (often referred to as V1 and V2), and the V-3 cannon. Terror bombing with V-weapons killed approximately 18,000 people, mostly civilians. The cities of London, Antwerp, and Liège were the main targets (Serrien 2016).

Other participants (I1, I2, and C3) felt no vibrations, and depended on hearing persons when there was an alert. Participant I4/C6, for example, noticed that planes flew over by paying attention to the reactions of the hearing pupils in her school:

> In our school, there were not only deaf children, but also hearing pupils with speech disorders. We were playing in the playground. Suddenly all the hearing children looked up. We thought: "That is silly, there is nothing to see?" But then we saw all these silver stars in the sky. They were American planes, on their way to Mortsel to drop bombs. [. . .] Our school, too, was damaged during that bombing. [. . .] We were very shocked.
> (I4/C6)

Participant I6 also recalls that she saw the airplanes of the famous bombing raid of the German arms factory in Mortsel and that, as a result, the windows of the girls' school in Antwerp were broken. Participant C3 states that she once saw V2 bombers flying over when she was at home. She beckoned her mother, so that she could also see them, but her mother immediately pulled her away from the window.

On other occasions, participant I4/C6 had to rely on hearing persons to notify her that the air-raid sirens went off. One particular time, the sisters warned her. She explains how the school was evacuated during an alert:

> The younger children slept on the first floor, and we, the older children, slept on the second floor together with the teachers. They also boarded at the school. There was a wooden floor. The teachers would stamp their feet hard on the floor. We sensed the vibrations and knew we had to get up. We got up, and it was dark. We did not get fully dressed, but just put on a black coat. We went to the first floor to wake the younger children. They also put on their coats, and then we all went to the basement. There we waited until the alert was over, and then we returned upstairs. [. . .] My friend, who was in the same class as me, always had convulsions [authors' note: an epileptic seizure] when we had to go down.
> (I4/C6)

Participant I3/C5 was not awakened by the vibrations, but by the light during a bomb alert:

> The siren often went off during the night, when everyone was asleep. We all went to hide in the basement. The teachers woke up from the noise, and they woke us up by flashing the lights. We all went downstairs to hide. When the danger was over, we went back upstairs to sleep. That happened time and time again.
> (I3/C5)

Apparently, one of the deaf pupils was a very sound sleeper, according to the same participant:

> One night in 1942, the alarm had already sounded twice, and we had gone into hiding for nothing. When the alarm went off for the third time that night, we decided to just stay in

> bed. Then a bomb fell. Many buildings in our street were destroyed. Our toilets were completely broken. We all got up, but could hardly see anything because of all the dust. It was completely dark. We carefully went to the basement. It was dark and cold when we got there, but we were happy we were unharmed. In the basement, they counted us, and it turned out that two children were missing. We waited until morning, when it became light again, to go and have a look. One boy slept in a bed with a high iron headboard and a slightly lower footboard. A window had broken next to him and had fallen out of the wall onto the bed. It rested on the high frame of the bed. And that boy was still sleeping peacefully! So, he was still alive. I do not remember exactly what had happened to the other boy, but everyone had survived. The teachers were naturally very relieved.
>
> (I3/C5)

Participant C4 was at the same school as participant I3/C5 and also talks about the bomb that fell on the school. On the way to the basement, there was broken glass, and when they went down that night in the dark on their bare feet, they all got shards of glass in their feet. He lays out exactly where the bomb had fallen:

> They had installed new toilets at our school, right next to the old ones. They had not demolished the old toilets. They were still there. The bomb fell right there, on the old toilets. It struck a deep crater.
>
> (C4)

According to him, it had been an English plane that had dropped the bomb on the school for the deaf in 1942. Afterwards, all students were taken home immediately. A little later, a German officer came to assess the damage. He saw what the bomb of the English plane had done and instantly put money on the table, so the school could build new toilets. It turned out that the German soldier used to be a teacher for the deaf himself.

Participant I5 also states that she often had to hide in the basement when the air-raid sirens went off. However, the basement of her parents' house was very small. That is why they had made a passage to the neighbors' basement. His basement was much larger and more comfortable to hide in. One day, a bomb fell in her garden when participant I5 was not at home. Later she would play with her brother in the crater the bomb had left. Figure 3 provides an impression of a destroyed residential area in Antwerp.

Finally, participant C1 talks about an inventive strategy of the allied bombers to warn the people that they were going to bomb German strongholds:

> A soldier on the plane dropped pieces of tinfoil from the hold of the plane. When we saw that tinfoil drifting down, we knew air strikes were coming and all went to hide in our basements.
>
> (C1)

This type of bomb alert thus was perfectly accessible for deaf people. That way, they could respond independently, without having to rely on hearing

Figure 3: A residential area in Antwerp destroyed, 1940 (Source: FelixArchief, Antwerp city archive, 736#60).

persons. The deaf participants in this study do not seem to have used inventive alarm systems such as those described in Pullen & Sutton-Spence (1993) (see Section 2.2).

3.3.5 The food rationing

All participants state that there was little food during the war as a result of the food rationing system, but that they were not really suffering too much from this. The family of participant I6 had found a solution for food shortage. Her parents hid a pig in their basement. They had to be careful, because the uncle of participant I6 worked for the service that handed out the food stamps. That is why the deaf girl always had to go and get the stamps, because they did not ask her questions, as she was deaf. Participant I4/C6 smuggled bread with her mother and later even by herself. Food was also scarce at the school for the deaf, says participant I3/C5:

> *All food was rationed. You received stamps and were not allowed to eat more than the value of those stamps. At the school for the deaf, there was also little to eat. My parents were both*

> deaf. My father worked on a farm. He helped cultivate the land there. For his work, he used to get bread or eggs, which he brought home. [. . .] I also took some of that bread to school. The other children did the same. We hid the bread in our lockers, which could be locked. After a meal, we went to our lockers, took the bread out and cut off a piece. We carefully dropped the crumbs onto a table so that we could eat them afterwards. (I3/C5)

There was also little to eat at the school for the deaf that participant I2 attended, but she lived on a farm and regularly brought food from home. That food was sometimes taken by the sisters (see Section 3.3.3). The farm where she lived was so productive that her parents could even sell apples and pears to other people.

3.3.6 The flight from the Nazis

Some participants fled to safer places. Participant C1 left with her family at the beginning of the war:

> We took our blankets off the mattress and put them together with our shoes and our clothes in a black-and-white striped bag we slung over our shoulders. [. . .] We could sleep on those bags at night. We fled to Westende because we wanted to take the boat to England. We went on foot. There were many people who fled. We walked in a long line via Ghent and Bruges to Westende. At night, we slept on the floor and ate what we could find. When we arrived, my family was already there, my grandfather as well. [. . .] My mother's brother and my father's brother came to tell us that we were too late. The boat had already left. Moreover, the Germans were advancing, so we had to return home on foot, back to Aalst. There were no trams or buses. [. . .] There were no horses any more, they were lying dead by the side of the road. [. . .] Many bombs fell, but after a while, it became quieter. The Germans had already taken the city. I went back to school and saw all my friends again. (C1)

Participant I5 also fled to Lo once. However, it was very crowded there, and the family only stayed for three weeks, then they went back home. Her father did flee to France, probably because otherwise he would have been forced to work, just like the father of participant I4/C6, who moved to the Netherlands for a while. Participant I3/C5 and his parents did not flee themselves, but all their neighbors did.

Participant I2 was probably in the most comfortable situation during the war. As mentioned in Section 3.3.5, her parents had a farm. They never had to flee and even took in refugees:

> Many people came to us during the war and slept in the hay barn with the animals. They all slept side by side, I saw them. [. . .] Many people came. Once we killed a pig to feed those people. Whole families were sleeping among the cows. (I2)

By contrast, because of her Jewish background, participant I1 (i.e., Lea Huysman, see footnote 3) was probably in the worst position of all participants. She not only had to flee, but also had to go into hiding, as already mentioned in the discussion of the documentary in Section 2.3. Her mother had asked the board of the deaf school whether she could hide there, but her request was refused. Consequently, there was no alternative but to flee the country:

> *I fled to France. We were in a village with many refugees. I was there with my father and mother, uncle and aunt, and their two children. First, we walked to Sint-Niklaas, and then we took the bus to Calais. We spent the night there. Many bombs fell. The following day, we took the train to France. Many refugees went to France. We stayed there for a few months, until all Belgians had to return home. We were not Belgian; my father was Dutch. So, we went to Toulouse, to a refugee camp with all Dutch people. We stayed there until September. My grandmother was still here* [authors' note: in Antwerp] *and said that everything was quiet and that we could come back.* (I1)

Later, her father was arrested (see also Section 2.3), and she lived in hiding with her mother for two years. She could never go outside or meet her friends. She says that she often felt lonely and read many books. Her mother always went outside to provide food, and the girl was very worried. Once they were able to escape from the Germans at the last minute:

> *The Gestapo rang the bell once at our house. The neighbor from downstairs, who was not a Jew, answered the door. They asked her if there were Jews, and the neighbor said: "No, come on in." I was upstairs. The neighbor showed the police her papers. She gestured to me that I had to hide. My mother and I fled. Fortunately, the Gestapo had not seen us, because they were standing with their backs to the window.* (I1)

Later, they could go to a different safe house. The mother of participant I1 provided fake passports for her and her daughter. Just before the liberation, the two fled again, this time to Philippeville, near Namur. They stayed there until the end of the war.

3.3.7 The arrest of Jewish people

From 1941, Jews were forced to wear the Star of David, participant I1 explains. Her father was Jewish and was arrested by the German police not much later. They had told them that if the men came along, the women and children would be left in peace, but that turned out to be a lie. Her father first went to France to work, and, according to Lea, in September 1941, he was brought to the Kazerne Dossin in Mechelen. From there, he was taken to Auschwitz.

Later, there were raids in the neighborhood where participant I1 lived with her mother:

> One night, I remember very well, in August 1942, they carried out a raid. I lived in Borgerhout, and around our house, they had invaded every house except ours. So, they rounded up many people around us, but not in our house. (I1)

After that, mother and daughter fled and lived in hiding for two years. It is striking that her mother had written the word 'deaf' on the travel suitcase of participant I1. She probably thought that that would protect her daughter.

Interestingly, the other participants in this study also refer to the stories of the two deaf Jewish girls from Antwerp, Anna van Dam and Lea Huysman. Almost all of them seem to know their story.

3.3.8 The sterilizations

In the interviews we conducted ourselves, the participants were given the opportunity to spontaneously talk about their memories of WWII. The only question the interviewer consistently asked in every interview, was whether the participants knew that deaf people in Germany were systematically sterilized (see also Section 2.1). With the exception of participants I1 and I2, they all responded that they knew nothing about forced sterilizations. Participant I1 is the only one who brought up the subject herself. When she went to visit her uncle in America after the war, she met a German deaf couple on the boat, and they told her that they had been sterilized. Participant I2 does not know anybody who has been sterilized, but she learned about the sterilizations from others. In the other data, collected for the *Seniorenproject*, the topic is not mentioned (on the topic of sterilization, see also Mittelstädt & Hosemann and Brockmann & Kozelka, this volume).

3.3.9 Encounters with German soldiers

Encounters with German soldiers were experienced as fairly smooth and non-threatening by almost all participants. Participant I3/C5 states that during the four-year war, they often had to show their identity card to the Gestapo, but that everything else went as normal. Participants I1 and I6 say they were never afraid when meeting Germans in the street. In contrast, participant C1 was scared of them, and even now sometimes still gets scared when seeing policemen in the street. The Gestapo were the worst, according to her. Participant

I3/**C5** remembers, in the corpus data, that, as a young boy, he was frightened by a German soldier's aggressive behavior:

> Our street crossed a small alley that ended on the main road. My father, mother, and I were walking. I peeked curiously around the corner of the alley and saw German troops marching in the main street. A German soldier saw me and pointed his gun at me. My father immediately pulled me away. (I3/**C5**)

In the interview we conducted with the same participant, he reports that one day he witnessed an arrest by the German police:

> We played soccer with eight other children in the street where I lived. Suddenly two uniformed men from the Gestapo arrived. They rang the bell of a house on our street. It was the home of a boy I was playing with. He had three older brothers. They wanted to arrest the second oldest brother. The Germans rang the bell, and we were all holding our breath. But they did not find the second brother at home. He was hiding behind a kind of wooden tower that we had made during a game. The two Germans were looking for him, but could not find him. The father of the family was arrested. We watched how they took him. He came back later. (I3/C5)

A curfew was imposed during the war, which meant that one had to be home by 11pm with windows and doors closed, as participants I3/C5 and I4/C6 recall. Participant C3 was almost arrested, because she had accidentally not respected the curfew:

> I went swimming. An officer was talking to some Germans. We had to be in by 9pm, but I was late because I had been chatting with some deaf friends. I suddenly noticed that it was already late. I walked very quickly to the tram stop, but had to wait a long time for the tram. Finally, it came. I ran into an officer, and he pointed his gun at me. He thought I was a Jew, but I said that was not true and showed my identity card. I said I had been chatting too long and therefore was late. Then it was OK. When I got home, I got a beating from my father. "Make sure that never happens again!", he said. (C3)

Participant C4 seems to have come into contact with German soldiers the most. He was arrested and almost deported by the Germans twice. The first time, he happened to be in the wrong place at the wrong time:

> A train was running between Antwerp and Essen, on which cannons were transported. The white brigades [authors' note: a resistance group] had exploded a bomb there. I was in the area gathering wood. The Germans arrested 300 people in the area. They were gathered in a group. I was there myself. My boss had seen that and called my father. My father wanted to come and pick me up, but the Kapellen police told him my mother should come. If my father came, they would just trade him for me. If my mother came, we could both go home. My mother came, and she negotiated for hours with an – armed – officer about my release. Finally, I was allowed to go home. The others were deported to Germany to work. (C4)

On another occasion, he, again, manages to get away just in time:

> The Germans had knocked down electricity poles. I thought that was beautiful wood, so I stole it and cut it to pieces. [. . .] Somebody had betrayed me. The Germans came to us with their guns ready. I had a large cart, and together with [name sign] – who is now deceased – I went to collect the wood. We met the German soldiers who stopped us. They talked to each other, but of course, we did not hear that. Then we suddenly ran away really fast with the cart. The Germans still called after us, but we kept running until we got home. At home, we opened the gate, quickly drove the cart in, and closed the gate again. (C4)

German soldiers stayed at the school of participant I2. They had fun and laughed a lot. However, the deaf girl could not understand what they were saying. At the school for the deaf of participant C1, neither German nor British soldiers were allowed to stay overnight, much to the regret of the teenage girls:

> Germans once came to our school. They asked whether they could stay the night. The sisters said they could not, because it was a school for deaf and blind children. The Germans went away, and everyone was relieved. Then one day British soldiers came and asked if they could spend the night. Everyone was excited. We were twelve years old, so . . . But unfortunately, the sisters did not allow it. (C1)

3.3.10 The liberation

In general, the participants have good memories of their contacts with American and British soldiers. C1, C2, and I3/C5 explain that they got chocolates or other sweets from them. Two participants even had a British or an American soldier visiting their home. Participant I6 tells that an American soldier lived with them for three weeks. He was a friendly man. One day, however, his officer came. He asked participant I6 whether it was true that the soldier had stayed overnight with them. When she confirmed this, the officer became very angry, and the soldier had to go with the officer immediately. Her father, in turn, was angry with the girl because she had told it to the officer, but she had not known any better and regretted it a lot. One year later, she suddenly received a large parcel from America through the mail. It was from her American friend and contained presents: clothes and jewelry.

Participant I3/C5 received a very short visit from a British soldier, as he recalls in the interview we conducted:

> I still remember that the soldiers entered the city in large groups. My parents – who were also deaf – and I were still asleep. My father got up in the morning and opened the shutters on the windows. He saw British soldiers in the street. They had arrived the night before. He was startled. The soldiers had knocked hard on all doors, but the neighbors had told them that we were deaf, so they had left us alone; the doors of all our neighbors were open, only

> ours was still closed. We were shocked when we saw this, but a British soldier came to reassure us. "We knew that you were deaf", he said. My father invited him in to wash and shave. He was very friendly. He gave us white bread, chocolate, and British cigarettes. (B/C5)

Participant C1 not only saw the allied troops coming, but also the German soldiers leaving:

> My mother heard noise outside. We opened the window and saw Germans leaving with everything they got. It was about 1 or 2 o'clock at night. The British advanced. [. . .] Then came the Americans, and they gave us chocolates. That was nice. (C1)

4 Discussion: Deaf children and World War II

The aim of this study is to document and analyze the experiences of Flemish deaf people during World War II and to determine which of those experiences may be related to their deafness. The research shows that the experiences of the deaf participants are to a large extent the same as those of their hearing peers. Yet, being deaf does seem to have influenced certain experiences of the participants. Obvious examples are: not being able to hear the air-raid sirens, the knocking on the door, or someone calling. More striking – and more interesting – is the lack of (access to) information, and possibly[5] also a lack of opportunities to take initiative and make decisions for yourself.

It is important to note that the participants were young at the time of the Second World War: most were between six and 13 years of age. While many Flemish hearing children and teenagers are currently fairly well informed about important societal events, this was much less the case 80 years ago. There were much less media, and for most children and teenagers, access to press resources, such as newspapers, was far from obvious. Moreover, the way adults treated children differed as well – also within the family. The literature sometimes refers to these changes in parenting relationships as the transition from a "bevelshuishouding" ('household characterized by commands') to an "onderhandelingshuishouding" ('household characterized by negotiations') (see, for example, de Bois-Reymond et al. 1990). In general, children were not expected to participate in adult conversations, and while currently, most parents value the opinion of their (young) children, and children are often involved in family decision making, that

---

[5] We write "possibly" here because this is less apparent from the stories in our own research, but it does appear from the literature, see, for example, the research of Pullen & Sutton-Spence (1993).

was certainly not the case at the time. In the past, children were sometimes even expected to participate in actions or activities without being able to decide for themselves whether they wanted to or not, and they were not always aware of the importance – or the danger – of their actions. We refer, for example, to participant I4/C6's account of the smuggling in Section 3.3.5. We are aware of similar stories from (hearing) family members and acquaintances who have experienced the war as children or young people.

In contrast to their hearing peers who usually lived at home full-time, most Flemish deaf children and teenagers stayed in boarding schools at that time, and they spent relatively little time with their parents and brothers and sisters (Buyens 2004). The participants' stories show that incorrect information was sometimes provided within the boarding schools – remember, for instance, the testimony by participant C2 about the sisters telling them that the German soldiers were doctors (Section 3.3.2). Furthermore, the stories reveal that the information was insufficiently accessible because only spoken language was used.

Although this study has not highlighted it, we know from other research and testimonies that the communication between hearing family members and deaf children was often very limited, and that the deaf children were often ill-informed. In Van Herreweghe & Vermeerbergen (1998), a deaf woman compares her position as a deaf child in a hearing family to that of a pet:

> *You could say that as a small child, I belonged to the family somewhat like a pet. That may sound harsh, but I still feel it can be compared to that. People who love their pets take very good care of them, but they do not have a conversation with the pets, certainly not an in-depth conversation, nor do they give the animals any information.*
> (Van Herreweghe & Vermeerbergen 1998: 153; our translation)

The same woman reports that, on several occasions, the lack of information led to (very) negative experiences; for example, she did not know that a beloved nephew had died, she totally panicked during a medical intervention, and she was not involved in the mourning of the family after the death of a sister. She states:

> *As a child – and later as a teenager – it often happened that I did not understand situations that I saw or experienced. My sisters could hear it when my parents were arguing upstairs, and so they also knew what it was about, but I only saw the angry faces and felt the tense atmosphere. All I could do was trying to guess what was going on. Sometimes I guessed right, but very often I was wrong.*
> (Van Herreweghe & Vermeerbergen 1998: 154; our translation)

In the end, she just gave up guessing and did not try to understand anymore. Possibly, this reflects the same attitude of resignation we witness in participant I3/C5 from the present study when he says:

> But the deaf did not understand much. They barely cared. (I3/C5)

In summary, we can state that the lack of information shown in our study may be related to the fact that the participants were young at the time of the Second World War, but that their deafness also played a major role. Communication with the hearing environment, at home but also at school, was often (very) limited. Moreover, deaf children and teenagers were not able to retrieve information from (over)hearing what adults were saying to each other, and there was virtually no access to the media at that time. Obviously, this was very different for hearing children.

During the interviews, the participants sometimes mentioned that they did not understand or know something at the time, and that they only realized much later what a certain incidence was about. However, this is not always stated explicitly, and it is therefore not always clear whether a certain memory is original or has taken shape only later. We know that over time, events are often perceived – and described – in a somewhat distorted way, which may involve adding details to or dropping details from the original event. As de Bois-Reymond et al. (1990) point out:

> Human memory is not reliable in all respects, certainly not when it concerns facts or feelings that are far back in time and may relate to painful experiences. Moreover, it is a well-known fact in biographical research that respondents tend to see their live in a more positive way afterwards than it actually was or at least to reconstruct events based on new experiences. (de Bois-Reymond et al. 1990: 96; our translation)

Kayzer (1995) cites the words of psychologist Elizabeth Loftus, an expert on human memory:

> It is almost a miracle that we remember anything the way it really happened. Our memories are constantly falsified, they age, or they are simply destroyed. Memories are important, without a doubt, but given that they are constantly moving and transforming, the question arises of how we can hold on to something like "the truth". (Kayzer 1995: 9; our translation)

The story of the deaf student, who just sleeps through the bombing of the building, told by participant I3/C5, for example, seems unbelievable to us (see Section 3.3.4), and other deaf persons had the same spontaneous reaction. Memory indeed is far from infallible, and again the young age of the participants during WWII will undoubtedly play a role here.

An important question that can be asked concerning the experiences of deaf people during WWII is whether Jewish people who were also deaf were facing double discrimination. Our study only provides a very limited answer to this question. The testimonies by Anna and Lea seem to indicate that life was indeed particularly tough for deaf Jewish people, especially in the camps. This is a possible topic for further research, as well as other forms of intersectionality. What about deaf women or deaf migrants, for example?

5 Conclusion

As we stated in the introduction, we see an increased – and probably still growing – interest in the past of the Deaf community in Flanders. It is highly welcome that organizations and federations are making efforts to document that past, for instance, by working on accessible archives.[6] This offers interesting possibilities for future historical research. In the context of compiling large-scale corpora for sign languages, the language use of elderly signers is also recorded. During such data collection, participants are regularly encouraged to recall memories of important events or their childhood. This, too, offers opportunities for research. However, as we ourselves experienced, transcribing spontaneous narratives from elderly deaf people can be challenging. Especially when deaf participants are addressing peers from the same region, this often leads to a regionally colored language use which is sometimes difficult to understand for L2 signers annotating the data. As a result, in this project, the number of analyzed clips from the Flemish Sign Language Corpus has remained more limited than we intended. An obvious suggestion for future research is to transcribe and analyze the other narratives from the corpus. Our limited exploration of the archives also strongly suggests that further interesting information can be found there as well.

Filmed interviews with eyewitnesses are important historical sources, for example with regard to our knowledge of the Second World War. Such interviews can be used for scientific research and for educational purposes, for instance, in the media and in education – where they increasingly replace live testimonies.

Primary witness accounts may also provide leads for more specific, targeted search activities in archives, which in turn can contribute to our knowledge about historical events. However, interviews with deaf eyewitnesses are often relatively scarce. We cannot be certain as to why that is the case. It might be related to misunderstandings about the linguistic status of sign languages and,

---

6 As an example, we refer to the efforts by *Doof Vlaanderen*, the Flemish Deaf association, to digitalize its archive. This is done together with a group of volunteers, who give up their free Saturdays for this.

as a result thereof, about the communicative abilities of signers. Or perhaps, the interviewers did not have the financial means to engage a sign language interpreter, or they simply were not aware of this option.

It is unfortunate that deaf eyewitnesses are often excluded, as there can be no doubt that their testimonies lead to a more comprehensive perspective on and thus a better understanding of important events and major periods in world history.

References

Beelaert, Bram, Christine Bruyneel & Kaat Leeman. 2009. *Vive la parole? Milaan 1880 als scharniermoment in het dovenonderwijs* [Milan 1880 as turning point in deaf education]. Gent: Fevlado-Diversus.

Bergman, Jerry. 1999. Darwinism and the Nazi race holocaust. *Creation Ex Nihilo Technical Journal* 13(2). 101–111. Retrieved from: https://www.trueorigin.org/holocaust.php.

Biesold, Horst. 1999. *Crying hands. Eugenics and Deaf people in Nazi Germany*. Washington, DC: Gallaudet University Press.

Biesold, Horst. 2002. Teacher-collaborators. In Donna F. Ryan & John S. Schuchman (eds.), *Deaf people in Hitler's Europe*, 121–163. Washington, DC: Gallaudet University Press.

Buyens, Maurice. 2004. *De dove persoon, zijn gebarentaal en het dovenonderwijs* [The deaf person, his sign language, and deaf education]. Leuven: Garant.

Crasborn, Onno & Han Sloetjes. 2008. Enhanced ELAN functionality for sign language corpora. In Onno Crasborn, Thomas Hanke, Eleni Efthimiou, Inge Zwitserlood & Ernst D. Thoutenhoofd (eds.), *Construction and exploitation of sign language corpora. 3rd Workshop on the Representation and Processing of Sign Languages*, 39–43. Paris: ELRA.

Collier, Basil. 1976. *The battle of the V-weapons*. Morley: The Elmfield Press.

Doof Vlaanderen, last retrieved May 30, 2019, from https://www.doof.vlaanderen/.

Du Bois-Reymond, Manuela, Els Peters & Janita Ravesloot. 1990. Jongeren en ouders: van bevelshuishouding naar onderhandelingshuishouding. Een intergenerationale vergelijking [Youth and parents: from a household characterized by commands to a household characterized by negotiations. An inter-generational comparison]. *Amsterdams Sociologisch Tijdschrift* 17(3). 69–100.

Friedlander, Horst. 2002. Holocaust studies and the Deaf community. In Donna F. Ryan & John S. Schuchman (eds.), *Deaf people in Hitler's Europe*, 15–31. Washington, DC: Gallaudet University Press.

Heberer, Patricia. 2002. Targeting the "unfit" and radical public health strategies in Nazi Germany. In Donna F. Ryan & John S. Schuchman (eds.), *Deaf people in Hitler's Europe*, 49–70. Washington, DC: Gallaudet University Press.

Kayzer, Wim. 1995. *Vertrouwd en o zo vreemd. Over geheugen en bewustzijn* [Familiar and yet so strange: on memory and conscience]. Amsterdam & Antwerpen: Uitgeverij Contact.

Kwalitan, last retrieved April 11, 2019, from https://www.kwalitan.nl/index.php?s=1&k=-1#tekst_top.

Lindwer, Willy & Tom Linszen. 2008. *Anna's stille strijd* [Anna's silent battle; documentary]. AVA Productions, The Netherlands. https://www.youtube.com/watch?v=5tKqFIJOuOE&t=1452s; last retrieved April 11, 2019.

Mostert, Mark P. 2002. Useless eaters: disability as genocidal marker in Nazi Germany. *The Journal of Special Education* 36(3). 155–168.

Opfer der Vergangenheit [Victims of the past]. 1937. Movie, last retrieved April 11, 2019, from https://www.ushmm.org/online/film/display/detail.php?file_num=3213

Pullen, Gloria & Rachel Sutton-Spence. 1993. The British Deaf community during the 1939–1945 war. In Renate Fischer & Harlan Lane (eds.), *Looking back. A reader on the history of Deaf communities and their sign languages*, 171–176. Washington, DC: Gallaudet University Press.

Proctor, Robert N. 2002. Eugenics in Hitler's Germany. In Donna F. Ryan & John S. Schuchman (eds.), *Deaf people in Hitler's Europe*, 32–48. Washington, DC: Gallaudet University Press.

Raemdonck, Liesje & Ingeborg Scheiris. 2007. *Ongehoord verleden. Dove frontvorming in België aan het begin van de 20ste eeuw* [Unknown past: deaf activism in Belgium at the beginning of the 20th century]. Gent: Fevlado-Diversus.

Rombouts, Lisa. 2016. *Een stille strijd: de situatie van Dove personen in Vlaanderen tijdens de Tweede Wereldoorlog* [A silent battle: the situation of deaf people in Flanders during the Second World War]. Antwerp, Belgium: KU Leuven Master's thesis.

Ryan, Donna F. 2002. Introduction. In Donna F. Ryan & John S. Schuchman (eds.), *Deaf people in Hitler's Europe*, 1–7. Washington, DC: Gallaudet University Press.

Schuchman, John S. 2002a. Misjudged people: the German Deaf community in 1932. In Donna F. Ryan & John S. Schuchman (eds.), *Deaf people in Hitler's Europe*, 98–113. Washington, DC: Gallaudet University Press.

Schuchman, John S. 2002b. Hungarian Deaf Jews and the holocaust. In Donna F. Ryan & John S. Schuchman (eds.), *Deaf people in Hitler's Europe*, 169–201. Washington, DC: Gallaudet University Press.

Serrien, Pieter. 2016. *Elke dag angst* [Every day fear]. Antwerpen: Horizon.

Van Herreweghe, Mieke & Myriam Vermeerbergen. 1998. *Thuishoren in een wereld van gebaren* [Feeling at home in a world of signs]. Gent: Academia Press.

Van Herreweghe, Mieke, Myriam Vermeerbergen, Eline Demey, Hannes De Durpel, Hilde Nyffels & Sam Verstraete. 2015. *The VGT corpus. A digital open access corpus of video and annotation material in Flemish Sign Language.* University of Ghent & KU Leuven,

Vermeerbergen, Myriam & Mieke Van Herreweghe. 2018. Looking back while moving forward: the impact of societal and technological developments on Flemish Sign Language lexicographic practices. *International Journal of Lexicography* 31(2). 167–195.

Visual Box. 2014. *1001 gebaren*. Aflevering 2 [1000 signs, episode 2; documentary]. Last retrieved April 11, 2019, from https://vimeo.com/user14202278/review/89611413/4db800c1ad.

Jordina Sánchez-Amat, Raquel Veiga Busto, Xavi Álvarez, Santiago Frigola, Delfina Aliaga, Miguel Ángel Sampedro, Gemma Barberà, and Josep Quer

The Francoist dictatorship through the Deaf lens

1 Introduction

During the conversation with Amalia,[1] the interviewee summarized the coexistence of two opposing political sensitivities within her family during the Franco regime as follows:

> My husband hated Franco, and we disagreed on this. But I understood his position and he mine, of course. My father was a Francoist and was in favor of Franco because it was thanks to him that my grandmother was saved. And yet, Franco was responsible for the execution of my father-in-law. It was a very hard time. (Amalia)

The experience of this marriage illustrates the complexity of the situation in which the population found itself after the coup d'état against the Second Spanish Republic in 1936.[2] The subsequent Civil War (1936–1939) ended with the victory of the participants in the coup and led to a dictatorial regime, with general Francisco Franco at its head, as self-proclaimed Spanish Head of State. Both the victors and the defeated suffered a severe post-war period of extreme economic scarcity (*"If we return again [to the ration cards], I shoot myself"*, says Juana), but the social rupture caused by the war and Francoisms' denial of any type of reconciliation (Hernández & del Arco 2011) aggravated the suffering of the defenders of the Republic.

During the Franco regime, the government used several mechanisms to maintain a hierarchical social order, subsumed under the label "New State". These mechanisms emanated from three pillars: the Church, the army, and the single party, always subject to the government (Riquer 2010). Education was monopolized by the Church, which imposed moral conservatism, promoted traditional

---

[1] For the sake of anonymity and due to data sensitivity, the interviewees' names that appear in the article are fictitious, and we also refrain from providing source codes for the fragments quoted from the actual interviews.

[2] The failed coup d'état on 18 July 1936, led by right-wing military forces, was followed by a Civil War between the regions that joined the coup (so-called National faction) and the area where the legitimately elected government, under the Second Republic, continued to operate (the Republican faction).

customs, and followed the values of the regime. There was a strong repression and violence against the defeated and opponents, which in turn served as a lesson to the rest of the population: goods were seized, at least 50,000 people were executed during the post-war period, and the prison population in 1942 exceeded more than 10 times that of 1933 (Riquer 2010: ch. 3). With the law of February 10, 1939, which set standards for the cleansing of civil servants, dissidents were purged in the public and private sector (professors and teachers, personnel in transportation, the Justice system, Post and Telegraphs, journalists, workers in industry and commerce, banks, and others).

There was a high level of social control: The judiciary was subject to the government, and numerous legal provisions were enacted to maintain the status quo; for instance, political parties and unions were prohibited, and attitudes contrary to the regime (e.g., demonstrations, strikes, etc.) were classified as acts of military rebellion (Riquer 2010: ch. 3). There was also strong censorship in journalism, literature, film, music, and other artistic expressions, and the functioning of associations was strongly controlled. The regime oppressed all cultural, ideological, and linguistic diversity in the interest of the national Catholic state it had established. In the economic sphere, the government protected and favored the bourgeoisie and reduced the rights of workers.

The memories of the Civil War impacted strongly on the population, increasing their fear of reviving it and getting them to trust the regime as the way out of that situation (Hernández 2014). This resulted in a "time of fear" (Riquer 2010: 177), which caused the society's response to the regime to be largely passive and depoliticized. However, the role of fear in citizens' attitudes towards the regime has been nuanced. While investigations of social behaviors under dictatorial regimes highlight the effects of mechanisms to terrorize, coerce, and repress citizens, they also indicate that these mechanisms can only partially explain the passivity or conformity of the citizens, that it would only be "one side of the coin, whose reverse is made up of accommodation, acceptance, or consent" (Hernández 2014: 92). An important factor to take into account is the desire on the part of the populace for normalcy and for an ordinary life, which often led to the acceptance of the conditions imposed by the regime (Hernández 2016).

In this chapter, we present a first approximation to how 19 deaf people (seven signers of Catalan Sign Language, LSC, and 12 signers of Spanish Sign Language, LSE) perceived the Franco dictatorship, based on oral sources, and taking into account the complexity of the mechanisms that operate in their perspectives. As Font (2004: 51) states, "in the field of political attitudes under the dictatorship, complexity, paradoxes, inconsistencies and contradictions are the most abundant, and any simplifying determinism has no place". We show the complexity of the perceptions, experiences, and attitudes of a sample of deaf people from different areas of the Spanish State during the Franco dictatorship concerning various domains. The participants who contributed to our study ranged between 70 and 93 years of age at the time of data collection; the average age of the sample is 80.4 years. Eleven of the people interviewed were born before 1940, and eight were born thereafter. Ten women and nine men were interviewed. The informants come from seven autonomous communities: Andalusia (2), Asturias (1), Catalonia (7), Galicia (2), Madrid (3), Valencia (3), and Castile and Leon (1). Only four of the participants have at least one deaf parent. The sample was selected for convenience reasons and it is therefore very diverse. In addition, the interviews were semi-structured and were conducted without the specific objective of studying the perceptions of Franco. For both reasons, the results obtained must be interpreted with caution. We analyzed the interviews based on pre-established categories, which we will address in turn, namely politics (Section 2), education (Section 3), family and moral values (Section 4), work (Section 5), and participation in associations and social contexts (Section 6).

2 Politics

Most interviewees who express their views on the political regime of Francoism value it positively, emphasizing that there was less corruption, more security, and more control than in later times:

> There are many people who say that they did not live well with Franco, and that he was very bad. But I remember Francoism as a good time, I prefer that time. There was no corruption, no homosexuality. And today, there is a lot of freedom for everything. (Inés)

> Many people were against Franco, but I led a very pleasant life [. . .], without fear in the streets, very quiet. Now I am much more scared because I have already been robbed several times. It seems that in democracy, there is hardly anyone sent to prison and that a little hard hand is missing, people are not afraid. (Nieves)

Pedro also expresses similar considerations. When giving his opinion on the current political situation and about his interests in politics, he states:

> I think that with Franco, it was calmer. Now they talk a lot, but they are liars alike, and they still mooch the same. I believe that with Franco, at least it was a single person who did it. [. . .] I don't like politics. (Pedro)

According to Riquer (2010), forced depoliticization, one of the objectives pursued by Franco, was achieved by means of repression, which led the population to fear talking about politics. The previous testimonies, especially the one by Pedro, are an illustration of the achieved goal. Notably, however, the interviewees were not direct witnesses of Franco's violence and the oppression during the war or the first post-war period, because they were either very young at that time or not even born yet. In fact, no interviewee expresses feelings of fear towards the regime. So, how did Franco achieve the depoliticization of these people?

The interviews present us with indications that the effect of fear on our participants materialized indirectly, by first influencing those who informed them through the family, the educational institutions, and the media.

As for the information transmitted by their families, most interviewees report that they did not receive too much information about the Civil War from their parents. Those who did, namely Inés, Jose, Carlos, Emili, and Encarna, be it first-hand or through third-party accounts, highlight the suffering and hunger faced by the population. Emili also recalls the mass exile, especially that of children, to France via the Catalan border. After narrating the participation of his uncle in the Battle of Cabo de Palos in 1938, Antonio also reports on the various attempts by his uncle to flee to French territory, the controls carried out by the falangists,[3] and the subsequent executions of the Republicans who participated in the battle.

On the other hand, some interviewees, like Encarna, Lola, and Inés, highlight the importance of family and neighborhood networks to survive the extreme scarcity experienced during the war and the post-war period. For example, Encarna remembers that his maternal grandfather, who was better off, shared the food he had with the residents of the town *"because they had nothing and were hungry"*. Next to the general hunger, goods and food plundering was perpetrated by the regime's soldiers. According to Óscar, his mother told him that after killing the pigs, they buried the meat under stones to prevent Franco's soldiers from stealing it – a common practice as confirmed by other people from neighboring towns. The interviewees who had already been born when the Civil War began did not clearly understand what was happening at the time. In their stories about the war, both

---

3 *Falange Española Tradicionalista y de las Juntas de Ofensiva Nacional Sindicalista* ('Spanish Traditionalist Falange of the Assemblies of the National-Syndicalist Offensive') or *Movimiento Nacional* ('National Movement') was the only official party under Franco rule. It created several sectoral organizations: *Frente de Juventudes* ('Youth Front'), *Sección Femenina* ('Female Section'), *Central Nacional Sindicalista* ('National Sindicalist Center'), among others. Interestingly, our interviewees refer to the participants in the coup d'état as *falangistas* ('falangists'), and they do not use the very common term *nacionales* ('nationals'). As for the defenders of the Republic, most interviewees call them *comunistas* ('communists'), the term *rojo* ('red') is less frequently used, but none of the interviewees calls them "Republicans" or "anarchists".

Rosa and Juana remember that, when there were bombings, their families or teachers helped them to protect themselves and to move to shelters.

Some interviewees' narratives report on family stories more explicitly related to political experiences, but these explanations during the interview hardly denote any critical interpretation of the facts.

For example, Inés, who lived in Valencia – which belonged to the Republican zone during the Civil War –, when asked whether her family were falangists or communists, provided the following explanation about her father's experience:

> Inés: *My father was in jail for two years. Because he found a cap, and put it on, not knowing what it was.*
>
> Interviewer: *A cap of what?*
>
> Inés: *A cap of the communists. He found it, put it on, and they accused him. Then he was imprisoned for two years.*

Her account does not reveal when and who imprisoned him, either the Francoists or a Republican faction other than communists, although it was an episode that marked her family's life.

According to Frederic, his whole family, with the exception of his father, left Barcelona (also belonging to the Republican zone) when the Civil War began. He states:

> *On the door of the floor of Aribau Street, we put a sign that said "Cura" ['priest'], so that the communists would not enter. And my grandfather did the same at his door. The communists respected him and did not enter. My father lived there. [. . .] [In the end,] he joined the falangists to hide, so that the military did not know that he was a communist.* (Frederic)

Without doubting its truthfulness, this story is confusing, and it seems that evidence to support this event is lacking, as the reason for a priest to be safe in a Republican area is unclear. Actually, while the Francoists executed many priests considered to be Republicans, it is also known that priests were intensely persecuted by both the communists and the anarchists. Yet, it appears that Frederic does not perceive such a gap, and that he accepted the explanations by his family without questioning them.

All this seems to suggest that parents avoided delving into these issues, and that this avoidance might be the result of the silence that the dictatorship had imposed through fear.

Carlos, in turn, claims that he began to become aware of what had happened as he grew up, and that he started to notice the people mutilated from the war and the hungry people. His story is exceptional, as it shows that during the dictatorship he was critical towards it:

> *I was very young. I was one year old at the time. Then they imprisoned my father. I did not begin to realize things until I started growing up, and I began to see many mutilated people on the street who lacked one or both legs, or with one arm missing. There were many people who were hungry, who had nothing to eat, and the Franco regime did not care. It was a dictatorship, there were no votes, and all public officers were handpicked by Franco.*
>
> (Carlos)

The data also suggests that being deaf aggravated the misinformation situation in which the population as a whole was immersed. Lola points this out:

> *The school was religious, and they allowed almost no talking about politics. I did not understand. With my parents, I talked about everything, and at school that caught everyone's attention. Without deaf parents, communication was delayed.* (Lola)

As this informant suggests, the children of signing deaf parents had earlier access to a language, and thanks to that, they could access the information that was transmitted within their family. In contrast, communication difficulties between hearing parents and their deaf children affected the depth of the conversations and thus the possibility of accessing content from third-party dialogues.

Several participants explain that they were not aware of the repressive activities of the dictatorship. *"Later on, I discovered [that there was censorship in the cinema] by reading. At that time, I was not aware of all these things"*, explains Lola. Similarly, Encarna was only told years later, since during the Franco era, media were controlled and censored,

> *[. . .] that Franco was very bad because many people were shot in the Valle de los Caídos [Valley of the Fallen, a mausoleum built by Franco; authors' note] once its construction was finished. [. . .] This information was not in the newspapers, but has been made public now [. . .]. Those were things that I didn't know at the time.* (Encarna)

Still, access to information after the end of the Franco regime and knowledge of the atrocities that the dictatorship had committed does not lead all respondents to have a negative view of the regime. *"I know there were many things that were not good with Franco, there was a dictatorship, censorship, etc. But there was a lot of safety"*, admits Nieves. Holding an equally ambiguous position, when asked what time was better, Juana responds *"I would not know what to tell you, because, of course, there are things I did not know, I saw on television, like there were skulls of people [. . .], killed by the Francoists"*, but she did not provide a clear answer to the question.

This indeterminacy is also present in other stories. Amalia, on the one hand, explains that *"before, in Franco's time, there was a lot of authoritarianism, everything was very quiet, and now there have been many changes, politics is very different"*. On the other hand, she admits that

> [. . .] now there is more culture than there was before, when we had less training. [. . .] Over time, I understood things better, and I also gave my children more freedom, I didn't exercise the control they exercised over me at that time. Therefore, I understand the two periods. (Amalia)

Lola expresses a similar ambivalence when recalling the Franco regime:

> Well, without knowing what came next, that period was positive for us, the deaf. It is true that there is now much more openness, but at that time, we were fine, too [. . .]. It is true that society was not so open. [. . .] During the Franco regime, there were many things that were prohibited. (Lola)

Juana offers one of the few testimonies that explicitly expresses the desire for normalcy described by Hernández (2016). After being asked about her experience of Franco, she replies: *"I didn't pay much attention, at that time, I was quite young, and I wanted to have fun more than anything else"*.

To understand the apparent contradiction presented by certain stories – which admit to knowing the brutality of Francoism but, at the same time, are reluctant to judge it and, to some extent, even show their approval of the regime – it is essential to take into account the mechanisms employed by the dictatorship to achieve these attitudes: misinformation, repression, and social control. In addition, the economic growth of the 1960s, known as "developmentalism",[4] which followed the hardships experienced by the interviewees or their parents during the post-war period, contributed to the positive perception of Francoism and the idea that a normal life was possible under the dictatorship.

3 Education

After the coup d'état, the educational system underwent a profound modification by annihilating previous Republican educational principles, such as secularism or co-education. In fact, among the first measures taken by the National

---

[4] During the 1960s and early 1970s, a period known as "developmentalism", Spain experienced a pronounced economic growth characterized by development of the industrial and service sectors, external (mainly European) and internal emigration, depopulation of the countryside, among other phenomena. Whereas Francoism attributed it to the regime's development policies, according to Riquer (2010: ch. 11), the European post World War II economic expansion would have had a major impact on it.

Defense Board in September 1936 and, as of October of the same year, by the so-called Committee on Culture and Education, were the obligatory nature of the Catholic religion (mandatory religion classes and prayer, mass attendance in boarding schools, etc.), the implementation of segregation by sexes, and the prohibition of teaching in languages other than Spanish (Morente 2001b; Alfonso 2002). Likewise, the regime initiated the ideological clearance of the teaching staff with the aim of neutralizing the regime's opponents (Morente 2001a,b). The Franco regime re-established the hegemony of the religious apparatus within the educational system: during the Franco dictatorship "formal education was always under the direct or indirect control of the Catholic Church" (Viñao 2014: 22). However, it was neither the case that literacy was universal, nor was it the case that access to education occurred uniformly. In fact, there are notable differences in the age of access to schooling among the interviewees: with one who started school at 3.5 years, and one who went to school at 15.5 years. The total period of schooling also differs, ranging from 3 to 16 years. In many cases, economic difficulties led to the selection of the school based on it being free of charge, and sometimes students left school due to the tight economic situation in the family, because they could not afford the uniform, as in the case of Teresa, or transportation, as in the cases of Lola and Francesc.

With the exception of one interviewee, all were enrolled in deaf schools, some of which also had blind students. In addition, some interviewees at some point attended schools with hearing students or received training from private teachers, especially to be trained for work. Due to distances and economic difficulties, interviewees who did not live near the school, or did not have relatives in the area, were enrolled in boarding schools. This is how Lola narrates her experience:

> *I was only returning [home] in the summer, but not during the other holidays, like Christmas, Easter, or any other time. I was not the only one. There were many other pupils who did the same. We stayed at the boarding school mainly because of the cost of transportation back then.* (Lola)

The widespread misery of the post-war period and the lack of investment in educational institutions are also reflected in the precariousness of food supply in schools. Inés and Óscar remember the scarcity and poor quality of food, but *"we would eat it because we were hungry, and there was nothing else"*, as Inés mentions.

Education was a central tool for the transmission of the national-catholic values of the regime, among which religion occupied a prominent place. According to Lola, *"the influence of religion was very strong; even your skirt riding up a bit was considered a sin, and you had to go to confession. For everything, we had to confess, and everything was a sin"*. We also find stories that report on the obligation to attend mass every day that existed in some institutions (Inés and Nieves), as well as on the importance attached to the study of the Catholic religion. As Inés adds: *"We did sewing, embroidery, drawing, but especially lots of catechism, lots of religion, every day"*.

As the story of Inés already suggests, the education system also contributed to spreading an unequal view of women, whose social role was limited to the care of the family and the home. At school, women's subalternity was transmitted through instruction in tasks considered typical of their sex, such as sewing or embroidery. The organizational model of the school itself is testimony of the unequal vision on men and women, given that in practically all the institutions, the students were segregated according to sex, and contact between them was strictly prohibited.

In general, sign language was banned in the classroom and, depending on the institution, also in the courtyard, although in some schools, it was used during specific activities. At Lola's school, for example, a form of Sign-supported Spanish was used in lessons about religion that were held on Saturdays. This fact could be interpreted as an indication of the concern to make religious content completely accessible to students. Despite the ban, some teachers and nuns signed with varying degrees of fluency, and even within the same institution, one could find very different levels of language skills. In addition, in some of the institutions, there were also deaf teachers, especially in artistic subjects (such as drawing and painting), which all interviewees value positively. For example, Jose and Antonio, alumni of the deaf leader Félix Jesús Pinedo – an unusual case of a deaf teacher who dedicated himself to the teaching of the Spanish language – highlight the clarity of his explanations and their speed of learning: *"When he arrived as a teacher, we all made great progress. [. . .] Our world grew with him"*.

No interviewee received a degree at the end of their studies, only a certificate with their marks. According to Pedro, son of deaf parents, the training was very basic: *"I learned more at home, reading the newspaper, with the explanations that my father gave us, than I learned in school"*. Other interviewees, like Juana, indicate that after the school period, they had to work hard to continue learning. Yet, the available resources and the educational practices were not homogeneous among the different schools. In fact, several interviewees highlight the superior quality of education in the schools of Madrid and Deusto (Bilbao). Antonio compares the differences between the two schools in which he was enrolled as follows:

> *In Santiago de Compostela, the training was more basic, a bit limited. There were 70 students per teacher. In Madrid, the situation was much better. There were 15 students per teacher, in smaller groups, and there were some deaf teachers of drawing and painting, and with them I learned a lot.* (Antonio)

All interviewees agree that the current educational situation for young deaf people has improved, as there are now deaf people studying at high schools and even going to university.

The educational method was oralist and based on rote learning: *"We had to memorize, repeat like a parrot"*, Lola mentions. The dominant educational practice was to copy or read what the teacher wrote on the blackboard. Juana recalls:

> *I did not understand anything or learn much. [. . .] We talked in pairs in front of the mirror to practice, but we did not understand what we were doing, nor did we know if we did it right or wrong, because the teacher did not pay attention to us.* (Juana)

A good part of the interviewees agrees that the educational system gave much importance to spoken language skills. Being questioned about his opinion on the weight of language in education, Francesc states: *"We didn't need to learn to sign because there were already associations, but to speak . . . yes"*, which clearly illustrates the asymmetric situation of the teaching of sign language as opposed to that of spoken language.

The focus on the spoken language skills of the deaf would sometimes lead to public exhibitions of their command of spoken language, as is evident from the following quote:

> *When the director of the "Caixa de Pensions"* [a bank; authors' note] *came to the "Puríssima" school [in Barcelona], they always called me and another pupil to show that we spoke very well. In this way, he believed that all of us spoke equally well. The nuns tricked him, those wretches!* (Teresa)

In the institution of Carlos, however, speech therapy education was restricted to students from wealthy families, who received classes after the other students had finished school hours. Possibly as a consequence of the importance given to spoken language skills, several interviewees use the same rhetoric, which associates quality of education with oral skills, as shown by Emili's assertion, *"I was the best in my class; I was the one with the best voice of all"*.

Despite the institutionalization of oralism, all interviewees, with the exception of the children of deaf parents, who already knew how to sign, learned to sign in school. In the absence of adult language models, students learned sign language from their peers through observation, albeit with initial difficulties: *"When I arrived, I didn't know anything about sign language, I didn't understand what people were saying"* (Juana), and the feeling of otherness: *"I saw the school children waving their hands, and it seemed strange"* (Francesc). The situation was no different for those students who had learned sign language at home and who expressed their amazement at discovering the sign language of the school. Pedro, for instance, states that *"at first, I didn't understand what they were saying, because it was so different"*. Despite this, children of deaf parents could become language models for other students, as Nieves' recollection shows:

> *I always used sign language and also taught it to others because my parents were deaf. They always punished me for that [. . .], I was the queen of punishments, but I didn't care if they punished me a lot, I already knew it was forbidden, and even so, I always signed.*
> (Nieves)

The depoliticization of the population to which Franco was aspiring took place at the school, by means of the direct prohibition against talking about politics (compare Lola's quote in Section 2), by the omission of information, or by the legitimization of the dictatorial regime. In addition, other more subtle tools were used to transmit and maintain social order, such as the implementation of a rigid discipline in boarding hours, which is reported by Inés: *"We had dinner very early, about half past seven or eight, and we had to go to sleep. At six or seven in the morning, we would get up to go to mass: all the blessed days in the morning!"*. Likewise, depoliticization was also achieved in the school through the exercise of physical repression, symbolic violence (term taken from Bourdieu (1977)), that is, by subtle forms of domination aimed at reproducing social inequalities (unequal vision of men and women, inequality of sign languages with respect to spoken languages, etc.), and submission to authority. Punishment of sign language use was widespread and added another recurring motive for punishment: contact between deaf peers of different sexes. As stated by Amalia: *"If you greeted a boy, the nun would put you on your knees in a corner with the arms extended as punishment"*. Such contacts could even be penalized with expulsion from school. Catholic fundamentalism even led to sanctioning mere eye contact: *"The only place we were allowed to be together at the same time was in the church, each on a bench, but if the boys looked at the girls, they were slapped on the back of their neck immediately"*, says Lola. Isabel indicates that dancing was also not allowed, and, according to Inés, if there was no silence at bedtime, students were punished by being locked in the closet.

Other punishments involved the prohibition of visiting the family, as Nieves explains, slapping on the hands, as Amalia mentions, or the obligation to spend the night outside. This is how Lola tells about the experience of their schoolmates:

> *They cried a lot and were afraid to stay outside because if they peed on the bed or did something wrong, the punishment that the nuns imposed on them was to force them to spend the night outside or to beat them.*
> (Lola)

Despite the prohibition against contact with partners of the opposite sex, in the school of Nieves, one of the punishments imposed on girls who wetted their bed consisted in the following: *"They made you wrap yourself in the same sheet and go for a walk to the boy's school so that everyone would laugh at you"*. Besides physical and symbolic violence, interviewees also report on sexual violence: *"Several female pupils told me that the priest used to touch them"*, explains Lola.

Despite the negative experiences described, the assessment of the school period is positive in the majority of interviewees. Several narratives highlight why they evaluate their educational period positively. First, the majority of the interviewees learned sign language by accessing education. Juana, for instance, explains, *"I learned sign language thanks to the school, because they didn't know how to sign in town"*. In addition, even if the educational method is questioned by interviewees, during that period they became literate and acquired knowledge considered relevant for their future work. Lola refers to this when she says: *"I learned to read, even if it was like a parrot, but I learned thanks to the nuns. Otherwise, I would never have learned because my mother could not read"*. Second, the existence of a strong bond with deaf classmates was very important:

> *For me, the school was not a second home, but the first one. Home came second. In the school, we were all very close, we supported each other a lot. [. . .] Besides, I was the only deaf person in my family, I was an only child, I felt very isolated, so I liked going to school very much.* (Jose)

Likewise, living with other older deaf people lead to acquiring new knowledge and skills. Last but not least, the repression of the school system was compensated for by the expression of affection or reward by at least some of the nuns and teachers towards some interviewees. Lola, for instance, recalls:

> *All these negative things happened, but for me, there were also many positive experiences, because the nuns were affectionate to me, they encouraged me, and they rewarded me, they raised my self-esteem every time I did something right.* (Lola)

In the case of Nieves, however, the repression exerted by the nuns is mirrored by the widespread repression, also existing in the family environment, as shown in the next section.

4 Family and moral values

Traditional family and conservative values were part of the ideological basis of the "New Order" that Franco's dictatorship established. The roles of men and women in the public and private spheres were clearly defined. Marriage, which was considered indissoluble, and procreation were considered basic purposes, and family structure, as a transmitter of those values, was extremely hierarchical.

In general, women in Franco's era had few rights: a man had to tutor her, and her radius of action was mainly domestic, while public life was reserved for men. A married woman was expected to play the role of housewife and mother and to take care of children, husband, and parents. If she wanted to work, she had to ask her husband for permission (see Section 5). Lola describes the social pressure to be a mother: *"Sometimes they also told me, 'What a pity that you are not going to have children, you will not have anyone to take care of you'"*. All female interviewees explain that the household chores were mainly assumed by them, but only Encarna admits that her husband wanted *"a person who knew how to cook, sew, buy . . . ; that was what interested him, otherwise, he didn't want her"*. Although, according to their narratives, most of the interviewees seem to have accepted the role assigned to them as women, many express that they were bored at home, which might indicate an only partial acceptance of their role in society (several female interviewees even started working due to boredom).

Several interviewees, especially women, point out that they had short courtships before getting married (Rosa, Juana, Encarna, Carme, but also Pedro). This may be related to what was expected of women, namely that their goal in life was to get married. Lola tells that, in addition to a lack of offspring, society *"was also very sorry when people did not marry, when women stayed single. This was said a lot, too, that it was important to marry, even if it was late, to marry someone, no matter who"*. Encarna, who married at the age of 23 years after two years of dating, shares that *"everyone would tell me 'Come on, come on!', and I would answer 'Oh, leave me alone'. I thought that I was not in a hurry, and they would tell me 'You are very silly'"*.

The interviewees report that their parents had a major influence on their lives, mainly with regard to their work life (see Section 5) and their affiliation to the deaf association (see Section 6), and that they were very demanding with them. When talking about the strictness at schools Nieves admits that *"parents were also hard on us. Many people forget families and think that only the nuns were like that, but they were all the same"*. The fact that parents demanded punctuality, for instance, was highlighted in four interviews, with Nieves, Lola, Encarna, and Amalia. In all cases, the curfew imposed by the families was 10pm. Nieves explains that *"other schoolmates had to run because, if they didn't, they would not eat until the next day!"*. Lola adds that, next to punctuality, her father forced his daughters to socialize only with girls until they got married, which suggests that the parents were anxious to preserve the reputation of their daughters before marriage.

The conservative values instilled into the interviewees are also manifested in their opinions about relationships, separations and divorces, or sexuality. With respect to the current high number of divorces, Lola expresses the opinion that *"today relations go very fast; there are many divorces, and I think it is very good that people divorce, but I also think that some patience is needed"*. The rejection of separations is more evident in the discourse of Encarna: *"At that time, life was better. Now, there are many problems, many separations, and at that time, there was none of this"*.

Likewise, Nieves remembers, on the one hand, how couples could not walk arm in arm through the village until they got married – in contrast to what happened in the city (Seville) – and, on the other hand, that nowadays, it is *"too much. They kiss, and they can even fuck in the street [. . .]. There is nothing in between."* Carme also recalls meeting her future husband when she was 15 years old. Because of a balance problem, he was unstable, and, wanting to help him, she innocently grabbed his arm, provoking reproachful looks for having touched a man. The morality of the time also prevented them from spending their first night as newlyweds in a hotel, because she was still 17 years old, and the hotel did not allow them to enter. Regarding their perspective on homosexuality, in general, most interviewees who talk about the topic do so with respect (Lola, Encarna, Rosa, Frederic, and Nieves), although they explain that during the Franco era, they did not know many homosexual people.

Given their different regional, linguistic, and class backgrounds, the experiences of the interviewees during their first socialization within the family are very diverse. However, the language issue is essential in most interviews. As indicated in the previous section, most interviewees grew up in hearing families and did not learn sign language until they started school. In the family environment, most claim to have communicated using a mixture of gestures, vocalizations, proper signs, and mime. Although some of the interviewees, namely Carlos and Antonio, admit to having communicated using signs with their family, the veto on sign language occasionally infiltrated the family sphere on the advice of school teachers. For example, Antonio states:

> *My mother told me that both in the school in Santiago and in Madrid, they asked her not to sign during holidays, that it was prohibited. [. . .] When I was older, my mother told me that she had regretted following their instructions in this regard.* (Antonio)

In other cases, the family went through a process of rejecting the use of sign language by their deaf child. According to Frederic,

> *at the "Puríssima" school [in Barcelona] I signed, and then at home, too, but my family didn't like to sign because they said it was ugly, which made me sad. So, I stopped signing and continued to speak.* (Frederic)

Despite the situations described, some interviewees report that they did not experience communication problems in the family, like in the case of Frederic. However, for other informants, the absence of a common language could lead to poor communication. For example, after narrating the imprisonment of his father and being interrogated by the interviewer for more details, Héctor states:

> Héctor: *I was curious, but it was very difficult for him to explain more.*
>
> Interviewer: *Sure, because communication wasn't good, right?*
>
> Héctor: *Sure, and he didn't sign anything.*

Óscar indicates that his brother warned him against using the communist greeting because he could get shot. However, initially he did not understand the warning, in part due to Óscar's young age at that moment, to his lack of background information, and to the lack of a language in common with his brother (as suggested by how Óscar narrates the way his brother talked to him, which is closer to mime or gestures than to sign language):

> *I knew that they had taken several people from the village and shot them, because there were several widows, and my brother told me, 'You see, they were communists, and they killed them for that', but I didn't know very well what he was talking about. Then in Santiago [at school], they started telling me more about those things; the director talked to me about greeting like the fascists, not like the communists, and there, I began to understand a little what was going on.* (Óscar)

In many cases, and even without fully sharing a common language, relatives, or, in their absence, neighbors or friends, interpreted for the deaf in order to meet their communicative needs (Encarna and Carlos). Jose, however, describes his experience as unsatisfactory:

> *At first, I went with my mother, but we didn't understand each other so well [. . .]. When the Confederación Nacional de Sordos de España ['National Confederation of the Deaf in Spain']⁵ interpretation service was created, I stopped going with my mother and always went with an interpreter.* (Jose)

Once being married to another deaf person, almost everyone claims to have communicated in sign language with their partner. An exception is the case of Nieves, who states that when she met her ex-husband, they used spoken language with each other, but once they got married, he began to sign. Still, he used to prevent her from using sign language in the street:

> *He did not accept that he was deaf. If we walked on the street signing, he became very angry because he did not want people to look at us. [. . .] He said: 'When we go out into the street, we use spoken language'. [. . .] He had a real complex about being deaf.* (Nieves)

---

5 The predecessor of the current State Confederation of the Deaf in Spain.

Although in married life both partners used sign language with each other, the language practices adopted within each family were rather diverse: Some did not sign to their children (Héctor); in other cases, communication between parents and children took place in the two modalities (Antonio and Emili), or in one language or the other depending on the parent. Pedro, for instance, says: *"With my wife, they [the children] use sign language, because she prefers so, but they also use spoken language. While with me, they use spoken language."* Sometimes, the fact that children did not know sign language could lead to a breakdown in communication. Encarna, for instance, explains:

> Encarna: *I used spoken language a lot, but my husband used more sign language.*
>
> Interviewer: *So, how did your husband communicate with your children?*
>
> Encarna: *In sign language, but many times, they told me 'Mom, what does he say?', they asked me 'What is he saying?', because they didn't understand him.*

In the case of Jose, the poor signing skills of their children are explained by the lack of complete socialization in this language. In addition, he highlights the centrality of associations of deaf people as an environment for socialization and the transmission of sign language:

> Jose: *[My children] only know the sign language we use in the family, which is more basic. Beyond that, no.*
>
> Interviewer: *Why not?*
>
> Jose: *Well, because they didn't want to come to the association. They just signed with the family.*

5 Work

In post-war Spain, progress achieved in social and labor conditions during the Second Republic by the popular classes were halted by the Franco dictatorship in order to restore "class power" (Sola 2014: 104), favoring the bourgeoisie. Until the 1950s, the regime established an autarkic economic policy, which sought self-reliance, the reduction of foreign trade, and intervention by the government, based on the Labor Law of 1938 and the 1940 laws of Trade Unity and Basis of the Trade Union Organization, among other provisions. The regime fixed workers' wages until the enactment of the Collective Agreements Act of 1958 (Sola 2014) and established that both employers and workers be integrated in vertical unions, that is, in government-dependent bodies that controlled workers and repressed them if they undertook industrial actions (Molinero & Ysàs 1993). Economic and labor policies caused a strong inflation, a decrease in consumption, a limitation in the growth of the industrial sector, and a pronounced economic inequality (Riquer 2010: ch. 5). As a result of these, rationing was established, and the clandestine market became widespread.

Given this economic depression, the Stabilization Plan was promulgated in 1959, which led to a growth in employment and productivity and to progressive industrialization (Riquer 2010: ch. 8). In this context, we note that most of the 19 people we interviewed had jobs that could be considered similar to those of the general population – taking into account the circumstances of the time, the deafness of the interviewees, and the fact that they did not have an official degree, not even for elementary studies (except for Pedro who obtained the title of draftsman through a correspondence course, and Lola who explains that she never needed degrees until she, as an adult, was asked to produce her primary school certificate). In fact, "[during the 1950s and 1960s] the expectations for the deaf students to stay and progress in the school system are low", and most of them did not pass the high school entrance exam (Alcina 2014: 303). As for their training, some draftsmen among the interviewees report that they learned the trade from a private teacher, usually a deaf person with or without official qualification who knew the craft, and since the training was in sign language, they managed to learn. In contrast, other interviewees, like Jose and the husband of Encarna, attended an official study academy, at which only spoken language was used, and they state that it was impossible for them to learn.

Although compulsory schooling was from six to 12 years of age until 1962 or 1964 (Egido 1994; Amich 2012), the age at completion of the studies varied from institution to institution. The Labor Contract Act of 1944 established 18 years as the threshold of working age, although under certain circumstances, it allowed a reduction to 14 years, or even lower ages, such as in agricultural work or in family workshops (Amich 2012). In fact, the initial age of employment of our interviewees just after finishing their studies ranges between 14 and 18 years. An exception is Óscar, who started working to help his father at seven-eight years of age, and was schooled from 15 to 20 years of age. Almost everyone's first job was obtained through the mediation of a relative, mostly the father or mother, uncle, cousin, or grandfather.

All interviewed men worked. The majority report to have worked as a draftsman, in addition to a woman who also had this profession, and some clarify that what they really did was to trace the work of some architect (Jose, Carlos, and Nieves). There were also quite a few who worked at a printing press, either as a bookbinder or a typesetter. Three interviewees worked in the metal industry as blacksmiths or in a factory of profiles and metal objects.

In applying the objectives of the "New Order", which established that the man was the economic provider of the family and relegated women to the role of mother and wife, the legislation was geared towards impeding the emancipation of women. However, despite what had been established by the Labor Court, according to which "the State [. . .] will free the married woman from the workshop and the factory" (art. II.1, p. 6179), a considerable number of the women interviewed also worked, four of them in the sewing industry, and others in other traditionally female professions (cleaning, hairdressing, etc.). Probably, the poor economic situation of the time pushed them to work, often in the informal economy.

As established by the Labor Contract Law, "the married woman, with the authorization of her husband" (art. 11 d) could be employed. We witness the effect of this provision in some accounts given in the interviewees. Amalia, for example, says:

> *When we got married, my husband wanted me to stop working and dedicate myself to being a housewife, and my father said, 'No kidding, you keep working here at the hairdresser [. . .], because if you do not work, then you will not have anything'.* (Amalia)

She therefore decided to continue working, which her husband accepted. In the case of Nieves, despite having a job she liked, and at a place where she was very comfortable with her workmates, she obeyed her husband; she says that *"his idea was [for me] to have children soon and to stop working"*, which she later regretted. Juana explains that when she got married, she also stopped working, but that over the years, she got bored and started cleaning a lady's house.

The case of Lola is a further interesting example of the hardness of the Franco era. She narrates that from a young age, she took care of the donkeys that pulled the waterwheel that drew water, so that the donkeys would not stop. Later, when they had a generator, she was in charge of turning it on because she had the necessary strength, and she also milked the goats, etc. She then worked in various trades until she became a laborer in a team of street workers at the town hall, composed mostly of men, and ended up working as a cleaner in a hospital.

The workweek was from Monday to Saturday, with rest only on Sunday, and none of the interviewees talks about working conditions, vacations, etc. Some of them, like Teresa, worked in the black economy sector without the right to unemployment or Social Security benefits; most do not say so explicitly, but the conditions of work they describe (at home, for parents, etc.) suggest that this was the situation. It was very common to have more than one job, hard work on a piecework basis, and often at the home of the parents of the interviewees, who forced their children to help them (as, for instance, in the case of Pedro and Óscar). Teresa, for example, had to go find a particular fabric at a far-away place, bring it home for her mother to sew, and once finished, take it back and bring back more. In addition, two interviewees (Teresa and Pedro) report that they had to accompany their mothers to the house of clients to whom they provided hairdressing at home. Carme worked as a seamstress and in a thermometer company until her mother-in-law told her to quit; from then on, they sewed all kinds of garments at home.

Four of the people interviewed became owners of their own businesses and two, managers. Héctor was in charge of a Mercedes dealership abroad, and later had his own car mechanics workshop in Seville, but he was in permanent conflict with his father, who always insisted that he should have a hearing partner. Amalia set up her own hairdresser salon as a freelancer and did all the necessary paperwork with the help of her mother-in-law. Frederic's mother set up a dental prosthesis laboratory at home, which he later took over and in which he worked until his retirement. Francesc had worked in the tailor shop of his grandfather since he was 14 years; the grandfather transferred the shop to his father and uncle, and finally Francesc took it over by paying a monthly fee to his uncle.

Regarding communication with co-workers and clients, the seven interviewees who mention this topic all state that they experienced little difficulties. Of those who ran a business, Amalia explains that she mainly communicated with clients through lip-reading. In contrast, Nieves tells that her ex-husband employed hearing people, and that he did not hire deaf people because it would have been more difficult for them to communicate with clients, while her father, who had a photography shop, knew what his customers wanted by pointing to samples and asking them: *"What kind of photos do you want? Half body, full body . . . ? I didn't see that there were major communication problems, and he had a great ability to communicate".*

Of the interviewees who worked as employees, Carlos and Rosa had deaf colleagues, and they consider that both with them and with hearing fellow workers, the communication was good. As for communication with hearing colleagues, two interviewees (Carlos and the husband of Inés) remember it as very positive, as they worked in the same company for a long time. The way of communicating was varied: They either used writing (Carlos and Pedro with their boss), a mixture of sign language, oral language, and gesture (Rosa), or relied on the mediation of a co-worker (Jose). Only Pedro reports that his deafness had been perceived as a problem by his boss, who told him: *"It is a pity, because if you were hearing, I would always keep you with me".*

Regarding a comparison between the working situation of the deaf during the Franco era and the current situation, some interviewees believe that nowadays, the deaf are better prepared as they have access to an education that allows them to receive an official and approved title, something that in their times was impossible or unnecessary (Jose, Inés, and Lola). However, they also point out that in their time, despite the lack of adequate labor legislation that would defend the most vulnerable against the abuse of employers, the deaf had better and more varied jobs in general, especially manual ones, were well respected, and received a salary in line with the average. Similarly, Lola recalls that back then,

> there was no talk of disability, the deaf were paid the same as hearing peers, and it was much easier for them to find work. On the other hand, deaf people now sell ONCE [blind and deaf-blind organization] coupons or work in special work centers. (Lola)

According to the interviewees, although there are currently a lot of training possibilities and more protection for the deaf, paradoxically the jobs are worse and very limited, and mostly in out-sourced cleaning companies.

6 Associations and social contexts

During the Civil War, and especially in its last days, the Franco government began to establish the basis for controlling the country and started to put pressure on groups with an ideology conflicting with that of the regime, prohibiting those associations that were not loyal to the National Movement (see footnote 3), and at the same time promoting those associations linked to the Catholic religion, falangism, the military, etc. The promulgation of the decree of January 25, 1941, on the regulation of the exercise of the right of association contributed to the control and repression of associations. In the province of Barcelona, for example, out of 3,599 associations registered before the war, only 300 were still registered in the 1940s (Riquer 2010: 344).

As for associations for deaf people in Spain, before the Civil War, several had already existed. In 1935, the First Assembly of Societies of Deaf-mutes was organized in Barcelona. According to Carlos, the presidents of seven associations met at the congress to discuss ideas for a better future, at the initiative of the Catalan deaf leader Àngel Calafell.[6] As a result, the *Federación Nacional de Sociedades de Sordomudos de España (FNSSE)* ('National Federation of Societies of Deaf-mutes of Spain'), the current *Confederación Estatal de Personas Sordas (CNSE)* ('State Confederation of the Deaf in Spain'), was founded on June 15, 1936, during

---

6 In his memoirs, Calafell (2011: 130), like Carlos, says that seven delegations attended the event. Besides, he states that there were ten deaf associations at that time in Spain, whereas Marroquín (1985: 63) mentions the existence of 15 associations in 1935.

the Second Assembly of Societies of Deaf-mutes (Calafell 2011: ch. XIV). The National Federation was born in Barcelona and constituted in Madrid (Yuste 2003: 64). However, its activities were stopped by the start of the Civil War on July 18, 1936 – similar to what happened to some other associations.

According to Carlos, during the war, as Franco's troops advanced, many deaf people from Spain went into exile and sought refuge in Catalonia, which was still a Republic (see footnote 2). Once there, Àngel Calafell tried to find a place for them to stay, as Carlos and Carme mention. In fact, in Barcelona, there was the *Refugio de Guerra para Sordomudos* ('War Shelter for Deaf-mutes') since late 1937 (Calafell 2011: 142). Juan Luis Marroquín, then president of the *Asociación de Sordomudos de Madrid* ('Association of the Deaf-mutes of Madrid') and of communist ideology (*"as was known by all"*, according to Jose), fearing for his own safety in Madrid, also travelled to Barcelona, where he was welcomed by Calafell, as explained by Carlos, and stayed there for several years. Calafell, in Catalonia, and Marroquín, in Madrid, were two recognized and important deaf leaders, and later Félix Jesús Pinedo, too, as the interviewees remark. At that time, the fact that Calafell wrote not only in Spanish but also in Catalan, was considered as highly remarkable, as Nieves explains. As for Marroquín, he was considered a role model, like a second father, for many deaf people.

When the war was over, the decree that established tough regulations regarding the creation and the promotion of associations linked to religion also influenced the deaf community. The *Organización Nacional de Acción Católica del Sordomudo de España* ('National Organization of Catholic Action of the Deaf-mutes of Spain') was founded in opposition to the National Federation (Calafell 2011: ch. XXI). The first local Catholic Action association was set up in Madrid in 1939 (Jose), followed by Barcelona, in 1941 (Calafell 2011: ch. XIX), Valencia, Valladolid, and Mallorca, in 1942 (Barceló-Coblijn 2018), among others. Estanislao Martín, director of the Madrid school for deaf children "Ponce de León", and a fervent Catholic with a close relationship with Franco, according to Francesc, promoted the creation of local deaf associations of this organization across Spain, always led by people linked to the regime. Jose used to go to the Catholic Action in Madrid, and he points out that *"it was of right-wing ideology, and there was little talking. People would speak well of Franco [. . .]. Since Franco had won, people would tell and speak very little"*.

Therefore, at that time, two types of associations co-existed. On the one hand, there were those we call "traditional", which were disconnected from religion and politics and had the main objective of being a social club for deaf people. These traditional associations included those that predated and had survived the Civil War and also those that were created afterwards with a similar philosophy. On the other hand, there were the Catholic associations, which were created after the triumph of Francoism.

The creation of the Catholic associations was accompanied by a strong pressure on the traditional deaf associations. As reported by Jose, when the *Acción Católica de Sordomudos de Madrid* ('Catholic Action of Deaf-mutes of Madrid'), which was right-wing, was founded, it attacked the Association of the Deaf-mutes of Madrid, the traditional one. This caused the regime to investigate whether there was communist propaganda in the association and, should that be the case, to close it. The majority of members of the traditional Madrid association indeed sympathized with communism even if they did not express this during the postwar period. Still, according to Jose, when the Deaf association in Madrid began to face serious problems, members begged Marroquín, who was still in Barcelona, to return, which he did. According to Carlos, Marroquín then also got involved in the National Federation. Finally, as explained by Jose, the problems with the regime ended when the deaf association was joined by a Francoist hearing person, who confirmed that they were all falangists and that there were no communists. From then on, Marroquín, despite his ideology and philosophy contrary to Francoism, continued his struggle to work for the deaf. Jose tells that when Marroquín went to meet Franco, it was to improve the lives of deaf people, to request money, but that his ideology remained the same. Since 1950, Marroquín, as president of the National Federation (Martos Contreras 2016),[7] travelled to different parts of the territory to contribute to the creation and development of the traditional associations, not the Catholic ones, as Francesc explains.

In Barcelona, the *Casa de Sordomudos de Barcelona* ('House of Deaf-mutes of Barcelona') also suffered from pressures, just like the Association of the Deaf-mutes in Madrid. Calafell (2011: ch. XIX) reports that the foundation of the association *Acción Católica de Sordomudos de Barcelona* ('Catholic Action of Deaf-mutes in Barcelona') created quarrels within the city's deaf community. To overcome these conflicts and to unify the associations, a Moral Order Commission was created, which ordered the expulsion of three individuals from the House: one for being homosexual, another one for prostitution, and the third one, who was Calafell's second partner, for not being married by the Church (Calafell 2011: ch. XXI). Carlos describes this situation as resulting from the values of the time: *"During the Franco regime, this was not accepted, it was not allowed. We had to respect the sanctity of marriage"*. Carme also remembers this particular situation.

---

[7] According to Martos Contreras (2016), when the National Federation was reinstated in 1950, after the First National Congress of the Deaf one year before, the central office was in Barcelona; however, due to the centralist mentality of that period, it was moved to Madrid in 1953.

She explains that, due to the mentality of the time, Calafell and his second partner were said to be lovers. The reality was that they could not marry because he was separated from his ex-wife but not yet divorced, as this was prohibited by the Francoist regime.

The nature of the co-existence of traditional and Catholic associations led deaf people who wanted to join an association to have to choose between one of the two types. However, religion was not the main reason to associate with the Catholic ones. Teresa mentions sign language, rather than religion, as her personal motivation for going to a religious association. During the last years of the Franco Regime, some Catholic associations changed their characteristics or even split up. One of these was the Barcelona-based Cerecusor: they maintained the Catholic association and created another non-religious one, the two being located at the same place. In this way, Cerecusor could join the National Federation, which did not allow the affiliation of Catholic associations, explains Francesc. Likewise, according to Francesc, creating a parallel traditional association was also a strategy for receiving double funding, from the Church and from the government, since the Catholic associations eventually received less financial support from the Church.

Normally, deaf school alumni were directly affiliated with deaf associations, although this was not always the case. Their parents sometimes were against their joining an association, as happened to Rosa, who was told by her angry mother not to go to the association. Francesc describes the process of entering the association as follows:

> My parents did not want me to be a member of the deaf association. They thought that if I went, my way of speaking would get worse. [. . .] I would escape and arrive home late, and told them that I was going out with friends. I was doing this more and more, and my father was getting irritated. But I usually got bored with hearing people. My father punished me, he scolded me. [. . .] As time went by, my mother and sister accepted what I was doing, since I enjoyed it. In the end, I signed up for the association. (Francesc)

In addition, the associations also attracted people who had never attended deaf schools. Encarna, who despite having two deaf brothers did not know sign language, recalls how she entered the association:

> One day, I was going with my brother down the street. He was 17 years, and I was 19. We saw a group of deaf people. We approached them, greeted them, but we did not understand anything they said [. . .]. At that time, sign language gave me a lot of headache, because I wasn't used to it. Then, little by little, from the age of 21, when I became a member of this association [. . .], I began to meet more people. [. . .] I learned sign language in the association. Deaf people taught me. (Encarna)

Franco's gender policy, aimed at minimizing the public life of women (Molinero 2004), also had an impact on women's participation in associations, as described by Pedro, son of deaf parents: *"At that time [in the first years of the post-war period], it was forbidden for women to associate, but my mother used to go to the association anyways"*. Women could only access as companions, but they did not appear as members. By 1950, women began to be allowed as members, says Pedro. Still, in some Catholic associations, when mass was celebrated, men and women sat separately. In addition, other religious events were organized specifically for women by women, and for men by men, as Frederic mentions.

The interviewees also shared other anecdotes that show the strong influence of the regime's conservative values in the associations. For example, the son of Rosa was banned from the association in the early 1970s for five years for wearing long hair. Antonio recalls that in the Catholic Action of Deaf-mutes of Madrid *"fines were imposed for misbehavior, of 10 pesetas, because there was a moral statute at that time. Morality was given a lot of importance"*. Antonio also tells how movies were inspected in an association because some people believed they were pornographic.

The fact that some associations did not accept as members people who were already member of another type of association (Catholic or traditional) affected people. Sometimes, according to Rosa, during parties held outside the association, people would fall in love with someone who was associated with another type of association. If they ended up being a couple, then one of them normally left his or her association to join the other one. Occasionally, even a young couple that fell in love would leave the association in which their parents were to join the other one. Right after the beginning of post-Francoism, regional federations began to be set up. The first one that was founded in Spain was the *Federación de Sordos de la Comunidad de Valencia* ('Federation of the Deaf of the Community of Valencia'), as Lola reports. According to her, once democracy had been established and the monarchy restored, attitudes did not immediately change, since the Francoist atmosphere was still alive. It took some years for the change to be noticed.

7 Concluding remarks

The accounts by the deaf people we interviewed highlight that the Franco Regime has had an impact on all the aspects of their lives that we have analyzed. Likewise, we have observed in the sample studied, as have other studies on attitudes towards Francoism (Font 2004), a great complexity in the perceptions of the dictatorial regime.

The data obtained show in part what the mechanisms of the dictatorial government were in establishing the "New State". We have mainly found evidence for this in the stories about the educational system in which the deaf interviewees were schooled, about the (mis)information they received during the Franco regime, and about the recent history of associations for deaf people. Education, which was basically in the hands of the Catholic Church, instilled submission to authoritarianism and to a hierarchical social structure, promoted the acceptance of the exercise of repressive control, and infused conservative and traditional moral values. As for the information they received, we have seen that many interviewees realized later that it was biased. Yet, the information that reached them from within the family was generally not questioned, and there is few data that would indicate that they saw as problematic what their relatives told them about the Civil War and Franco. Regarding the history of the associations during the Franco regime, we observe a clear impact of the regime on the associations' future, as the regime exercised social control through them, especially during the post-war period. However, only few interviewees mentioned episodes documenting the infiltration of Franco's values and of mechanisms of regime control into the associations.

Still, the actual effects of these mechanisms have been made visible in the interviewees' stories, mainly in their perspectives on political and moral values, but also in their stories about work experiences. In their remarks on politics, we have identified passivity, conformity, and depoliticization, attitudes already studied in previous research on Francoism (Font 2004). Also, some moral values expressed during the interviews are similar to those of the Franco era. Although in politics and moral values the interviews show a development and openness, this is not something that can be generalized over the whole sample or over the complete set of aspects analyzed. For example, while almost all respondents who talked about homosexuality rejected discrimination against gays and lesbians, thus showing a liberal mindset, there were more respondents who criticized the fact that divorces are currently so common, thus adhering to conservative values. Regarding their work experiences, we have not found direct criticism of Franco's measures such as the legal provisions that contributed to relegate women to the private sphere, the lack of welfare programs for deaf people (such as measures to improve the education of the deaf, interpreting services provision, work inclusion policies, etc.), or the high employment in shadow economy. Despite the problems at the time (economic and social inequality), interviews show a positive vision of the employment situation, which might contribute to their overall positive perspective on the regime.

Unlike other studies, we have not found evidence that would indicate that respondents were afraid of Francoism. We interpret this to be partly the result of the general misinformation of the time and also of the specific disinformation of the deaf community. Due to the fact that our group of interviewees consisted for the most part of deaf children of hearing parents, its members had little access to conversations between third parties and could not fully communicate with their parents. We therefore interpret the results from this lack-of-communication perspective. We conclude that the effect of fear was only experienced indirectly: the information that reached the interviewees was screened by hearing people, who probably had more information, but who either hid it or could not communicate it to their deaf relatives.

Based on the oral sources of 19 deaf people, this has been a first attempt to analyze how the deaf community that lived under the Franco dictatorship perceived it and how the regime impacted on their lives. Still, more research is needed to further support our findings, especially by increasing the sample size. Comparing the data according to the interviewees' age group (those that were born before and after 1940), gender, and origin, among other factors, would lead to a broader knowledge of the subject of study, as well as conducting new interviews explicitly focusing on this topic, and taking into account the results of this research for the design of the interviews. Most importantly, more evidence is needed to support the results that differ in part from previous studies conducted with hearing people, that is, the role of fear and misinformation in the attitudes of the deaf population towards Francoism.

Acknowledgements: This contribution has been possible thanks to the SIGN-HUB project, which has received funding from the European Union's Horizon 2020 research and innovation program under grant agreement No 693349, and to the Government of the Generalitat de Catalunya (2014 SGR 698). We wish to warmly thank all participants for their generosity in sharing their cultural and linguistic heritage, that is, their life stories, and the Deaf associations for providing the space to conduct some of the interviews. We would also like to express our sincere gratitude to the book editors for their careful and helpful comments.

References

Alcina, Alfredo. 2014. *La política educativa de las enseñanzas de sordomudos en España a través del Colegio Nacional de Sordomudos de Madrid (1875–2000)*. Universidad Nacional de Educación a Distancia.
Alfonso, José Manuel. 2002. La orientación católica de la enseñanza (1936–1939): principales disposiciones normativas. *Papeles Salmantinos de Educación* 1. 31–57.
Amich, Cristina. 2012. El trabajo de los menores de edad en la dictadura franquista. *Historia Contemporánea* 36. 163–192.
Barceló-Coblijn, Lluís. 2018. Aproximació sociolingüística a la llengua de signes a les Illes Balears. *Llengua, Societat i Comunicació* 16. 45–54.

Bourdieu, Pierre. 1977. Sur le pouvoir symbolique. *Annales: Économies, Sociétés, Civilisations* 32(3). 405–411.

Calafell, Àngel. 2011. *La meva vida silenciosa (1909–1962)*. Barcelona: Octaedro.

Egido, Immaculada. 1994. La evolución de la enseñanza primaria en España: organización de la etapa y programas de estudio. *Tendencias Pedagógicas* 1. 75–85.

Font, Jordi. 2004. "Nosotros no nos cuidábamos de la política". Fuentes orales y actitudes políticas en el franquismo. El ejemplo de una zona rural, 1939–1959. *Historia Social* 49. 49–66.

Hernández, Claudio. 2014. Más allá del consenso y la oposición: las actitudes de la "gente corriente" en regímenes dictatoriales. Una propuesta de análisis desde el régimen franquista. *Revista de Estudios Sociales* 50. 87–100.

Hernández, Claudio. 2016. En busca de la paz prometida: actitudes de normalización durante el primer franquismo (1936–1952). *Ayer: Revista de Historia Contemporánea* 104(4). 177–201.

Hernández, Claudio & Miguel Ángel del Arco. 2011. Más allá de las tapias de los cementerios: la represión cultural y socioeconómica en la España franquista (1936–1951). *Cuadernos de Historia Contemporánea* 33. 71–93.

Marroquín Cabiedas, Juan Luis. 1985. Fundación – Primera etapa 1936/49. In *Resumen histórico de la C.N.S.E. en sus bodas de oro*, 61–63. Confederación Nacional de Sordos de España. Retrieved from http://www.cnse.es/uploaded/publicaciones/bodas.pdf.

Martos Contreras, Emilia. 2016. *Personas mayores y diversidad funcional física e intelectual durante la transición a la democracia*. Almería, Spain: Universidad de Almería PhD dissertation.

Molinero, Carme. 2004. Mujer, represión y antifranquismo. *Historia del Presente* 4. 9–12.

Molinero, Carme & Pere Ysàs. 1993. Productores disciplinados: control y represión laboral durante el franquismo (1939–1958). *Cuadernos de Relaciones Laborales* 3. 33–49.

Morente, Francisco. 2001a. La depuración franquista del magisterio público. Un estado de la cuestión. *Hispania* 61(208). 661–688.

Morente, Francisco. 2001b. La muerte de una ilusión: el Magisterio español en la Guerra Civil y el primer franquismo. *Historia y Comunicación Social* 6. 187–201.

Riquer, Borja de. 2010. *La dictadura de Franco*. Sabadell: Crítica/Marcial Pons.

Sola, Jorge. 2014. El legado histórico franquista y el mercado de trabajo en España. *Revista Española de Sociología* 21. 99–125.

Viñao, Antonio. 2014. La educación en el franquismo (1936–1975). *Educar em Revista* 51. 19–35.

Yuste de Santos, Jesús. 2003. *Juan Luís Marroquín, la fuerza de la unidad*. Madrid: Fundación CNSE.

Part IV: **"He signs like me, we are the same":**
        Linguistic and educational perspectives

Jami N. Fisher, Julie A. Hochgesang, Meredith Tamminga, and Robyn Miller

Uncovering the lived experiences of elderly Deaf Philadelphians

1 Introduction

This chapter provides a general overview of the social, linguistic, and educational experiences of elderly Deaf[1] people from the Philadelphia area in the mid-Atlantic region of the United States. The information presented comes from a synthesis of data from the *Philadelphia Signs Project*, a collection of conversational interviews in American Sign Language (ASL) with Deaf Philadelphians. A review and analysis of these conversations reveal several predominant themes, highlighting the commonalities and differences amongst elderly Deaf Philadelphians.

Such points of discussion give insight into the evolving lived experience of elderly Deaf Philadelphians as shaped by their education, their work, and their socialization patterns from youth to the present day. These anecdotes make known the underlying values and connections coming from a shared Deaf experience, as well from having a shared sign language variety that anecdotally distinguishes members of this community from Deaf people from other regions in the United States. These interviews and conversations also uncover a hidden narrative implicit within the history of Deaf Philadelphians: The experiences of Black[2] Deaf Philadelphians were, in many ways, markedly different than those of white Deaf residents, particularly with respect to education locale and avenues for accessing a signed language. Ultimately, this review and synthesis of narratives by elderly Deaf Philadelphians will contribute to the historical record of local Deaf experiences as they are presented and documented now and in years to come.

---

[1] Convention over the last several decades has been to use a lower-case "d" to indicate audiological status and an upper-case "D" to indicate a Deaf cultural affiliation. A concern is that this distinction singles out only certain members of the larger Deaf community. Also, there are recent conversations among anthropologists and ethnographers (see https://twitter.com/EHowlett/status/1196692684787900416?s=20 for Twitter thread discussion) problematizing the capitalization of "deaf". The authors believe that all Deaf people share common experiences in navigating a majority-hearing world, and that this experience transcends educational location or signing ability. Thus, we will use the capital D inclusively throughout, to refer to all people who share these experiences.

[2] We are capitalizing Black here to reflect a cultural affiliation and not simply ethnicity or race.

For the purposes of this chapter, we have defined elderly as age 55 or above to include the diverse perspectives of multiple generations of elderly Deaf participants. At the time of the interviews, the ages ranged from 55–89 years old. We have analyzed a total of 15 participant and community-consultant contributions. Three of the 15 identify as Black, twelve are white; ten are women, five are men. The majority of participants come from hearing families, with three coming from a Deaf family with at least one Deaf parent and/or sibling. Some taught hearing family members to sign after they had learned a sign language at school, but most came from families who knew no sign at all (see Appendix A for details).

2 Background on the Philadelphia Signs Project

The Philadelphia Signs Project is a specialized corpus containing ASL conversational interviews between Deaf Philadelphians who are regular users of ASL. Its foundations are in the Philadelphia Deaf community's desire to document their self-noted regional dialect of ASL. At current count, we have almost 35 participants including 15 who are considered to be elderly or senior citizens.

The data collection protocol, drawing from previous work in ASL sociolinguistics (Lucas et al. 2001), is modeled on the sociolinguistic interview methods laid out by Labov (1984). The interview questions elicited narratives about the Philadelphia Deaf ASL users' lived experiences. The interviewers, all Philadelphia Deaf natives with strong ties to the local Deaf community and institutions, guided the interactions but gave considerable conversational latitude to the people being interviewed. Each interview was video-recorded from two perspectives: one capturing a frontal view of the participant, and the other capturing both the participant and the interviewer simultaneously.

The data[3] reside temporarily in cloud storage accessible to the research team, but will eventually be shared publicly online. Both interview and elicitation data have been annotated in ELAN (Wittenburg et al. 2006). Current data processing efforts focus on the minimum annotation required to make primary data accessible (e.g., Himmelmann 2006; Johnston 2010): adding both a loose translation into English and ID glosses for individual signs using the SLAAASh data annotation protocols (Hochgesang 2015). The ELAN annotation files are directly linked with the ASL Signbank External Controlled Vocabulary (Hochgesang et al. 2019) to ensure consistency of ID glosses both within our data and with other ASL

---

[3] These include primary video data as well as project metadata.

documentation projects. The quotes included throughout this chapter were translated by the first author rather than taken from the annotations.

We began our documentation efforts focusing on those participants who attended *Pennsylvania School for the Deaf* (PSD; see Figures 1 and 2), because the locus of sign language transmission tends to be through schools for the Deaf. However, throughout the course of our interviews, we found that many Deaf people in Philadelphia did not attend PSD. In particular, elderly Deaf people of color are sparsely represented in the PSD alumni community, despite the fact that demographic statistics would suggest – and photographic evidence[4] shows – that Deaf people of diverse racial and ethnic backgrounds lived in the Philadelphia

Figure 1: Front entrance of the Pennsylvania School for the Deaf (PSD), Mount Airy Campus, 1960.

---

4 Figure 3 is a photo hanging in the PSD Deaf Cultural Heritage Center from 1947 of the Silent Social Club, a club for Black Deaf people. There are at least 100 people in this photo. Based on personal communication with elderly Black Deaf Philadelphians, one of whom was at this gathering, we understand that this event was broadly regional in nature, drawing from the eastern half of the country, from the south, mid-west, and northeast (Anon., personal communication, 13 January 2019). Some commented that this gathering was a kind of support network for Black Deaf people, with different cities hosting guests from around the country traveling for camaraderie and social purposes.

Figure 2: Front entrance of Pennsylvania School for the Deaf (PSD), Mount Airy Campus, 1960.

area and attended social gatherings for Deaf people (see Figure 3).[5] Therefore, we broadened our inclusion criteria to any signing Deaf person who spent their formative years in Philadelphia. At the time of writing, we have connected with the *Pennsylvania Chapter of Black Deaf Advocates* (PCBDA), a local chapter of the *National Black Deaf Advocates*,[6] to recruit additional participants and document the experiences of Deaf racial and ethnic minority groups in Philadelphia.

---

5 After the 1980s, the population of Deaf minorities diversified beyond Black Deaf communities. We are working to include participants from various backgrounds amongst younger generations.
6 The *National Black Deaf Advocates* is an advocacy organization of Black Deaf and Hard-of-Hearing people in the United States, whose mission is "to promote the leadership development, economic and educational opportunities, social equality, and to safeguard the general health and welfare of Black Deaf and hard of hearing people" (National Black Deaf Advocates 2019).

Figure 3: Black Deaf Silent Social Club photo from 1947.

Most of the information used for analysis comes from the Philadelphia Signs Project interviews. At times, we felt some of the comments in the conversations warranted some follow-up, which, when possible, we did through in-person and videophone conversations. In some cases where we found gaps in the historical information, we were connected with community members not part of the project. We include the insight of those consultants as well. Those conversations are cited as personal communication.

3 Documenting Deaf experiences

Deaf histories and stories have typically been shared across generations in what Bahan (2006) calls a "face-to-face tradition", wherein Deaf people share and learn from each other through signed stories and storytelling. Historically, these stories could only be shared from person to person since sign languages have no conventionalized written form. The advent of film enabled documentation and proliferation of stories and histories in the signed modality which, in turn, serve to preserve the memories and stories of Deaf people. It is in this tradition that we set forth on documenting the histories and language of members of the Philadelphia Deaf. We are far from the first to document for the sake of posterity; indeed, in an authoritative attempt to push back against the oralist onslaught in Deaf education, the National Association of the Deaf raised funds to preserve its sign language in the newly developed film medium (see, for example, George Veditz's 1913 "Preservation of the Sign Language"). While some Deaf people themselves have used film to document the everyday lives of Deaf people (see Supalla 1991, 1995), many of the stories of the face-to-face tradition have been lost to the changing landscape of Deaf community interactions, not to mention rapid technological changes that can render recording mediums obsolete in a decade or less.

Some scholars have made deliberate efforts to preserve these stories in naturalistic form. Bahan and Bauman collected what they call "Deaf Life Stories" from 2001–2006 in order to understand American Deaf people's experiences (Bahan & Bauman 2005; Bahan 2018). Lucas et al. (2002) documented ASL conversations from seven different regions in the United States to better understand regional differences in ASL. Meanwhile, the 2011 work of McCaskill et al. was one of the first to document publicly and analyze how Black ASL differs from the pan-regional variety used by white Deaf Americans. Since then, other efforts to document and understand regional variation in ASL have slowly come forward. It is in this vein that we attempt to document and understand the Philadelphia variety of ASL.

A rich depiction of socio-historical context is exceedingly important in understanding the lived reality of a particular group of people in a specific time and place. For example, Hill (2017) details how socio-historical context is essential in understanding the development of Black ASL. Meanwhile, Barron (2017) describes how students in Canadian Deaf residential school settings banded together to combat oralist pedagogy and practices in the late 1880s–1920s. To these ends, Fisher et al. (2018) provided an initial overview of the Philadelphia Deaf community vis-à-vis education policy and language use at PSD. We chose the PSD site for our initial foray into contextualizing the Philadelphia Deaf community because of the pervasive – yet perhaps reductionist – presumption that sign languages proliferate from Deaf person to person primarily within the Deaf school context. However, upon deeper investigation, we recognize that a signing Deaf school experience was not the only way that Deaf people come to learn ASL in Philadelphia. The following section briefly recaps the history of PSD and discusses how alternative educational options may have been chosen – this is important background to our discussion of education, language, and race in the experiences of elderly Deaf Philadelphians.

4 A brief history of Deaf education in Philadelphia

Education for Deaf children in Philadelphia came not long after the first manualist Deaf school was established in Hartford, Connecticut, in 1817. The *Pennsylvania*

Institution for the Instruction of the Deaf and Dumb (PIDD)[7] was founded in 1820 by Philadelphia merchant David Seixas. It began as a manualist school, espousing an instructional methodology centered on sign language and hiring Deaf teachers as instructors. Over the years, the school followed the trend toward oralism; by 1910, it was entirely oralist, with a purported total banishment of signs for Deaf students (Hutchinson 1912: 11). But by all accounts, Deaf children at PSD persisted in their use of signs in dormitories, playgrounds, and in vocational settings. Furthermore, the vocational school still employed Deaf teachers, even though only hearing teachers were employed in teaching academically tracked (nonvocational) students. Though Deaf students would be punished – sometimes physically – for using signs in class, many of our participants tell stories of their persistence with respect to signing, giving implicit and explicit nods to the integral nature of signed language to their lives.

Not everyone who was Deaf in Philadelphia attended PSD. Some attended the oralist day program at the *W.H. Martin School* (see Figure 4) or a parochial program at the *Archbishop Ryan Memorial Institute for the Deaf*,[8] also historically oralist. The coexistence of these programs for the Deaf is well-known in Deaf circles in Philadelphia, but the reasoning behind families sending their children to one school over the other is less understood. PSD was a residential school that drew from a broad area beyond the city of Philadelphia. This meant that families of Deaf children who lived outside the city – especially in rural areas – typically only had one option for schooling: PSD. Families who lived in the city, however, could choose from PSD, the *Martin School*, or the *Archbishop Ryan School*. Through our data and anecdotal accounts from community members, we know that one factor in how families decided to educate their Deaf children was the recommendations of physicians, who overwhelmingly recommended oralist programs.[9] This is unsurprising since the oralist model and assimilationist

---

[7] The school has had three names during its existence: *Pennsylvania Institution for the Deaf and Dumb* (PIDD), which was changed to *Pennsylvania Institution for the Deaf* (PID) in 1925, then to *Pennsylvania School for the Deaf* in 1934. We will refer to the school as it was called contemporaneously, unless our participants name it differently. The name PSD will be used for general references to the school not connected to a particular time.
[8] Now known as *Archbishop Ryan Academy for the Deaf*.
[9] It should be noted that some of our participants and community contacts reported instances where families of Deaf children were told to send their child to a school or institution for mentally handicapped children. Others have reported knowing Deaf Philadelphians who had never attended school at all. These are tragic artifacts of hearing hegemony that must be acknowledged. We do not, however, have direct accounts of these people's experiences, so we do not address them in detail here. For a full account of one Black Deaf person mistakenly institutionalized for over six decades, see Burch & Joyner (2007).

Figure 4: W.H. Martin School (photo credit: Wikipedia Contributors 2019).

mentality pervaded the United States from the late 1880s until the early 1970s. Another factor affecting school choice is the day-school versus residential model; several participants commented that their families wanted to see their children daily and thus selected the day-school model (i.e., *Martin School* or *Archbishop Ryan School*) over PSD's residential model. Many of our white participants commented that they started out at the *Martin School* when reaching school age and then transferred to PSD when older, often following other peers who transferred from the day-school program.

The enrollment patterns for Black students at PSD was different than that of white students.[10] Two of our Black participants commented that upon reaching

---

10 In the interviews and conversations, there is no mention of enrollment of other students of color (Latinx, Asian, for example) at PSD until the 1970s and 1980s, which is why we do not

school age (six or seven years old), they started at a program like the *Martin School* but very quickly transferred to PSD because their families were not satisfied with the quality of education or progress there (see 160402_CherylA_A_1_17: 28–17:30 and 150131_JanieC_A_1:27–1:38[11]). But these cases seem to be somewhat exceptional: Our engagement with Black Deaf community members and organizations in Philadelphia reveals that a high percentage of Black Deaf Philadelphians did not attend PSD at all, with families typically opting for dayschool programs only.[12] Some of our Black participants and other consultants speculate that Black families were reluctant to send their children to live in a residential setting run by white dorm supervisors, who were both culturally different from – and potentially hostile to (as we discuss later) – Black students. There is also repeated commentary from our Black participants and other community members that many Black Deaf children were simply kept home by their families, thereby forgoing formal education entirely.

We recognize that the schooling decisions and the factors that influence them are personal in nature, and reasonings vary from family to family. However, these decisions were also constrained by larger political and socioeconomic factors which, in the aggregate, had a significant impact on the racial and ethnic makeup of each school. More specifically, the collective effects of family decisions on where to educate their Deaf children manifested in *de facto* racial segregation of Deaf children in Philadelphia which ultimately impacted how and when – or whether – they learned ASL during their school years. This segregation influenced participants' social and linguistic experiences as Deaf Philadelphians in ways we will discuss below.

---

mention them here. In fact, we know of very few Latinx and of no Asian Deaf people prior to the 1970s attending any of the local schools for the Deaf in Philadelphia. It is probable that they were part of the Deaf population in Philadelphia, but we have no data on them – anecdotal or otherwise – before the 1970s and 1980s.

11 Our filename convention is YYMMDD_ParticipantName_CameraView_#, in which YYMMDD are the digits for the year, month, and day, e.g., January 10, 2020 is thus 200110.

12 Based on anecdotes from participants and other consultants, some themselves Black, as well as school photographs and other archival information, the number of Black students at PSD was historically quite low – sometimes only three or four in the whole school at a given time – until the 1970s and 1980s. We also see PSD becoming more frequently populated with Black students in the 1970s with a full integration after 1984 when the School District of Philadelphia and PSD reached an agreement to close the *Martin School* program for Deaf students for children kindergarten through eighth grade (ages 5–14) and PSD to close its high school program (ages 14–21). This integration had other impacts on the social makeup of the school. See Fisher et al. (2018) for more details.

5 Emerging themes in the lives of elderly Deaf Philadelphians

Common themes emerged from the analysis of elderly participants' conversations. Far and away, the majority of themes are positive recollections of connections to other Deaf peers, initially through schooling, but also throughout their lifetimes. Participants regularly commented on how schools, sports, and other Deaf community gathering places had greatly impacted their lives, which is commonly noted in the literature (e.g., Burch 2002; Edwards 2012). Yet, not all are positive memories. We see repeated accounts of oppressive mindsets and cruelty of hearing people toward our participants, whether they be in the school experience or in the broader community. In the school context, these are most clearly the manifestation of oralist pedagogy, which had lasting impacts on all of our participants in their formative years and beyond. Outside of school, hearing hegemony was simultaneously a force that pushed Deaf people together and gave them motivation for resistance (see Jankowski (1997) and Burch (2002) for historical analysis).

We focus here on three themes of importance to our elderly Deaf Philadelphian participants: (i) the social and linguistic impacts of residential schooling (Section 5.1); (ii) variation and change over time in Philadelphia ASL (Section 5.2); and (iii) a preliminary glimpse into the educational and social experiences of Black Deaf Philadelphians (Section 5.3). Under the first theme, we include first-day-of-school accounts provided by many of our participants, which contextualize the individual and collective school experiences that have proven to be formative in the participants' lives. Under the second theme, we discuss participants' attachment to and opinions of Philadelphia lexical variants, as well as social and communicative influences on their decisions to use or repress Philadelphia-specific signs. Under the third theme, we discuss the overlooked experiences of Black Deaf Philadelphians, exploring the factors that facilitated and inhibited integration with white Deaf Philadelphians in the time when our participants were growing up. Although far from comprehensive, these themes present new insight into the lived experiences of elderly Deaf Philadelphians.

5.1 Theme 1: Social and linguistic impacts of residential schooling

For those participants who attended PSD, there was an overwhelming sentiment that commonality of school experiences was a unifying factor both socially and linguistically. It is unsurprising that the Deaf school experience in Philadelphia would bring together otherwise disparate individuals; Deafness was the sole factor that pooled together students, often from distant towns and sometimes from a variety of religious and ethnic backgrounds. One of our participants recalls affectionately, *"My good friend . . . [and I], we had the same problems. I was too young. He was too fat."* [150727_JayB_CU_1_13:25–13:33]. Despite their differences, they bonded and were *"friends for a lifetime"* [150727_JayB_CU_1_16: 52–16:54]. In all, our participants commonly harbored high regard for the social connections and lifelong friendships that a Deaf school experience afforded them (see Appendix B for time stamps and links to corresponding video clips).

In the residential school context, participants experienced milestones that shaped their lives forever. Many recall disorientation and trauma of being dropped off at a residential school for the first time while also revealing quick relief in learning their first signs from their Deaf peers. Our participants who attended the *Martin School* solely did not reveal any particularly notable first-day experiences, so they are not included here. Some who attended *Martin School* and then transferred to PSD did note a difference in their experiences, which are included below.

For most of our participants, first-day-of-school and dormitory experiences are rife with memories of initial awkwardness and discomfort at the transition to the residential school from home. One participant, Peggy, recounts how uncomfortably large PSD seemed to her upon arrival and expresses discomfort on her face at this memory [160307_PeggyS_A_1_8:30–8:38]. She later says (see Figure 5 for an image of the dormitory, Cresheim Hall, that she refers to in the quote):

> *[The dormitory, Cresheim Hall] was huge compared to my small house.*
> [160307_PeggyS_A_1_10:21–10:26]

> *[. . .] it was huge, with stairs up to the dormitory with rows and rows of beds. [. . .] I was scared to go to bed. I went into bed and everyone was stone-cold asleep, but I was wide awake, scared.* [160307_PeggyS_A_1_10:42–10:54]

Another participant, Cheryl, recalls:

> *When I transferred [to PSD], it was really awkward for me. I became homesick. When I was at the Martin School, I would commute from home to school daily, and I was accustomed to that. But at PSD, I would just stay. It was disorienting. I was like, "MOMMMM! WHERE'S MOM?", and I would cry. I would ask them to go home. And the dorm supervisor would say, "Sorry, you stay here until Friday". And I'd just sit there still, tucked into my bed. Others would say, "Hey! Come on! Come play!" And my friends would be playing around me.*
> [160402_CherylA_CU_1_14:38–14:53]

Figure 5: Cresheim Hall (elementary school) at PSD Mount Airy Campus; photo circa 1950s.

Of course, much of the consternation can be attributed to the fact that these were very young children – ranging in ages from 6 to 11 – who were leaving home for the first time. Additionally, the residential school setting was often a significant change from home life with respect to size, number of students, and everyday routines. Recurring reflections on these experiences are testimony to the lifelong imprint first-day-of school experiences have on participants' lives.

Compounding the first-day anxiety was a repeated notion that the hearing parents did not or could not fully and clearly communicate their plans for residential schooling to their Deaf children. This unfortunate phenomenon is grounded in the fact that participants typically did not have well-established language foundations before arriving to school. With the exception of participants who came from a Deaf family, there was no common language for communication beyond home signs and other gestures, which also ostensibly added to the first-day transition confusion. One participant, Irene, recalls that her Deaf father *"could not communicate with his father at all [emphatic expression]"*, and that communication amongst her immigrant grandparents and the rest of her Deaf family at home was *"not easy"* [170930_IreneK_A_1_12:

27–12:50]. An example of this limited communication is shown by Peggy, who describes being carefully escorted by her mother, grandmother, and dorm supervisor to the PSD dormitory, and then only upon saying goodbyes did she realize her family was leaving her. She thus protested their departure with dismay and in tears [160307_PeggyS_A_1_9:07–9:21].

Interestingly, several participants suggest that their quick acquisition of sign language served to mitigate these feelings of confusion and tumult. For example, Peggy immediately follows her expressions of fear and apprehension of her new school environment with the fact that she *"picked up signing and learned it fast"*, as she went along in the day-to-day activities at PSD [160307_PeggyS_A_1_9: 21–9:29]. Cheryl also suggests her disorientation was ameliorated by her socialization and language exposure at school when she says,

> It was different and disorienting [at first] but then I was like, "Oh!", and I would learn [the sign language]. Then it became easy to socialize. Then the dorm was better than home.
> [160402_CherylA_CU_1_16:02–16:07]

After agreeing with the interviewer's question whether transferring from the *Martin School* to PSD made her happier and more comfortable, she says,

> Yes. I would make modifications [to what I saw signed around me], and I would sign away. [She depicts examples of how she grew to be proficient and it made her a more social person at school]. Oh, I enjoyed it so. Really enjoyed it. I learned a lot. Yes.
> [160402_CherylA_CU_1_18:07–18:22]

Not everyone had a disorienting experience on the first day. One participant, Harrison, one of the few elderly Deaf participants in the Philadelphia Signs Project with Deaf family members, describes his peers' stunned reaction when he showed he already knew sign. He says,

> When I started PID, I was already skilled in sign because my parents were Deaf. The other kids were shocked [mouth agape] that I already knew sign. [They said,] "You're new and you're already skilled in sign! How?", and I said, "MOTHER-FATHER DEAF. BROTHER DEAF." They were all shocked."   [160307_HarrisonS_A_1_26:52–27:12]

In fact, four out of five of Harrison's siblings attended PID/PSD, which clearly afforded him the luxury of an easier transition to residential schooling.

Many, if not all, of our participants also described similar peer reactions to the arrival of a new student. Peggy recalls a lot of buzz over being the new girl when she arrived, which she found rather jarring. She describes entering the building with her suitcases and upon entering, *"throngs of girls came over saying, 'New girl! New girl!', and I just looked at them completely scared"* [160307_PeggyS_A_1_8: 58–9:07]. Wilma also describes her first night at PSD, explaining that she arrived late in the evening, and while unpacking her clothes and getting ready for bed, everyone just watched her, saying "Who is the new girl?" She was taken aback by all the attention [151101_WilmaJ_A_2:26–2:46].

For many participants, dormitory life was ultimately recalled quite positively. Rachel states,

> I enjoyed PSD. Loved it really [. . .] [because] there was more socializing. After dinner and study hour, there was more time with everyone to just chat away until bedtime. [Unlike] when I was home, I would just twiddle my thumbs. I couldn't stand it. I loved PSD very much. [151001_RachelA_2:48–3:09]

Cheryl remarks,

> [Despite the difficult beginning,] I continued [living in] the dorm and I enjoyed it. It was a good experience being able to communicate with Deaf people.
> [160402_CherylA_CU_1_15:11–15:16]

PSD often appealed to the social inclinations of Deaf students from other day-school programs. Sherry talks about the fact that she transferred to PSD because many of her friends from the *Martin School* were doing the same to play sports or to have a better social life. It was at that time that she learned to sign [150723_SherryD_A_1_24:06–24:49]. Pinky describes his tenacity in commitment to learning sign through his Deaf peers, despite never formally enrolling in PSD. He explains,

> I learned a lot of sign when I was eleven years old. For five years, every day I would go to PSD and learn, without being explicitly taught [. . .] At that time, I was hard-of-hearing, and most hard-of-hearing [people] were iffy with signing [ability]. Me, no. I was stubborn. I acted like a Deaf person, so I would go there, and I learned a lot for five years. That's how all the students knew me and were used to me. They thought I was actually a PSD student. I wasn't. But they knew me very well and have all these years.
> [150820_PinkyK_Part1_A_5:19–5:55]

For these Deaf Philadelphians, PSD encompassed all things important to a developing Deaf child: It was a place where one could explore a full social life in the residential school setting; sign language proliferated despite its official banishment; and Deaf peers – even ones not officially matriculated at the school – connected with one another, facilitated by their use of a signed language.

5.2 Theme 2: The Philadelphia variety of ASL

Reflections on sign language and its use pervade the interviews. Indeed, the transmission, suppression, and persistence of the sign language (as it is often referred to by our participants) are commonly identified themes in the experiences of signing Deaf people in general (see Brevik 2005; Padden & Humphries 2006; Jankowsky 1997; Edwards 2012; amongst many others). Two interesting linguistic sub-themes emerge from the conversations: The first is that many of the elderly Deaf see a marked distinction between the signing they learned and used growing up versus what is commonly known now as ASL; the second is that the variety of ASL that they use can be readily identified by themselves and others as distinctly Philadelphian.[13] Participants' linguistic self-reflections and analyses reflect pride in the use of the Philadelphia variety; a recognition and lamentation that the Philadelphia variety is being lost to more commonly used forms; an awareness of their own acquiescence to more commonly used forms in situations where Philadelphia signs would be viewed as conspicuous and perhaps criticized; and, in some cases, a dogged resistance to losing Philadelphia signs to the pan-regional variety of ASL.

5.2.1 Theme 2a: Differences between older and younger signers

One interesting occurrence within the interviews is a repeatedly demonstrated resistance to using the label ASL to describe participants' own signing while growing up. Many draw a clear distinction between the signing they used versus ASL used today. This may reflect the fact that the term 'American Sign Language' was not recognized until Stokoe's (1960) seminal observations, well after the formative years of our participants. One participant, Peggy, first describes her own signing growing up as *"home signs"*, presumably in reference to what she used with her hearing family at home. But later, she is asked by the interviewer, *"So, in your time, did you have that term, ASL?"* to which she responds,

> *No, well, we talked the same, but did we think of it as ASL? Now, I learn ASL is an abbreviation for [or synonymous with] talking.*[14]   [160307_PeggyS_A_1_27:14–27:32]

This description affirms the notion that their reluctance to call their old signing ASL might be because this was not the term used growing up.

---

[13] When participants talk about Philadelphia ASL, they exclusively mention lexical distinctions (Fisher et al. 2016). At the time of this writing, we do not have evidence that differences in the Philadelphia variety and the pan-regional ASL extend beyond the lexical level.

[14] Peggy actually uses the sign for TALK, as opposed to SIGN or PRODUCE-SIGN. All three signs can be found in the ASL Signbank (https://aslsignbank.haskins.yale.edu; Hochgesang, Crasborn & Lillo-Martin 2019) by searching for the gloss: TALK [ID gloss 289], SIGN [ID gloss 256], PRODUCE-SIGN [ID gloss 937]. If using the ID gloss number to locate the sign, use the following URL, then add the number after the last slash: https://aslsignbank.haskins.yale.edu/dictionary/gloss/.

However, others' comments on sign language use complicate this theory, showing, on the one hand, a more diverse use of signing and, on the other hand, what should, according to the participants, be categorized as ASL. In particular, one participant, Jay, objects to calling his signs ASL. Instead, he describes his signing as *"oral signs"* (Jay B, personal communication, 24 August 2017). When asked to explain what this means, he says that with ASL,

> *the mouth is closed shut [using no mouth movements]. And I understand none of it. With mouth movements and non-manuals, I catch the meaning and can understand better [. . .] ASL is produced [gestures all over the signing space] but I look [primarily in the head region]. With the closed mouth, I can't find the signs. Other people have no problem.*
> [Jay B, personal communication, 24 August 2017]

His descriptions and clarifications suggest that these "oral signs" are akin to what we now call SIM-COM[15] or perhaps a signing style that favors the structure of English rather than ASL. He explains that he learned this style of signing *"from the old PSD back in the 1930s and 40s"* from *"classmates from school [and] schoolmates outside of class"*. He continues, *"When I was in the vocational school, I learned more. Playing sports, I learned more signs"*, clearly distinguishing this signing and communication mode from what was used within the strictly oralist pedagogy wherein *"lip-reading, speech, [and] some subjects like reading and writing, arithmetic"* were exclusively used (Jay B, personal communication, 24 August 2017).

Jay does remark that some of his peers who signed like him changed their signing style to be more like what is currently known as ASL after socialization with other Deaf Philadelphians. He explains:

> *Many changed later. Leaving school, being involved in their homes, I met them at Deaf clubs or tournaments, and some changed. Few are still the same. For example, you know [name removed]? [. . .] He signs like me. We are the same. His wife [name removed], she was strongly involved in [a local Deaf organization]. Her signs changed. Now she signs [like ASL]. [. . .] Some old timers are the same. Many changed.*
> [Jay B, personal communication, 24 August 2017]

Jay's account of sign language use in the 1930s and 40s suggests an interesting distinction in the signing styles of the Deaf Philadelphians who spent most to all of their time in the academic track at PSD versus those who attended predominantly vocational classes (see Figure 6).[16] The academic classes were strictly oralist in nature; any signing produced in those settings resulted in

---

[15] SIM-COM stands for simultaneous communication, or when you sign and speak at the same time; for the sign, see ASL Signbank ID gloss 3289.
[16] See Fisher et al. (2018) for pedagogical approaches in academic versus vocational settings at PSD with respect to sign language use.

Figure 6: Morris Hall (vocational school), PSD Mount Airy Campus; photo circa 1960.

punishment. His time in the vocational classes and in extracurricular programming – settings where rules against sign language use were more lax – afforded him opportunities to learn more sign language. It is quite possible, then, that his "oral signs" are more of a signing style that incorporates the grammatical structure of English – what he used in his academic classes – but borrows the signs from ASL – what he learned from his peers in the vocational track and in sports. In all, his comments suggest that there were cohorts of students like him, revealing signing diversity within the PSD alumni community.

The last example of personal reflection on sign language use and its evolution over the years comes from Harrison, one of the oldest participants in the project, age 89 at the time of recording. Coming from a Deaf and signing family, Harrison rejects the view that the signs he used and what is known now as ASL are one and the same. He says, *"We would SIGN [ID gloss 256], not PRODUCE-SIGN [ID gloss 937]. Like, my parents, my father's brother, in school, my teacher"* [160307_HarrisonS_A_2_24:28–24:47].[17] When asked more specifically if the signing in the past was the same as signing today, Harrison says, *"Oh, it's changed.*

---

17 The sign PRODUCE-SIGN mentioned in the quote means something like "to sign more ASL". Signs mentioned in this and the following quotes as well as in the text can be found at ASL Signbank (see footnote 14) by searching for the ID gloss; in the text and within the quotes, we only provide the ID gloss number between brackets.

A lot. Many changes. Like what? I used to sign SHOES *[ID gloss 393], it was like this, shoes [depiction of sliding feet in]. They're all different"* [160307_HarrisonS_A_2_24: 54–25:14]. This exchange suggests that the changes Harrison has noticed reflect lexical differences rather than a structural change.

5.2.2 Theme 2b: Differences between Philadelphia ASL and other varieties

All of our participants were acutely aware and proud of their distinct variety of Philadelphia signing. They repeatedly recount the tensions that emerge from using this variety, bringing to life the social forces that underpin language variation and change. The differences just discussed between old and new forms intersect with regional specificity: the signs that people identify as Philadelphian are typically older signs, while the new signs reflect contact with other communities. Importantly, some elderly Philadelphians show dismay at the use of the newer forms, expressing a preference to keep their "old" signs. Others, however, concede to the fact that the newer, more commonly used signs are more clearly understood and were later, sometimes reluctantly, adopted by some participants. In the end, the lexical variants evident in the Philadelphia variety of ASL are the most salient indicators distinguishing a Deaf Philadelphian from signers hailing from other parts of the U.S. Unsurprisingly, then, lexical variation was one of the most repeated themes amongst all of our participants in the project.

One important factor that supports the maintenance of the Philadelphia ASL variety among elderly deaf Philadelphians is a tendency to stay within the Philadelphia Deaf community and/or limit contact with younger generations of Deaf Philadelphians. Sometimes participants would bring attention to their own signing differences by comparing their signs with others from outside communities, by comparing their own signs with those who left and came back, or by comparing their own old way of signing with their currently used form.

Cheryl describes her own acquisition of Philadelphia lexical variants and discusses how they are distinct from currently used or more common forms. She explains,

> *I would learn sign [at school and] I was like, "Oh!" I would take them as my own. The signs were old-fashioned.*[18] *Like* SCHOOL *[ID gloss 247] was signed [looks like dragging luggage] or [looks like moving a piece of paper in front of the face].* WORK *wasn't like [ID gloss 1450], it was [flat hand, one-handed shake].* [160402_CherylA_CU_1_15:56–15:59]

---

[18] Cheryl and others often use the words "old-fashioned" to describe the older Philadelphia variants or signs of older Deaf Philadelphians.

And though many highlighted the older variants specifically, it was common for participants to use the older forms of the Philadelphia variety without any commentary, thus suggesting that it was the more favored or only variant in their lexicon. Caroline, for example, describes her vocational schooling at PSD to be centered on cooking and sewing, and she expresses consternation that there was a lot of teacher turnover in the cooking program. She uses a form of COOK (Figure 7), which is no longer commonly used among Deaf Philadelphians [160307_CarolineZ_A_1_9:35].

Figure 7: Two segments of the old Philadelphia form of COOK; the movement is repeated.

Meanwhile, other participants make reference to the Philadelphia variety, noting its distinct difference from others. Peggy identifies the Philadelphia sign for PICNIC-CHEST [ID gloss 3295], but points out that some sign it differently, and that there is *"diversity"* in the use of that sign (e.g., PICNIC variants on ASL Signbank) [160307_PeggyS_A_1_32:08–32:16]. Harrison explains, *"I used to [sign] SQUIRREL-EAT [ID gloss 2623; Figures 8 and 9], but my son-in-law, who was at Gallaudet, signs SQUIRREL$_{neut}$ [ID gloss 739]"* [160307_HarrisonS_A_2_23:47–23:56].

Harrison makes passing reference to Gallaudet, which is culturally significant and the source of social and linguistic hierarchies within the Philadelphia Deaf community and beyond. Gallaudet[19] stands as a symbol of engagement with the

---

[19] Gallaudet University in Washington, D.C., USA, is the first postsecondary institution for deaf and hard-of-hearing people in the world. It was established in 1864.

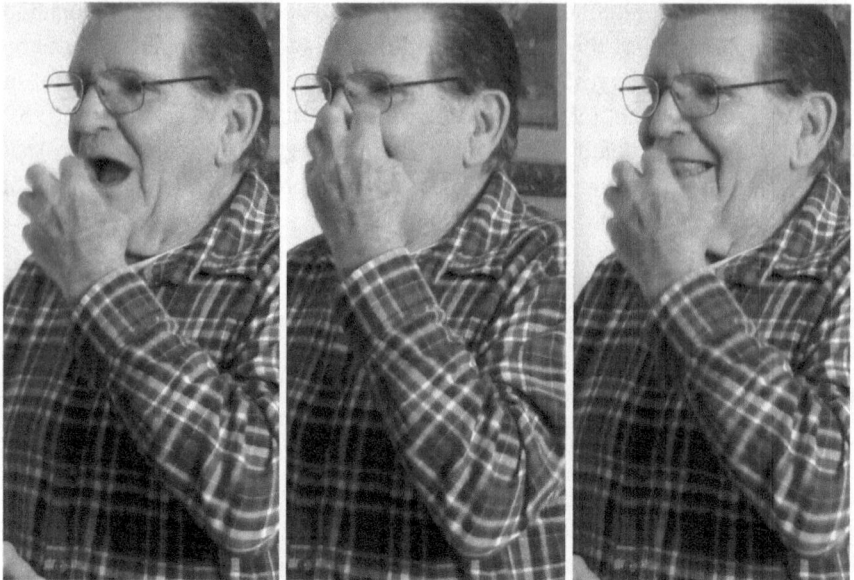

Figure 8: SQUIRREL-EAT, Philadelphia variant; 3 segments shown; the movement is repeated.

Figure 9: SQUIRREL-EAT, Philadelphia variant, side view of handshape.

Deaf world outside Philadelphia; the linguistic mark left by the Gallaudet experience reflects that engagement. Participants of all ages describe feeling disoriented or facing negative linguistic judgments when communicating with signers from outside communities. This was particularly noted in descriptions of attending Gallaudet and/or the high school on its campus, *Model Secondary School for the Deaf* [MSSD].[20,21] Under pressure to communicate clearly and fit in socially with signers from other areas, Philadelphia signers may shift toward linguistic forms that are used pan-regionally. Affiliation with Gallaudet is also an indicator of educational attainment, which may bring a boost in social (and perhaps economic) status but may also suggest a degree of alienation from Philadelphian identity. Convergence to outside signs was not necessarily viewed positively by Deaf Philadelphians who never left. For example, when Peggy is asked, "In your time, did the older Deaf people's signing look different?", she responds:

> *Yes, it was different. I would look up at them[22] and [she names a Philadelphia acquaintance's husband], he was from Gallaudet. He would come back for football games from Gallaudet [imitates his air of superiority], and he would fingerspell everything as if he was so advanced. I couldn't read the signs. Some of the communication, I couldn't catch because I was little and couldn't read the signs. Now, now that we are adults, we all sign the same.*
> [160307_PeggyS_A_1_30:12-30:49]

Based on the conversations from the interviews, it is apparent that Peggy and her family have, in later years, traveled extensively and met Deaf people from all over the U.S. Thus, it is not clear whether her last comment – *"as adults, we all sign the same"* – is a reflection on her own signing style having converged with pan-regional ASL, or whether she simply considers herself a more mature Philadelphia signer now, as compared to the younger signer in her memory. Regardless, in the recollection of this memory, she depicts a clear distinction between the signing style and the self-perceived higher social status of the visitor with a Gallaudet education, as compared to her own experience as a younger Deaf Philadelphian. In any case, her comment is an important glimpse into

---

20 Both of these schools draw from Deaf communities around the U.S. Gallaudet, as a college and now university, unsurprisingly attracts people from all over the U.S. and world. MSSD is a federally funded high school for Deaf students on Gallaudet's campus. Since it is federally funded, neither families nor school districts have to pay tuition to attend. This became an attractive option for Deaf Philadelphians looking for high school options between 1984 and 2000, when PSD no longer had a high school program on its campus. There was public school programming available as another option, but since neither cost money for families, many chose the residential Deaf school as a logical next step to a Deaf day-school model.
21 We also see this experience in younger generations of Deaf participants leaving Philadelphia for MSSD (see Fisher et al. (2016) for examples).
22 She was a young child then; her sign positioning suggests she means literally to look up at these people.

the social factors that impact language use and the effects that they have within the Philadelphia Deaf community.

5.2.3 Theme 2c: Maintaining or moving away from Philadelphia signs

In comparing both age groups and regional varieties in the previous two subthemes, we note a recurring tension between maintaining the older Philadelphia variants and succumbing to external forces that favor more commonly used, panregional lexical variants. Harrison acknowledges these external forces in his reflection on his own signing style. Asked whether he knew "any old Philadelphia signs", he says,

> I'm mixed [in my signing style], Deaf/hearing, old/young, WPSD[23] signs/PSD signs, different schools for the Deaf. You know I've traveled to and been in about 20 or 21 schools for the Deaf. [160307_HarrisonS_A_2_31:42–32:12]

In discussing her sign for EASTER [ID gloss 2883] – a sequential combination of RABBIT [ID gloss 59], BIRD [ID gloss 361], and the Philadelphia variant for WHITE-EGG [ID gloss 2617] signed in sequence – Peggy explains that she used that sign because *"everyone else around her did"* though upon going *"out into the world [outside Philadelphia]"*, she realized that the pan-regional variety, EGG [ID gloss 447], was much more commonly used [160307_PeggyS_A_1_27:47–28:30].

Some participants show that their transition to newer and more commonly used variants was more forced than voluntary. For example, Sherry explicitly states that she had to *"learn [the younger generation's signs]"* when she became a teacher's aide in a preschool class at PSD. She describes being *"corrected repeatedly"* for using her older variety and even experienced misunderstandings from the children's different sign usage [150723_SherryD_A_1_26:14–26:43]. Her reluctance to give up her old signs is most evident when she points out that she very quickly returned to the older sign variety – *"Not completely, but moving in that direction"* – upon retiring from her PSD job and socializing with her friends from the old PSD [150723_SherryD_A_1_27:45–28:00]. Clearly then, it is not just geography and experience with signers from other communities that influences the use of the older Philadelphia variety; younger generations, many of whom never had contact with the older generations of Philadelphia signers, also have an effect on the use or minimization of the Philadelphia variety.

---

[23] *Western Pennsylvania School for the Deaf* in Pittsburgh, Pennsylvania.

Not everyone shifted their behavior in response to these external pressures, however. A few show a conscious effort to resist the newer forms, choosing to maintain their older signs. Caroline talks about socializing with other Deaf senior citizens at a local gathering and explains that though she *"learns many new signs"* from her peers, who have modernized their own signing, she still uses her old PSD signs. She explains, *"They all understand me. Do I have to think about only new [signs]? No! I know everyone there and keeping my old signing [style] is fine."* [160307_CarolineZ_A_1_14:40–15:12]. She later mentions, *"Some of [the Deaf people] out there alert me that I must use the newer signs and eliminate [using] the old [ones]. I can't. I can't [do that]. I still use my old signs."* [160307_CarolineZ_A_1_20:39–20:50]. Meanwhile, Jay's comments reveal the pervasive value of these older signs, despite their uncommon usage today. He explains, *"I still use old signs. People make fun of me. But they really cherish [these signs that I use] because I'm like a relic."* (Jay B, personal communication, 24 August 20).

A few of the participants mention conflicts in staying with their old signs, particularly when socializing with younger generations of signers. Janie finds the more contemporary Philadelphia signing *"confusing"* [151031_JanieC_CU_6:38]. Furthermore, she is criticized by younger signers for using older forms like CHOCOLATE-CANDY [ID gloss 3082; see Figure 10] and PIE [ID gloss 3294], which she finds startling [151031_JanieC_CU_6:44–6:48]. She explains,

> My grandson[24] signs a little differently. [I see the signs] and I know they're new. [I] accept [their use]. I see the new signs and ask, "What's that?" He explains to me, and then I'm clear. How awful [the signs] are. [151031_JanieC_CU_7:09–7:22]

Overall, she finds herself preferring the older signs, explaining, *"It's hard to keep up with the young [signers], but I still use my old signs. I stay [the same]."* [151031_JanieC_CU_6:52–6:57]. Sticking with the older variant is not always easy, especially when it has a different meaning than intended. Sherry shows her struggle with her use of the old Philadelphia sign for 'dog', knowing that the more commonly used meaning of this sign is a racial slur. She says:

> It's hard for me to sign FS-DOG [the newer, fingerspelled variant]. In the past, [my son] would tell [his wife], "My mother uses this Philadelphia sign for 'dog'." [His wife] was like, "Hold on [don't use that sign]." I have to be mentally controlled [not to] [. . .] When I talk to other Philadelphians, I'd [probably] use this older sign for 'dog' because we all have common [knowledge of what it means]. [150723_SherryD_A_1_6:46–7:13]

---

[24] She signs "grandson" differently than some older Deaf Philadelphians, using the two-handed sign for GRANDMOTHER [ID gloss 862] and adding SON [ID gloss 1095] immediately after.

Figure 10: Philadelphia-area sign for CHOCOLATE-CANDY.

5.3 Theme 3: Educational and social experiences of Black Deaf Philadelphians

The thematic reflections detailed above are inclusive of all Deaf Philadelphians regardless of race. However, we feel it is imperative that we highlight the experience of Black Deaf Philadelphians in this next section, as their stories have been largely overlooked in the Philadelphia Deaf community history. One of the many pernicious outcomes of racism is how it supplants and suppresses the lived experiences and history of minorities within a community. Until now, the little documentation that exists on the Philadelphia Deaf experience – particularly in the archives and history of the *Pennsylvania School for the Deaf* – mostly centers on white Deaf people and their experiences. The history heretofore implicitly and explicitly marginalizes the lived experience of a significant subset of the Philadelphia Deaf community. The discussion and analysis in this chapter is thus a modest first step in bringing Black Deaf Philadelphians' stories into the written historical narrative about the broader Philadelphia Deaf community.

In their documentation and analysis of Black Deaf experiences and sign language use in the American South, McCaskill et al. (2011) uncover what they call the "hidden treasure" of Black ASL, the dialect used by Black Americans. The authors refer to Black ASL as a hidden treasure because its use and users were historically overshadowed by white Deaf people's experiences and signs. In many ways, we have found similar stories in the education and lives of Black Deaf Philadelphians: They were more likely to attend oralist day schools than their white Deaf peers; they learned ASL, but much later and from different sources than their white Deaf peers; their stories and signs are also not prominent in the Philadelphia Deaf community, as much of the historical documentation centers on a PSD educational experience. We believe that as in the southern Black Deaf communities, this separate schooling impacted Black Deaf Philadelphians both linguistically and socially.

Anecdotes from the community and commentary from conversations within our project corroborate the fact that there was a very small population of Black Deaf students at both PSD and the *Martin School* at the time our participants attended school (1930s–1970s). Jay, a lifelong Philadelphia resident and the first Deaf member of the PSD Board of Trustees, confirms that during his years there (entering in 1938), PSD was *"all white [students]. [. . .] Martin School was the same. Maybe one [Black] person."* (Jay B, personal communication, 24 August 2017). In the 1970s, PSD began to see more Black Deaf students, though most were shifted into vocational rather than academic programming (Anon., personal communication, 25 January 2019). In the 1970s and early 1980s, most of the Deaf children of color attended the *Martin School*, likely resulting from the fact that it was a public school in the city of Philadelphia, where most of the Deaf students of color resided.[25] A much larger influx of Deaf students of color including Latinx and Asian Deaf children moved to PSD in the mid-1980s after an agreement with the PSD Board and the School District of Philadelphia resulted in the closure of *Martin School* and PSD's high school program, leaving all Deaf students residing in the City of Philadelphia with only one option for kindergarten through 8th grade (ages 5–14) education: PSD (see Fisher et al. (2018) for more detailed information).

Because our recruitment efforts were originally focused on PSD, most of what we have learned from our participants about racial dynamics within the Deaf community relates to experiences at PSD. While the span of years that our participants attended PSD saw monumental social and educational shifts, social and residential segregation and racist attitudes from classmates and

---

25 The passage of federal Public Law 94–142, Education for All Handicapped Children Act, of 1975 may have also had a large impact on this school as a preferred option for Deaf students of color; this law required that students be placed in the Least Restrictive Environment – one that mandates maximum opportunities to interact with non-disabled peers. The *Martin School*, being a public school program, would have satisfied these criteria, whereas PSD would have been considered a more restrictive option and thus a last resort for educating Deaf children residing in the city of Philadelphia.

educators had lasting impacts on Black Deaf students in both subtle and overt ways. We now understand our original focus on PSD as itself a reflection of a white-centric view of the community, motivating us to seek out participants with different educational backgrounds in our current and future recruiting. The inner workings and effects of systemic racism in the Philadelphia Deaf community are complicated and will require careful unpacking in future work dedicated to the topic; our current evidence base and theoretical understanding are too incomplete to undertake such unpacking here. However, we include the following anecdotes as a preliminary way of highlighting some of the racialized dynamics and experiences that Black Deaf Philadelphians have encountered over the past century, acknowledging that the topic will require more attention than we are able to allot in this chapter.

During the 1930s through the 1950s, there were few Black Deaf children who attended PSD. One participant, Janie, entered PSD in 1944 and stayed until 1957. During that time, she recalls being one of only four Black students in all of PSD, with no Black teachers or dorm supervisors (Janie, personal communication, 6 March 2017).[26] Another Black Deaf consultant, who attended PSD from 1934–1950, corroborates this account, noting that during his time, there were three Black boys and two Black girls in all of PSD (Anon., personal communication, 13 January 2019). Both recall being required to sleep on separate floors designated for Black Deaf children and having to use restrooms that were the farthest away from everyday activity. Contrary to these residential experiences, there is no evidence of PSD classrooms being segregated at any point in its history. Both Janie and other participants and consultants confirm this to be fact (Janie, personal communication, 6 March 2017). Meanwhile, by Cheryl's time at PSD (1960s), dormitory segregation was ended. She says, *"We were all integrated. I enjoyed that and could play [with anyone]. We learned to communicate with each other and would play."* [160402_CherylA_CU_1_15:41–15:56].

For some participants, their educational trajectory and ability to comfortably socialize amongst white Deaf peers was dictated by racist mindsets of administrators, dorm counselors, and their white Deaf peers. For example, one Black Deaf consultant to our project recalls being placed into the vocational track upon arriving to PSD, despite having exceptional grades at the *Martin School*. Her parents, both Deaf and active in the Civil Rights movement, were

---

26 Janie is part of our participant cohort. Some of the anecdotes mentioned here were taken from a follow-up conversation with her – recorded but not part of the study – to clarify and enrich some of her experiences known to the authors but not included in the original conversation. The same is true for comments from Jay. If the cited comments are not from the formal interview, they are cited as personal communication, as we do here.

infuriated by the motion and confronted school administrators, resulting in her appropriate placement into the academic track (Anon., personal communication, 25 January 2019). Unlike the classroom, social extra-curriculars were segregated. Janie explains that dorm counselors required that

> at parties, Black students had to be in one group, while white students had to be in a separate group. This prevented students from one group to be interested in [dating] a person from another group. [Janie, personal communication, 6 March 2017]

She also recalls being rejected and taunted by her white Deaf peers, being made to play undesirable characters in group games, enduring repeated tormenting in the cafeteria and on the playground, and being *"prohibited"* by a dorm supervisor from going to prom with a white Deaf peer, who very much wanted her to be his date (Janie, personal communication, 6 March 2017).

Some teachers and dorm counselors actively intervened in curtailing racist behavior. Janie mentioned that some of the teachers *"favored her"* and forcefully told the students who were picking on her to *"Stop!"*, saying that *"Black people are the same; they are human. [The teacher] was really supportive"* and often checked in to be sure she was okay (Janie, personal communication, 6 March 2017). She also recounted one incident in which one of her Black Deaf friends wanted to leave PSD due to ever-present bullying and other racist acts. Janie's friend was afraid to tell the supervisor in fear of retaliation, but Janie told the supervisor anyway, hoping that it would bring an end to the abuse. The dorm supervisor then called a meeting with all of the kids in the dorm, insisting that everyone *"try to socialize with one another"*. After this, she recalls, *"the Black Deaf students were so relieved. [As a result, they] slowly [. . .] began to socialize with one another and that segregation faded away."* (Janie, personal communication, 6 March 2017).

Though some participants found racism and prejudice to be an impediment to a fully realized social experience at school, other Black Deaf community members found that other privileges or abilities allowed them to traverse social boundaries that might not have otherwise been open to them. For example, one participant, Sandra, a Black woman who is one of our small group of participants from the *Martin School*, explicitly mentions having no problem with hearing students at the *Martin School* – a deaf and hard-of-hearing program within a mainstream setting – because she grew up around hearing people [181009_SandraW_A_1_4:12–5:16]. This experience may be connected to the fact that she also recalls no personal experiences with racism while in school. She notes, *"Everybody was friendly with each other, like a team. It was good."* [181009_SandraW_A_1_4:00–4:08]. Of course, another possibility is that students attending the *Martin School* encountered less racism than students attending PSD. However, even in the context of the more extremely white-dominant PSD environment, another community consultant expressed certainty that she was more socially accepted amongst her white peers because of her intelligence and place in the academic track (Anon., personal communication, 25 January 2019).

Athleticism and participation in sports were a notable domain in which Black Deaf students gained entree into social circles that might otherwise have been prohibited. Historically, sports and athleticism have been revered amongst Deaf students and Deaf communities in the U.S. They are an avenue through which participants can demonstrate unity through "emphasizing sportsmanship, teamwork, and physical abilities" while simultaneously providing opportunities to share and express a common culture and signed language connections (Burch 2002: 77). Our participants' narratives show how participation in sports not only served as a vehicle for integration with white Deaf peers, but also allowed Black Deaf students to garner a kind of prestige, respect, and privilege that might not have been otherwise granted. Cheryl, known as a gifted athlete during her time at PSD, documents the ease with which she engages with white Deaf community members. She explains:

> *I have a lot of experience with white Deaf people because I would go to their sporting events, and I was involved in those sports for many years [. . .] [For her, socializing with] whites [is] easy."* [160402_CherylA_CU_2_1:55–2:26]

One male consultant, who was known for his singular athleticism, expresses having no problem socializing with his white peers then and now. His status as a star athlete, by his report, helped significantly (Anon., personal communication, 13 January 2019). Janie also recalls that when playing sports, she did not experience any bullying at all by her peers (Janie, personal communication, 6 March 2017).

Athleticism was not always enough to traverse racial boundaries in the world outside school. The same consultant mentioned above, who expressed ease in socialization at school, shared a heartbreaking story in which he tried to enter the *Silent Athletic Club* (SAC) and was turned away at the door simply because he was Black. It was 1950 and, at that time, the SAC bylaws explicitly expressed that Black people were prohibited. He shared that he was quite *"sad"* by the encounter, but has moved past these feelings well over sixty years after the unexpected confrontation (Anon., personal communication, 13 January 2019). He then explains that a few years later, he was allowed to be a part of the club, not because of a dissipation of prejudice, but more probably due to the draw of having such a gifted athlete on the club's sports teams.

Even outside of athletics, not all of the people of color in our corpus look back on their school experiences with memories of racism, prejudice, and isolation. In fact, there is certainly evidence of interracial camaraderie, friendship, and socialization noted in many of the interviews as well as in our supplementary conversations with Philadelphia Deaf community members. In some cases, Black students at PSD presented themselves as more comfortable socializing with white Deaf people, retaining this preference in the years after leaving PSD. We find this preference notable as, anecdotally, it is not congruent with the experiences of Black Deaf people who did not attend PSD. As we will discuss below, Black students at PSD had far more opportunities to socialize with and learn the ways of their white Deaf peers than they did with Black Deaf peers. Of our participants, Cheryl was the most explicit about her preference for socializing with white Deaf people over Black Deaf people, explaining that,

> *I have a lot of experience with them. I grew up with white [people]. I have socialized with them, and I'm used to them. [. . .] In comparing them, I find white folks to be better because I have good connections and relationships with them.*
>
> [160402_CherylA_CU_1_28:56–29:36]

She then clarifies, *"Am I against anyone? No. We're all the same [. . .] Whites are good [to me] [. . .] I have experience with both."* [160402_CherylA_CU_1_28: 56–29:36].

Another one of our consultants, an elderly Black Deaf man, feels similarly to Cheryl. He remarks that though he has many Black Deaf friends, some of whom attended the *Martin School* and some who have no formal education, he socializes mostly with white Deaf people because that is who he grew up with. He also mentions the fact that PSD afforded him an education, one that was not extended to some of his Black Deaf peers. He admits that their lack of an education impacts his connection to them socially because they have less in common (Anon., personal communication, 13 January 2019). For Black Deaf Philadelphians, a PSD education may have elevated them academically while socially alienating them from their Black Deaf peers. None of the participants who attended only the *Martin School* expressed this same preference for socializing with white Deaf peers rather than Black Deaf peers.

It is important to note that because many Black Deaf people attended a dayschool program, their opportunities to learn ASL from their peers diverged from the traditional school-based peer-to-peer model.[27] Thus, many Black Deaf people

---

[27] Here, we are not talking about the academic part of school, but the residential and extracurricular part, where signing was tolerated and proliferated.

in Philadelphia came later, if at all, to learning ASL. Our participants and consultants suggest that Black Deaf people who attended day-school programs learned to sign through connections with other community members at church and church-related functions[28] or in their neighborhoods. The few Black Deaf people who attended PSD would come back to the neighborhood on weekends and in the summer and socialize with other Deaf people who attended day-school programs. It has been reported that their signs mixed with the home signs used by the neighborhood-based Deaf Philadelphians to create a variety that is anecdotally distinct from that of the white Deaf Philadelphians. Indeed, one of our participants, Cheryl, repeatedly points to this distinction in signing between Black and white people. For example, she says, *"Black people [have] old-fashioned [signs]"* [1604020_CherylA_CU_1_29:37–29:56] and *"[...], the people from the Martin School, their signing is different."* [1604020_CherylA_CU_2_1:28–2:02]. And though *Martin School* was the favored school for Black Deaf Philadelphians, it should be noted that not all Black Philadelphians had the opportunity to attend school at all. Furthermore, the Black PSD alumni in our project mentioned a clear educational distinction between the Black Deaf people who attended PSD versus those who did not, at least within the elderly population. It is clear from these conversations that Black Deaf people who went to PSD and who stayed through graduation perceived themselves as *"better educated"* than their peers who had not. It is suggested, then, that a PSD education afforded Black Deaf Philadelphians opportunities that may not have otherwise been attained elsewhere, especially if they were not able to thrive in the oralist model of education.

The historical, social, and linguistic experiences of Black Deaf Philadelphians have heretofore been overlooked both in the local community and in the academic literature. While this section focuses primarily on Black Deaf experiences in education, our data show that there is a rich social history to be uncovered as well. For example, it was not until we were reviewing conversations with some of our

---

28 One example from later in the history is the *Society for Helping Church*, whose mission is to "provid[e] a holistic inclusive ministry where Deaf, hard-of-hearing, and hearing persons grow spiritually together while empowering Deaf and hard-of-hearing persons to funchtion [sic] well within a Deaf world", and which has been facilitating relationships between Deaf and hearing people since 1976 (Society for Helping Church). In this setting, hearing and Deaf members of Black communities in Philadelphia come together in fellowship with the additional benefit of church members adept at signing and/or speaking to communicate home and school activities and needs to one another. Here, Black Deaf children who attended the *Martin School* in the 1970s and later were exposed to signing by those in the ministry as well as other Deaf parishioners. This organization was thus a bridge between signing and non-signing community members, both Deaf and hearing.

elderly Black Deaf participants that we even understood that there was a separate social club for Black Deaf Philadelphians, the *Reed Street Deaf Club*, formed in response to the discrimination, prejudice, and oppression exerted by some white Deaf community members in other Deaf clubs in Philadelphia (the *Silent Athletic Club* in the Hunting Park section of Philadelphia and the *Central City Deaf Club* on 13th Street). The *Reed Street Deaf Club* was mentioned in passing in one interview with an elderly Black Deaf Philadelphian, but it was never discussed in detail during the interview with her or any of the initial interviews with other participants. In fact, one of our interviewer-participants, a white elderly Deaf male, who considers himself to be highly knowledgeable of Philadelphia Deaf history and strongly connected to many local community members across the generations, was completely unaware of the *Reed Street Deaf Club* and was shocked to know of its existence, since he had memories of many Black Deaf people attending the other local Deaf clubs.[29] It was only during follow-up conversations with our participants and reflections of one of the authors of this paper that we could piece together details on this club as a social space formed for and by Black Deaf people in response to racism and prejudice experienced at the main Deaf clubs in Philadelphia. It is directly from these passing anecdotes that we gleaned these clues on the distinct Black Deaf Philadelphian experience, pointing us toward the great importance of broadening our participant pool going forward.

6 Conclusion

Our focus on elderly Deaf participants in the Philadelphia Signs Project has brought rich insight into the multifaceted history of the Philadelphia Deaf community. The participants discussed in this chapter have seen many decades of social, educational, and linguistic change in their lifetimes. The stories we have presented here were selected to highlight recurring themes about the importance of educational institutions in Deaf social life, the attachment of Deaf Philadelphians to their traditional styles of signing, and changes taking place in Philadelphia ASL. We have also explored the ways in which these educational, social, and linguistic experiences were racially mediated, with a special

---

[29] Again, many of the conversations about Black Deaf inclusion at the predominantly white Deaf clubs revealed that Black Deaf people were often exceptional athletes who played on club sports teams. This falls in line with white acceptance of Black Deaf people when it was convenient and beneficial – like in sports competitions – and not necessarily for everyday social activity.

focus on the lives of Black Deaf Philadelphians. In the latter part of the 20th century, and continuing today, social and educational awareness around the racial and ethnic diversity of Deaf people in Philadelphia has increased. As we continue our data collection, we will seek out participants from racial and ethnic groups that were not well represented in our earlier PSD-centric recruiting. In partnership with local organizations representing and led by people of color and in collaboration with community members across the generations, we aim to accurately document the varied social and historical forces that contribute to American Sign Language use in Philadelphia.

Acknowledgements: We would like to give our deepest thanks to the following people and organizations. Without their participation, enthusiasm, energy, and support, this project would not be possible:
- our participants, including consultants wishing to remain anonymous;
- the interviewers: Randy Fisher, Janessa Carter, Domonic Gordine;
- the Pennsylvania School for the Deaf; Deaf-Hearing Communication Centre; Pennsylvania Chapter of Black Deaf Advocates;
- the University of Pennsylvania School of Arts and Sciences Dean's Office, Research Opportunity Grant;
- annotators from Gallaudet University: Julie Hochgesang, Kaylee Bodtke, Nicole Carlo, Heather Hamilton, Jamila Hubbard, Franklin Jones, Jr., August Klett, Ginette Redmond, Robin Spigner;
- our research assistants: Payton Matous, Carmen Lugo, and Elana Chapman.

References

Bahan, Benjamin & H. Dirksen Bauman. 2005. Narrative, identity, and theory in Deaf studies. From https://research.gallaudet.edu/Presentations/2005-09-14.ppt; retrieved February 15, 2019.

Bahan, Benjamin. 2006. Face-to-face tradition in the American Deaf community. In H.-Dirksen L. Bauman, Jennifer L. Nelson & Heidi M. Rose (eds.), *Signing the body poetic: Essays on American Sign Language literature*, 21–50. Berkeley, CA: University of California Press.

Bahan, Benjamin. 2018. *Communicating Deaf theory: A data-driven approach*. Presentation at Transformations: Gallaudet Deaf Studies Conference, November 1–3, 2018. Gallaudet University. Washington, DC.

Barron, Sandy. 2017. "The world is wide enough for us both": The Manitoba School for the Deaf at the onset of the oralist age, 1889–1920. *Canadian Journal of Disability Studies* 6 (1). 63–84.

Brevik, Jan-Kare. 2005. *Deaf identities in the making: Local lives, transnational connections*. Washington, DC: Gallaudet University Press.

Burch, Susan. 2002. *Signs of resistance: American Deaf cultural history, 1900 to World War II*. New York: New York University Press.

Burch, Susan & Hannah Joyner. 2007. *Unspeakable: The story of Junius Wilson*. Chapel Hill, NC: University of North Carolina Press.

Edwards, Rebecca A. 2012. *Words made flesh: Nineteenth-century Deaf education and the growth of Deaf culture*. New York: New York University Press.

Fisher, Jami N., Julie Hochgesang & Meredith Tamminga. 2016. Examining variation in the absence of a 'main' ASL corpus: The case of the Philadelphia Signs Project. In *Proceedings of the 7th Workshop on the Representation and Processing of Sign Languages: Corpus Mining*, 75–80. LREC, Portorož, Slovenia, May 28, 2016.

Fisher, Jami N., Meredith Tamminga & Julie A. Hochgesang. 2018. The historical and social context of the Philadelphia ASL community. *Sign Language Studies* 18(3). 429–460.

Hill, Joseph C. 2017. The importance of the sociohistorical context in sociolinguistics: The case of Black ASL. *Sign Language Studies* 18(1). 41–57.

Himmelmann, Nikolaus. 2006. Language documentation: What is it and what is it good for? In Jost Gippert, Nikolaus P. Himmelmann & Ulrike Mosel (eds.), *Essentials of language documentation*, 1–30. New York: Mouton de Gruyter.

Hochgesang, Julie A. 2015, updated 2016. *SLAAASh ID glossing principles and annotation conventions*. Manuscript, Gallaudet University and Haskins Laboratories, http://bit.ly/2jGbPfU.

Hochgesang, Julie A., Onno Crasborn & Diane Lillo-Martin. 2019. *ASL Signbank*. New Haven, CT: Haskins Laboratories and Yale University, https://aslsignbank.haskins.yale.edu/.

Hutchinson, Emlen. 1912. *Annual report of the board of directors of the Pennsylvania Institution for the Deaf and Dumb, 1910–1911*. Philadelphia: Institution Printing Office, Mount Airy.

Jankowski, Katherine A. 1997. *Deaf empowerment: Emergence, struggle, and rhetoric*. Washington, DC: Gallaudet University Press.

Johnston, Trevor. 2010. From archive to corpus: Transcription and annotation in the creation of signed language corpora. *International Journal of Corpus Linguistics* 15. 104–129.

Labov, William. 1984. Field methods of the project on linguistic change and variation. In John Baugh & Joel Sherzer (eds.), *Language in use: readings in sociolinguistics*, 28–53. Englewood Cliffs, NJ: Prentice Hall.

Lucas, Ceil, Robert Bayley, Mary Rose & Alyssa Wulf. 2002. Location variation in American Sign Language. *Sign Language Studies* 2(4). 407–440.

McCaskill, Carolyn, Ceil Lucas, Robert Bayley & Joseph Hill. 2011. *The hidden treasure of Black ASL: Its history and structure*. Washington, DC: Gallaudet University Press.

Padden, Carol & Tom Humphries. 2006. *Inside Deaf culture*. Cambridge, MA: Harvard University Press.

National Black Deaf Advocates. 2019. About us. Available at: https://www.nbda.org/content/about-us; retrieved February 1, 2019.

Society for Helping Church, Inc. 2013–2018. About: Our church. Available at: https://www.societyforhelping.org/about; retrieved March 2, 2109.

Stokoe, William C. 1960. Sign language structure: an outline of the visual communication systems of the American Deaf. *Studies in Linguistics Occasional Papers* 8. Buffalo: University of Buffalo Press [Re-issued 2005, *Journal of Deaf Studies and Deaf Education* 10 (1).3–37].

Supalla, Ted. 1991. Deaf Folklife Film Collection Project. *Sign Language Studies* 70(1). 73–82.

Supalla, Ted. 1995. *Charles Krauel: A profile of a Deaf filmmaker*. San Diego, CA: Dawn Sign Press.

Veditz, George. 1913. Preservation of the sign language. *Library of Congress*. Available at: https://www.loc.gov/item/mbrs01815816/; retrieved May 7, 2019.

Wikipedia contributors. November 14, 2019. Bache-Martin Elementary School. In *Wikipedia, The Free Encyclopedia*. Retrieved from https://en.wikipedia.org/w/index.php?title=Bache-Martin_Elementary_School&oldid=926159172 at 17:17, December 28, 2019.

Wittenburg, Peter, Hennie Brugman, Albert Russel, Alex Klassmann & Han Sloetjes. 2006. ELAN: a professional framework for multimodality research. In *Proceedings of LREC 2006, 5th International Conference on Language Resources and Evaluation*. ELAR.

Appendix A

Interviewee First Name	Last Name	Age at time of recording	1a. Are you Deaf or Hard-of-Hearing?	1b. Were you born that way? If not, when did you become deaf or hard-of-hearing and why?	2. Are you female or male?	5a. What schools you attended? Please list all (including year and age).	5b. And what kind (deaf, hearing, mainstreamed)?	6. What is your highest level of education?	8b. How many siblings do you have?	8c. Are any Deaf?	8d. Do any sign?	9a. What languages do you use?	9b. When did you learn each?	9c. How and where did you learn them?	9d. Which one is your primary language?	10. What is your ethnicity?
Cheryl	A	62	Deaf	yes	female	PSD (entered 1964)	Deaf	vocational/ 12th grade	n/a	n/a	yes taught siblings	ASL	age 7	PSD	ASL	Black
Rachel	A	72	Deaf	yes	female	Martin School (1946–1955); PSD (1955–1960)	Deaf	high school	3	no	yes	ASL	age 5	Martin School	ASL	Russian, Jewish
Jay	B	84	Deaf	yes	male	Houston Public School (1937; 5 y.o.); Pennsylvania School for the Deaf (1938; 6 y.o.; Friends Select School (1948; 16 y.o.); University of Pennsylvania (1951; 19 y.o.); Drexel Institute of Technology (1957; 25 y.o.); Temple University (Ph.D.) (1962; 30 y.o.)	Deaf (PSD); hearing (all others)	Ph.D.	1	no	no	English and Philadelphia sign language (ASL)	English (2 y.o.); ASL (6 y.o.)	Parents, PSD	English	German, Russian
Janie	C	77	Deaf	no (Whopping cough – toddler)	female	Martin School, PSD (graduated 1957)	Deaf	Business School	4	no	no	ASL	PSD	PSD – peers	ASL	Black

(continued)

Interviewee First Name	Last Name	Age at time of recording	1a. Are you Deaf or Hard-of-Hearing?	1b. Were you born that way? If not, when did you become deaf or hard-of-hearing and why?	2. Are you female or male?	5a. What schools you attended? Please list all (including year and age).	5b. And what kind (deaf, hearing, mainstreamed)?	6. What is your highest level of education?	8b. How many siblings do you have?	8c. Are any Deaf?	8d. Do any sign?	9a. What languages do you use?	9b. When did you learn each?	9c. How and where did you learn them?	9d. Which one is your primary language?	10. What is your ethnicity?
Albert	D	82	Deaf	yes	male	PSD	Deaf	high school		yes–both parents; siblings	yes	ASL	from family	home	ASL	White
Sherry	D	75	Deaf	yes	female	Martin School (1945–1954; 5–14 y.o.); PSD (1954–1957; 14–17 y.o.); Levitan School (1958; 18 y.o.); Burroughs (1959; 19 y.o.)	Deaf (PSD, Martin); hearing (Levitan, Burroughs)		1	no	no	ASL, English	Martin School, PSD	Martin School, PSD	ASL	Jewish
Wilma	J	71	Deaf		female	PSD (Mt. Airy), starting age 5	Deaf (PSD)	12th grade				ASL	age 4 or 5 at PSD	school	ASL	Black
Irene	K	80	Deaf	born deaf	female	PSD 1942–1944 (elementary); Martin School 1944–1946; Archbishop Ryan (1946–1952); PSD 1952–1957	Deaf; oral mainstream; signed and oral; sign language (high school)	high school		yes–both parents, one sibling	yes	ASL	from family	from family	ASL	White
Pinky	K	87	Deaf	no (illness at age 7)	male		mainstream	12th grade		no		ASL	age 12	socializing with PSD friends	ASL	White

Uncovering the lived experiences of elderly Deaf Philadelphians

Name	Age	Deaf/HoH		Sex	School	Hearing/Deaf	Education	Siblings	Deaf siblings	Sign at home	Languages	Child	Parents	ASL	Ethnicity
Harrison	89	Deaf	no (10 y.o., but born CODA–signing since early childhood)	male	Hearing school (1931–1933; 5–8 y.o.); P– (1936); PSD (1937–1942; ~10–16 y.o.)	Hearing, Deaf (P–, PSD)	high school (unfinished)	3 brothers, 1 sister	yes – all became deaf (oldest born Deaf, other three Hard-of-hearing but became Deaf)	yes	ASL, English	Child (ASL); English (5 y.o.)	Parents	ASL	Swiss/German, Scottish
Peggy	84	Deaf	yes	female	PSD (1938–1952; 6–20 y.o.)	Deaf	high school	no	n/a	home sign (parents)	ASL, English	n/a	Deaf parents of friends	ASL	German, Irish
Sandra	78	Hard-of-Hearing	no	female	Martin School 1945; later mainstreamed	special program at Martin; mainstream	12 grade	no response	no	no	English; some ASL	Learned ASL in 20s	socializing with Deaf friends, school, and clubs	no response	Black
Caroline	80	Deaf	no (illness – 2 y.o.)	female	PSD (1943–1950; 7–14 y.o.); Hearing school (14/15 y.o. – ?)	Deaf, hearing	GED	5 brothers, 1 sister	no	yes	ASL, English	age 7	PSD	ASL	German
															Black
Contributors and consultants not in the video project															
Anon.	89	Deaf		male											Black
Anon.	late 50s	Deaf		female											Black

Appendix B

Timestamp citation	Reference and/or quotation	Link to video clip
160402_CherylA_A_1_17:28–30	Two of our Black participants commented that upon reaching school age (six or seven years old) they started at a program like the Martin School but very quickly transferred to PSD because their families were not satisfied with the quality of education or progress there.	https://repository.upenn.edu/elderly_deaf/51
160402_CherylA_CU1_14: 38–14:53	"When I transferred [to PSD], it was really awkward for me. [. . .] Others would say, 'Hey! Come on! Come play!' And my friends would be playing around me."	https://repository.upenn.edu/elderly_deaf/56
160402_CherylA_CU_1_16: 02–16:07	Cheryl also suggests her disorientation was ameliorated by her socialization and language exposure at school when she says, "It was different and disorienting [at first] but then I was like, 'Oh!' and I would learn [the sign language]. Then it became easy to socialize. Then the dorm was better than home."	https://repository.upenn.edu/elderly_deaf/52
160402_CherylA_CU_1_18: 07–18:22	"Yes. I would make modifications [to what I saw signed around me] and I would sign away. [She depicts examples of how she grew to be proficient and it made her a more social person at school]. Oh, I enjoyed it so. Really enjoyed it. I learned a lot. Yes."	https://repository.upenn.edu/elderly_deaf/49
160402_CherylA_CU_1_15: 11–15:16	"[Despite the difficult beginning] I continued [living in] the dorm and I enjoyed it. It was a good experience being able to communicate with Deaf people."	https://repository.upenn.edu/elderly_deaf/55

160402_CherylA_CU_1_15: 41–15:56	"We were all integrated. I enjoyed that and could play [with anyone]. We learned to communicate with each other and would play" "Oh!" I would take them as my own. The signs were old fashioned. Like SCHOOL was signed [looks like dragging luggage] or [looks like moving a piece of paper in front of the face]. WORK wasn't like it was [flat hand, one handed shake]."	https://repository.upenn.edu/elderly_deaf/53 and https://repository.upenn.edu/elderly_deaf/54
160402_CherylA_CU_1_15: 56–15:59	"Oh!" I would take them as my own. The signs were old fashioned. Like SCHOOL was signed [looks like dragging luggage] or [looks like moving a piece of paper in front of the face]. WORK wasn't like it was [flat hand, one handed shake]."	https://repository.upenn.edu/elderly_deaf/53
160402_CherylA_CU_2_1: 55–2:26	"I have a lot of experience with white Deaf people because I would go to their sporting events and I was involved in those sports for many years . . . . [For her, socializing with] whites [is] easy."	https://repository.upenn.edu/elderly_deaf/45
160402_CherylA_CU_1_28: 56–29:36	"I have a lot of experience with them. I grew up with white [people]. I have socialized with them and I'm used to them . . . in comparing them, I find white folks to be better because I have good connections and relationships with them." She then clarifies, "Am I against anyone? No. We're all same . . . .Whites are good [to me] . . . I have experience with both."	https://repository.upenn.edu/elderly_deaf/48
1604020_CherylA_CU_1_29: 37–29:56	Cheryl, repeatedly points to this distinction in signing between Black and white people. For example, she says, "Black people [have] old fashioned [signs]" and "the people from the Martin School, their signing is different".	https://repository.upenn.edu/elderly_deaf/47
1604020_CherylA_CU_2_1: 28–2:02	"the people from the Martin School, their signing is different"	https://repository.upenn.edu/elderly_deaf/46

(continued)

Timestamp citation	Reference and/or quotation	Link to video clip
150131_JanieC_A_1:27–1:38	Two of our Black participants commented that upon reaching school age (six or seven years old) they started at a program like the Martin School but very quickly transferred to PSD because their families were not satisfied with the quality of education or progress there.	https://repository.upenn.edu/elderly_deaf/37
151031_JanieC_CU_6:38	"confusing"	https://repository.upenn.edu/elderly_deaf/36/
CHOCOLATE [151031_JanieC_CU_6:44] and PIE [151031_JanieC_CU_6:48]	She is criticized by younger signers for using older forms like CHOCOLATE (https://aslsignbank.haskins.yale.edu/dictionary/gloss/3082/) [151031_JanieC_CU_6:44] and PIE [151031_JanieC_CU_6:48] (https://aslsignbank.haskins.yale.edu/dictionary/gloss/3294/), which she finds startling.	https://repository.upenn.edu/elderly_deaf/34 and https://repository.upenn.edu/elderly_deaf/33
151031_JanieC_CU_7:09–7:22	"My grandson signs a little differently. [I see the signs] and I know they're new. [I] Accept [their use]. I see the new signs and ask 'What's that?' He explains to me, and then I'm clear. How awful [the signs] are."	https://repository.upenn.edu/elderly_deaf/35
151031_JanieC_CU_6:52–6:57	She finds herself preferring the older signs, explaining, "It's hard to keep up with the young [signers], but I still use my old signs. I stay [the same]."	https://repository.upenn.edu/elderly_deaf/32
072715_JayB_CU_1_13:25–13:33	"My good friend . . . [and I], we had the same problems. I was too young. He was too fat."	https://repository.upenn.edu/elderly_deaf/2

ID	Quote	URL
072715_JayB_CU_1_16:52–16:54	Despite their differences, they bonded and were "friends for a lifetime".	https://repository.upenn.edu/elderly_deaf/30
160307_PeggyS_A_1_8:30–8:38	One participant, Peggy, recounts how uncomfortably large PSD seemed to her upon arrival and expresses discomfort on her face at this memory.	https://repository.upenn.edu/elderly_deaf/23
160307_PeggyS_A_1_10:21–10:26	"[The dormitory] was huge compared to my small house."	https://repository.upenn.edu/elderly_deaf/19
160307_PeggyS_A_1_10:42–10:54	"It was huge, with stairs up to the dormitory with rows and rows of beds. . . . I was scared to go to bed. I went into bed and everyone was stone-cold asleep, but I was wide awake, scared."	https://repository.upenn.edu/elderly_deaf/18
160307_PeggyS_A_1_9:07–9:21	Peggy, who describes being carefully escorted by her mother, grandmother, and dorm supervisor to the PSD dormitory, and then only upon saying goodbyes did she realize her family was leaving her. She thus protested their departure with dismay and in tears.	https://repository.upenn.edu/elderly_deaf/21
160307_PeggyS_A_1_9:21–9:29	Peggy immediately follows her expressions of fear and apprehension of her new school environment with the fact that she "picked up signing and learned it fast" as she went along in the day-to-day activities at PSD.	https://repository.upenn.edu/elderly_deaf/20
160307_PeggyS_A_1_8:58–9:07	She describes entering the building with her suitcases and upon entering, "throngs of girls came over saying, 'New girl! New girl!' and I just looked at them completely scared."	https://repository.upenn.edu/elderly_deaf/22
160307_PeggyS_A_1_27:14–27:32	"So, in your time, did you have that term, ASL?" to which she responds, "No, well, we talked the same, but did we think of it as ASL? Now, I learn ASL is an abbreviation for [or synonymous with] talking."	https://repository.upenn.edu/elderly_deaf/16

(continued)

Timestamp citation	Reference and/or quotation	Link to video clip
160307_PeggyS_A_1_32: 08-32:16	Peggy identifies the Philadelphia sign for PICNIC (https://aslsign bank.haskins.yale.edu/dictionary/gloss/3295/) but points out that some sign it differently and that there is "diversity" in the use of that sign.	ttps://repository.upenn.edu/elderly_deaf/13
160307_PeggyS_A_1_30: 12-30:49	"Yes, it was different. I would look up at them and . . . [she names a Philadelphia acquaintance's husband], he was from Gallaudet. He would come back for football games from Gallaudet [imitates his air of superiority] and he would fingerspell everything as if he was so advanced. I couldn't read the signs. Some of the communication I couldn't catch because I was little and couldn't read the signs. Now, now that we are adults, we all sign the same."	https://repository.upenn.edu/elderly_deaf/25
160307_PeggyS_A_1_27: 47-28:30	EASTER, Philadelphia variant	https://repository.upenn.edu/elderly_deaf/14
160307_PeggyS_A_1_27: 47-28:30		https://repository.upenn.edu/elderly_deaf/15
170930_IreneK_A_12:27–12:50	One participant, Irene, recalls that her Deaf father "could not communicate with his father at all [emphatic expression]" and that communication amongst her immigrant grandparents and the rest of her Deaf family at home was "not easy".	https://repository.upenn.edu/elderly_deaf/38

151101_WilmaJ_A_2:26–2:46	Wilma also describes her first night at PSD, explaining that she arrived late in the evening and while unpacking her clothes and getting ready for bed, everyone just watched her, saying "Who is the new girl?" She was taken aback by all the attention.	https://repository.upenn.edu/elderly_deaf/3
151001_RachelA_2:48–3:09	"I enjoyed PSD. Loved it really. . . . [because] there was more socializing. After dinner and study hour, there was more time with everyone to just chat away until bedtime. [Unlike] when I was home, I would just twiddle my thumbs. I couldn't stand it. I loved PSD very much."	https://repository.upenn.edu/elderly_deaf/11
181009_SandraW_A_1_4:12–5:16	Sandra explicitly mentions having no problem with hearing students at the Martin School because she grew up around hearing people.	https://repository.upenn.edu/elderly_deaf/8
181009_SandraW_A_1_4:00–4:08	"Everybody was friendly with each other, like a team. It was good."	https://repository.upenn.edu/elderly_deaf/10
160307_HarrisonS_A_1_26:52–27:12	"When I started PID, I was already skilled in sign because my parents were Deaf. The other kids were shocked [mouth agape] that I already knew sign. [They said,] "You're new and you're already skilled in sign! How?" and I said, "MOTHER-FATHER DEAF. BROTHER DEAF." They were all shocked."	https://repository.upenn.edu/elderly_deaf/43
160307_HarrisonS_A_2_24:28–24:47	"We would SIGN not PRODUCE-SIGN. Like, my parents, my father's brother, in school, my teacher."	https://repository.upenn.edu/elderly_deaf/44
160307_HarrisonS_A_2_24:54–25:14	When asked more specifically if the signing in the past was the same as signing today, Harrison says, "Oh, it's changed. A lot. Many changes. Like what? I used to sign SHOES, it was like this shoes (depiction of sliding feet in). They're all different."	https://repository.upenn.edu/elderly_deaf/40

(continued)

Timestamp citation	Reference and/or quotation	Link to video clip
160307_HarrisonS_A_2_23: 47–23:56	"I used to [sign] SQUIRREL-EAT, but my son-in-law who was at Gallaudet signs SQUIRREL."	https://repository.upenn.edu/elderly_deaf/42
160307_HarrisonS_A_2_31: 42–32:12	Asked whether he knew "any old Philadelphia signs," he says, "I'm mixed [in my signing style] Deaf/hearing, old/young, WPSD signs/ PSD signs, different schools for the Deaf. You know I've traveled to and been in about 20 or 21 schools for the Deaf."	https://repository.upenn.edu/elderly_deaf/39
150723_SherryD_A_1_24: 06–24:49	Sherry talks about the fact that she transferred to PSD because many of her friends from the Martin School were doing the same to play sports or to have a better social life. It was at that time that she learned to sign.	https://repository.upenn.edu/elderly_deaf/6
150723_SherryD_A_1_26: 14–27:43	For example, Sherry explicitly states that she had to "learn [the younger generation's signs]" when she became a teacher's aide in a preschool class at PSD. She describes being "corrected repeatedly" for using her older variety and even experienced misunderstandings from the children's different sign usage.	https://repository.upenn.edu/elderly_deaf/5
150723_SherryD_A_1_27: 45–28:00	Her reluctance to give up her old signs is most evident as she points out that she very quickly returned to the older sign variety – "Not completely, but moving in that direction" – upon retiring from her PSD job and socializing with her friends from the old PSD.	https://repository.upenn.edu/elderly_deaf/4

150723_SherryD_A_1_6:46–7:13	"It's hard for me to sign FS-DOG [the newer variant]. In the past, [my son] would tell [his wife], 'My mother uses this Philadelphia sign for 'dog'. [His wife] was like, 'Hold on [don't use that sign].' I have to be mentally controlled [not to] . . . . When I talk to other Philadelphians, I'd [probably] use this older sign for 'dog' because we all have common [knowledge of what it means]."	https://repository.upenn.edu/elderly_deaf/7
150820_PinkyK_Part1_A_5:19–5:55	"I learned a lot of sign when I was eleven years old. For five years, every day I would go to PSD and learn, without being explicitly taught . . . At that time, I was hard-of-hearing and most hard-of-hearing [people] were iffy with signing [ability]. Me, no. I was stubborn. I acted like a Deaf person so I would go there and I learned a lot for five years. That's how all the students knew me and were used to me. They thought I was actually a PSD student. I wasn't. But they knew me very well and have all these years."	https://repository.upenn.edu/elderly_deaf/12
160307_CarolineZ_A_1_14:40–15:12	She explains, "They all understand me. Do I have to think about only new [signs]? No! I know everyone there and keeping my old signing [style] is fine."	https://repository.upenn.edu/elderly_deaf/63
160307_CarolineZ_A_1_20:39–20:50	"Some of [the Deaf people] out there alert me that I must use the newer signs and eliminate [using] the old [ones]. I can't. I can't [do that]. I still use my old signs."	https://repository.upenn.edu/elderly_deaf/64

Rose Stamp, Svetlana Dachkovsky, and Wendy Sandler
Time will tell: time and discourse as 'motion through space' in early Israeli Sign Language (ISL)

1 Introduction

Narrating personal stories plays an important role in human communication, serving as a vehicle for sharing life experiences, on the one hand, and for construing one's identity, on the other. Discourse structure may be characterized by various types of coherence, and what makes a discourse coherent is the range of ways in which its elements are connected to each other.

Temporal relations are one of the most important types of connectivity in narration, and such relations are crucial for two reasons. First, during a narrative, we reconstruct the chronological sequence of events in a story; and second, temporality is a property of discourse itself, since the text unfolds in time. There are several means for marking temporal relations in a narrative, for example, time expressions, such as *one hour later*, or *then*, and certain temporal categories associated with verbs, such as tense and aspect. In many cases, these time expressions are rooted in conceptual metaphors of motion through space, either through the representation of **time** as motion through space, or of **discourse** as motion through space. Consequently, time expressions can express both chronological temporality and discourse temporality.

In this chapter, we focus on a time expression[1] used by signers of Israeli Sign Language (ISL), henceforth glossed as TIME-PASS (see Figure 1). The repeated, forward-moving, circular motion of the two hands produced in this sign expresses the succession of time periods. It is therefore a clear example of metaphorical extension of space to represent time (Smart 1949; Traugott 1978; Lakoff 1993; Deutscher 2006; *inter alia*). Here, we explore the forms and functions of this sign, used frequently by elderly signers of ISL – members of the first generation of signers of this young language.

While the meaning of the sign consistently refers to the passage of time, we noticed that the form of TIME-PASS can be expressed with two different prosodies.

---

[1] In this study, we use the term *time expression* to refer specifically to a sign glossed as TIME-PASS, in the context of the wider literature on discourse markers in spoken and signed languages as part of Section 2. We reserve the use of *discourse marker* and *temporal adverbial* to refer more specifically to each function of TIME-PASS, as explained in the discussion.

https://doi.org/10.1515/9783110701906-012

In one, which we call TIME-PASS1, the rotating movement of the hands is repeated several times and the sign occupies its own separate intonational phrase. In the other, TIME-PASS2, the sign appears at the beginning of an intonational phrase that includes other signs, and is much reduced in length and number of reduplications. Our goal in this study is to determine whether these two different forms for the same time expression represent two different discursive functions. We conclude that this formational bifurcation is indeed a reflection of different functions: ISL signers extend the metaphor of 'time as motion through space' into the realm of discourse, and distinguish two distinct functions for this expression, even in the early stages of language formation.

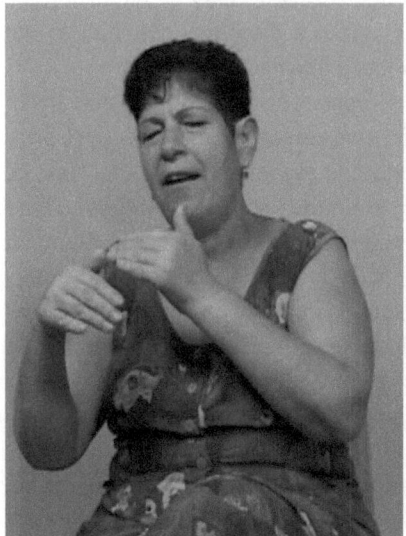 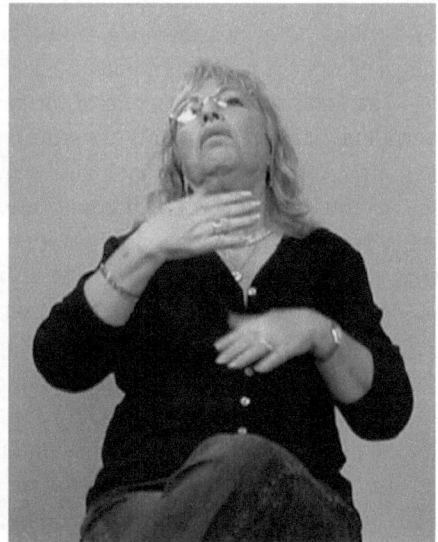

Figure 1a and b: Example of TIME-PASS in its two forms; (a) TIME-PASS1 accompanied by head down and open mouth with a prosodic break before and after; (b) TIME-PASS2, produced with upward head movement, and prosodically connected to subsequent signs. In both forms, the two hands circle one another.[2]

We begin in Section 2 with an overview of spoken language discourse markers and the contribution of prosody in determining their role. We continue in Section 3 by describing what is known about discourse markers in sign language, and go on to provide an introduction to sign language prosody, laying

---

[2] See Figures 4–8 for images of these signs in prosodic context.

the groundwork for our investigation. In Section 4, methodology, we describe our coding system and analytical procedure. We then present the formational part of our results in Section 5, showing that the sign TIME-PASS in our dataset can be categorized into two distinct prosodic displays with accompanying non-manual markers. In Section 6, we go beyond form, and demonstrate the various functions performed by TIME-PASS1 and TIME-PASS2 according to our results. TIME-PASS1 functions as a discourse marker connecting larger episodic units, and in this way structures the discourse. TIME-PASS2 links sequences of events within an episode, connecting the temporal relation between the events themselves. In Section 7, we conclude from our investigation that the 'space is time' metaphor is adopted and exploited for two different functions, even in the early stages of the development of a sign language.

2 Temporality in narratives

Structuring a story in a coherent way makes for effective communication (Gernsbacher & Givón 1995; Graesser et al. 1997; Noordman & Vonk 1997). According to many theories of discourse connectedness, relations between different conceptual units account for coherence in discourse (see Hobbs 1979; Mann & Thompson 1986; Sanders et al. 1993).

One of the central types of coherence in narration is expressed through temporal relations. Unlike other discourse genres, narratives are intrinsically based on time and events. Another reason for the preponderance of temporal relations in this genre is that narratives construe their own "narrative time" (Ricoeur 2010). That is, narratives both reconstruct the chronological sequence of events in a story, and convey the temporality of the discourse itself, since the text unfolds in time. We refer to these two roles as 'discourse temporality' and 'event temporality' in what follows.

In Labov's (1972) model, a narrative is primarily a way of evoking and shaping experience in time; that is, clauses that are ordered temporally and correspond to an inherent temporal relation between events (e.g., *We went to the market and I bought cheese*) are more central to the text and serve to convey the point of a story more than sequences of clauses with no temporal relation. According to a later paradigm, the context of time and space can evoke and shape cultural and personal identities in a narrative (Bakhtin 1981; Schiffrin 1996).

All natural languages have developed a rich repertoire of devices to express temporal relations. Haspelmath (1997) and Klein (2013) consider the main ways in which language expresses time – inherent lexical features of the verb, the categories of tense and aspect associated with verbs, and various types of discourse markers, such as *before* or *a week ago*. Different devices expressing temporality interact and complement each other.

The devices expressing temporal coherence can convey chronological unfolding of events in a story plot, on the one hand, and the unfolding of discourse, on the other (Fleischman 1991). For example, shifts in aspect marked on verbs can be used to differentiate between foregrounded (the main plot) and backgrounded events (circumstances) in a narrative, so that imperfective (continuative and habitual) verbs often mark backgrounded events or episode boundaries, whereas the main plot and event sequencing is realized through verbs with end points (e.g., Richardson 1994; Ricoeur 2010; *inter alia*).

Discourse markers, the main focus of this paper, can also signal temporal transitions among central events during a narrative, and organize the discourse itself (Fraser 2009: 296). On the one hand, they can signal the transition between *sequences of events* and their *contiguity* (Haspelmath 1997). On the other hand, they concern the speaker's communicative intention and discourse management, that is, "how the speaker intends the basic message to relate to the whole discourse" (Fraser 1990: 387). Such markers include transitions and connections between *bigger discourse frames* or "paragraphs" (Chafe 1984; Schiffrin 1987), structural relations between conversational actions in terms of order and hierarchy (e.g., *backgrounded* versus *foregrounded events*), negotiation of a speaker's attitude toward the narration ("stance") (Du Bois 2007), such as disregard or attention, or other *evaluative* meanings (Schiffrin 1987; Maschler 2012). These markers have been described as "assessment tools" (Haegeman & Hill 2013), that is, expressing different aspects of subjective evaluation and interpretation, ranging from surprise or relief (like some uses of *already*) to subjective importance (conveyed by particular uses of *then* or *now*) (Brinton 2010; Schourup 2011).

A given marker need not perform only one of these roles. Discourse markers in general often draw on metaphorical associations from the spatial domain to express either event temporality or the unfolding of a discourse (see, e.g., Clark 1973; Lakoff & Johnson 1980; Gentner 2001; Evans 2004). For example, Hebrew *rega* ('one sec', Maschler 2012) and English *now* can be used to relate successive events, but also to request clarification or to interrupt the interlocutor, signaling a more pragmatic function related to the unfolding of the narrative. This is true not only of individual time expressions but also of verbal forms. For example, Chodorowska-Pilch (1999) shows how the verbal form *vamos* (literally 'we go' in Peninsular Spanish) is used as a politeness discourse marker which allows the speaker to create distance from the content of an utterance and in turn create interpersonal distance. Moreover, cross-linguistically, the imperfective aspect does not only convey the progress of an event in time, but often expresses discourse managing functions by signaling backgrounded and incremental information (Richardson 1994).

What is it that disambiguates the functions of time expressions in the discourse? The two major functions of time expressions described above – discourse temporality and event temporality – are distinguished in two ways: by prosodic and contextual features (Couper-Kuhlen 1996; Dehé & Wichmann 2010; Vandenbergen et al. 2010; Gonen et al. 2015; see Maschler & Schiffrin 2015 for a useful overview). In the next section, we summarize literature dealing with the contribution of prosody and of context in distinguishing the functions of discourse markers. This discussion informs our choice of coding categories in the analysis of the two functions of TIME-PASS in the present study.

2.1 Prosody and discourse markers

The first two decades of discourse marker research paid very little attention to their prosody (Aijmer 2002: 262). Instead, researchers were more concerned with the distributional or contextual analysis of discourse markers. More recently, however, researchers have studied the correlation between various functions of a discourse marker and particular intonation contours and durational features (e.g., Aijmer 2002; Dehé & Wichmann 2010; Vandenbergen et al. 2010).

Couper-Kuhlen (1996) conducted a pioneering study regarding prosody and the function of discourse markers, analyzing 200 examples of *because*, extracted from a four-hour corpus of British and American spoken discourse. She examined speakers' pitch, loudness, and timing in the configuration of causal clause combining that was lexically marked by *because*. The study brings evidence for two distinct intonational patterns associated with causal clause combining in English: the first pattern with a unifying pitch contour integrating two turns, and the other with a pitch reset between the turns. For instance, her study shows that if *because* follows the main clause without a pitch reset, i.e., without a change of the intonational contour between the two clauses, the semantic link between the clauses is simply a causal relation between the events, as in example (1) (Couper-Kuhlen 1996: 407).

(1) A: *Why were you not that concerned about the time?*
    B: *(I wasn't concerned about the time) because I am not a fast runner.*

In contrast, when the pitch of two turns is not integrated, the turns can be interpreted as interactional sequences, such as justification for a prior assessment, or a prior question/ request, as in example (2).

(2) A: *I think it's the second largest.*
B: *Are you sure?*
A: *Because they have like twelve thousand applicants, and they only take eight thousand.*

Prosodic features of this kind figure prominently in Schiffrin's (1987) and Maschler's (2012) definition of prototypical discourse markers as syntactically detachable elements with a range of prosodic contours, operating on different planes of discourse. Prosodic properties of a particular marker are then correlated with its different functions, establishing a relation between the two (e.g., Maschler & Dori-Hacohen 2012; Auer & Maschler 2016).

Time expressions also divide between the two functions, event temporality and discourse temporality. For example, in a spoken Hebrew corpus study, Gonen et al. (2015) analyzed 106 occurrences of *aXʃav* 'now'. They found that this word functions either as a temporal adverbial or as a discourse frame shifter, and that each function had systematically different durations. It is this distinction that we find in ISL's TIME-PASS.

2.2 Context and discourse markers

While prosody appears to be one of the determining factors, in most cases, context[3] can reflect much finer and more precise distinctions between different functions of time expressions (Maschler 1997). For example, prosody and context together differentiate the discourse-structuring and event-sequencing uses of *anyway* (Ferrara 1997), and a "reaction" or turn-continuer use of *yeah* (Jucker & Smith 1998).

The context of a discourse marker, that is, the types of expressions that accompany the discourse marker in the immediate environment, is strongly associated with its function. Evers-Vermeul (2005) reviews a number of studies that suggest an interaction between context and the function of discourse markers. She claims that the speaker, when using a multifunctional word, exploits its context in order to disambiguate different functions.

Prosodically non-integrated expressions are not strongly associated with any particular grammatical or syntactic features in their immediate environment (Maschler & Schiffrin 2015), and often function to connect larger units of

---

[3] The context of a discourse marker refers to the type of signs or predicates which accompany the discourse marker in the immediate environment (before or after).

text.⁴ These discourse markers are often found in contexts with other discourse markers that have similar functions. There is a general tendency to employ more discourse marker clusters at the most prominent frame shifts in discourse (cf. Clover 1982; Enkvist & Wårvik 1987; Maschler 1997). For example, Maschler (1997) demonstrates that the Hebrew discourse marker *rega* ('one sec') is preceded and followed by other discourse markers regulating the information flow (*bekitsur* 'anyway', *az* 'so', and *ve* 'and').⁵

In contrast, discourse markers which serve as time adverbials or conjunctions are found in very specific environments. By their very nature, discourse markers are closely related to temporal properties of verbs, since both temporal expressions and verbal forms move the story ahead or allow for the jumping backwards or forwards in time (Wårvik 2011). Therefore, verbs are considered to be informative indicators of the function of the discourse marker in question (Hutchinson 2004; Tagliamonte 2005). For example, time-frame adverbials, such as *in an hour*, usually come together with predicates that have inherent end points (e.g., *arrive*), i.e., telic verbs. Conversely, time-span adverbials, such as *for an hour*, usually accompany predicates with no inherent end points (e.g., *walk*).

2.3 Interim summary

In sum, a prototypical marker of discourse-structuring is usually defined as a prosodically and structurally independent unit (Chafe 1994). In terms of its pragmatic contribution, it must have interactional and discourse structuring functions in the context in which it occurs, for example, by being preceded or followed by other discourse or evaluative expressions. Markers of event-sequencing (i.e., those time expressions which connect sequences of events) are more prosodically and syntactically integrated, co-occurring with other time expressions and particular types of predicates (Maschler 2002).

In the present study, these generalizations will form the basis for our predictions regarding the functions of TIME-PASS in ISL narratives. In line with the studies discussed above, our analysis aims to unravel how TIME-PASS exploits contextual and prosodic properties in a diversity of meanings – both discourse-structuring and event-sequencing. In order to base our predictions on the specific features of

---

4 For instance, prosodically non-integrated *weil* ('because') in German does not assign the dependent clause word order (SOV) in contrast to its prosodically integrated counterpart (Kempen & Harbusch 2016).
5 Outside their functions as discourse markers, the literal meanings are: *rega* 'moment'; *bekitzur* 'in short'; *az* 'then'.

the visual-spatial modality, the following section surveys what is known about discourse connectivity as well as the roles of prosody and of verbal aspect in sign language discourse.

3 Discourse and discourse markers in sign languages

Sign languages are often described as 'discourse oriented'; that is, discourse and pragmatics play an important role in determining the structure of sign language sentences (Shepard-Kegl 1985; Lillo-Martin 1986). Ironically, though, research at the discourse level of sign languages has been scarce or has focused only on a small number of specific discourse markers. For example, some linguists have explored the features one might expect to see in a narrative or a lecture. Roy (1989) asked subjects to comment on what makes a 'good' lecture after watching a lecture produced in American Sign Language (ASL). One feature noted by the subjects was the role of discourse markers in the organization of the lecture. Roy (1989) looked at two discourse markers in ASL, NOW and NOW-THAT, and concluded that they enhanced the coherence of the lecture.

Other studies tackle isolated manual discourse markers whose discursive status is transparent, because of their relation to widely used gestures (e.g., Roy 1989; Hoza 2011; McKee & Wallingford 2011). The most well-researched discourse marker is PALM-UP, in which the hand is held open with palm facing up; this marker has been studied in various sign languages (e.g., McKee & Wallingford 2011; van Loon 2012), in co-speech gesture research (e.g., Kendon 2004; Müller 2004), and in both (Cooperrider et al. 2018). It serves multiple functions, some of which are shared across more than one sign language. PALM-UP has been defined (i) as a presentation gesture in Danish Sign Language (Engberg-Pedersen 2002), (ii) as a particle of indefiniteness in ASL (Colin, Hagstrom & Neidle 2003), (iii) as a turn-exchange regulator and mitigator in ASL (Hoza 2011), Sign Language of the Netherlands (van Loon 2012) and Swedish Sign Language (Mesch 2016), (iv) as an interrogative and negative particle in Turkish Sign Language (Zeshan 2006), (v) as a discourse marker used to close the turn, to connect clauses, and to express modality in Norwegian Sign Language (Amundsen & Piene Halvorsen 2011), and (vi) as a modality marker in Catalan Sign Language (Jarque 2014).

Few studies have looked at how particular discourse markers can perform multiple functions. An exception is the study of the sign PALM-UP in New Zealand Sign Language (McKee & Wallingford 2011), which found that this frequently occurring discourse marker is able to express cohesive, evaluative, interactive, and frame-setting functions (see also Hoza (2011) for other exceptions).

Similar time expressions to the one investigated in this study have been described in gesture and in sign language research (Selvik 2006; Ladewig 2011). Ladewig (2011) explores the metaphoric meaning of a cyclic gesture very similar in form to TIME-PASS. She describes a cognitive model underlying the form and function of this gesture, and concludes that this cyclic gesture has a stable form-meaning relationship, likening the gesture to the metaphor 'time is motion through space' (Smart 1949; Traugott 1978; Lakoff 1993; Deutscher 2006; *inter alia*). The movement of the sign, also found in Norwegian Sign Language, reflects a spatial metaphor in which recurrent time periods (e.g., days, months, years, eras) may be metaphorically associated with cycles, or, more directly, with a circular movement (Selvik 2006).

3.1 Prosody of rhythm and non-manual signals in sign language

A distinct component of the grammatical system of sign languages is prosody, which includes rhythm, intonation, and prominence. As in spoken languages, prosody interacts with syntax and segmental phonology, as well as with semantics, information structure, and discourse organization (Sandler 1999).

We concentrate here on prosodic constituents at the level of the intonational phrase (IP), the basic domain of intonational alignment. Intonational phrase boundaries in ISL are marked by the timing and prominence of manual cues – pause, hold, reduplication, and/or enlargement of the final sign in the phrase (Nespor & Sandler 1999).[6] Intonation, a component of prosody, is realized as facial expressions and head movements (Reilly, McIntire & Bellugi 1990; Nespor & Sandler 1999; Dachkovsky & Sandler 2009). The alignment of manual cues (e.g., hold or reduplication) with face and body movements (e.g., raised brows or torso tilt) is what makes the IP boundary so salient, as can be seen in Figure 2 below – an ISL sentence meaning *'The cake that I baked is tasty'*. The sentence consists of two intonational phrases, indicated in the figure caption by capital 'I' after the brackets, and separated by a double line, and of three phonological phrases, indicated by capital 'P' after the brackets,

---

[6] Here we follow Nespor & Sandler's designation of cues such as hold, reduplication, or pause as signaling prominence or strength, in relation to other constituents in the prosodic phrase, thus establishing a rhythmic alternation.

and separated by a single line in the figure. In this particular utterance, the IP-final sign BAKE has more repetitions than the citation form of the sign, and TASTY ends with a long hold. Similar cues have been found at IP boundaries in other sign languages, such as ASL (Dachkovsky et al. 2013) and German Sign Language (DGS; Herrmann 2010). We follow studies of spoken languages in proposing that intonational phrases can roughly correspond to thought units (e.g., Du Bois 1985; Chafe 1994).

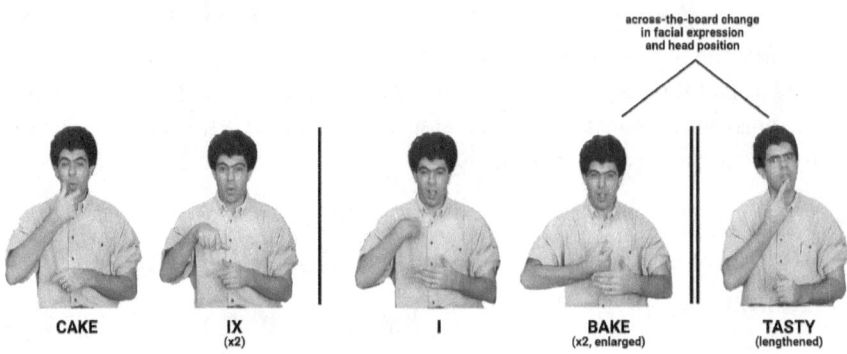

Gloss: [[CAKE IX] $_P$ [I BAKE] $_P$] $_I$ [[TASTY] $_P$] $_I$
Transl. 'The cake that I baked is tasty.'

Figure 2: An ISL complex sentence consisting of two intonational phrases and three phonological phrases. In the image, 'IX' stands for an indexical pointing sign; the single line marks a phonological phrase boundary; and the double line indicates the IP boundary. In the gloss, Intonational phrases are marked by 'I', and phonological phrases are marked by 'P' (adapted from Nespor & Sandler 1999).

Non-manual markers corresponding to intonation are equally important for interpreting sign language constituents (Baker & Padden 1978; Liddell 1980; Nespor & Sandler 1999). The non-manual markers of facial expression and head position align temporally with the manual markers, and all markers change across the board between IPs (Nespor & Sandler 1999). So, in the sentence in Figure 2, the entire first intonational phrase is marked by raised eyebrows, squint, and forward head movement, which all change in unison at the IP boundary.

Like linguistic intonation in spoken languages, linguistic facial expressions and head movements in established sign languages signal various pragmatic functions, such as the illocutionary force of an utterance (assertions vs. questions), continuation and dependency across clauses, as well as information structure distinctions (Dachkovsky et al. 2013; Sandler et al. 2019). Figure 2 illustrates that head movement down is typical of the end of the intonational phrase in ISL, while head up characterizes the beginning of a new intonational phrase. Other recent research has attributed similar status to head movements in Finnish Sign Language (Puupponen 2018) and Austrian Sign Language (Lackner 2013).

In addition to prosody, manual rhythmic signals and non-manual cues can make morphological distinctions in sign language. Specifically, reduplicated hand movements and particular facial expressions mark adverbial and aspectual modification of a verb (Fischer 1973; Klima & Bellugi 1979; Liddell 1980; Sandler 1990; Wilbur 2003, 2009; Meir & Sandler 2008). Figure 3 below illustrates the marking of continuative aspect (e.g., *I've been studying for a long time*) in ISL (Meir & Sandler 2008). It shows that the aspectual modification of a verb is signaled by reduplicated slow hand movements and by a particular facial expression (specifically, an open mouth configuration). As markers of aspectual distinctions, rhythmic cues together with non-manual features are associated with verbs and characterize events.

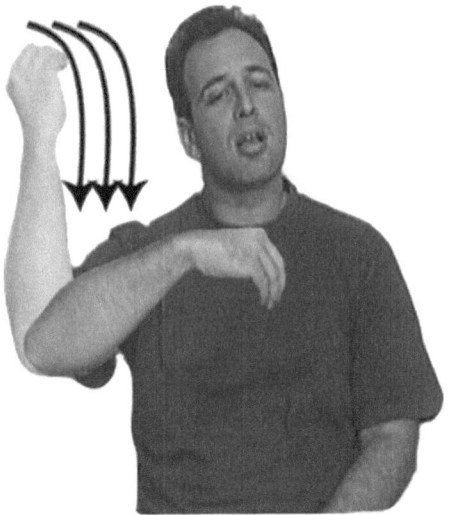

Figure 3: Marking of continuative aspect in ISL (Meir & Sandler 2008: 93).

In sum, particular patterns of rhythmic cues and non-manual signals play important roles in determining both prosodic constituency (intonational phrases) and grammatical categorization (predicates versus other sentence elements).

Building on the generalizations reported in the spoken and sign language literature, we predict that discourse-structuring time expressions will have the following characteristics. They should stand as prosodically separate expressions, occupying their own intonational phrase. They will often occur in close proximity with other discourse markers and other cues of backgrounded information, such as verbs denoting continuous or habitual events. Event-sequencing time expressions, on the other hand, will have features of syntactic integration. Specifically, we expect to see them positioned at the beginning of an intonational phrase. We predict that they will occur in environments where the adjacent verbs are telic and/or have clear end points, since a sequence of events presupposes their start and end.

4 Methodology

This section begins by introducing the community under investigation, the Israeli deaf community, followed by a description of the data we analyzed, narratives elicited from seventeen elderly deaf ISL signers, representing an early stage in the development of the language. We then proceed to present our coding categories, informed by the theoretical research described above.

4.1 The community and our participants

Israeli Sign Language is the established language of the deaf community in Israel (Meir & Sandler 2008). It is a young sign language, roughly 90 years old, which arose with the formation of the deaf community around the 1930s, together with the establishment of the first Israeli School for the Deaf in 1932 in Jerusalem. Immigrants from all over the world contributed to the signing used by a small number of deaf Jews and Arabs already in Jerusalem. Vocabulary items have been traced in particular to immigrants from Germany, as well as to immigrants from elsewhere in Europe, North Africa, and the Middle East. A conventional local sign language evolved, and today, ISL is used by roughly 10,000 people in a wide range of settings, including the educational system, deaf social and cultural institutions, interpreting programs, and the media. The linguistic structure of ISL has been investigated in earlier work (e.g., Meir 1998, 2010; Nespor & Sandler 1999; Meir & Sandler 2008), and its emergence and change has more recently become the object of study (e.g., Meir et al. 2013; Dachkovsky 2018; Dachkovsky et al. 2018).

The narratives elicited as part of this study form part of a collection known as the ISL Narratives Archive, which we describe in more detail below.

4.2 The data: the ISL Narratives Archive

Seventeen videos were analyzed from an archive of spontaneous life stories collected as part of various projects at the University of Haifa. The archive consists of roughly fifty narratives collected during several filming sessions from the year 2000 to 2018, by Prof. Wendy Sandler and by the late Prof. Irit Meir, and assistants. Narratives range in length from 2 to 54 minutes.

A sample of four of the deaf narratives from the archive is fully accessible to the public, in collaboration with the SIGN-HUB (Horizon 2020) project and the University of Tel Aviv, together with Prof. Naama Friedmann. The aim of the SIGN-HUB project is to preserve, research, and foster the linguistic, historical, and cultural heritage of deaf signing communities, primarily in Europe (see Pfau, Göksel & Hosemann, this volume, for details). The four ISL narratives include subtitles in English and Hebrew and are accessible via the SIGN-HUB project webpage. All participants included in our sample represent the elderly population (aged 70+), which was the focus of the relevant part of the SIGN-HUB project.

4.3 Coding and analysis

A total of 133 tokens of TIME-PASS were coded from the narratives. As noted in the introduction, this marker was chosen as the subject of investigation because of its frequent use in the signing of the older deaf population, indicating an early structure in the language. Narratives were divided into intonational phrases based on manual signals, such as pause, hold, and reduplication, which correspond to phrase-final lengthening in ISL, and are reliable signals of intonational phrase boundaries, often accompanied by blinks (Nespor & Sandler 1999). We coded for the manual rhythmic cues and the aligned non-manual cues accompanying each TIME-PASS token (see Table 1). In this study, the intonational phrase was the basic unit in the analysis of the distribution of non-manual signals marking discourse relations. An intonational phrase usually corresponds either to a full clause or to a temporal clause-initial stage-setter, such as 'during the winter'. All coding was implemented using ELAN, a video annotation software (Crasborn & Sloetjes 2008). Based on predictions derived from previous studies (see Section 2.2), we coded the presence of other time expressions, discourse markers, and verbs within the context of each TIME-PASS token (as shown in Table 1).

Table 1: Coding categories.

Manual cues	Aligned non-manual cues	Context
Duration: the length of the sign (in secs)	Head movement: head up or down during the sign production	Other time expressions with time quantification (e.g., THREE-YEARS, AGE FOUR)
Presence of hold/ pause: after/ before the sign	Head nods accompanying the sign production	Other discourse markers expressing discourse or evaluative stance (e.g., SO-SO, ANYWAY)
Cyclic reduplication: the number of cycles produced during the sign	Open mouth during the sign	Verbs with implied end points (e.g., ARRIVE, MOVE-HOUSE)
Position of the sign in the intonational phrase (IP): either at the start, end, or constituting an IP by itself		Verbs without implied end points (e.g., WALK, STUDY)

5 Results

It was the observed prosodic bifurcation between instances of TIME-PASS that inspired this study, and we begin with quantified results for prosodic markers to confirm that observation. Based on the coding described in Section 4, two characteristic displays were identified. We initially distinguished the two TIME-PASS markers on the basis of type of head movement and number of repetitions. We refer to them here as TIME-PASS1 and TIME-PASS2. There were 52 examples of TIME-PASS1 and 51 examples of TIME-PASS2.[7] We then sought independent evidence from context that these were indeed two different markers. Here, we describe the results in terms of manual rhythmic cues (Section 5.1) and non-manual cues (Section 5.2) of TIME-PASS1 and TIME-PASS2. Context will be discussed in Section 5.3.

---

[7] We note that thirty examples were excluded because they present a mixed display and could not be clearly categorized. While this is not a negligible quantity, it is compatible with the fact that the language of our participants represents an early stage, and is in a state of flux, and we leave those instances for future research.

5.1 Manual rhythmic cues

We took the following rhythmic cues into account: position of the sign in the intonational phrase and intonational phrase marking, such as holds, pauses, reduplications, or size of sign. As shown in Table 2 below, TIME-PASS1 typically constitutes an intonational phrase by itself (65%), and it has a longer duration (1.2 secs) with multiple iterations of the cyclic motion (2.24 cycles). In contrast, TIME-PASS2 is typically reduced in length and cycles (0.75 secs, 1.02 cycles), and it tends to occur at the beginning of an intonational phrase (67%).

Table 2: Summary of the characteristics of each time expression category.[8]

	TIME-PASS1	TIME-PASS2
Manual rhythm/constituency		
Duration	1.2secs (average)	0.75secs (average)
Cyclic reduplication	2.24 (average)	1.02 (average)
Position in intonational phrase	65% alone	67% beginning
Non-manual markers		
Head up	37%	85%
Head down	63%	15%
Head nods	53%	32%
Open mouth	20%	4%
Context		
Other time expressions	7%	45%
Other discourse markers expressing discourse stance or evaluation	58%	12%
Verbs or predicates with end points	15%	70%
Verbs or predicates without end points	60%	10%

---

8 The numbers here represent the percentage of total TIME-PASS tokens with the specified feature.

5.2 Non-manual markers

We based our clustering on the non-manual features which were consistent across the majority of tokens; these include head movements, such as up and down, as well as head nods, and open mouth. Our results revealed that TIME-PASS1 is typically accompanied by a characteristic head movement: downward head movement (63%) and in some cases head nods (53%). In contrast, TIME-PASS2 is typically accompanied by an upward movement of the head (85%). In addition, open mouth sometimes accompanied TIME-PASS1 (20%), but was rarely found with TIME-PASS2 (4%).

5.3 Context

Our results indicate that there are contextual patterns with each TIME-PASS (see Table 2). TIME-PASS1 tends most often to be preceded by predicates without an implied end point (60%), such as actions in progress or incomplete actions, like STUDY or GROW. In contrast, this context is very rare with TIME-PASS2 (10%). TIME-PASS1 also occurs with discourse markers expressing discourse stance or evaluation, such as WELL, DOESN'T-MATTER, WHATEVER (58% for TIME-PASS1 versus 12% for TIME-PASS2). Instead, TIME-PASS2 is often followed by other time expressions, such as THREE-YEARS, EXACTLY-THEN, or AFTER (45% for TIME-PASS2 versus 7% for TIME-PASS1), and by verbs or predicates with implied end points (70% for TIME-PASS2 versus 15% for TIME-PASS1).

In sum, the contexts of the two types of TIME-PASS are very different by all measures. While TIME-PASS1 tends to co-occur with other cues of backgrounding information, TIME-PASS2 occurs in environments where the punctuality and the end points of events are emphasized. In the following discussion section, we provide specific examples of each type of TIME-PASS, and explore how each TIME-PASS display offers multiple yet distinct functions in the discourse.

6 Discussion

The findings of our study reveal that elderly signers of early ISL already use two distinct prosodic profiles, in relatively equal proportion, for the same lexical expression of TIME-PASS. In this section, we discuss the contributions of prosodic cues and of context in distinguishing these functions.

6.1 Two types of TIME-PASS: general characteristics

6.1.1 Manual rhythmic cues

TIME-PASS1 constitutes an intonational phrase by itself. That is, there is an intonational boundary immediately preceding and following TIME-PASS1. In contrast, TIME-PASS2 was not produced in a separate intonational phrase, but rather appeared at the beginning of the intonational phrase, followed by more material within the same IP, so that the IP boundary preceded the sign only. In this sense, it serves as an introduction to the rest of the material in its intonational phrase. The strength of the boundaries around TIME-PASS1 was stronger than that preceding TIME-PASS2. This was determined based on prosodic signals of the kind described in Section 3.1 – that is, the boundaries preceding TIME-PASS1 were longer, with more holds, and/or multiple iterations or a larger production of the cyclic motion of the sign. TIME-PASS2, however, is reduced in length, either with fewer iterations of the cyclic motion or more restricted in size.

6.1.2 Non-manual markers

Now we turn to the non-manual markers which accompany each time expression in our study. The longer duration and multiple iterations of TIME-PASS1 are often accompanied by head nods, downward head movement, and open mouth, which are indicators of action in process (Meir & Sandler 2008). The end of the intonational phrase is also marked by movement of the head down.

TIME-PASS2, in contrast, is accompanied by a movement of the head up. In ISL, head up is common for marking the beginning of an intonational phrase, but it also signals continuation and topic (Dachkovsky et al. 2013). This seems to suggest that TIME-PASS2 functions in a similar way to a time adverbial. In some cases, we also see that signers produce a mouthing of a Hebrew word (e.g., *aXarai* 'after' or *aXar kaX* 'afterwards') along with TIME-PASS2, signaling its function as an event-sequencing device.

6.1.3 Context

TIME-PASS1 is freer in its context than TIME-PASS2. We see that TIME-PASS2 is restricted to particular types of grammatical environments. In most cases, TIME-PASS2 is accompanied by either time expressions (e.g., *3 years, age 2*, etc.) or telic (end point) verbs (e.g., *arrive, move, leave*). In this context, TIME-PASS2 functions more like 'afterwards' or 'then' by helping to relate events more efficiently. Since sign languages do not mark tense on verbs, TIME-PASS2 serves as an effective way to mark these relations. In this sense, TIME-PASS2 acts as a temporal adverbial or conjunction.

At a more global discourse level, TIME-PASS1 seems to bridge together two segments of text at a higher level of discourse (i.e., larger chunks). TIME-PASS2, alternatively, with its more restricted syntactic context, relates segments at a clausal level.

In the next section, we will discuss and illustrate these two distinct functional profiles of TIME-PASS1 and TIME-PASS2 on the basis of stories presented by two older ISL signers. These two stories provide a magnifying lens for highlighting the unique properties of the two distinct time expressions sharing the same basic manual form.

6.2 Functions of TIME-PASS1 and TIME-PASS2 illustrated by real stories

In light of what we discussed in Section 2, we will consider the functions of TIME-PASS1 and TIME-PASS2 in turn.

6.2.1 TIME-PASS1

The functions of TIME-PASS1 deduced from its rhythmic and non-manual marking, as well as from its context, will be demonstrated on the basis of the first signer's story below.[9] Examples are numbered to relate them to the description that follows; for every example, we specify in which figure it is illustrated. There are other time expressions in the narratives, but we focus on the numbered examples to explicate our findings most clearly. Material in square brackets was added by the authors for clarity.

> Narrative 1 by S., who emigrated to Israel from Algeria, filmed in 2005
> *My mother told me that when I was very young, I was seriously sick, and this was the reason I became deaf. It was around the outbreak of the war [WWII], and my father was recruited into the army and sent to France. It was a rough time, **I was sick, there was war and difficulties, whatever. <u>After some time</u>, father returned** [example 2 (Figure 5)]. My mother was so happy. Everything was good. Over the next few years, he went back and forth to the*

---

9 The text represents a summary of what was produced by the signer. Some details are missing. For the full story, see the SIGN-HUB archive.

army. This was when my mother got pregnant. My brother arrived into the world and then my sister. **Mother was pregnant again; <u>all the while</u>, I continued to be sick** [example 1 (Figure 4)]. *I was sick for so long but there were no doctors back then. It was a hard time for my mother, with a growing family. I wanted to go to school, I wanted to learn but I was too scared. I had to speak at school, and I was too afraid to use my voice. Then mother got pregnant again. We were ten children in the end. I worked hard to look after the home. I would do the cooking, the laundry, the cleaning. Meanwhile, my sister refused to help at all. I also looked after my grandmother, I cared about her a lot. At this time, it was difficult being a Jew in Algeria. We were scared. When we heard that there was a war, we packed our bags in the middle of the night and left. We headed to France, and from there to Israel. After emigration, it was tough.* **<u>Time passed</u> and everything settled down: eventually, we were all close to each other – my mother, sister, grandmother, and me** [example 3 (Figure 6)]. [S.; 2005; 00:00–04:15]

TIME-PASS1 is abundant in S.'s whole story and helps to structure it. The sign fulfils a number of distinct, though overlapping, functions: (i) backgrounding, (ii) evaluation, and (iii) episode connecting between larger units. We will exemplify each function separately, using different result categories as pieces of evidence in our argumentation.

(i) Backgrounding function

A crucial distinction in every narrative is the juxtaposition between central events of the narration, its skeleton, and backgrounding events that convey the circumstances of the main events of the story (Hopper & Thompson 1980; Labov 2010). In our dataset, TIME-PASS1 is often used to signal the boundary between backgrounding (less central) and foregrounding (more central) parts of the narrative. Seventy percent (70%) of the TIME-PASS1 tokens convey this function. In such cases, they delineate the backgrounding sections. This function of TIME-PASS1 is often cued by other discourse markers in the text, such as SO-SO, WELL, etc. In this function, TIME-PASS1 is often adjacent to the predicates that convey repeated or continuous events or states, such as *sick for a long time, grow bigger, study hard*, etc. In this sense, TIME-PASS1 indicates a transition from her explanation of the circumstances to a new discourse segment with an event more central to the line of the narration.

This use of TIME-PASS1 echoes the cross-linguistic use of linguistic devices signaling narrative background. Multiple typological studies have demonstrated that among the most frequent backgrounding devices are subordinate constructions, as well as imperfective forms used to represent the internal temporal composition of a verb (Givón 1987; Cristofaro 2005; *inter alia*).

As for subordination, the research on emerging sign languages has convincingly demonstrated that early stages of language development lack overt syntactic subordination devices (Sandler et al. (2011) on Al-Sayyid Bedouin Sign Language; Dachkovsky (2018) on ISL). The present study puts the previous findings into a new perspective. Although early stages of sign language emergence lack subordination as a backgrounding device, our findings show that specific lexical items, such as TIME-PASS, can be used to mark the crucial distinction between background and foreground in the discourse.

For example, in S.'s story, the severe and untreated illness that led to her deafness is presented as the background for the dramatic story about the whole family, whose existence is shaken by world war, national revolution, and forced emigration. These constitute the main sequence of events in the narrative. In example 1, illustrated in Figure 4, TIME-PASS1 occurs at the boundaries of the backgrounding unit in which S. talks about her illness, thereby presenting it as a backgrounded circumstance of the main narrative events.

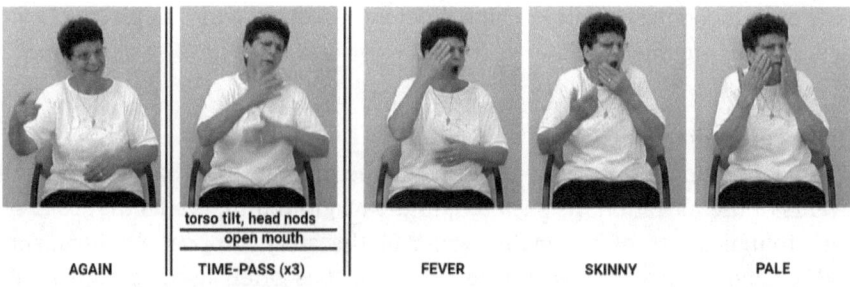

Figure 4: Example 1 – TIME-PASS1 with backgrounding function.
Mother was pregnant again; // all the while, // I continued to be sick. (01:22–01:25)

TIME-PASS1 in this example is produced in its own intonational phrase and is accompanied by repeated head thrusts. The cyclic motion of the sign is reduplicated four times cuing the continuative temporal nature of the predicate, which is emphasized by the open mouth expression. The opposing head tilts mark the boundary between the background and foreground units in the narrative.

(ii) Evaluative function

The backgrounding function of TIME-PASS1 is intrinsically connected to another pragmatic function that it can fulfil – evaluation. The division between background and foreground in discourse does not reflect the objective flow of events, but rather is sensitive to their subjective construal (Givón 1991; Langacker 2004), in which one event is viewed as more central (foreground), and another event is presented as more peripheral and circumstantial (background). Since the reason for the foreground-background construal is subjective and not objective, it is inevitably highly dependent on the presenter's evaluative stance and point of view. Therefore, it is only natural that TIME-PASS1 often bears an evaluative function as well – it helps to downgrade the information by signaling that it is of low communicative or personal value, parenthetical, and not obligatory for the interlocutor's knowledge.

This function was also very common in our dataset – it was present in more than half of all of the TIME-PASS1 examples. The low communicative informational value is often cued by non-manual signals of disregard or uncertainty, such as lowered lip corners, furrowed and slightly raised brows. In terms of their context, all the instances of evaluative TIME-PASS1 are accompanied by other downgrading discourse markers expressing uncertainty or lack of involvement, such as WELL, WHATEVER, DON'T-KNOW, NO-IDEA, etc., as in example 2 from S.'s story (shown in Figure 5).

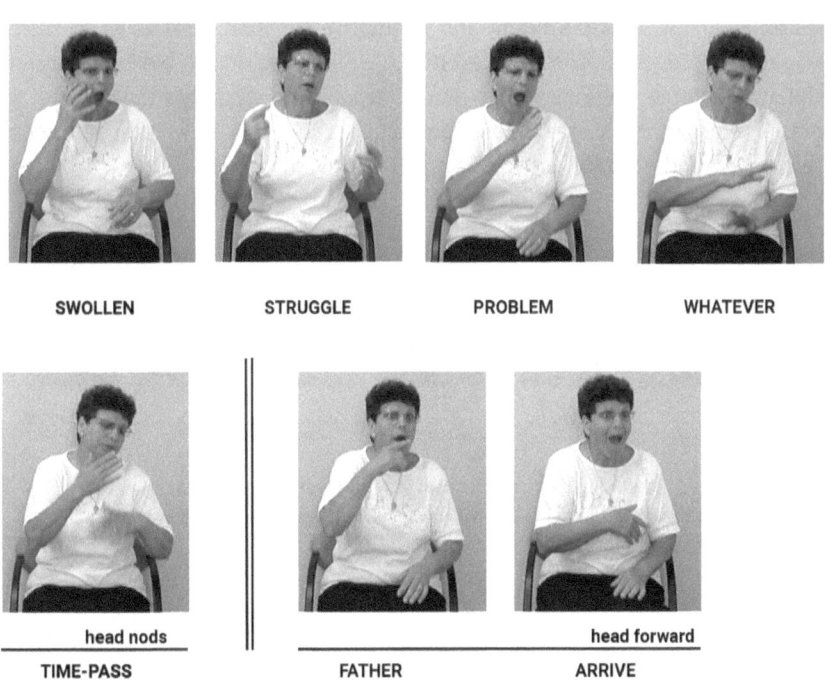

Figure 5: Example 2 – TIME-PASS1 with evaluative function.
I was sick. There was war and difficulties, whatever. After some time, father returned.
(00:54–01:03)

In this example, S. lists different difficulties experienced during her childhood (e.g., illness, war, fights, etc.), but by the act of summarizing them with a single general term PROBLEM followed by a downgrading discourse marker WHATEVER, the signer shows that those difficulties were not central in their life back then; they were overridden by more important events, such as her father's return from the war. This effect is strengthened by the change in the head position: it is held backward on the background part but is thrust forward on the more prominent event. As in the previous example, here as well, TIME-PASS1 occupies the whole intonational phrase, and the cyclic hand movement is repeated multiple times. The change between the backgrounded, downgraded circumstances (her illness) to the central line of the story (her father coming back) is also underlined by the shift in the verb type: the former is expressed by the continuative states (SICK, SWOLLEN), whereas the main event manifests with the verb with a clear end point (ARRIVE).

(iii) Episode-connecting between larger units

In addition to the backgrounding and evaluative function, TIME-PASS1 in many cases separates larger units of the narrative, i.e., major episodes. We see an example below (example 3 in Figure 6), where S. separates the family's time in Algeria from their emigration to Israel. More specifically, she recalls how, after settling in Israel, the life of the family settles down and returns to its normal flow.

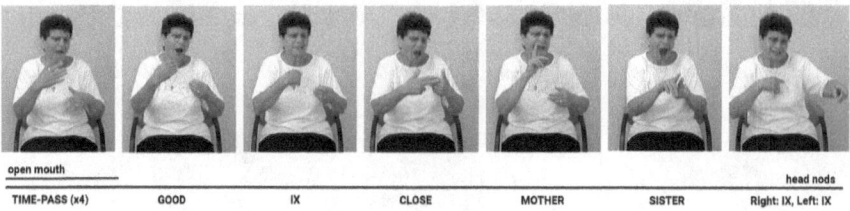

Figure 6: Example 3 – TIME-PASS1 as an episode divider between larger units.
Time passed // and everything settled down. // Eventually, we were all close to each other – my mother, sister, grandmother and me.[10] *(04:11–04:15)*

TIME-PASS1 occupies an entire intonational phrase, which supports the interpretation that it expresses a whole proposition, separate from the surrounding propositions. As intonational phrases can be considered as roughly corresponding to

---

10 The signer produces two pronouns simultaneously to mean 'grandmother and me'.

thought units (e.g., Chafe 1984; Du Bois 1985), we can loosely translate the TIME-PASS1 to mean 'time went on', which stands as a separate event.

The rotating hand movement is reduplicated four times, which suggests that the event is imperfective or uncompleted, another characteristic of backgrounding. The accompanying non-manual markers support this interpretation: the sign is accompanied by open mouth, characteristic of continuous temporality, as explained above (see Figure 3). The rhythm of the repeated hand movements is mirrored by repeated head thrusts.

A similar use of imperfective verb forms to mark major episode boundaries has been attested in spoken languages as well, for example, in the narrative of Beowulf (Richardson 1994). In that study, the author discusses verbal aspect as one of the principal means of structuring and organizing narratives. In the context of older signers' narratives in our data, the use of the imperfective marking on TIME-PASS1 as a narrative structuring device has an even greater significance. Dachkovsky et al. (2018) found that older signers, in contrast to younger signers, almost exclusively exploit lexical markers (e.g., THAT'S-IT, FINISH, etc.), and not grammatical devices like aspectual inflections, to separate larger narrative episodes. The use of TIME-PASS1 described here falls nicely into this category, and facilitates efficient discourse organization in the absence of other grammatical cues.

In sum, TIME-PASS1 has a very rich meaning potential, often expressing multiple pragmatic and discourse functions simultaneously. All of these functions are rooted in the metaphor of time and discourse unfolding gradually and evenly, similar to motion in space. The gradualness and regularity of the unfolding are underscored by rhythmic and non-manual markers. Rhythm is conveyed by manual reduplications, and intonation by non-manual markers such as head movements. The presence of other discourse markers helps to specify the use of this metaphor in terms of the narrative progression.

In contrast, TIME-PASS2, discussed in the following section, lacks this pragmatic and discourse potential. It is pragmatically bleached and restricted to specific structural environments.

6.2.2 TIME-PASS2

This use of TIME-PASS2 is demonstrated on the basis of the second story, told by signer R.

> Narrative 2 by R., who was born in Israel, filmed in 2006
> When I was little, I got sick and became deaf. The doctors back then didn't understand what deafness was. **At age two, I got sick. Afterwards at age 3, I recovered.** [example 4

(Figure 7)]. *The doctors decided that I was retarded so when I was three, I was sent to an institution for retarded children. I was there for a year. Finally, when I was four, the doctors realized that I wasn't retarded, and I was sent to a school in Jerusalem. At the same time, it was the Second World War. Times were hard, there was no food, and we were stuck in bomb shelters all the time. One day, when I was seven years old, I remember we were in the shelters, and I couldn't take it anymore, and so I escaped out into the streets of Jerusalem. The streets were filled with tanks and British soldiers. The soldiers came up to me and gave me candy. It was a big deal but my teacher was furious because I had disappeared, and so I was punished. It was completely worth it, it is an experience that I will never forget.*

At the school in Jerusalem, they forced us to speak and not sign. I was an excellent student. At the age of nine, Neev school was founded in Haifa, and I moved from Jerusalem to attend school there. I was there until eighth grade. There was no junior high school back then. My teacher saw that I had the potential to continue with my studies. I begged my parents, and they agreed. **After the (deaf) class was formed, and (after) the teacher arrived, I moved to another school** [example 5 (Figure 8)]. *It was hard work, there was no provision back then. I had to get by from reading my friends' notes and working hard at home. But I made it, and I finished twelfth grade. The head teacher called a meeting with my parents. They asked me about my future plans, and I said that I expected to become a seamstress, but the head teacher insisted that I should set my sights higher and that he thought I was good enough to go on to college. My parents were delighted. So, that's what I did. I went to college and became a teacher, and over the years I have continued to study. This is why I am still working today because I continue to learn new skills.*

[R.; 2006; 00:00–7:40]

The results presented in Section 5 demonstrate that TIME-PASS2 almost never occurs as a separate intonational phrase, instead appearing at the beginning of the intonational phrase together with the following proposition. In other words, it does not make a proposition of its own but rather precedes a proposition. It is typically phonologically reduced, rarely resulting even in one full rotation of the hands, unlike TIME-PASS1, which is produced with multiple reduplicated movements. Therefore, TIME-PASS2 does not convey an action in progress. Open mouth, characterizing an action in progress in TIME-PASS1, is missing in the TIME-PASS2 occurrences. Below we delve into the specific functions of TIME-PASS2.

(i) Connective function

Unlike TIME-PASS1, which usually demarcates backgrounding information and, as a result, connects larger stretches of text, the connective function of TIME-PASS2 is different. It signals the connection between two individual events or episodes and conveys a change of state, or succession of events rather than one event backgrounding another. Therefore, TIME-PASS2 is typically followed by time adverbials such as THREE-YEARS ('three years later'), AGE NINE ('at age 9'), JUST-THEN, and so on. The vast majority of predicates in the intonational phrase introduced by TIME-PASS2 are telic, with an endpoint, or resultative, emphasizing a change of state, as shown in example 4, illustrated in Figure 7 below. The example is taken from the very beginning of R.'s story, in which she recollects one of the most crucial changes in her life – the moment she became deaf, as a result of illness.

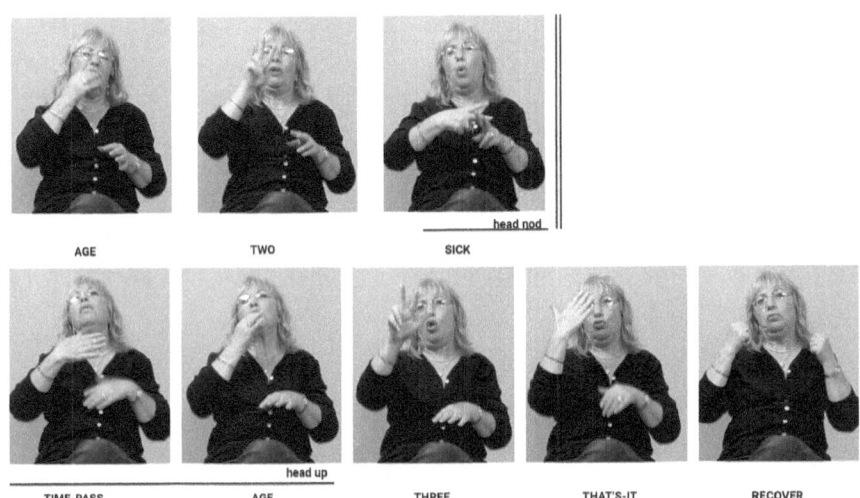

Figure 7: Example 4 – TIME-PASS2 with connective function.
At age two I got sick. // Afterwards at age 3 I recovered. (00:10–00:14)

TIME-PASS2 here introduces a new intonational phrase and, together with it, presents a chain of events. As suggested by many researchers (e.g., Chafe 1984; Dubois 1989; Langacker 2004), a new intonational phrase represents a new thought unit and typically signifies a new proposition. Moreover, the predicate (RECOVER), used in the same proposition with TIME-PASS2, is resultative – emphasized by the use of the discourse marker THAT'S-IT. Taken together, these characteristics signal that TIME-PASS2 acts as a connector between two successive events. In this function, the time expression only appears at the beginning of the IP it modifies.

(ii) Completion of events: Perfective function
Another function of TIME-PASS2 is related to the first, but is more specific. In some contexts, it signals that the change of events or states is due to the completion of preceding events. In this case, the function of TIME-PASS2 is similar to

that of the perfective aspect, and different from the verbs denoting the internal temporal structure of an event, which, as we have seen, contextualize TIME-PASS1. Instead, TIME-PASS2 occurs in the context of a sequence of events, in which the occurrence of one event is contingent on the completion of another, as shown in example 5 (Figure 8).

Figure 8: Example 5 – TIME-PASS2 used in perfective function.
After the (deaf) class was formed, // and (after) the teacher arrived, // I moved to another school. (04:06–04:08)

As we can see in this example, the events are contingent upon one other, so that the completion of one event leads to the next event. Moreover, all the predicates (CLASS-FORM, ARRIVE, MOVE) in the sequence above are telic, i.e., with implied end points. TIME-PASS2, then, connects to a telic predicate.

In sum, TIME-PASS2 does not seem to express purely discourse functions. It expresses temporal relation to what follows, similar to 'then' or 'afterwards'.[11] This is strengthened by the fact that in some examples, like the second instance of TIME-PASS2 shown in example 5 (Figure 8) above, the signer mouths the word

---

11 We speculate that TIME-PASS2 acts as either a temporal adverbial, conjunction, or preposition since it connects events at a clausal level. To understand which of these options (temporal adverbial, conjunction or preposition) is more likely is beyond the scope of this paper and we hope to revisit this in future work.

'after' in Hebrew. Its functions are related to particular structural properties of the narration, and it connects specific events within the same bigger episode.

7 Conclusions

The roles of different visible actions of the body are crucial for understanding sign language structure (Sandler 2012, 2018). But all too often, the importance of multi-articulatory analysis is overlooked in other studies. Our results indicate that rhythmic and non-manual cues are crucial for disambiguating different functions of time expressions in sign language. Sign languages, as visual languages, offer us an opportunity to easily observe the function reflected in the linguistic marking of form (see Sandler et al. 2019). In this study, we observed two rhythmic and non-manual displays which reflect different functions represented by the same lexical sign in ISL, TIME-PASS: discourse temporality and event temporality. Our study supports the notion that changes in form represent nuances in the conceptual representation of a narrative. An area for future research is to see if these functions are expressed differently in younger generations, as the language develops over time.

Our findings can be compared with those of Ladewig (2011). In her study, she found that speakers draw on the widely accessible metaphor 'time is motion through space'. Our results show that this metaphor is also prominent in sign language (see also Friedman 1975; Brennan 1983; Sutton-Spence 2010, 2016), providing further support for this metaphor in human cognition. Drawing on Fleischman (1991), we see in our results that signers expand its meaning to convey 'motion through discourse'.

This particular study focused on the elderly deaf population in Israel – the first generation of a recently emerged sign language. We still observe the continued development of this language today, by studying younger generations (Dachkovsky 2018; Dachkovsky et al. 2018). The signing of older signers is often overlooked in other studies, perhaps on the assumption that signers in this generation would not exhibit features of a fully functional language. Our results indicate that this is a mistake. Older signers demonstrate earlier grammatical patterns of a sign language. In an early stage of the development of ISL, the lexical sign TIME-PASS is effectively used and extended to two clearly distinguishable functions, as we have shown. Older signers produce the lexical sign with different prosodic profiles, expressing different structural functions in discourse, supported by our analysis of contexts. Our study points to the importance of studying the signing of older people to understand how conceptually complex relations are expressed in early stages in the life of a language. The narratives we collected are thus important, not just from a historical and cultural perspective, but also from a linguistic perspective.

Most importantly, discourse markers in the older signers' narratives both evoke and shape cultural and personal identities of the founders of the contemporary deaf community in Israel. These signers use space to represent concepts of time in TIME-PASS to construe these identities. Individual narratives cumulatively build a multi-colored yet coherent history of the Israeli deaf community, and of the diverse history of the country as a whole. We are privileged to study and archive them – seizing the opportunity before TIME-PASSes us by.

References

Aijmer, Karin. 2002. *English discourse particles: Evidence from a corpus*. Amsterdam: John Benjamins.
Amundsen, Guri & Rolf Piene Halvorsen. 2011. *Sign or gesture? Two discourse markers in Norwegian Sign Language (NSL)*. Presentation at the 33rd Annual Conference of the German Linguistic Society (DGfS), Göttingen.
Auer, Peter & Yael Maschler (eds.) 2016. *Nu and its relatives: A discourse marker across the languages of Europe and beyond*. Berlin: Walter de Gruyter.
Baker, Charlotte & Carol Padden. 1978. Focusing on the nonmanual components of American Sign Language. In Patricia Siple (ed.), *Understanding language through sign language research*, 27–57. New York: Academic Press.
Bakhtin, Mikhail M. 1981. *The dialogic imagination: Four essays* (ed. by Michael Holquist). Austin, TX: University of Texas Press.
Brennan, Mary. 1983. Marking time in British Sign Language. In Jim G. Kyle & Bencie Woll (eds.), *Language in sign: An international perspective on sign language*. London: Croom Helm.
Brinton, Laurel J. 2010. *Pragmatic markers in English: Grammaticalization and discourse functions*. Berlin: Walter de Gruyter.
Chafe, Wallace. 1994. *Discourse, consciousness, and time*. Chicago: University of Chicago Press.
Chafe, Wallace. 1984. How people use adverbial clauses. *Annual Meeting of the Berkeley Linguistics Society* 10. 437–449.
Chodorowska-Pilch, Marianna. 1999. On the polite use of *vamos* in Peninsular Spanish. *Pragmatics* 9(3). 343–355.
Clark, Herbert. 1973. Space, time, semantics, and the child. In Timothy E. Moore (ed.), *Cognitive development and the acquisition of language*, 27–63. New York: Academic Press.
Clover, Carol J. 1982. *The medieval saga*. London: Cornell University Press.
Colin, Frances, Paul Hagstrom & Carol Neidle. 2003. A particle of indefiniteness in American Sign Language. *Linguistic Discovery* 2(1). 1–21.

Cooperrider, Kensy, Natasha Abner & Susan Goldin-Meadow. 2018. The palm-up puzzle: Meanings and origins of a widespread form in gesture and sign. *Frontiers in Communication* 3: 23.

Couper-Kuhlen, Elizabeth. 1996. Intonation and clause combining in discourse: The case of because. *Pragmatics* 6(1). 389–426.

Crasborn, Onno & Han Sloetjes. 2008. Enhanced ELAN functionality for sign language corpora. In *Proceedings of the 3rd Workshop on the Representation and Processing of Sign Languages: Construction and Exploitation of Sign Language Corpora*, 39–43. Paris: ELDA.

Cristofaro, Sonia. 2005. *Subordination*. Oxford: Oxford University Press.

Dachkovsky, Svetlana. 2018. *Grammaticalization of intonation in Israeli Sign Language: From information structure to relative clause relations*. Haifa, Israel: University of Haifa PhD dissertation.

Dachkovsky, Svetlana, Christina Healy & Wendy Sandler. 2013. Visual intonation in two sign languages. *Phonology* 30(2). 211–252.

Dachkovsky, Svetlana & Wendy Sandler. 2009. Visual intonation in the prosody of a sign language. *Language and Speech* 52(2–3). 287–314.

Dachkovsky, Svetlana, Rose Stamp & Wendy Sandler. 2018. Constructing complexity in a young sign language. *Frontiers in Psychology* 9 (2202).

Deutscher, Guy. 2006. *The unfolding of language: An evolutionary tour of mankind's greatest invention*. New York: Holt Paperbacks.

Du Bois, John W. 1985. Competing motivations. In John Haiman (ed.), *Iconicity in syntax*, 343–366. Amsterdam: John Benjamins.

Du Bois, John W. 2007. The stance triangle. In Robert Englebretson (ed.), *Stancetaking in discourse: Subjectivity, evaluation, interaction*, 139–182. Amsterdam: John Benjamins.

Dubois, Betty Lou. 1989. Pseudoquotation in current English communication: 'Hey, she didn't really say it!' *Language in Society* 18(3). 343–360.

Engberg-Pedersen, Elisabeth. 2002. Gestures in signing: The presentation gesture in Danish Sign Language. In Rolf Schulmeister & Heimo Reinitzer (eds.), *Progress in sign language research: In honor of Siegmund Prillwitz*, 143–162. Hamburg: Signum Press.

Enkvist, Nils Erik & Brita Wårvik. 1987. Old English Þa, temporal chains, and narrative structure. In Anna Giacalone Ramat, Onofrio Carruba & Giuliano Bernini (eds.), *Papers from the 7th International Conference on Historical Linguistics (Current Issues in Linguistic Theory* 48), 221–237. Amsterdam: John Benjamins.

Evans, Vyvyan. 2004. *The structure of time: Language, meaning and temporal cognition*. Amsterdam: John Benjamins.

Evers-Vermeul, Jacqueline. 2005. *The development of Dutch connectives: Change and acquisition as windows on form-function relations*. Utrecht: University of Utrecht PhD dissertation.

Ferrara, Kathleen. 1997. Form and function of the discourse marker *anyway*: Implications for discourse analysis. *Linguistics* 35(2). 343–378.

Fischer, Susan D. 1973. Two processes of reduplication in the American Sign Language. *Foundations of Language* 9(4). 469–480.

Fleischman, Suzanne. 1991. Discourse as space / discourse as time: Reflections on the metalanguage of spoken and written discourse. *Journal of Pragmatics* 16(4). 291–306.

Fraser, Bruce. 1990. An approach to discourse markers. *Journal of Pragmatics* 14(3). 383–398.

Fraser, Bruce. 2009. An account of discourse markers. *International Review of Pragmatics* 1. 293–320.

Friedman, Lynn. 1975. Space, time, and person reference in ASL. *Language* 51. 940–961.
Gentner, Dedre. 2001. Spatial metaphors in temporal reasoning. In Merideth Gattis (ed.), *Spatial schemas and abstract thought*, 203–222. Cambridge, MA: The MIT Press.
Gernsbacher, Morton Ann & Talmy Givón. 1995. *Coherence in spontaneous text*. Philadelphia, PA: John Benjamins.
Givón, Talmy. 1991. The evolution of dependent clause morpho-syntax in Biblicial Hebrew. In Elizabeth Closs Traugott & Bernd Heine (eds.), *Approaches to grammaticalization*, 257–310. Philadelphia, PA: John Benjamins.
Gonen, Einat, Zohar Livnat & Noam Amir. 2015. The discourse marker *axshav* ('now') in spontaneous spoken Hebrew: Discursive and prosodic features. *Journal of Pragmatics* 89. 69–84.
Graesser, Arthur C., Keith K. Millis & Rolf A. Zwaan. 1997. Discourse comprehension. *Annual Review of Psychology* 48. 163–189.
Haegeman, Liliane & Virginia Hill. 2013. The syntacticization of discourse. In Raffaella Folli, Christina Sevdali & Robert Truswell (eds.), *Syntax and its limits*, 370–390. Oxford: Oxford University Press.
Haspelmath, Martin. 1997. *From space to time*. Munich: Lincom.
Herrmann, Annika. 2010. The interaction of eye blinks and other prosodic cues in German Sign Language. *Sign Language & Linguistics* 13. 3–39.
Hobbs, Jerry R. 1979. Coherence and coreference. *Cognitive Science* 3(1). 67–90.
Hopper, Paul J. & Sandra A. Thompson. 1980. Transitivity in grammar and discourse. *Language* 56(2). 251–299.
Hoza, Jack. 2011. The discourse and politeness functions of HEY and WELL in American Sign Language. In Cynthia Roy (ed.), *Discourse in signed languages*, 70–95. Washington, DC: Gallaudet University Press.
Hutchinson, Ben. 2004. Acquiring the meaning of discourse markers. In *Proceedings of the 42nd Annual Meeting of the Association for Computational Linguistics (ACL-04)*, 684–691.
Jarque, Maria J. 2014. *Metatextual discourse markers in Catalan Sign Language (LSC): Their emergence and the role of gesture*. Presentation at Spanish Cognitive Linguistics Association X International Conference, Badajoz.
Jucker, Andreas & Sara W. Smith. 1998. And people just you know like 'Wow': Discourse markers as negotiating strategies. In Andreas Jucker & Yael Ziv (eds.), *Discourse markers: Description and theory*, 171–202. Amsterdam: John Benjamins.
Kempen, Gerard & Karin Harbusch. 2016. Verb-second word order after German *weil* 'because': Psycholinguistic theory from corpus-linguistic data. *Glossa* 1. 1–32.
Kendon, Adam. 2004. *Gesture. Visible action as utterance*. Cambridge: Cambridge University Press.
Klein, Wolfgang. 2013. *Time in language*. London: Routledge.
Klima, Edward S. & Ursula Bellugi. 1979. *The signs of language*. Cambridge, MA: Harvard University Press.
Labov, William. 1972. Language in the inner city. Studies in the Black English Vernacular. In William Labov (ed.), *The transformation of experience in narrative syntax*, 354–396. Philadelphia: University of Pennsylvania Press.
Labov, William. 2010. Oral narratives of personal experience. In Patrick C. Hogan (ed.), *Cambridge encyclopedia of the language sciences*, 546–548. Cambridge: Cambridge University Press.

Lackner, Andrea. 2013. *Linguistic functions of head and body movements in Austrian Sign Language (ÖGS): A corpus-based analysis*. Graz, Austria: University of Graz PhD dissertation.

Ladewig, Silva H. 2011. Putting the cyclic gesture on a cognitive basis. *CogniTextes. Revue de l'Association Française de Linguistique Cognitive* 6. https://doi.org/10.4000/cognitextes.406.

Lakoff, George & Mark Johnson. 1980. *Metaphors we live by*. Chicago: University of Chicago Press.

Lakoff, George. 1993. The contemporary theory of metaphor. In Raymond W. Gibbs Jr. (ed.), *Metaphor and thought, 2nd ed.*, 202–251. New York, NY: Cambridge University Press.

Langacker, Ronald W. 2004. *Foundations of Cognitive Grammar II*. Stanford, CA: Stanford University Press.

Liddell, Scott K. 1980. *American Sign Language syntax*. The Hague : Mouton.

Lillo-Martin, Diane. 1986. Two kinds of null arguments in American Sign Language. *Natural Language and Linguistic Theory* 4(4). 415–444.

Mann, William C. & Sandra A. Thompson. 1986. *Rhetorical structure theory: Description and construction of text structures*. Marina del Rey, CA: Information Sciences Institute.

Maschler, Yael. 1997. Discourse markers at frame shifts in Israeli Hebrew talk-in-interaction. *Pragmatics* 7(2). 183–211.

Maschler, Yael. 2002. The role of discourse markers in the construction of multivocality in Israeli Hebrew talk-in-interaction. *Research on Language and Social Interaction* 35. 1–38.

Maschler, Yael. 2012. Emergent projecting constructions: The case of Hebrew *yada* ('know'). *Studies in Language* 36(4). 785–747.

Maschler, Yael & Gonen Dori-Hacohen. 2012. From sequential to affective discourse marker: Hebrew *nu* on Israeli political phone-in radio programs. *Discourse Studies* 14(4). 419–455.

Maschler, Yael & Deborah Schiffrin. 2015. Discourse markers: Language, meaning & context. In Deborah Tannen, Heidi E. Hamilton & Deborah Schiffrin (eds.), *The handbook of discourse analysis*, 189–221. Malden, MA: Wiley Blackwell.

McKee, Rachel & Sophia Wallingford. 2011. 'So, well, whatever': Discourse functions of palm-up in New Zealand Sign Language. *Sign Language & Linguistics* 14(2). 213–247.

Meir, Irit. 1998. Syntactic-semantic interaction in Israeli Sign Language verbs: The case of backwards verbs. *Sign Language & Linguistics* 1. 3–33.

Meir, Irit. 2010. The emergence of argument structure in two new sign languages. In Malka Rappaport Hovav, Edit Doron & Ivy Sichel (eds.), *Syntax, lexical semantics, and event structure*, 101–123. Oxford: Oxford University Press.

Meir, Irit, Carol A. Padden, Mark Aronoff & Wendy Sandler. 2013. Competing iconicities in the structure of languages. *Cognitive Linguistics* 24(2). 309–343.

Meir, Irit & Wendy Sandler. 2008. *A language in space: The story of Israeli Sign Language*. New York: Lawrence Erlbaum.

Mesch, Johanna. 2016. Manual backchannel responses in signers' conversations in Swedish Sign Language. *Language & Communication* 50. 22–41.

Müller, Cornelia. 2004. Forms and uses of the palm up open hand: A case of a gesture family? In Cornelia Müller & Roland Posner (eds.), *The semantics and pragmatics of everyday gestures*, 233–256. Berlin: Weidler.

Nespor, Marina & Wendy Sandler. 1999. Prosody in Israeli Sign Language. *Language and Speech* 42(2–3). 143–176.

Noordman, Leo & Wietske Vonk. 1997. The different functions of a conjunction in constructing a representation of the discourse. In Michel Fayol & Jean Costermans (eds.), *Processing interclausal relationships in production and comprehension of text*, 75–93. Hillsdale, NJ: Lawrence Erlbaum.

Puupponen, Anna. 2018. The relationship between movements and positions of the head and the torso in Finnish Sign Language. *Sign Language Studies* 18(2). 175–214.

Reilly, Judy Snitzer, Marina McIntire & Ursula Bellugi. 1990. The acquisition of conditionals in American Sign Language – grammaticized facial expressions. *Applied Psycholinguistics* 11. 369–392.

Richardson, Peter. 1994. Imperfective aspect and episode structure in 'Beowulf'. *The Journal of English and Germanic Philology* 93(3). 313–325.

Ricoeur, Paul. 2010. *Time and narrative (Vol. 3)*. Chicago: University of Chicago Press.

Roy, Cynthia B. 1989. Features of discourse in an American Sign Language lecture. In Ceil Lucas (ed.), *The sociolinguistics of the Deaf community*, 231–251. San Diego, CA: Academic Press.

Sanders, Ted, Wilbert P.M. Spooren & Leo Noordman. 1993. Coherence relations in a cognitive theory of discourse representation. *Cognitive Linguistics* 4. 93–133.

Sandler, Wendy. 1990. Temporal aspects and ASL phonology. In Susan Fischer & Patricia Siple (eds.), *Theoretical issues in sign language research. Volume I: Linguistics*, 7–36. Chicago: University of Chicago Press.

Sandler, Wendy. 1999. The medium and the message: Prosodic interpretation of linguistic content in Israeli Sign Language. *Sign Language & Linguistics* 2(2). 187–215.

Sandler, Wendy. 2012. Dedicated gestures in the emergence of sign language. *Gesture* 12(3). 265–307.

Sandler, Wendy. 2018. The body as evidence for the nature of language. *Frontiers in Psychology* 9: 1782.

Sandler, Wendy, Mark Aronoff, Irit Meir & Carol Padden. 2011. The gradual emergence of phonological form in a new language. *Natural Language and Linguistic Theory* 29(2). 503–543.

Sandler, Wendy, Marianne Gullberg & Carol Padden. 2019. Editorial: visual language. *Frontiers in Psychology* 10: 1765.

Schiffrin, Deborah. 1987. *Discourse markers*. Cambridge: Cambridge University Press.

Schiffrin, Deborah. 1996. Narrative as self-portrait: Sociolinguistic constructions of identity. *Language in Society* 25(2). 167–203.

Schourup, Lawrence. 2011. The discourse marker *now*: A relevance-theoretic approach. *Journal of Pragmatics* 43(8). 2110–2129.

Selvik, Kari-Anne. 2006. *Spatial paths representing time: A cognitive analysis of temporal expressions in Norwegian Sign Language*. Oslo: University of Oslo PhD dissertation.

Shepard-Kegl, Judy A. 1985. *Locative relations in American Sign Language word formation, syntax and discourse*. Cambridge, MA: MIT PhD dissertation.

Smart, J.J.C. 1949. The river of time. *Mind* 58(232). 483–494.

Sutton-Spence, Rachel. 2010. Spatial metaphor and expressions of identity in sign language poetry. *Metaphorik.De* 19 (www.metaphorik.de/19/sutton-spence.pdf).

Sutton-Spence, Rachel. 2016. Metaphor in sign language poetry. In Elisabetta Gola & Francesca Ervas (eds.), *Metaphor & communication*, 249–264. Amsterdam: John Benjamins.

Tagliamonte, Sali. 2005. So who? Like how? Just what?: Discourse markers in the conversations of young Canadians. *Journal of Pragmatics* 37(11). 1896–1915.

Traugott, Elizabeth Closs. 1978. On the expression of spatio-temporal relations in language. In Joseph H. Greenberg (ed.), *Universals of human language, Vol. 3: Word structure*, 369–400. Stanford, CA: Stanford University Press.

Vandenbergen, Anne-Marie, Anne Wichmann & Karin Aijmer. 2010. How prosody reflects semantic change: A synchronic case study of 'of course'. In Kristin Davidse, Lieven Vandelanotte & Hubert Cuyckens (eds.), *Subjectification, intersubjectification and grammaticalization*, 103–154. Berlin: De Gruyter Mouton.

Van Loon, Esther. 2012. *What's in the palm of your hands? Discourse functions of palm-up in Sign Language of the Netherlands*. Amsterdam: Universiteit van Amsterdam MA thesis.

Wårvik, Brita. 2011. Connective or 'disconnective' discourse marker? Old English Þa, multifunctionality and narrative structuring. In Anneli Meurman-Solin & Ursula Lenker (eds.), *Connectives in synchrony and diachrony in European languages*. Helsinki: Varieng. www.helsinki.fi/varieng/journal/volumes/08/warvik/.

Wilbur, Ronnie B. 2003. Representation of telicity in ASL. *Chicago Linguistics Society* 39. 354–368.

Wilbur, Ronnie B. 2009. Effects of varying rate of signing on ASL manual signs and nonmanual markers. *Language and Speech* 52(2–3). 245–285.

Zeshan, Ulrike. 2006. Negative and interrogative structures in Turkish Sign Language (TİD). In Ulrike Zeshan (ed.), *Interrogative and negative constructions in sign languages*, 128–164. Nijmegen: Ishara Press.

Part V: **"Goodbye, hearing world!":** Creating a safe environment for the elderly Deaf

Judith Reiff-de Groen and Peter van Veen
De Gelderhorst: a home full of signs

1 Introduction

In Ede, in the center of the Netherlands, rests *De Gelderhorst*, a unique residential and care center for the elderly deaf. The center is visited regularly by deaf people from all over the world, who intend to set up something similar in their own country, something that, however, has not yet been realized.

In this chapter, we first offer a brief outline of the history of *De Gelderhorst* (Section 2). Subsequently, in Section 3, we describe the current developments within the institution. Our aim is to contribute to the understanding that the continuity of this unique institution cannot be taken for granted. The target group is changing, as more and more elderly deaf people decide to live independently at home for longer, and therefore requires a different approach.

Residents, employees, and managers, but also external parties, have cooperated in the development of a new vision for the future of the center. Deaf and hearing people, young and old, have worked together on this task. The process of arriving at this new vision for the future has been at least as important as the final result, which has been achieved based on ideas put forward by the people who live and work at *De Gelderhorst*, following the motto: "Nothing about us without us".

2 A brief history of *De Gelderhorst*

"Twenty years ago, there was no thought of opening such a home. It sometimes seemed as if people forgot that deaf people also have souls. Today, however, through love and sacrifice, this home, Our Own House, has come into being. The joy of this is further enhanced by the realization that society has begun to show more understanding of and interest in the problems of the deaf community." (*Ons Bondblad* 1953: 28; our translation). It was July 11, 1953, when Jan Leenhouts, member of the board of the Dutch Christian Union of Deaf People, uttered these words at the opening of *Dovenvreugd*, a villa in the town of Baarn, which would later grow into *De Gelderhorst* in Ede, the only center for elderly deaf people of this size in Europe. In this section, we sketch the history of *De Gelderhorst* over the past 80 years, based on information provided in Van Veen (2012, 2013).

2.1 Deaf initiative

The history of *De Gelderhorst* actually goes back further than that summer day in Baarn over 65 years ago. Thirteen years earlier, a week before the occupation of the Netherlands in the Second World War, on 2 May 1940, Ascension Day, employees of the deaf institute Effatha in Voorburg and deaf people who had attended school there came together to establish an association for Christian deaf people. Their aim was to "look after the spiritual and material interests of its members". It was mainly hearing people who took the lead, but soon after its foundation, the association had a number of deaf members in prominent positions. Two of them were the brothers Bram and Jan Leenhouts. The association was given the name *Nederlandse Christelijke Bond van Doofstommen* (NCBD; 'Dutch Christian Union of the Deaf-mute').

The brothers Leenhouts were two active and socially engaged deaf people. For a long time, they had noticed that there were many elderly deaf people who lived in isolation, and they decided that something had to be done. Soon after the establishment of the NCBD, they approached Cornelis Timmer, the director of Effatha, who was also chairman of their association for the deaf, with the idea of establishing a kind of home for them. Timmer's interest was piqued, and so was that of the rest of the board of the NCBD. Due to the war, however, the plans were put on hold. Following the liberation, fundraising for *Ons Eigen Huis* ('our own house') was soon initiated. *Ons Bondsblad*, the magazine of the NCBD association, which first appeared in 1946, reported on the plans in May of that year. At the beginning of 1953, the deaf members had raised sufficient funds, which allowed the board to purchase a villa in Baarn. A few months after the purchase, the *Stichting tot Oprichting en Instandhouding van Christelijke Tehuizen voor Doofstommen* ('Foundation for the Establishment and Maintenance of Christian Homes for the Deaf-mute') was established, and the board named the new home *Dovenvreugd* ('Deaf's delight/joy'). "In this name, the board has expressed their fervent wish for this house to become a great joy for the deaf", the foundation explains.

2.2 *Dovenvreugd*

One year after the foundation, thirteen elderly deaf people lived in *Dovenvreugd* (see Figure 1). This number was rising rapidly, and after only a few years, the villa became too small. The elderly all slept on the first floor of the villa: the couples together and the rest in a dormitory where the beds were separated by curtains. There was room for 23 residents. In a sense, *Dovenvreugd* functioned like a kind of family substitute, as there were no comparable facilities in the

Figure 1: Nurse H.P. Walter (second from left) with *Dovenvreugd* residents.

Netherlands. In the early years, the daily management was in the hands of Mr. and Mrs. Bos, who became a kind of father and mother for the residents. When it came to decision-making, the deaf people themselves did not have much to contribute. They needed to be well cared for, and the hearing board and staff members knew how to do that. This patronizing attitude towards the deaf is characteristic of that time.

In spite of frequent requests from deaf people for more involvement in decision processes, it wasn't until the end of 1957 that Jaap Rodenburg became the first deaf member of the board of the Foundation for the Establishment and Preservation of Christian Homes for the Deaf. In 1965, the deaf Mrs. E. van Wijk joined the board of the foundation, followed by the deaf Jan Leenhouts and Bram Scheele a year later.

In the early years, the members of the board were regularly involved in the daily affairs of the home. This involvement was not limited to praying with the residents, but also included the purchase of equipment, the admission of new residents, and addressing complaints like one according to which "one of the female patients is asking the other residents for money, takes strong drinks and was caught in the bedroom of a male patient" (Van Veen 2013: 28).

Among each other and with staff members, the residents communicated in spoken language, supported by some signs. Most residents did not master sign language, as they had been raised at one of the five schools for the deaf in the Netherlands, where the oral method had been used.

Over the years, housing became overcrowded. After a tour in 1968, the new board member Kooij writes in a letter: "I must say that the accommodation is unacceptably sober. This observation is one that the lady director must in no way take as a criticism of her, because everything was tidy and clean, but it is such an assault on personal freedom and homeliness (if four women have to share a room – sectioned off with curtains), that I can well imagine that the government body responsible for supervision might forbid any further admissions." (Van Veen 2013: 39).

In the mid-sixties, the board was already convinced about the construction of a larger home. During this period, retirement homes were springing up like mushrooms. Yet, at the same time, there was a debate as to whether a home exclusively for the deaf was required. For the board of *Dovenvreugd*, however, there was no question, and they started to look for a location for a new home.

2.3 *De Gelderhorst* in Ede

In 1968, the board of the foundation bought a plot of land in Ede, a medium-size town in the center of the Netherlands, and in 1971, a year before the move to Ede, Marius Veldhoen was appointed as the new director. In addition to the construction of the new building, he was also involved in the selection of new residents. He, too, was confronted with the question: Who should be accepted as resident? In 1971, he writes a letter to a number of social services in various municipalities, from which residents have applied for the new home. The letter describes how the home struggles with its target group. Veldhoen writes: "The unfortunate truth is that the deaf often suffer an isolated existence in a world of hearing people. We therefore believe that those who partly for this reason can't manage to live independently in society, even if they are under 65 (but too old for a family replacement home) should be eligible for accommodation in our home." (Van Veen 2013: 41).

In 1972, the residents of *Dovenvreugd* moved from Baarn to Ede. From that moment on, the home was named *De Gelderhorst*. The name, which has been created by Dick Rodenburg (Van Veen 2013: 44), combines *Gelder*, which refers to *Gelderland*, the name of the province, where Ede is located, with *horst*, which can be translated as 'nest'. A year later, the building on the Pollenstein is festively opened, and Queen Juliana visits the new location with 75 single rooms and 28 rooms for couples. Care advances with leaps and bounds, but does not differ much from that of regular retirement homes. The difference lies in the target group. The personal contact between the residents contributes more to their well-being than provisions like extra lighting, special light signals, vibrating alarms, and additional staff.

Soon after the opening, there is again a waiting list. *De Gelderhorst* is also growing into a meeting place for deaf people who live elsewhere. Aside from a few deaf volunteers, staff members are still all hearing. What does change gradually is that the residents, just as in regular homes, have more say through the establishment of a residents' committee. Communication is still conducted in spoken language supported by some signs.

In the 1980s, the emancipation of the deaf gained momentum: the deaf community claims its rights and draws attention to the problems they encounter in daily life, and topics such as sign language, Deaf culture, and equality rise to the top of the agenda. Little by little, it also became clear that there are many deaf people with psychological problems. For many years, there had been a lack of attention for this particular group within the deaf community, let alone that professional help was made available for this target group. Research conducted among the residents of *De Gelderhorst* in the mid-eighties revealed that many of them had social-emotional or psychiatric problems. The fact that some of the residents had been negatively affected in their youth by the boarding school life at one of the deaf institutions or by life-long exclusion had hardly been recognized until then. In addition to the emancipation of the deaf community, *De Gelderhorst* faced another challenge during that period. In the 1960s and 1970s, many homes for the elderly were built in the Netherlands. The first residents were relatively young and had limited health issues, but this changed as the group aged. However, in older deaf people, staff members often did not recognize the symptoms due to existing communicative barriers.

2.4 New directions

The above-mentioned developments within the deaf community and the care for the elderly forced *De Gelderhorst* to change its policies at the beginning of the 1990s. With the arrival of the new director Jan Tempelaar in 1989, *De Gelderhorst* initiated a new course. Sign language, Deaf culture, and an extensive network in the deaf community became a priority, and communication and emancipation were established as central concepts. Soon after Tempelaar's arrival, employees were required to learn Sign Language of the Netherlands, deaf employees were hired, and interpreters made their entrance.

In 1991, the Ministry of Welfare, Public Health, and Culture commissioned a study under the title 'Estimate of the need for places in nursery homes for the elderly deaf' (*Behoefteraming verzorgingshuisplaatsen voor oudere doven*). The results, once again, raised the old question of whether a single central home for the elderly deaf is desirable. The report concludes: "For older deaf people, it is desirable that care home locations specifically for the deaf are available in areas/regions where many deaf people live. The distance to the only care home currently available for the deaf is experienced as a major problem. It has also been shown that deaf people have a great need for contact with other deaf people. In that context, there is also a great need for forms of living outside the care home where people can live in each other's proximity." The researchers recommend that in five regions, at least ten places should be created within an existing care facility specifically for deaf persons. "In these five nursing homes, there will thus be supported living or forms of group housing. Personnel and technical facilities must meet the specific requirements for the living of and the caring for older deaf people. This has far-reaching consequences for *De Gelderhorst*. A step-by-step development will be necessary, in which *De Gelderhorst* itself can play an active role by contributing its own specific expertise". Yet, in the years following the research, the advice is not practically implemented.

In the mid-nineties, a growing number of forms of care are introduced, such as, for instance, nursing home care and daytime care facilities. In order to better comply with these various forms of care and to further develop Deaf culture, plans are made for a new building in Ede. The design is attuned to the specific needs of the deaf with ample light to facilitate various forms of visual communication, such as sign language. 81 care homes are also developed on the site. On April 22, 1998, Queen Beatrix officially opens the new building with the unveiling of a bronze ornament displaying the name of *De Gelderhorst*.

2.5 Emphasis on Deaf culture

On the Willy Brandtlaan, the new location, *De Gelderhorst* (see Figure 2) is further developing into a home with various forms of care, an emphasis on Deaf culture, and an increase in the number of deaf employees. In the course of time, many foreign visitors come to learn from the concept. *De Gelderhorst*'s network is growing significantly, especially within the Dutch deaf community. In 2010, the results of a study into the housing requirements and care needs of elderly deaf people, commissioned by the *Lectoraat Dovenstudies* ('Deaf Studies') of the University of Applied Sciences Utrecht, are published (Ursem

Figure 2: *De Gelderhorst* in Ede (The Netherlands) now (© De Gelderhorst).

2010). The final report has the revealing title *Dovencultuur is de verbinding* ('Deaf culture is the link'). A statement on the back of the report reads: "The most important result that emerged from this research is that in all their [i.e., elderly deaf people; authors' note] wishes and needs, Deaf Culture is the common thread. Without contact with one another, they feel excluded because, as one of the interviewees said, "Soort zoekt soort" ('Birds of a feather flock together'). Hence, the title 'Deaf culture is the connection'. This should be the starting point for all policies concerning elderly deaf people."

Bringing elderly deaf people out of their isolation has always been an important goal of *De Gelderhorst*. By taking them out of a hearing environment and bringing them together, loneliness is prevented. Simply put, in combination with loving care, one could call this the policy which governed the first 35 years. Social developments, however, forced *De Gelderhorst* to change direction at the end of the 1980s. Deaf people, just like other cultural minorities, demanded rights at that time. They wanted to have a say and no longer be treated as needy. The professionalization of care also gained momentum, and more attention was paid to socio-emotional problems. At the beginning of the 1990s, the management chose to strengthen the role of Deaf culture, the participation of residents, the attention for, among other things, deaf-blind people and nursing home care, the contact with the deaf community at home and abroad, day recreation throughout the country, and the hiring of deaf personnel. These changes made *De Gelderhorst* the unique institution it is now.

3 *De Gelderhorst* – an island?

3.1 A new vision for the future

Much has been written for and about deaf people by hearing people. This is also true for the present chapter, and that although *De Gelderhorst* tries to live up to the well-known motto "Nothing about us without us".

In Section 2, we sketched the history of *De Gelderhorst*. This recollection illustrates that it was often the hearing, who determined what is best for the target group. Remember, however, that it had been elderly deaf people, who had founded a residential community in Baarn and later in Ede. Yet, it was hearing people, who set up the care home and later the nursing ward; and again, it was the hearing, who determined that the vision for the future of *De Gelderhorst* had to be revised. So, what is *De Gelderhorst*'s vision for the future? In Table 1, we provide an overview of our mission and our core tasks.

Table 1: Mission and core tasks of *De Gelderhorst*.

Our mission	– At *De Gelderhorst*, we create a suitable home for elderly deaf people. – We do this by respecting the Deaf culture and by supporting and stimulating our residents and employees in their development. – Making decisions for oneself and self-confidence are at the heart of that development. – Sign language is the connecting factor in everything we do.
Our core tasks	– We offer a wide range of care and services: from supporting independent living to providing extensive care. – We do this in a living and working environment that is future-proof and oriented both inwards and outwards. – Our knowledge center is a hub for the distribution of knowledge and development both within the Netherlands and internationally.

The process of arriving at a new vision has been a valuable experience. In the following, we describe this process in more detail. It also marked the start of a new phase, namely the phase in which it was decided to strengthen the connections of 'the island' *De Gelderhorst* (see Figure 3) with 'the mainland'; in other words, to make the internal world of *De Gelderhorst* known to and integrate it in the outside world.

Figure 3: The 'island' *De Gelderhorst* (© Gelderhorst).

Members from all levels of *De Gelderhorst*'s organization – residents, employees and managers, as well as external parties – cooperated intensively in the development of the new vision. Crucially, deaf and hearing people worked together. The process of arriving at the new vision of the future was at least as important as the final result, which stems from the ideas of the people who live and work at the facility.

Until a few years ago, *De Gelderhorst* was a kind of island in Ede. The organization mainly sought contact with its own target group. It had limited or even no contact with the care and nursing homes in the region as there seemed to be insufficient common ground. *De Gelderhorst* mainly organized meetings for deaf people and invited deaf people from all over the world to visit 'the island'. 'The island' was a great place to be: the language of communication was Sign Language of the Netherlands (*Nederlandse Gebarentaal*, NGT), the residents felt at home and cared for. In short, they were overall satisfied. After all, they had each other.

The hiring policy was aimed at hiring as many deaf employees as possible, regardless of their intellectual level. In the world of the deaf, *De Gelderhorst* therefore had a good reputation. However, at the same time, inquiries among the target group revealed that there were also some deaf people who believed that *De Gelderhorst* was an inward-oriented community with much social control (Hiddinga et al. 2017).

Organizations in the region also held a different opinion. Representatives of the hospital and the regular care institutions experienced *De Gelderhorst* as an enclosed stronghold, overly confident and demanding of its surroundings. After all, *De Gelderhorst* asked hospital staff to learn signs and to adapt their attitude and behavior to the deaf people – all of this, of course, with the best intentions for the target group.

These statements may sound harsh and are perhaps somewhat exaggerated, but it was clear to the management of *De Gelderhorst* that they would have to reflect on the future of this unique organization. After all, for the time being, the institution *De Gelderhorst* is the only one of its kind, and elderly deaf people still describe ending up in a care or nursing home for hearing people as a nightmare scenario (see Hiddinga et al., this volume). For many of them, the existence of *De Gelderhorst* is a source of peace of mind and thus contributes to quality of life and well-being, even for those who never come to live there (Hiddinga et al. 2017).

3.2 Working jointly towards the new vision: Core values

This reflection on the future of *De Gelderhorst* was initiated in the autumn of 2017. Two external supervisors assisted *De Gelderhorst* in this effort. They did this together with a development team (*regie-team*), a team of employees that organized a range of activities and supervised the whole process. The aim was to encourage residents, management, and employees to think about the desired course for *De Gelderhorst*, in order to achieve a result that is supported throughout the organization.

Initially, start-up meetings were organized for the employees. The purpose of these meetings was to explicitly ask the participants for input on the guiding question "What are your views and thoughts regarding the present and the future of *De Gelderhorst*?" Four sub-questions addressed the following components:
- Foster – What behavior do we want to maintain?
- Stimulate – What behavior should we exhibit more?

- Appreciate and let go – What behavior used to be appropriate but no longer is?
- Disappear – What behavior do we really want to get rid of?

The meetings were very well attended and provided useful input (see Figure 4, in which the outcome of the meetings is visualized). Employees were happy to contribute to the process, despite some initial unease as they had not been involved in decision-making in this way before.

Figure 4: Input from the start-up meetings for employees, November 2017, as visualized by the external advisers Tanja ten Berge (Ten Berge Organisatieadvies) and Thomas Verhiel (Thover). The header reads "On the way to the future" (© De Gelderhorst).

In Table 2, we provide an overview of the input and wishes for the future brought forward by the employees during the start-up meetings.

Taken together, the employees' input during the start-up meetings provided much clarity and ideas for future direction, and it laid the initial foundation for determining the core values of *De Gelderhorst*: pride, equality, and innovation, as explained below.

Table 2: Input from the employees during the start-up meetings in November 2017.

Employees' input	– We have a strong desire to maintain the current atmosphere, culture, and communicative environment.
	– We value diversity, togetherness, and security.
	– At the same time, this strong culture of care also has its downsides:
	  (i) Are we pampering employees and residents too much?
	  (ii) Are we bringing shortcomings to each other's attention, or are we making exceptions?
	  (iii) Do the above values not also promote an island culture in which every department focuses on itself? And do we want to move away from that?

Employees' wishes for the future	– We maintain the great diversity, and we are proud of what we are collectively: an inclusive and equal environment for deaf and hearing people. – We want to be Deaf with a capital D: proud self-confident Deaf people with a rich culture. – We want to support residents in increasing their self-reliance and their ability to make decisions for themselves. – We want to show more courage and be open to innovation. – We want to develop in an open atmosphere – cooperatively rather than competitively – into proactive employees who can work independently. – Our service and care provision received a 5-star rating: it is a beautiful product tailored to the needs of the target group. – We open our house to the broad target group of deaf people, including their families and the neighborhood. – We want to restrict the rules and the workload to a normal level.

- **Pride:** refers to the way in which memories, knowledge, and interests of the residents are collected and are given a place; genuine attention and respect, both in the process and in the realization, make the difference.
- **Equality:** is about stimulating one's self-reliance and decision-making abilities. If you focus on people's qualities and challenge them accordingly, people can do much more than they think. Equality is also about facilitating that different target groups and generations meet one another and discover what they can do for each other.
- **Innovation:** novel and different forms of visualizing memories, including methods for visualizing the residents' memories, knowledge, and interests by means of certain modes of working. This also involves making this a

journey in and of itself: by allowing oneself to be nourished in the outside world, one can gain much inspiration and observe one's actions from a different perspective.

Employees also expressed concrete wishes for the realization of housing, care, and the professionalization of both these domains. Their wish to treat residents in a more equal way is remarkable. They want to contribute to the residents' self-reliance and their ability to make decisions for themselves. Furthermore, the employees believe that the culture of the deaf and the communicative environment should be maintained. They are concerned that these values will be phased out gradually and will be considered less important.

This concern is partly due to the fact that the older generation of deaf people is decreasing, and that this will also reduce the feeling of togetherness and the need to do things together. Moreover, there is uncertainty about what effect the increase in the number of people with cochlear implants (CI) will have on the Deaf culture, not to mention the new possibilities afforded by communication technology and social media.

The development team also spoke with a delegation of residents about their ideas and wishes concerning the future of *De Gelderhorst*. The illustrator Olivier Rijcken made an effort to visualize the ideas brought forward by the residents (Figure 5).

Following these meetings, the development team made an 'inspirational journey'. The aim of this 'journey' was to gain inspiration, literally and figuratively, beyond the walls of *De Gelderhorst*. To that end, members of the development team jointly travelled by bus through the Netherlands and visited the 'Sign Language Coffee Bar' in Amsterdam, where they met Ctalents (ctalents. nl), an agency that helps people with visual and hearing impairments on the labor market. The journey continued to *Vreedenhoff*, a residential care facility in Arnhem, where also students live. *Vreedenhoff* implements a special form of daytime care aimed at collecting and giving a place to memories, knowledge, talents, and interests of the residents. The last destination of the trip was a visit to the Canon of Dutch History in the Open Air Museum in Arnhem: a beautiful way to depict stories and history.

Following the start-up meetings and the journey, additional expertise and ideas were also collected from a number of external guests during a roundtable meeting. People with specific expertise and experience in the field of Deaf culture or some other relevant topic were asked whether they were willing to share their knowledge and ideas and to translate them into concrete advice for the future of *De Gelderhorst*.

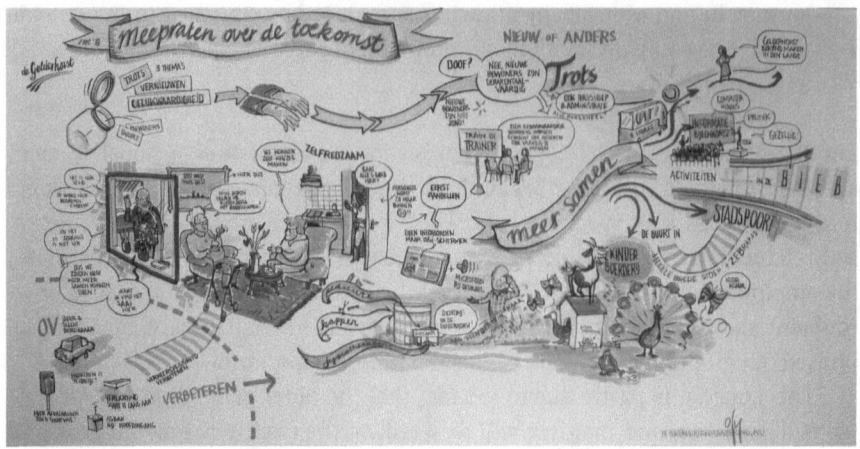

Figure 5: Visualization of the residents' ideas and wishes for the future. Some indications regarding the content: in the banner on the top, it reads "Joining discussions about the future"; in the banner on the right "more together"; the letters on top (*Nieuw of anders*) mean "new or different"; the letters on the bottom left (*Verbeteren*) "improve" (© De Gelderhorst).

The approach was as follows: at different tables, 20 guests discussed various topics with 20 employees and a representation of residents: housing, care and services, and development. For each of these topics, a link was established with the three core values. The result was an incredibly inspiring and enjoyable afternoon during which the participants, with enormous commitment and energy, contributed concrete ideas about the future of *De Gelderhorst*. Despite the various themes that were discussed, there was a clear common thread in the advice resulting from the meeting:
- Make use of and further expand your knowledge and expertise, and be recognized as a knowledge center;
- Bring in the outside world and benefit from it: work together with other parties in order to advance and substantiate technological developments;
- Be flexible and offer tailor-made solutions: concerning the way in which facilities are built, choices regarding where and how people want to live, facilities to be offered, and different target groups.

In order to arrive at a sound vision for the future, the external supervisors also engaged in extensive discussions with stakeholders, such as the directors of the health care institutions in the region (hospitals, mental health care institutions, and care and nursing homes), health insurance companies, the alderman of the municipality of Ede, representatives of organizations for the deaf, and other stakeholders of the deaf.

The discussions yielded the following key messages: (i) maintain and improve what you are already good at for this special target group and create greater awareness for your qualities; (ii) also focus on innovation: broaden the view on your target group, the needs and wishes of future generations, and respond to developments such as the increasing complexity of all issues related to care – all of this should be done in close interaction with the outside world.

A SWOT analysis (Strengths, Weaknesses, Opportunities, and Threats) including DESTEP components (Demography, Economy, Socio-cultural, Technology, Ecology, and Politics) also formed an important part of the process that led to the vision of the future. Next to the management of *De Gelderhorst* and the development team, the supervisory board also made a significant contribution to this process, the results of which are too far-reaching to be presented here in detail. It is, however, beneficial to give an impression of important results that have been incorporated in the vision for the future.

3.3 Opportunities and challenges

De Gelderhorst should be proud of its unique concept of a large residential, care and nursing home for a small target group – a place where so many of the target group live and work together – and also proud of the extensive knowledge and skills regarding the organization in the domain of care for deaf people and communicating and working with them. Caution, however, is also required. With 'equality' as a core value, it is important not to 'pamper' and patronize the deaf residents and employees. When it comes to 'pride', the organization itself should also demonstrate this core value. The outside world is far too unfamiliar with the expertise and skills accumulated at the *De Gelderhorst*, and the organization must therefore make an effort to bring the inner world out into the open.

Meanwhile, there are plenty of opportunities. Given an increased demand for nursing and care, due to the aging of the target group, and technological advances in the field of communication and care, *De Gelderhorst* must also open its doors to the outside world. For example, in the field of nursing and care, there is still much to learn. A major opportunity is that *De Gelderhorst* has a considerable size, a concentration of deaf residents (240), and a good mix of deaf and hearing employees (200, of whom 40% are deaf). The size of the institution facilitates good communication for both residents and employees, and thus allows for nursing and care of optimal quality, way better than what could be achieved in a smaller institution.

What *De Gelderhorst* must anticipate in the coming years are the changes that will take place in the target group, for instance, the fact that older deaf people may want to have more personal control and stay in their homes for longer, the increasing complexity of the demand for care, multicultural aspects, and an increase in the number of people who received a CI at a young age. *De Gelderhorst* will have to develop a keen sense and intuition for the coming generations of elderly deaf people. While *De Gelderhorst* is the largest and in fact the only institution for elderly deaf people, it still remains a small player in the market. The organization will have to deal with that, too.

Taken together, based on all the input and the multifarious factors described above, the vision for the future (see Section 3.1) has been established.

4 *De Gelderhorst* builds bridges

Now that the phase of 'dreaming' has more or less ended, the phase of 'daring, doing' (Tiggelaar 2005) has begun. This means that the organization is working together with residents and employees to ensure that the core values (pride, equality, and innovation) are indeed reflected in people's behavior. A lot of energy, however, is also put into the implementation of the core tasks (as described in Table 1).

The core values require constant attention from both residents and employees. For this reason, another group has been formed in 2019, which is held responsible for this: the 'Core Group'. The members of this group, a mix of deaf and hearing staff members, are the so-called 'frontrunners'. The Core Group has since organized a successful meeting about the core value Pride, during which residents and staff members presented cards to each other, on which they wrote down, for different contexts, why they are proud, as shown in Figure 6.

In this way, people were stimulated to talk to each other about what pride is, and what it means to them when someone is proud of you – a topic that people do not commonly communicate about explicitly. Older deaf people in particular seem to need more encouragement in this respect.

There is often a debate within the organization about Equality, the second core value. For sure, debates about this value are a good thing. At least, there is now a conscious reflection on what this core value means for *De Gelderhorst*. The Canadian Prime Minister, Justin Trudeau, once made the following statement:

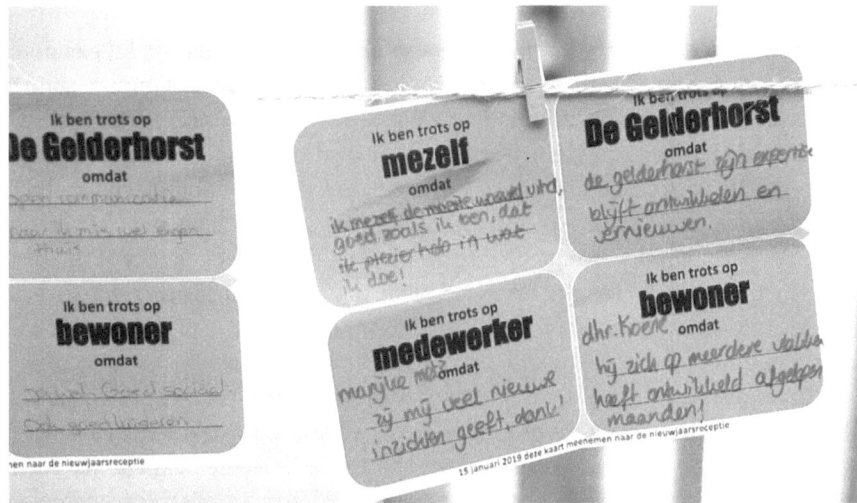

Figure 6: Core value Pride (Dutch *trots*); the printed text on the card reads "I am proud of *De Gelderhorst* / resident / myself / staff member because . . . " (*Ik ben trots op De Gelderhorst / bewoner / mezelf / medewerker omdat . . .*).

"Diversity is a fact, inclusion is a choice" – and we wholeheartedly agree with this statement. *De Gelderhorst* has chosen inclusion for its residents and employees, along with participation and integration. After all, that's what being equal is all about. Equality manifests itself in the behavior of deaf and hearing people towards each other. Some practical examples are:
- Allowing for equal access to situations by ensuring that all participants can follow the conversation during meetings: providing communication in sign language or writing, paying attention to light and how participants sit, avoiding background noises, etc. A meeting should never start before the interpreter is there.
- This also goes two ways, as the hearing participants also want to be able to follow the deaf participants. This also requires an effort from a group of deaf people in a context in which only a single hearing person is present, for example, slower signing, more facial expressions and, if possible, the use of (supporting) oral communication.
- It is no longer a question of deaf versus hearing. In personnel policy, 'deaf' no longer necessarily equals 'good', rather, it is quality that counts, irrespective of hearing status.

In order for quality to prevail over deafness, *De Gelderhorst* must support the deaf person in such a way that they are also able to deliver quality. An example of this type of support is that the organization is in the process of implementing *Tolkcontact* (which allows for making calls with the help of NGT interpreters) for all deaf employees. Equality implies that deaf employees are also able to communicate with suppliers, doctors, and employees of the pharmacy. Another example concerns education and training. The Communication, Training & Advice department, for instance, ensures that training for emergency situations and evacuation exercises are arranged such that deaf and hearing employees can work together in an optimal way. The fire brigade and the police are involved in this.

The older residents of *De Gelderhorst* struggle with the concept of equality at times. They learn from the staff how they can arrange a taxi for themselves, organize their tax returns, etc. However, sometimes residents experience such instructions as a setback in comparison to the care and assistance of former times. It is therefore important that the employees explain that providing instructions does not imply a decrease in loving care, but that it serves to reduce patronization. The saying "Give a man a fish, and you feed him for a day. Teach a man to fish, and you feed him for a lifetime" is considered wise words at *De Gelderhorst*.

The head of the Facilities Department (FD) deals with such issues in a relaxed manner. For example, the residents who live independently were informed by the energy supplier by letter that every address would receive a new electricity meter, which would be installed free of charge, provided that the resident would have this done by appointment before a certain date. After that date, the installing would no longer be free of charge. The head of FD suspected that many residents would have difficulties with the complicated formulations in the letter and would therefore ignore them. The head therefore did two things. First, he sought contact with the energy supplier and asked them for some lenience with the residents of *De Gelderhorst*. Second, he organized an informative hour for the residents, to assist those who had encountered difficulties with the letter in making an appointment. The core of this is that, on the one hand, you show understanding for the culture of the deaf person, which commonly makes the deaf person used to being helped. But on the other hand, you also contribute to a gradual change of this cultural habit by helping older deaf people to become more independent. Ultimately, it will give them a feeling of satisfaction and pride, and they are also aware of this.

One of the core tasks of *De Gelderhorst* is to realize a living environment that is future-proof and oriented both inwards and outwards. This task is related to the third core value, Innovation, and it has several aspects. For example, this concerns changes in the care demands of residents and the requirement to adapt the facilities accordingly. Originally, residents had a great need for long and unobstructed lines of sight, lots of glass, and open spaces – this is what Deafspace is all about. But residents suffering from dementia suffer from loss of decorum. Therefore, in order to preserve the privacy of residents, the so-called Deafspace now has to be designed differently; for example, more small enclosed sitting rooms will be created, open spaces will be less open, and glass surfaces will be covered in certain places.

Creating a living environment that is oriented inwards and outwards also implies, among other things, that *De Gelderhorst* increases contact with the hearing world. To that end, the organization works together with Opella, a large regional housing and care organization for elderly hearing people. The cooperation is based on equality and reciprocity and involves the following components. First, *De Gelderhorst* has started offering communication workshops for Opella employees. The core of these workshops is 'See and be seen', with non-verbal communication as the key to a successful experience, primarily for the client but, of course, also for the employee. Contact and communication with a demented elderly person can proceed much smoother once a number of elements from Deaf culture are implemented. For example, the participants from Opella indicate that sign language users can teach them a lot about strategies for approaching and making contact. Not only the deaf elderly benefit from colleagues in the care sector adopting certain Deaf culture practices, but such practices can also be enormously beneficial for hearing elderly people. To give a few examples, eye contact enables you to establish and maintain contact. Also, a verbal message is commonly supported by body language and appropriate facial expressions. Seeing and interpreting such non-verbal signals, which are commonly used in signed communication, can help the interlocutor in understanding the message. In addition, natural signs can be used to support the meaning of words, for instance, pointing to or showing objects in order to provide context. By means of a touch, contact can be made and a feeling of closeness can be conveyed (see Figure 7 for an illustration).

In addition, *De Gelderhorst* and Opella have plans to establish a system of job rotation, in which employees take on an internship in each other's organization and provide feedback in both directions. *De Gelderhorst* strongly believes that working together with hearing care organizations has added value for both parties. In this way, *De Gelderhorst* builds bridges, so to speak (as visualized in Figure 8).

Another example of 'bridge-building' is the cautious collaboration that is developing between a local primary school and *De Gelderhorst*. This collaboration started with a few NGT lessons that the sign language teachers gave to

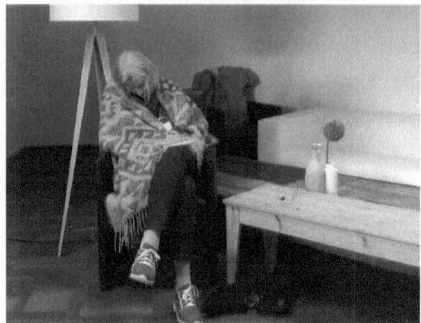 

Figure 7: Impressions from the workshop 'See and be seen'.

Figure 8: *De Gelderhorst* builds bridges.

groups 7 and 8 (see Figure 9). The pupils and teachers from the school were enthusiastic and wanted to know more about deaf people and their culture.

Around Christmas, the pupils visited *De Gelderhorst* to offer self-made cards to the residents. To prepare for the visit, they first received an NGT lesson

Figure 9: School children receive a sign language lesson.

in which they learned some Christmas terms and the Christmas wishes. Since spring 2019, a group of residents has been working in the school's vegetable garden. The pupils learn the necessary signs which they can use to communicate with the residents while working in the garden. This cooperation is also beneficial for both parties. On the one hand, the children learn to deal with the diversity of people and to behave in a tolerant manner. In this way, *De Gelderhorst* hopes to cultivate young, enthusiastic future volunteers. On the other hand, the residents also greatly enjoy the interaction with the children, who make uninhibited contact with them (see Figure 10).

Another core task relates to the fact that *De Gelderhorst* is a knowledge center that functions as a hub when it comes to distribution of knowledge and development. Without exception, national and international visitors are impressed by the way in which the organization shapes living, care, and well-being. *De Gelderhorst* also distinguishes itself from other institutions in the way in which deaf and hearing employees work together. A great deal of energy is invested by *De Gelderhorst*'s teachers and employees to propagate a communicative living environment which is characterized by the use of NGT as primary language, the use of specific practices that suit the target group, but also by the consistent use of interpreters and by striving to translate written Dutch into NGT as much as possible. Thanks to a presentation in NGT, for instance, both employees and residents are able to understand the requirements of the General Data Protection Regulations (GDPR).

Figure 10: School children and residents working together in the school garden.

De Gelderhorst has noticed that the outside world, and especially the hearing outside world, is not sufficiently aware of our expertise and skills. It is certainly desirable and possible to bring this knowledge to the outside world and to 'market' it much better. For instance, too few organizations know that our teachers provide advice and workshops on how, within a company, hearing employees can interact optimally with a single deaf colleague. Moreover, our lecturers and nurses can give very specific advice to hearing care organizations on how to deal with a single elderly deaf person suffering from dementia.

Taken together, we conclude that, at present, *De Gelderhorst* actually still does too little for the target group. In part, this shortcoming concerns marketing, but continuing development in order to meet the needs of the target group is also important.

5 Conclusion: 'People walk across the bridges'

This chapter touched upon the history of *De Gelderhorst*, described its vision for the future, including the core values that have been established, and sketched how this vision can be realized. The organization has given itself

Figure 11: Traffic crosses the bridges in both directions.

several years to grow. In the coming years, *De Gelderhorst* will continue to invest energy in the realization of suitable living and working conditions for its special target group, within and outside its own organization. The focus will continue to be on developments in both the deaf and the hearing community, such that – staying faithful to our 'bridge' metaphor – people can and will cross the bridges that have been built (Figure 11). In all these efforts, the most important guideline is to always adhere to the motto "Nothing about us without us".

References

Hiddinga, Anja, Nienke Sijm, Michou Benoist, Madeleine Herzog, Maja de Langen, Katya Buts & Meike Brock. 2017. *Verslag activiteiten project verhuizen . . .. Waarom? Daarom* [Report on the activities regarding the moving project . . . Why? That's why]. University of Amsterdam, Amsterdam Institute for Social Science Research (AISSR). Available at: https://dare.uva.nl/search?identifier=b832ed68-84fc-4cd8-8143-7e6b52865954.

Ons Bondsblad, Maandblad van de Nederlandse Christelijke Bond van Doofstommen (July/August 1953) [Monthly Journal of the Dutch Christian Association of Deaf-mutes].

Tiggelaar, Ben. 2005. *Dromen, durven, doen* [Dream, dare, do]. Amsterdam: Spectrum.

Ursem, Janet J.A. 2010. *Dovencultuur is de verbinding: verslag van een pilotonderzoek naar de woonwensen en zorgbehoeften van oudere doven* [Deaf culture is the link: report of a pilot study into the wishes regarding living and the care needs of elderly deaf people]. Utrecht: Hogeschool Utrecht, Kenniscentrum Educatie van de Faculteit Educatie.

Van Veen, Peter. 2012. *Verhaal halen bij doven – een geschiedenis* [Stories from the deaf – a history]. Deventer: Van Tricht uitgeverij.

Van Veen, Peter. 2013. *Thuiskomen in De Gelderhorst: 60 jaar oog voor oudere Doven*. Ede: De Gelderhorst. [English translation: *Coming home at De Gelderhorst: 60 years awareness of elderly deaf people*. Ede: De Gelderhorst, 2013].

Anja Hiddinga and Research Collective 'Beyond Hearing. Cultures Overlooked'

Growing old together: aging deaf people and the politics of belonging

1 Introduction[1]

While traditionally, the church, family and private charities have all been important in the care for elderly and needy people in The Netherlands, long term care has moved into the marketplace through a series of rearrangements over the past few decades. In "the most major reconfiguration of the Dutch welfare state ever" (Putters 2014: 9), state budgets for care are shrinking and policies focused on substantial cost reductions put in place. Private stakeholders sell their services and products, while people in need of care have become 'consumers', managing their own budgets (Kremer 2006). In the state-proclaimed 'participation society', informal networks of family and friends take responsibility for whatever else is needed.

Costs for long term care, traditionally with a strong collective nature (Da Roit & Le Bihan 2010), account for a large proportion of total health care costs in The Netherlands.[2] With a graying population, the demand for long term care arrangements continues to grow, and budgets for elderly people and people with chronic conditions or disabilities are particularly threatened by current policies. Institutional housing and care facilities for elderly and disabled people are rapidly disappearing.

---

[1] This chapter is largely based on an earlier article: Hiddinga, Anja & Collectif de recherche 'Beyond Hearing. Cultures Overlooked'. 2018. Vieillir ensemble ou les expressions d'un sentiment d'appartenance. Les personnes sourdes en institution aux Pays-Bas. *Ethnologie Française* XLVIII(3). 515–526. We are grateful to the publishers of the journal for granting permission to use it.

The research reported in this chapter was supported by a grant from *Stichting Handgebaar*, Ede, The Netherlands.

[2] Central National Statistics office of The Netherlands, CBS 2017: https://opendata.cbs.nl/stat line/#/CBS/nl/dataset/83039ned/table?fromstatweb, accessed 20th February 2020.

Note: 'Beyond Hearing. Cultures Overlooked' is a mixed deaf-hearing team composed of the first author and a changing mix of collaborators – Maja de Langen, Lisa Hinderks, Meike Brock, Katya Buts, and Samoa Greeve – who gathered information, reported findings, and discussed the results of research pertaining to Deaf culture. Although Anja Hiddinga takes full responsibility for this chapter, we wish to present it as the outcome of our shared intellectual and political concerns regarding equality and the empowerment of Deaf people.

https://doi.org/10.1515/9783110701906-014

All the more surprising then that the country's center for elderly deaf people, *De Gelderhorst*, is nevertheless thriving. In the rhetoric of supply and demand prominent in today's care business, *De Gelderhorst* claims to be THE service provider for elderly deaf people now and in the future, and planned extensions to the complex have indeed been realized.[3] At present, it accommodates a total of 175 residents. The majority of them make use of assisted living in well-equipped two-room apartments, some 60 smaller apartments are available for individuals who need more intensive care, and 13 for those who need nursing care.[4] *De Gelderhorst* receives high scores in quality evaluations of care institutions, and a waiting list testifies to its continued attraction for the target population.[5] Located in a small provincial town in the East of the Netherlands, the center nevertheless has a nation-wide function, and residents come from all over the country. The buildings with wide, open spaces and unbroken lines of vision are designed especially for deaf people, and technological provisions facilitate communication with and among residents (Figure 1).

Given current policies and support for non-institutional and individualized care, the success of *De Gelderhorst* is perhaps unexpected. This might have something to do with the clientele the center aims to attract, according to its mission statement: "an emancipatory group of Deaf[6] people with its own culture and language."[7] Looking to make the most of existing possibilities, *De Gelderhorst* seeks to provide an environment in which these elderly can grow old in a 'good' way. But what do elderly deaf understand 'good' care to be? For them, what could be the appeal of an institutional environment to spend their last years of life? What does the center's concept of care entail, and what are elderly deaf people's motivations to move or not move there?

Examining the situation in *De Gelderhorst* allows us to explore the complexity and heterogeneity of care situations (Purkis & Ceci 2015) and of recipients of care. In trying to analyze the way infrastructures and services of care relate to the situation of individuals, we view care services and resources offered at *De Gelderhorst* as part of a dynamic 'carescape' (Bowlby 2012), where exchanges of

---

[3] Year report 2013 De Gelderhorst, *Begrepen Worden*.
[4] See the website: www.gelderhorst.nl.
[5] Report National Inspection Health Care: https://www.igz.nl/actueel/nieuws/verscherpt-toezicht-bij-stichting-de-gelderho.aspx, accessed 20th February 2020.
[6] We are aware of the (politicized) discussions regarding deaf/Deaf distinctions. We have tried to reserve the capital D to refer to deaf people, organizations, or activities that self-consciously identify as part of a cultural group.
[7] Mission statement on website www.gelderhorst.nl, accessed 20th June 2017.

Figure 1: Lobby of *De Gelderhorst*; © Monte Gardenier.

political and social ideas about care take place over space and across time. This framing encompasses both the care that *De Gelderhorst* provides as well as claims to belonging to a deaf sociality. The notion of carescape has been developed by Bowlby and others, particularly to analyze the interweaving of formal and informal care, of caring and being cared for. In our research, we use this concept to focus on the interrelations between socio-economic developments (austerity), Deaf emancipation, and individual needs of deaf elderly. What is seen as constituting good care in *De Gelderhorst* involves changing discourses of cultural identity and belonging. As we will show, it is precisely the interconnectedness of the repertoires of care and belonging and the ways in which they resonate among potential clients that have enabled the growth of institutional care for elderly deaf in The Netherlands, despite an adverse socio-political climate.

The analysis presented here is part of an ongoing ethnographic study of the significance of deaf sociality and belonging for the quality of life of elderly deaf people. We draw on data from observations, interviews, and focus group discussions with elderly deaf, residents, and non-residents of *De Gelderhorst*. The in-depth semi-structured interviews usually took place at informants' homes and lasted 1.5–3 hours. Interviews were conducted in Sign Language of the Netherlands (*Nederlandse Gebarentaal*, NGT), in spoken, sometimes fragmented Dutch, or in a mixture of signs and speech, depending on the informants' preferred way of communicating.

The next section briefly sets out some background to better understand the situation of elderly deaf people in the Netherlands. In the remainder of this paper, we move on to *De Gelderhorst* and the questions pertaining to its success. Why do deaf elderly people want to move there? How does this relate to particular understandings of deafness and notions of good care?

2 Elderly deaf people in the Netherlands

As in most European and North American countries, the estimated 1,200–1,400 elderly deaf people in the Netherlands[8] grew up in a time when sign language was seen as primitive, and its use was forbidden (or strongly discouraged) in deaf education. Until well into the 20th century, most deaf schools imposed a regime of 'oral communication', punishing children for using signs and forcing them to learn to speak and lip-read the spoken language (Lane 1984). In the Netherlands, all five schools for the deaf had such oral regimes in varying degrees of strictness (Rietveld-Van Wingerden & Tijsseling 2010; Tijsseling 2014). Moreover, many deaf children had to live in schools' residential facilities and could visit their (almost always hearing) families only a few times a year. The expertise and policies of the deaf schools were virtually unquestioned and, due to this, children's communication – both at school and at home – was experienced as fractured and fraught with misunderstandings. It is no surprise then, that the communication policies of the deaf schools, the ideas behind them, and the regimes imposing them, had great impact on these children. Memories of elderly deaf about these 'total institutions' (Goffman 1961) are often very negative (Breed & Swaans-Joha 1986; Rietveld-Van Wingerden & Tijsseling

---

[8] It is assumed that 10,000–15,000 Deaf people are living in The Netherlands. About 20% of them (i.e., 2,000–3,000) would be over 60. *De Gelderhorst* applies the rule of thumb of Prof. Johannes Fellinger to estimate the number of elderly deaf people that would be interested in moving to the center. According to this rule, only 50% of this group would see themselves as belonging to the Deaf community (personal communication Jan Tempelaar, former director of *De Gelderhorst*).

2010; Tijsseling 2014). In addition to this, the quality of education was unsatisfactory. Few elderly deaf people in The Netherlands today completed general secondary education, since in their youth, deaf schools only offered training for manual occupations. We regularly encountered elderly deaf regretting that they had not been able to fulfill their potential and had suffered setbacks in the hearing world because of it. The deaf schools controlled which social roles and behavior were appropriate for deaf people, ranging from occupations, to language for communication and partners for marriage (Rietveld-Van Wingerden & Tijsseling 2010; Tijsseling 2014).

This pattern of domination by the hearing world, of patronization and of control is characteristic of how deaf people were seen and treated. Like elsewhere in Europe and the US (see Becker 1983; Lane 1984), most elderly deaf people in The Netherlands today have been subject to these ideas and share a history of stigma, social exclusion, and dependency. This shared experience has been pointed out as being important for a sense of comfort and of belonging to a community of deaf people (Kusters & De Meulder 2013). Indeed, a shared history and the preservation of it in stories, places, and practices can be seen as constituting 'a practice of belonging' (Fortier 1999). So, how does one belong to a deaf community? In exploring this question, we have to take into account another important element.

Linguistic research in the 1950s and 1960s had shown that sign languages are fully-fledged languages, rather than primitive means of communication. This provided support for the notion that deaf sociality can constitute a *positive* source of identity: Deaf culture and Deaf identity written with capital D's (e.g., Lane 2005). The significance of linguistic claims in legitimizing a separate cultural space for deaf people can hardly be underestimated (Senghas & Monaghan 2002). Much of the literature on Deaf culture and belonging is indeed focused on the communication in sign language in deaf communities (De Clerck 2010). All in all, profound changes in the perception of deafness and sign language were instrumental in the development of a Deaf movement fighting for equality and autonomy. Deaf people's positioning as a cultural minority, by implication, thus also took shape in a discourse framed in terms of rights and entitlements (Kusters & De Meulder 2013; Lane 2005). In The Netherlands, the national organization for Deaf people, *Dovenschap*, represents Deaf interests from this cultural perspective and is actively engaged in supporting emancipation of Deaf people and empowerment in various arenas.[9]

---

9 See their website: www.dovenschap.nl.

These ideas have also been embraced in *De Gelderhorst* and have been made part of the institute's positioning in a care market in which it is challenged on the one side by policies aimed at the deinstitutionalization and socialization of care, and on the other side by a potentially reluctant clientele with negative memories of institutional settings. Noteworthy at *De Gelderhorst* are the use of NGT as in-house language and the large proportion (30%) of staff members, working in all different ranks and positions, who are themselves deaf.

Offering these provisions seems to presuppose particular ideas about belonging on the side of potential clientele. But how do elderly deaf themselves think about this? How does what *De Gelderhorst* has to offer relate to their sense of belonging when they consider moving, or not moving, to this specialized center?

3 Many ways of being elderly and Deaf

When asking about elderly deaf people's motivations, it is important to take into account the variety and diversity within this group. Indeed, we do not in any way want to suggest that deafness constitutes a 'reified fixity' (Yuval-Davis 2006: 199), predetermining people's ideas about the best ways to spend their later years in life. On the contrary, Deaf studies' scholars have pointed out the many ways in which one can be deaf (Monaghan et al. 2003), and have stressed the importance of intersectional approaches to deaf sociality (Kusters & De Meulder 2013). We can thus assume a multiplicity of deaf identities relating to a variety of deaf practices and senses of belonging. For example, given deaf people's history, one would expect fluent sign language communication to be an important element in the practice of deafness. The importance given to NGT as in-house language in the communication policies of *De Gelderhorst* supports such an idea. However, neither all people who are already living there, nor all those on the waiting list are fluent signers. This may have something to do with the educational regimes of their youth or the internalized reluctance to use signs. Whatever the reasons, residents vary widely in their mastery of the language: some of them sign fluently, but others use quite basic signs along with speech, and a few do not sign at all. Mrs. K., for example, an active member of deaf organizations and on the waiting list for *De Gelderhorst*, remarks:

> *Sign language is very important for the identity of deaf people. I myself don't use real sign language, but spoken language supported with signs.*

Some respondents even mentioned disadvantages of communicating in sign language, like Mrs. A., also on the waiting list, who refers to the visuality of the language and the small group of users:

> You always have to be careful among deaf people . . . They gossip . . . It's a small community, and people know a lot about each other. Privacy is problematic, because deaf people can see everything that's being talked about.

When discussing with elderly deaf people why they wanted to move to *De Gelderhorst*, it became clear that this was usually not so much because of the communication in sign language. Rather, reasons mentioned were that people – staff and fellow residents – would have the necessary understanding and experience with deaf people, would be patient, and make an effort to communicate with them. Hence, these practices of communication and the diversity in levels of signing as such constitute a more important foundation of belonging than a perfect mastery of NGT.

A related aspect of communication is also relevant to belonging. Where elderly deaf people talk about "the hearing world" and their efforts to connect with hearing people, negative experiences are paramount. As Mr. G., resident of the center, indignantly remarked:

> I've really had enough of contacts with hearing people. I'm really fed up. All my life I have done my best, always adapting, and now it's enough.

For some, this feeling of not-belonging in the hearing world is a strong motivation to move to *De Gelderhorst*. Mr. S., for example, phrased this particularly strikingly. He and his wife are pensioners and now live in a comfortable apartment in *De Gelderhorst*. In his working life, Mr. S. had had a good and well-paid job in a multinational company. When he retired at age 65,

> it was without a tear. Many of my colleagues were emotional at their retirement party. Not me! For me it was: "Good bye, hearing world, Gelderhorst, here I come!"

And while signing this, Mr. S. crumpled an imaginary piece of paper into a ball, throwing it 'out of the window' with great force.

Feeling excluded from the hearing world frequently figures in elderly deaf people's identity narratives. An 'escape' from this world can thus be seen as a negative motivation to want to belong to a deaf community of elderly in *De Gelderhorst*. In this way, practices of exclusion (Yuval-Davis 2006) are one side of belonging and help shape the desire to belong to the carescape realized at the center.

Figure 2: Resident of *De Gelderhorst* (the man in the picture is not quoted in this article); © Monte Gardenier.

These are not the only considerations taken into account when elderly deaf people contemplate a possible move. Some of our respondents expressed strategic rationales for moving at a fairly early age, while still in good health. Mr. and Mrs. A., for example, a couple in their early sixties, living in a comfortable modern house in a middle-sized town, explain:

> *Now, while we're young, we want to move to* De Gelderhorst *already, to better get to know the environment. If you wait until you're ill . . . . No, rather not. We want to move now we're still healthy.*

Another couple in their sixties, Mr. and Mrs. H., have similar thoughts, despite the fact that they hope to be able to stay in their own home as long as possible. Referring to the experiences of other people, Mr. H. mentions:

> *I have seen people with dementia looking for suitable elderly care, but couldn't go there because they were not listed. That's why I know: better now than later, and that's why we have listed ourselves early with* De Gelderhorst.

From these and similar quotes from our informants, it seems people want to move to *De Gelderhorst* because of the care they anticipate getting there when needed. Their Deafness is not a first motivation in their considerations. So, if not as a primary motivation, how *do* references to deaf identity and deaf practices come into the equation when elderly deaf people think about the future?

As to be expected, reference to deaf identity plays an important role for our informants when considering a move to *De Gelderhorst*, but not in a uniform way. We found people expressing different 'senses of belonging' when talking about spending the last phase of their lives in this institutional setting. Mr. Z., for example, outright positive about moving to *De Gelderhorst*, made reference to independence and equality he expects to find there:

> It has to do with equality. Everybody is equal there. That's nice. They will involve me in all sorts of things. Here in the neighborhood, they don't do that. Here I always have to ask, and I don't want to do that anymore, don't expect anything of it.

Such sense of identification with other deaf people also resonates in Mrs. V.'s words, although there is also reluctance and ambiguity in the way she expresses belonging:

> I don't really *want to go to* De Gelderhorst, *but I did sign up for the waitlist* . . . *because* . . . *because* . . . *I've always been part of the deaf world.*

The inevitability embedded in these words is quite contrary to the idea of being a client in a care market with a budget to organize care according to one's own preferences. Given that elderly deaf people suffered so much under the ideologies of institutional regimes in their younger years, this reluctance is not surprising. What do deaf residents hope to find at *De Gelderhorst* despite such hesitations? Could it be that the center functions principally as a space where deaf people can experience a form of community, as, for example, in a deaf club?

Researching activities and motivations of members of British deaf clubs, however, Atherton (2009: 443) talks about this belonging in terms of "a feeling as much as a place". As one of our respondents exemplifies:

> I feel deaf, I think differently, and hearing people don't understand that.

Indeed, as Sarah Wright (2015: 391) points out, "belonging can also exist despite the absence of any specific site at all". She remarks that belonging has escaped rigorous theorizing and finds belonging "to be more-than-human, to be bound up with emotion and affect, to becoming in relational ways" (Wright 2015: 405). Indeed, we take belonging as an inherently dynamic and relational notion (Yuval-Davis 2006), "at once a feeling, a sense and a set of practices" (Wright 2015: 391). In line with such a conceptualization, and trying to do justice to the multidimensional, diverse, and dynamic nature of belonging, we will explore how practices of deafness and practices of elderly care are involved in belonging to a deaf carescape at *De Gelderhorst*.

4 Practices of deafness and care

De Gelderhorst positions itself as a cultural institution and seeks to appeal to Deaf clients with a capital D. But who are these preferred clients, and what sort of care is offered to them? We will get a better picture of this when looking at the center's policy in selecting people from their waiting list. Here, we find the institute engaged in practices of exclusion in contacts with hearing elderly who have become deaf at a later age and whose mother tongue is spoken Dutch. These people have not experienced the social stigma attached to deafness, or the oralist regimes of the traditional deaf schools. On the waiting list of *De Gelderhorst*, there are some people who are either late-deaf or in the process of losing their hearing and who want to move to the center. Mrs. W., whom we discussed in more detail elsewhere (Hiddinga & De Langen 2019), for example, finds she belongs there because she is going deaf:

> When you go blind, you go to a blind-something. [. . .] I'm going deaf. De Gelderhorst *is for deaf people.*

A similar sentiment is expressed by Mrs. A., who has a progressive hearing loss and is now fully deaf, communicating through speech and lip-reading. When referring to elderly care in her hometown and its suitability for deaf people, she states:

> Nothing here is adapted to deafness, nothing at all. And in De Gelderhorst *everything is.*

However, neither deafness, nor the feeling of being lost because of it, are considered sufficient grounds for belonging to the carescape of *De Gelderhorst*. While Mrs. A. hopes to find

> [. . .] recognition of each other's stories, [. . .] of what you've been going through, and that you're not the only one,

she does not participate in the shared history of elderly deaf residents of *De Gelderhorst*, since most of her life she has lived as a hearing person. Mrs. A. and Mrs. W., as others on the waiting list with similar backgrounds, are cautioned by staff members that for them "living there is really not the best idea". This is not to say that these people are not aware that a medical diagnosis is not enough to fit in (Mrs. W talks about *"a world of difference between hearing and deaf"*). On the contrary, they make an effort to engage with what they see as required. But their attempts to learn sign language, their visits to the center's restaurant and to open days, still does not make them suitable candidates. This may come as a surprise, given the variety in the mastery of sign language among residents of *De Gelderhorst*. Here, cultural labels of deafness are imposed to exclude those who are not 'properly' deaf, which shapes this carescape in a particular fashion. Practices of deafness at *De Gelderhorst* are thus subject to institutional policies constructing deaf belonging in particular ways. This boundary setting is part and parcel of a politics of belonging (Yuval-Davis 2006).

These informants were among the very few people in our study who referred to their deafness as a primary motivation for moving to *De Gelderhorst*. As we noted earlier, most of our respondents primarily wanted to access the care possibilities offered. For some people, strategic reasons were decisive in wanting to move at a relatively young age, like the couple quoted earlier. More usual, however, was the intention to postpone moving as long as possible. Mr. R., for example, was typical in remarking:

> *I am on the waiting list of* De Gelderhorst, *but only to have access there when things are not going well with me. If I can't walk anymore or so . . . then I'll go. Not now.*

Such reactions are very similar to those of hearing elderly, as a recent national survey among Dutch people over 65 shows (Lijzenga & Van der Waals 2014). By far the majority of elderly in The Netherlands want to stay at home as long as possible, and elderly deaf people are no exception. Only when home care and informal networks cannot provide the support they need are people willing to move to a residential setting. At the same time, all the elderly deaf we interviewed who were still living in their own homes, were unanimous about wanting to go to *De Gelderhorst* and nowhere else when in need of intensive care. In fact, ending up in 'a hearing home' was sketched as a horror scenario. Mr. V., for example, left no doubts about his feelings:

> *A nursing home with hearing people? Never in my whole life . . . horrible! Then they don't understand you, and you'll be dead-lonely.*

In this vein, belonging can be understood as 'an emotional affiliation' (Wood & Wait 2011: 201), nurturing a basic human need. It is well-researched that loneliness, more precisely the *feeling* of loneliness, regardless of actual social interaction, has a significant impact on health and wellbeing (Cornwell & Waite 2009). As such, feeling that one belongs to a network that one could access, is thought to have a positive impact on health, regardless of whether that network is actually accessed. Indeed, many of the people wanting to move to *De Gelderhorst* are attracted to the idea of being easily able to socialize with their neighbors and to participate in social activities. Talking of their motives in wanting to move to the center, they mentioned good care, and the homely atmosphere. As Mrs. K., resident of *De Gelderhorst* explains:

> *It is safe here, cozy, everybody talks about the past, about the deaf schools they went to.*

Indeed, it was frequently referred to as a 'safe haven', 'home', 'a place where I belong'. Mrs. E., for example, finds *De Gelderhorst* a place where one can

> just have a small chat with anyone. Just someone you happen to meet. I wasn't looking for friends, but just being able to say a few words in passing . . . like people normally do.

The reference to normality is striking. Like a deaf club, *De Gelderhorst* may be one of few spaces where deaf people can have normal social interactions with others, not marred by misrepresentation and misunderstandings (Brien 1991). This feeling of normalcy is also echoed in an interview with one of the residents in a local newspaper, under the headline 'Finally my deafness is not a disability anymore' (van Veen 2013: 72). This is the positive aspect of the wish to escape from the hearing world: to enjoy deaf sociality in a deaf-friendly environment. What is seen as a disability in the hearing world disappears there. Such a situation is not specific to deaf people. In her study of Chronic Obstructive Pulmonary Disease (COPD) patients, Pols (2011) shows how in a specialized clinic, patients' sharing of differences that are problematic elsewhere, creates a sense of community. Not only does it provide a sense of normalcy, it also supports people in finding ways to lead a good life with this chronic condition.

One could imagine elderly deaf people nurturing feelings of suspicion and distrust of institutions of care – usually run by hearing people – because they would be reminded of the 'total regimes' (Goffman 1961) at residential schools in their youth. However, the carescape of *De Gelderhorst* engenders feelings of normality and belonging, which seem to take on a significance in notions of care and comfort. By bringing together a network of elderly deaf people, *De Gelderhorst* creates a space of belonging where deafness is 'undone' and a sense of being among equals is created, and where loneliness can be reduced regardless of levels of interaction. These practices of belonging at *De Gelderhorst* should therefore be seen as part of care itself (Wood & Wait 2011). Indeed, the very idea that such a place exists is a comfort to those who do not live there, or even intend to live there in the future. In this sense, the carescape of *De Gelderhorst* reaches well beyond the boundaries of it grounds or its buildings:

> With deaf friends . . . . The one says to the other: have you registered on the waiting list already? Yes? Me too. In case of . . . . You have to think ahead.

This remembered exchange points at one particular aspect of being elderly and deaf in The Netherlands. Talking about the center with deaf friends and listing oneself for a place there seem commonplace for elderly deaf people outside the center.

The extension outside the center's location is also apparent in our interviews with people outside *De Gelderhorst* who want to stay in their own house as long as possible. They think of the center as a safety net, a place on which they can always fall back. Mr. E. is an elderly man who lives by himself and suffers from a chronic disease. In an emotional exchange, he says about a possible move to *De Gelderhorst*:

> . . . when it comes to a certain point . . . There comes a moment that I'll have to surrender.

There is a sense of defeat in his words, but Mr. E. feels confident that in case he cannot manage by himself anymore, safety and security can be found in *De Gelderhorst*. No doubt part of this will have to do with the unwelcoming hearing world, but also with the kind of care offered by *De Gelderhorst*. Mr. E. communicates both in signs and in understandable spoken Dutch, however his greatest fear is that he would end up in a regular home where care workers would not understand him if he wanted to express his last wishes. He felt deeply reassured that – in case of utmost vulnerability – there was a place where they would, and where his dignity as a Deaf person would be respected.

5 Carescape *De Gelderhorst*

Old age and illness have classically been cast as periods of vulnerability, a recurring theme in the ageing literature (Hazan et al. 1984; Buch 2015). For elderly deaf people, this may be exacerbated by concerns they have about being able to communicate with hearing health care professionals. Care at *De Gelderhorst*, however, is specially tailored to meet the communication needs of elderly deaf, requiring staff not only to sign, but also to have the understanding and patience to invest time to communicate with elderly deaf people in care interactions. Furthermore, the building and care technologies are specifically designed with their needs in mind. This is likely to engender feelings of security and to contribute to a sense of belonging to the carescape of *De Gelderhorst*. The 'horror' frequently expressed by elderly deaf people imagining 'ending up' in a hearing home supports this idea. At the same time, it is living with a group of elderly deaf that provides the basis for feelings of security and belonging. Indeed, the familiarity of the social networks in *De Gelderhorst* was implicitly referred to in many of the interviews.

Moving to a care home may come at a price and is often construed as an exchange of independence for the promise of care. But this is not how elderly deaf experienced moving to *De Gelderhorst*. Although some expressed concerns about a potential loss of autonomy, more commonly people saw a move to the center as a way of retaining control over their lives. Mr. B., for example, gave as his reasons to move:

> *Not being lonely and able to live independently, that is important.*

Or, as one of the professionals working at *De Gelderhorst* remarked:

> *You see people grow and flourish in small things, but for us that's still wonderful to experience. Like for the first time in their lives going to the doctor on their own.*

At the same time, decreased independence does not necessarily mean an undesirable situation or bad quality of life, but can also imply what might be termed 'sheltered autonomy'. An elderly deaf couple on the waiting list for *De Gelderhorst* explains:

> *No, we are not moving there yet. We're waiting as long as possible. Then you'll even be grateful if you're being a bit cosseted.*

Indeed, it has been argued that relationships of care necessarily involve human interdependency and can form the basis of a system of ethics (Held 2006). In a secure environment, dependence can be a positive part of care and enable certain expressions of autonomy, rather than diminish it, as the literature on elderly care seems to suggest. This brings into question whether independence and dependence need to be thought of as incompatible opposites. As Hoppe (2012: 143) argues, ". . . being dependent or independent is not a personal trait, but something that is part of life and changes constantly". Her plea to use the notion of reciprocity instead, resonates with the expressed feelings of the above-mentioned couple. Of course, in *De Gelderhorst* a loss of autonomy would contradict the center's expressed loyalty to cultural notions of Deafness, but the point is more how the carescape of the center enables or disables expressions of autonomy. Struhkamp (2005) positions autonomy not so much 'in' people as in the arrangements of a social and material world through which they are enabled to 'do' things. In the carescape of *De Gelderhorst*, practices of belonging engender feelings of normality and peace of mind and provide a context in which autonomy may count for more than in a hearing environment, where elderly deaf have to fight for attention. Moreover, the center's mission to further Deaf culture shapes its institutional practices in terms of boundary setting, communication practices, employment policies, but also in terms of participation in Deaf culture activities outside the center. This may well provide a climate in which the co-creation (Wright 2015) of Deaf identity and deaf belonging can bring out new autonomies. While none of the elderly we talked to mentioned Deaf culture in their motivation to move to *De Gelderhorst*, such autonomy may be the basis for claims of rights and entitlements referring to a Deaf identity. A recent managerial conflict at the center, where residents stood up against a Board of Governors to defend 'their' Deaf culture, suggests precisely this (Hiddinga et al. 2020). Belonging to a deaf carescape, as at *De Gelderhorst*, may thus provide opportunities for autonomy that are not realized in hearing carescapes without the core ideal of belonging that underpins care in this center. In this way, care practices at *De Gelderhorst* can be seen as constituting a system of Deaf morality, in which equality and individual rights of deaf residents are fitting together with the trust and mutual consideration involved in their care.

Figure 3: Resident of *De Gelderhorst* (the woman in the picture is not quoted in this article); © Monte Gardenier.

Although the waiting list shows continued interest in coming to live at *De Gelderhorst* on the part of elderly deaf people, this may not be a sufficient condition for its continued existence. How the center manages to survive in a social climate where integration and inclusion of 'special' groups is seen as desirable and long-term care budgets are particularly targeted by cost reductions in health care, is a different matter. Towards the Deaf community, the center positions itself as a cultural institution. In debating with committees deciding on budgets for care, officers of the center regularly argue that 'their' residents cannot be treated in the same way as hearing elderly with similar health problems. In this arena of health care policies and politics, Deafness is presented as a medical condition, a disability. This line of reasoning forms a sharp contrast with the institution's references to emancipation and Deaf culture, a notion fundamentally opposed to the medical labeling of deafness. In this manner, the center navigates between the structural requirements and possibilities of the health care system on the one hand and loyalty to the cultural minority character of its potential clientele on the other.

6 Discussion

De Gelderhorst as a care facility for elderly deaf people has positioned itself successfully in the care field, despite budget cuts in long term care and pressures to reduce care facilities for special groups. Creative balancing of different labels of deafness in different arenas enables both the institute's financial viability and, at the same time, adherence to a cultural mission. Under present policies, playing the health care system like this is a precondition for the sustainability of a carescape of elderly deaf like that in *De Gelderhorst*. Moreover, the center's engagement in these politics of belonging renders elderly deaf visible by setting boundaries and constructing membership in a specific Deaf sociality.

Boundary setting is also used to limit belonging of potential clientele. Not every elderly deaf person qualifies as a suitable participant in deaf sociality at *De Gelderhorst*.

The center thus offers a space of belonging and a particular form of care in which deaf citizenship (Hiddinga & De Langen 2019) takes shape, encompassing different needs, feelings, and a variety of ways of being deaf.

The carescape at this center has flexibly incorporated changing ideas about deafness and sign language and fosters feelings of belonging far beyond its location. Widespread is the idea of *De Gelderhorst* as a safety net when the situation at home becomes untenable, if only to avoid ending up in a 'hearing' home. Indeed, being fed up with the daily struggle to belong to a hearing world, is frequently mentioned as a motivation to move to *De Gelderhorst*.

Obviously, wanting to participate in deaf sociality also plays a role in people's decisions to move to *De Gelderhorst*. Here, diversity and flexibility in practices of communication turn out to be more important for a sense of belonging than a perfect mastery of NGT. A strong foundation for belonging to deaf sociality at *De Gelderhorst* is elderly deaf people's shared history: "elements of the past, cobbled together to mold a communal body of belonging" (Fortier 1999: 59). Indeed, experienced social stigma, oralist regimes, and exclusion from the hearing world are important elements of this history. At *De Gelderhorst*, social arrangements of belonging are 'un-doing' deafness and engendering feelings of normality, equality, and togetherness, of security and peace of mind (even for those who will never live there), which are, in themselves, part of care. They also enable expressions of what we have called 'sheltered autonomy', which are constitutive of elderly deaf people's independence and, possibly, the development of a new Deaf identity.

Belonging to the carescape at *De Gelderhorst* involves deaf practices and care practices, people, language, buildings, and care technologies specifically adjusted to non-hearing care. In such a carescape, practices of belonging can enable new meanings of Deafness and care. All these together are constitutive of good care for elderly deaf people and will persuade critical deaf health care consumers to spend their golden years in this center.

References

Atherton, Martin 2009. A feeling as much as a place: leisure, deaf clubs and the British deaf community. *Leisure Studies* 28(4). 443–454.

Becker, Gaylene. 1983. *Growing old in silence*. Berkeley, CA: University of California Press.

Boot, Jan Maarten & Mat H.J.M. Knapen. 2005. *De Nederlandse gezondheidszorg* [The Dutch healthcare system]. Houten: Bohn Stafleu van Loghum.

Bowlby, Sophie. 2012. Recognizing the time-space dimensions of care: Caringscapes and carescapes. *Environment and Planning A* 44(9). 2101–2118.

Breed, Peter C.M. & Bernardine Swaans-Joha. 1986. *Doof in Nederland. Een exploratief onderzoek naar de leefsituatie van volwassen dove mensen in relatie tot opvoeding en onderwijs* [Deaf in the Netherlands: an exploratory investigation into the living situation of deaf adults in relation to upbringing and education]. Amsterdam: University of Amsterdam PhD dissertation.

Brien, David 1991. Is there a deaf culture? In Susan Gregory & Gilian Hartley (eds.), *Constructing deafness*, 46–52. London: Pinter.

Buch, Elana. 2015. Anthropology of aging and care. *Annual Review of Anthropology* 44. 277–293.

Cook, Glenda, Juliana Thompson & Jan Reed, 2015. Re-conceptualising the status of residents in a care home: older people wanting to 'live with care'. *Ageing and Society* 35(8). 1587–1613.

Cornwell, Erin York & Linda J. Waite. 2009. Social disconnectedness, perceived isolation, and health among older adults. *Journal of Health and Social Behavior* 50(1). 31–48.

Da Roit, Barbara & Blanche Le Bihan. 2010. Similar and yet so different: cash-for-care in six European countries' long-term care policies. *The Milbank Quarterly* 88(3). 286–309.

De Clerck, Goedele A. 2010. Deaf epistemologies as a critique and alternative to the practice of science: An anthropological perspective. *American Annals of the Deaf* 154(5). 435–446.

Fortier, Anne-Marie. 1999. Re-membering places and the performance of belonging(s). *Theory, Culture & Society* 16(2). 41–64.
Goffman, Erving. 1961. *Asylums: Essays on the social situations of mental patients and other inmates*. London: Penguin Books.
Hazan, Haim. 1994. *Old age: Constructions and deconstructions*. Cambridge: Cambridge University Press.
Held, Virginia. 2006. *The ethics of care: Personal, political, and global*. New York: Oxford University Press.
Hiddinga, Anja & Maja de Langen. 2019. Practices of belonging: claiming elderly care through deaf citizenship. *Citizenship Studies* 23(7). 669–685.
Hiddinga, Anja & Research Collective 'Beyond Hearing, Deaf Cultures Overlooked'. 2020. Empowerment of Deaf elderly in The Netherlands: residents of De Gelderhorst united. In Donald A. Grushkin & Leila Monaghan (eds.), *Deaf empowerment: resistance and decolonization*, 129–161. Laramie, WY: Elm Academic Press.
Hoppe, Silke. 2012. The negative side of independence. An exploration of the self and others. *Medische Antropologie* 24(1). 131–147.
Kremer, Monique. 2006. Consumers in charge of care: the Dutch personal budget and its impact on the market, professionals and the family. *European Societies* 8(3). 385–401.
Kusters, Annelies & Maartje De Meulder. 2013. Understanding deafhood: In search of its meanings. *American Annals of the Deaf* 157(5). 428–438.
Lane, Harlan. 1984. *When the mind hears: A history of the deaf*. New York: Random House.
Lane, Harlan 2005. Ethnicity, ethics, and the deaf-world. *Journal of Deaf Studies and Deaf Education* 10(3). 291–310.
Lijzenga, Jeroen & Theo van der Waals. 2014. *Woonvoorkeuren specifieke woonvormen voor ouderen: Een verhaal met veel gezichten. Rapport in opdracht van het Ministerie van Binnenlandse Zaken en Koninkrijksrelaties* [Preferences regarding specific types of living environments for elderly people: a story with many faces. Report on behalf of the Ministry of Internal Affairs and Kingdom's Relations]. Den Haag: Companen.
Monaghan, Leila, Constanze Schmaling, Karen Nakamura & Graham H. Turner (eds.) 2003. *Many ways to be deaf*. Washington, DC: Gallaudet University Press.
Pols, Jeannette. 2011. Breathtaking practicalities: A politics of embodied patient positions. *Scandinavian Journal of Disability Research* 13(3). 189–206.
Purkis, Mary Ellen & Christine Ceci. 2015. Problematising care burden research. *Ageing and Society* 35(7). 1410–1428.
Putters, Kim. 2014. *Rijk geschakeerd. Op weg naar de participatiesamenleving* [Richly nuanced: Towards a society of participation]. Den Haag: Sociaal en Cultureel Planbureau.
Rietveld-van Wingerden, Marjoke & Corrie Tijsseling. 2010. *Ontplooiing door communicatie: geschiedenis van het onderwijs aan doven en slechthorenden in Nederland* [Deployment through communcation: history of education for the deaf and hard-of-hearing in the Netherlands]. Antwerpen: Garant.
Senghas, Richard J. & Leila Monaghan. 2002. Signs of their times: Deaf communities and the culture of language. *Annual Review of Anthropology* 31(1). 69–97.
Struhkamp, Rita M. 2005. Patient autonomy: A view from the kitchen. *Medicine, Health Care and Philosophy* 8(1). 105–114.

Tijsseling, Corrie. 2014. *'School, waar?': Een Onderzoek naar de Betekenis van het Nederlandse Dovenonderwijs voor de Nederlandse dovengemeenschap, 1790–1990* ['School, where?': A study on the significance of Deaf education in the Netherlands for the Dutch deaf community, 1790–1990]. Utrecht: Utrecht University PhD dissertation.

Van Veen, Peter. 2013. *Thuiskomen in De Gelderhorst: 60 jaar oog voor oudere Doven*. Ede: De Gelderhorst. [English translation: *Coming home at De Gelderhorst: 60 years' awareness of elderly deaf people*. Ede: De Gelderhorst, 2013].

Wood, Nichola & Louise Waite. 2011. Editorial: Scales of belonging. *Emotion, Space and Society* 4. 201–202.

Wright, Sarah. 2015. More-than-human, emergent belongings: A weak theory approach. *Progress in Human Geography* 39(4). 391–411.

Yuval-Davis, Nira. 2006. Belonging and the politics of belonging. *Patterns of Prejudice* 40(3). 197–214.

List of contributors

Delfina Aliaga
University Pompeu Fabra
Barcelona
Spain

Xavier Álvarez
University Pompeu Fabra
Barcelona
Spain

Gemma Barberà
University Pompeu Fabra
Barcelona
Spain

Elisabeth Brockmann
Altenbeken
Germany

Jens-Michael Cramer
Georg-August-University
Göttingen
Germany

Svetlana Dachkovsky
University of Haifa
Israel

Buket Ela Demirel
Boğaziçi University
Istanbul
Turkey

Luca Des Dorides
National Institute of the Deaf
Rome
Italy

Hasan Dikyuva
Koç University
Istanbul
Turkey

Jami N. Fisher
University of Pennsylvania
Philadelphia
USA

Santiago Frigola
University Pompeu Fabra
Barcelona
Spain

Aslı Göksel
Boğaziçi University
Istanbul
Turkey

Menno Harterink
Zeist
The Netherlands

Anja Hiddinga
University of Amsterdam
The Netherlands

Julie Hochgesang
Gallaudet University
Washington, DC
USA

Jana Hosemann
University of Cologne
Germany

Elena Kozelka
University of Hamburg
Germany

Robyn Miller
Philadelphia
USA

Annika Mittelstädt
Georg-August-University
Göttingen
Germany

https://doi.org/10.1515/9783110701906-015

List of contributors

Roland Pfau
University of Amsterdam
The Netherlands

Josep Quer
ICREA-University Pompeu Fabra
Barcelona
Spain

Judith Reiff-de Groen
De Gelderhorst
Ede
The Netherlands

Research Collective 'Beyond Hearing. Cultures Overlooked'
(for this contribution: Meike Brock, Katya Buts, Samoa Greeve, Lisa Hinderks, and Maja de Langen)
University of Amsterdam
The Netherlands

Lisa Rombouts
KU Leuven
Belgium

Rita Sala
CNRS/University Paris 8
France
& University Ca' Foscari
Venice
Italy

Miguel Ángel Sampedro
University Pompeu Fabra
Barcelona
Spain

Jordina Sánchez-Amat
University Pompeu Fabra
Barcelona
Spain

Wendy Sandler
University of Haifa
Israel

Burcu Saral
Boğaziçi University
Istanbul
Turkey

Rose Stamp
Bar-Ilan University
Ramat Gan
Israel

Markus Steinbach
Georg-August-University
Göttingen
Germany

Meredith Tamminga
University of Pennsylvania
Philadelphia
USA

Elvan Tamyürek Özparlak
Boğaziçi University
Istanbul
Turkey

Süleyman S. Taşçı
Boğaziçi University
Istanbul
Turkey

Annemieke van Kampen
Royal Kentalis
Haren
The Netherlands

Peter van Veen
Van Veen Communication
Ede
The Netherlands

Raquel Veiga Busto
University Pompeu Fabra
Barcelona
Spain

Myriam Vermeerbergen
KU Leuven
Belgium
& Stellenbosch University
South Africa

Subject index

abortion 35–36, 172, 175–176, 200, 205
access (see *information*)
Al-Sayyid Bedouin Sign Language
  (ABSL) 342
American Sign Language (ASL) (see also
  Black American Sign Language) 1,
  159–160, 161fn., 162, 277, 278, 282,
  285, 286, 290–301, 305–306, 307,
  311–313, 316–318, 330, 332
– Philadelphia variety of 286, 290–300
annotation 27, 36, 45, 226, 244, 278–279,
  335
archive 3, 5, 6, 19, 21, 29, 41, 46, 51, 54,
  65fn., 68, 69fn., 71, 97fn., 123, 138, 218,
  222–223, 232, 235, 244, 285fn., 300,
  335, 340fn., 350
Aryan 171–172, 173, 178, 184–185, 191, 199
Asian Deaf 132, 135fn., 284fn., 285fn., 301
asylum 67, 69–70, 76–77
attitude 37, 59, 70, 80, 85, 107, 155, 160,
  173, 211, 218, 220, 243, 248, 253,
  270–272, 301, 326, 361
Auschwitz 224–225, 237
Austrian Sign Language (ÖGS) 333

barrier (see also *communication*) 51, 82,
  181–183, 193
bilingual(ism) 27, 45, 49–50, 68, 79–80
bimodal(ism) 49, 68
bisexual 135fn., 139, 150, 156, 163
Black American Sign Language (Black
  ASL) 132, 282, 300
Black Deaf 130fn., 132–134, 138, 277, 278,
  279fn., 280, 281, 283, 286, 300–303,
  305–308
– children/students 284–285, 303–306
– feminism 134
– Philadelphians 279fn., 286fn., 300–308
blind 104, 109, 135, 175, 197, 199, 215, 220,
  240, 254, 266, 365, 392
– school 94–96, 100, 198
– organization 106, 266
boarding school (see also *Deaf institute*,
  residential school) 24, 29, 40, 76–77,
  105, 146, 228, 231, 241–242, 254,
  257, 363
bomb(ing) 217, 222, 229, 232–234,
  236–237, 239, 243, 251, 346
borrowing / loan 159–162, 293
British Sign Language
– gay sign variation of 157fn.

care (see also *healthcare*) 28, 38, 188, 202,
  255, 259, 359–381
carescape 384–385, 389, 391–399
Catalan Sign Language (LSC) 4, 5, 7, 19, 27,
  248, 330
Catholic(ism) (see also *church*, *religion*)
  202, 208, 223, 248, 254–255, 257,
  266–269, 270, 271
church (see also *Catholic*, *religion*) 28, 172,
  202, 208, 219, 229, 231, 247, 254, 257,
  268–269, 271, 306, 383
Civil War (Spain) 247, 248, 250–251,
  266–267, 271
co-speech gesture (see *gesture*)
cochlear implant (CI) 118, 182, 371
coming-out 135, 138, 148–149, 153–154
communication
– barrier 24, 41, 47, 51, 150–151, 155–156,
  163, 187–188, 289, 363
– device / technology / system 30, 56–57,
  67, 85, 132, 282, 371–373, 384, 395, 399
– oral (see *oral communication*)
– problem / difficulty / gap 35, 36, 47, 70,
  72, 73, 82, 107–109, 112–113, 136, 151,
  154fn., 182, 186, 222, 243, 245, 252,
  260–262, 265, 303, 319, 376
communist / communism 171, 250fn., 251,
  261, 267–268
compensation 197–212

Danish Sign Language (DTS) 330
Darwinism 173, 174, 218–219
Deaf
– association (see also *Deaf organization*)
  39, 51, 53, 80, 92, 99, 102, 112, 113, 116,
  179, 217, 221, 259, 266–270

- beauty contest 121–122
- child(ren) 5, 49–50, 69, 77, 81, 84, 86, 146, 178–179, 186–191, 193, 197, 199, 220–221, 233, 241–243, 252, 271, 282–283, 285, 288, 301, 302, 306fn., 386
- club 23, 34, 51–53, 67, 85, 150, 221–223, 292, 307, 391, 394
- culture 37, 41, 47, 51, 77, 86, 123, 132, 134, 135, 136, 155, 363, 364–365, 371, 377, 387, 396–397
- education 36, 77, 94–97, 217, 220, 281, 282–285, 386
- history 1, 2, 6, 39, 41, 48, 65, 66, 68, 75, 77, 86, 136, 138, 277, 300, 307, 350, 387, 388, 398–399
- identity (see *identity*)
- institute/institution (see also *Deaf school*) 5, 29, 40, 68, 102, 360, 363
- organization (see also *Deaf association*) 29, 100, 113–116, 137, 222, 388
- school (see also *Deaf institute*) 22, 25, 48–50, 76, 77, 80, 81–82, 85, 94–96, 100, 103, 104fn., 109, 132, 155, 178, 186–192, 220, 223, 231–232, 235–236, 237, 254, 269, 279, 282, 287, 297fn., 334, 362, 386–387, 392, 393
- studies 21, 75–76, 136, 388
- teacher 2, 203, 234, 255, 283
- world 66, 136, 148, 150–151, 153, 154, 296, 391
deaf-mute 69–70, 73–74, 77, 81, 85, 173, 178, 180, 190, 202, 224, 266–267, 270, 360
Deaflympics 117–121, 149
Deafness
- acquired 172, 189, 191–192
- hereditary 175, 186, 191, 192, 199, 203, 215, 218
depoliticization 248, 249–250, 257, 271
deprivation 49, 79, 156, 201
dementia 377, 380, 390
discipline 69, 98, 172, 178, 179, 257
disability / disabled 93, 94, 96, 129, 131, 135, 173, 177, 181–183, 191, 198, 201, 210, 211, 218–220, 266, 301fn., 383, 394, 398

- studies 133, 173, 181–183, 193
discourse
- level 330, 340
- marker 323fn., 325, 327–330, 334, 336, 338, 341, 343, 347, 350
discrimination 53, 71, 79, 81, 84, 94, 107, 129, 130–131, 132, 134, 138, 146, 150, 155, 163, 171–172, 206, 220, 244, 271, 307
diversity 42, 248, 293, 308, 370, 375, 379, 388–389
divorce 85, 151, 259–260, 271
documentary 1, 6–7, 179, 223
dormitory 83, 105, 109, 147, 229, 283, 285, 287, 289–290, 302–303, 360

economy / economic 24, 93, 174, 178, 184, 185, 187, 190, 193, 199, 211, 220, 247, 254, 262–264, 271, 280fn., 297
- burden 177
- growth 85, 253
- value 174, 184
education (see *Deaf education*)
emancipation 42, 264, 363, 384, 385, 387, 398
employment / unemployment 94, 112, 263, 264, 271, 396
endogamy 83
equality / inequality 74, 147, 203, 255, 257, 263, 271, 363, 369–370, 373, 374–376, 387, 391, 397, 399
ethnic(ity) 24, 29, 133, 277fn., 279, 280, 285, 287, 308
eugenics 173–175, 179, 181, 186, 188–189, 193, 205, 208, 211, 216, 218–220
execution / execute 177, 184, 189, 193, 247, 248, 250
experience (see *memory* and *life stories*)
exogamy 83

face-to-face tradition 281
facial expression 108, 109, 157, 331–333, 375, 377
falangism / falangist 250fn., 251, 266, 268
feminism / feminist 83, 130, 134, 208
fingerspelling (see also *manual alphabet*) 25, 27, 95, 105, 297

Flemish Sign Language (VGT) 217, 225–226, 244
Finnish Sign Language (FSL) 333
food 102, 221, 250, 254, 346
– rationing 93, 221, 227, 230, 235–236, 263

gay 71, 132, 135–137, 140, 141–161, 271
gender 76, 82, 87, 129, 130, 133, 162
– policy 269
genetic 177, 184, 189, 211, 219
– defect/disability/disorder 171, 203, 219
– material 173, 176, 186, 190, 192, 193, 211, 219
– quality/value 173, 174, 184
German Sign Language (DGS) 4, 5, 19, 22, 26–27, 35, 46, 48, 56, 157fn., 203, 332
gesture 73, 80, 81, 84, 108, 109, 159, 237, 260, 265, 288, 330, 331
gossip 36, 150, 151, 154, 197, 389

hard-of-hearing 66, 102, 135fn., 202, 280fn., 290, 295fn., 303, 306fn.
health / healthy 171, 172, 176, 180, 182, 184, 189, 193, 197, 198, 200, 210, 219, 220, 280fn., 390, 393, 398
– care 372, 383, 395, 397–398
– court 175, 188, 197, 199, 200, 210
hearing world 66, 86, 151, 153, 154, 277fn., 377, 387, 389, 394, 395, 398–399
hereditary
– deafness (see *Deafness, hereditary*)
– disease 171, 174–177, 185, 193, 197, 198, 199, 201, 215, 220
– health court (see *health court*)
Hispanic Deaf 132, 135
HITLER CUT (sign for 'sterilization') 203
Holocaust 6, 174fn., 203, 218
home sign 288, 291, 306
homosexual(ity) (see also *gay, lesbian, Queer*) 24, 29, 42, 71, 129–163, 171, 218, 219, 249, 260, 268, 271
hospital 54, 69fn., 70, 93, 107, 108, 184, 204, 216, 219, 368, 372

identity 84, 129, 131, 133, 134, 137–138, 146–148, 152, 155, 162–163, 323, 387, 388
– Black 132
– cultural 3, 75, 171, 385
– Deaf 5, 7, 66, 67, 80, 84, 87, 135fn., 155, 156, 387, 391, 396–397, 399
– Jewish 134, 223
– Philadelphian 297
– sexual (incl. gay/lesbian/Queer identity see also *sexuality*) 71, 136, 141, 142fn., 148, 151, 153, 154, 156, 162
– shift 131, 156
ideology / ideological (see also *Nazi ideology*) 201, 211, 248, 254, 258, 266, 267, 391
immigration / immigrant 6, 85, 288, 334
impairment / impaired 5, 53, 96, 171–193, 197, 202, 210, 211, 220
inclusion / inclusivity 49–50, 132, 138, 271, 306fn., 307fn., 370, 375, 397
information
– access to 150, 155, 156, 252
– lack of (access to) 132, 136, 154, 163, 221, 230, 241, 242, 243
– provision of 228, 229–230
– structure 331, 332
International Sign 1, 7, 56
internet 24, 132, 155, 156
interpreter / interpreting 41, 51, 83–84, 108, 151, 155, 157fn., 221, 245, 261, 271, 334, 363, 375, 379
intersectional(ity) 66, 130–138, 146, 152, 158fn., 163, 244, 388
intonation(al) 327, 331, 345
– phrase 324, 331–334, 336, 337, 339, 342, 344, 346–347
Israeli Sign Language (ISL) 323–350
Italian Sign Language (LIS) 4, 5, 19, 20, 27, 30, 38, 68, 80, 81

Jewish 6, 134, 171–172, 177, 201–202, 218, 223–225, 227–228, 237–239, 243–244, 311–312, 334, 341

language variation (see *variation*)
Latinx Deaf 138, 284fn., 285fn., 301
legislation 53, 91, 92, 94, 173, 176, 264, 266
lesbian 133, 135–138, 141–146, 148–151, 153–157, 159–161, 271
liberation 76, 192, 224, 227, 228, 237, 240, 360
life stories / experiences 1, 5–6, 19–21, 30, 36–37, 40–42, 45, 46, 56, 67, 74, 76, 91–92, 123, 138, 140, 163, 282, 323, 335
lip-reading 49, 56, 77, 95, 107, 265, 292, 386, 392
loan (see *borrowing*)
loneliness 51, 80, 85, 133, 153, 237, 365, 393–394, 396

mainstream society (see also *society*) 37, 87, 129, 130fn.
manual alphabet (see also *fingerspelling*) 46–47, 56–57, 97, 106
marginalization / marginality 66–67, 70, 86, 129, 130fn., 131–132, 138, 162–163, 300
marriage / marry 23, 53, 71, 80, 82–83, 85–86, 104, 151, 172, 174, 176, 200, 219, 247, 258–262, 264, 268–269, 387
media 24, 28, 29, 30, 145, 223, 241, 243, 250, 252, 334, 371
medical / medication / medicine 54, 69fn., 102, 148, 175, 182, 184, 199–202, 205, 208, 211, 215–216, 220, 242, 392, 398
memory / experience / recollection 2, 6, 7, 23–25, 35, 37, 40, 46, 49–51, 65, 67, 71–74, 76–77, 91, 98, 107, 118, 120, 123, 130fn., 153, 211, 225–226, 229, 241–244, 257, 265, 277, 281, 297, 300, 317, 366, 370–371
– negative 21, 39–41, 53, 86, 93, 107–108, 110–111, 129–130, 133, 148–149, 151, 155, 202–206, 217, 221, 231, 238, 248, 250–251, 261, 286–287, 386, 388–389
– positive 21, 39, 112, 145, 147fn., 150, 157, 240, 258, 286, 290, 305, 307, 396
metaphor 153, 323–325, 326, 331, 345, 349, 381
military / paramilitary 93, 110, 119, 173, 178–179, 204, 205, 247fn., 248, 251, 266

– service 110–111, 172
minority 7, 24, 37, 41, 47, 48, 65, 75, 83–84, 129, 131, 132–133, 134, 136–137, 146, 160, 171, 177, 193, 280, 300, 365, 387
moral(ity) 182, 202, 205, 207, 210, 247, 258, 260, 268, 270–271, 397
mouthing 25, 27, 35–36, 80, 158, 203, 292, 339, 348

name sign 40, 71, 97, 99, 115–116
narrative / narration 3, 5–6, 67–68, 71, 74–76, 86, 244, 251, 258, 259, 261, 277, 278, 300, 304, 323, 325–326, 329–330, 334–335, 340–345, 349, 350, 389
National Socialism 171, 178–180, 183–184, 187, 193, 198, 200–202, 205–212
Nazi 223, 228, 236
– Germany/regime 48, 51, 53–54, 171–181, 186, 190, 193, 197, 199–203, 207–208, 210–212, 218–220
– ideology 174, 178–179, 183, 184–185, 187, 199, 201, 202, 208, 210, 218
negative memory (see *memory*)
network 7, 29, 82, 137, 150fn., 250, 279fn., 363, 364, 383, 393–395
New State (Spain) 247, 270
New Zealand Sign Language (NZSL) 330
non-manual (marker/signal) 292, 332–333, 335–340, 343, 345, 349
Norwegian Sign Language (NSL) 330, 331

oral communication 182, 265, 292–293, 375, 386
oralism / oral education 26, 35–36, 49–50, 77, 95, 138, 188, 256, 281, 282, 283, 286, 292, 301, 306, 362, 386, 392, 399
oppression 65–67, 76, 78, 81, 86, 130, 181, 201, 248, 250, 286, 307

paramilitary (see *military*)
patronization 361, 373, 376, 387
peers 23, 51, 107, 109, 135, 230, 241, 242, 244, 256–257, 266, 284, 286, 287, 289–290, 292–293, 299, 301, 302–306

people of color (see also *Black Deaf*) 135, 279, 305, 308
persecution 53, 171–172, 193, 201–203, 205, 208–210, 251
politics 24, 75, 92, 106, 135, 138, 172, 174, 177–179, 182, 184fn., 199, 201, 205–206, 208–212, 218, 221, 230, 247–248, 249–253, 257, 271, 285, 383, 385, 393, 398
Population Census of the Kingdom of Italy (1903) 81
positive memory (see *memory*)
prejudice 47, 48, 51, 80, 178, 180, 303, 304–305, 307
pride / proud 81, 145–146, 155, 157, 160, 171fn., 179, 291, 294, 369–370, 373–376
profession / professional life 23, 24, 48, 50–52, 83, 99, 108, 112, 263–264
prosody / prosodic 323–325, 327–330, 331–334, 336, 338–339, 349
punishment 80, 111, 147, 204, 257–258, 269, 283, 293, 346, 386

Queer 130–131, 133, 135–139, 140, 141fn., 156–158, 160, 162–163
questionnaire 4, 6, 20, 23–25, 27, 38, 92, 175, 227

race 129, 130–131, 133, 162, 171, 173, 177, 184, 199, 210, 218, 219, 277fn., 282, 300
racial hygiene 177, 179, 198, 199, 201, 202, 203, 218, 221
racial segregation (see *segregation*)
racism 173, 208, 300, 301–305, 307
rationing (see *food rationing*)
religion / religious (see also *Catholic, church*) 24, 31, 131, 171, 201, 205, 252, 254–255, 267, 269–270, 287
residential school (see also *boarding school*) 133fn., 282, 283–285, 286–290, 297fn., 301, 386, 394

school for the Deaf (see *Deaf school*)
Second World War (see *World War II*)
segregation 40, 132, 181, 254, 285, 301, 302, 303

sexuality (see also *identity*) 129, 131, 136, 138, 146fn., 150, 155, 205, 259
shame 73, 79, 80, 84, 120, 149, 160, 203, 209
SIGN-HUB project 2–7, 14, 20, 23, 25, 26, 28, 45, 65fn., 91, 139–140, 142fn., 146, 163, 335, 340fn.
Sign Language of the Netherlands (NGT) 4, 5, 19, 27, 31, 131, 140, 156fn., 158–162, 330, 363, 368, 376–379, 386, 388–389, 398
Sinti and Roma 171, 224
social 24, 28, 40, 51, 66–68, 73–74, 92, 129–131, 174, 178, 181–182, 201, 204, 211–212, 247, 257, 266, 277, 280, 286–287, 294, 297, 300, 362, 365, 393, 397
– control 85, 186, 205, 248–250, 252–253, 254, 262, 266, 271, 368, 387
– life 24, 86, 91, 92, 94, 96, 112, 192, 290, 307
society (see also *mainstream society*) 24, 48, 54, 76, 77, 82, 84, 87, 129, 134, 174, 179, 181, 182–183, 184, 186–187, 188, 191–192, 193, 201–202, 204, 209, 211, 218, 248, 253, 259, 359, 362
sociolinguistic(s) (see also *variation*) 2, 132, 278
soldier 93, 98, 102, 111, 179, 217, 224, 225, 228, 230, 234, 238–241, 242, 250, 346
Spanish Sign Language (LSE) 4, 5, 19, 27, 31, 248
speech 85, 95, 107, 109, 292, 386, 388, 392
– disorder 202, 233
– therapy 77, 256
spoken language 4, 6, 7, 24, 25, 41, 192, 242, 256–257, 261–262, 263, 324, 331–332, 345, 362, 363, 386, 388
sports 23, 112, 116–119, 121, 143, 178–179, 286, 290, 292, 293, 304, 307fn.
sterilization 48, 54, 172, 175–177, 179–181, 188–189, 191–193, 197–212, 219–221, 228, 238
– law (see also *Gesetz zur Verhütung erbkranken Nachwuchses*) 189, 198–200, 203, 205–212, 215–216, 219–220
stigma(tization) 77, 107, 109, 135, 160, 181, 183, 201, 211, 387, 392, 399
Swedish Sign Language (SSL) 330

taboo 143, 146, 149, 150, 155, 202, 204
teacher (see also *Deaf teacher*) 2, 27, 52, 77, 78, 82, 94, 95–96, 98, 102, 106, 107, 173, 178, 185, 186–190, 202, 203, 207, 220, 230, 231, 233–234, 248, 251, 254, 255–256, 258, 260, 263, 283, 293, 295, 298, 302, 303, 346, 348, 377–380
temporality 323, 325–326, 345
– event 325, 326–328, 349
– discourse 325, 326–328, 349
time expression 323–324, 326–327, 328–329, 331, 334–340, 347, 349
trauma(tic) 72, 110, 175, 197, 198, 203, 208, 211, 287
Turkish Sign Language (TİD) 4, 5, 19, 26, 27, 94, 96, 97, 106, 330

variation / variety / variant 5, 25, 27, 35, 75, 132, 157fn., 277, 286, 294, 298–299
– grammatical 25
– lexical 25, 132, 294–296, 298
– phonological 132, 142fn., 159–160

– regional 25, 26, 35, 160fn., 278, 282, 290–291, 294–295, 298
– sociolinguistic 2, 300, 306, 308
– typological 4
vocational school / education 51, 52, 96, 187, 283, 292–293, 295, 301, 302

welfare 98, 123, 179, 184, 271, 280fn., 364, 383
World War I / First World War 83, 92, 111fn., 173
World War II / Second World War 6, 24, 41–42, 79, 91, 92, 117, 155, 177, 199, 203, 205, 207, 217, 218, 221, 222, 225, 226, 241, 243, 244, 253fn., 342, 346, 360

younger generation 2, 27, 47, 140, 149, 154–155, 156, 163, 256, 280fn., 291, 294, 297, 298–299, 345, 349

Name index (incl. associations, laws, and schools)

1939–1945 Que Faisaient Les Sourds? ('1939–1945 What did the Deaf do?', movie) 6

Académie de la Langue des Signes Française ('Academy for French Sign Language') 6
Acción Católica de Sordomudos de Barcelona ('Catholic Action of Deaf-mutes of Barcelona') 268
Acción Católica de Sordomudos de Madrid ('Catholic Action of Deaf-mutes of Madrid') 268
Aktion T4 (Action T4 / T4 Program) 177, 184, 189, 219
Albreghs, Fritz 179–180
Altınkaynak, Kerim 96, 115, 121
Anna's stille strijd ('Anna's silent battle', movie) 223–224
Archbishop Ryan Academy for the Deaf (Philadelphia, USA) 283–284, 312
Asociación de Sordomudos de Madrid ('Association of the Deaf-mutes of Madrid') 267, 268
Atatürk, Mustafa Kemal 102, 111

Bann G (division of Hitler Youth for young Deaf people) 178–179, 189
Biesold, Horst 175, 203, 207, 209–210
Bock, Gisela 203, 208
Bouhler, Philipp 177
Brandt, Dr. Karl 177
British Union of Fascists ('Blackshirts') 222
Bund der "Euthanasie"-Geschädigten und Zwangssterilisierten (BEZ, 'Association for Victims of "Euthanasia" and Forced Sterilization') 208–209
Bundesentschädigungsgesetz (BEG, 'Federal Law of Compensation') 207–210

Calafell, Àngel 266–269
Carmona, Albert 95

Casa de Sordomudos de Barcelona ('House of Deaf-mutes of Barcelona') 268
Central City Deaf Club (Philadelphia, USA) 307
Christelijk Instituut Effatha ('Christian Institute Effatha') 146, 360
Confederación Estatal de Personas Sordas (CNSE, 'State Confederation of the Deaf in Spain') 261fn., 266

Dame di compagnia ('Lady-in-waiting', Turin, Italy) 82
Das Erbe ('The heritage', movie) 219
De Gelderhorst (home for elderly Deaf people, Ede, The Netherlands) 29, 156–157, 163, 359–381, 384–399
Deutscher Gehörlosen-Bund (DGB, 'German Deaf Society') 28
Dilsiz ve Körler Okulu ('School for the Mute and the Blind', İstanbul, Turkey) 100
Die Deutsche Sonderschule (DDS) ('The German Special School', journal) 173, 186, 188–190, 192
Doof Verleden Vlaanderen ('Deaf History Flanders') 217, 222
Doof Vlaanderen ('Deaf Flanders', Flemish Deaf Association, Belgium) 217–218, 222, 244fn.
Dovenschap (Dutch organization for Deaf people) 387
Dovenvreugd (home for elderly Deaf people, Baarn, The Netherlands) 359–362

Education Center for the Deaf (Osnabrück, Germany) 51
Efrand, Erol 96, 115–116, 119–121
Ehegesundheitsgesetz ('Marriage Health Law') 176
Eisermann, Heinrich 178
Epheta (Journal of the Association of the Catholic Deaf in Germany) 207

Federación de Sordos de la Comunidad de Valencia ('Federation of the Deaf of the Community of Valencia') 270
Federación Nacional de Sociedades de Sordomudos de España (FNSSE, 'National Federation of Societies of Deaf-mutes of Spain') 266
First National Congress of the Deaf (Barcelona, Spain) 268fn.
Francoist / Francoism 247–272

Gallaudet University (Washington, DC, USA) 295–297, 318, 320
Gesetz zur Verhütung erbkranken Nachwuchses (GzVeN, 'Law for the Prevention of Offspring with Hereditary Diseases', LPOHD) 171, 175–176, 184–185, 188, 193, 198, 215, 219
Gök, Süleyman 91, 96–106, 113, 115, 116, 119–121
Gökay, Fahrettin Kerim 103

Hitler, Adolf 172, 174, 177, 179, 201, 203, 216, 221
Hitlerjugend (HJ) ('Hitler Youth') 172, 178–179, 189, 193
Huysman, Lea 223, 225, 227fn., 228, 237–238

İnönü, İsmet 102–103
Institute of German Sign Language and Communication of the Deaf (IDGS, Hamburg, Germany) 51
İstanbul Dilsiz ve Âmâ Mektebi ('İstanbul School for the Mute and the Blind') 94–95
İstanbul Sağırlar Gençlik Spor Kulübü Derneği ('İstanbul Sports Club Association for the Deaf Youth') 119, 121
İzmir Dilsiz Mektebi ('İzmir School for the Mute') 95
İzmir Sağırlar Okulu ('İzmir School for the Deaf') 95

Kazerne Dossin (Mechelen, Belgium) 224, 237
Kip, Necati Kemal 95

La Vie Des Sourds Pieds Noirs Et Juifs D'Algérie ('Life of the Deaf Pieds Noirs and Jews of Algeria', movie) 6
Law 517 of 1977 (Mainstreaming Law, Italy) 67, 77
Leenhouts, Bram and Jan 359–361
Luczak, Raymond 135–136, 144

Madosa (Antwerp Deaf Club, Belgium) 218, 222–223
Maeße, Dr. Hermann 189–190
Mainstreaming Law, Italy (see *Law 517*)
Marroquín, Juan Luis 267–268
Martha King Memorial School for the Deaf (Merzifon, Turkey) 95
Martín, Estanislao 267
Milan Congress (1880) 65, 67, 76, 78, 79, 81, 84, 217
Model Secondary School for the Deaf (MSSD, Washington, DC, USA) 297
Morris Hall (Philadelphia, USA) 293

National Association of the Deaf (NAD, USA) 1, 281
Nederlandse Christelijke Bond van Doofstommen (NCBD, 'Dutch Christian Union of the Deaf-mute') 360
Nürnberger Ärzteprozess ('Nuremberg Doctors' Trial') 205
Nürnberger Gesetze (Nuremberg Laws) 205, 219

Opera Pia Sordomute Povere ('Pious Institution for Poor Female Deaf-mutes', Crema, Italy) 77
Opfer der Vergangenheit ('Victims of the past', movie) 220
Organización Nacional de Acción Católica del Sordomudo de España ('National Organization of the Catholic Action of Deaf-mutes of Spain') 267

Pennsylvania Institution for the Deaf (PID) 283fn., 289, 319
Pennsylvania Institution for the Instruction of the Deaf and Dumb / Pennsylvania

Institution for the Deaf and Dumb (PIDD) 283
Pennsylvania School for the Deaf (PSD) 279–280, 283fn., 300, 311
Philadelphia Signs Project 277, 278–281, 289, 307
Pinedo, Félix Jesús 255, 267
Pio Istituto delle Sordomute Povere ('Pious Institute for Poor Female Deaf-mutes', Bologna, Italy) 77
Pio Istituto per Sordomuti Poveri di Campagna ('Pious Institute for Poor Deaf-mutes from the Countryside', Milan, Italy) 77
Pio Istituto Sordomuti di Milano ('Pious Institute for Deaf-mutes of Milan', Italy) 77
Ponce de León 267
Public Law 94–142 (Education for All Handicapped Children Act 1975, USA) 301fn.
Purísima school (Barcelona, Spain) 256, 260

Quel Avenir Pour Les Personnes Agées Sourdes? ('What is the future of the elderly Deaf?', movie) 6

Rainbow Alliance of the Deaf (USA) 137fn.
Reed Street Deaf Club (Philadelphia, USA) 307
Refugio de Guerra para Sordomudos ('War Shelter for Deaf-mutes') 267
Reichsverband der Gehörlosen Deutschlands (ReGeDe, 'Reichs' Union of the German Deaf') 179–180
Roze Gebaar (Dutch Association for Deaf LGBTIQ people) 130, 139, 140–153, 154–156, 159, 160, 163

Sağır Dilsiz ve Körler Tesanüt Cemiyeti ('Solidarity Organization for the Deaf, Mute, and Blind', İstanbul, Turkey) 100, 106
Scheele, Bram 361
Seixas, David 283

Seniorenproject ('Senior Citizens Project', Belgium) 217, 218, 225–228, 238
Silent Athletic Club (SAC, Philadelphia, USA) 304, 307
Silent Social Club (Philadelphia, USA) 279fn., 281
Stichting tot Oprichting en Instandhouding van Christelijke Tehuizen voor Doofstommen ('Foundation for the Establishment and Maintenance of Christian Homes for the Deaf-mute') 360
Stokoe, William 65, 291

Taubstummen-Anstalten ('Institutes for the Deaf-mute') 173
Tez, Sevil 122
Timmer, Cornelis 360
Tulga, Refik 119
Turgut, Dr. Hamdi 96, 115, 116
Türkiye Sağırlar Tesanüt Derneği ('Solidarity Association of Turkey for the Deaf') 97, 100, 101, 103, 106, 113–115, 119
Türkiye İşitme Engelliler Milli Spor Federasyonu ('Turkey National Sports Federation for the Deaf') 116
Türkiye Sağırlar Milli Federasyonu ('Turkey National Federation of the Deaf') 115

University Medical Faculty (Göttingen) 54

van Dam, Anna (see also *Anna's stille strijd*) 223–225, 238, 244
van Wijk, E. 361
Verkannte Menschen ('Misjudged People', movie) 179–180, 220
Visser, Bea 139, 140, 141–143, 145, 146–149, 151, 159
Veditz, George 1, 281
Vlaams GebarentaalCentrum ('Flemish Sign Language Center') 217

W.H. Martin School (Philadelphia, USA) 283–285, 287, 289, 290, 301, 302, 303, 305, 306, 311–316, 319–320
Waltemathe, Ernst 207

We were there . . . We are here (movie) 1, 6
Western Pennsylvania School for the Deaf in Pittsburgh (WPDP) 298fn.

Yıldız Sağırlar Okulu ('Yıldız School for the Deaf', İstanbul, Turkey) 92, 95, 97fn., 103, 105, 116, 122, 116–117

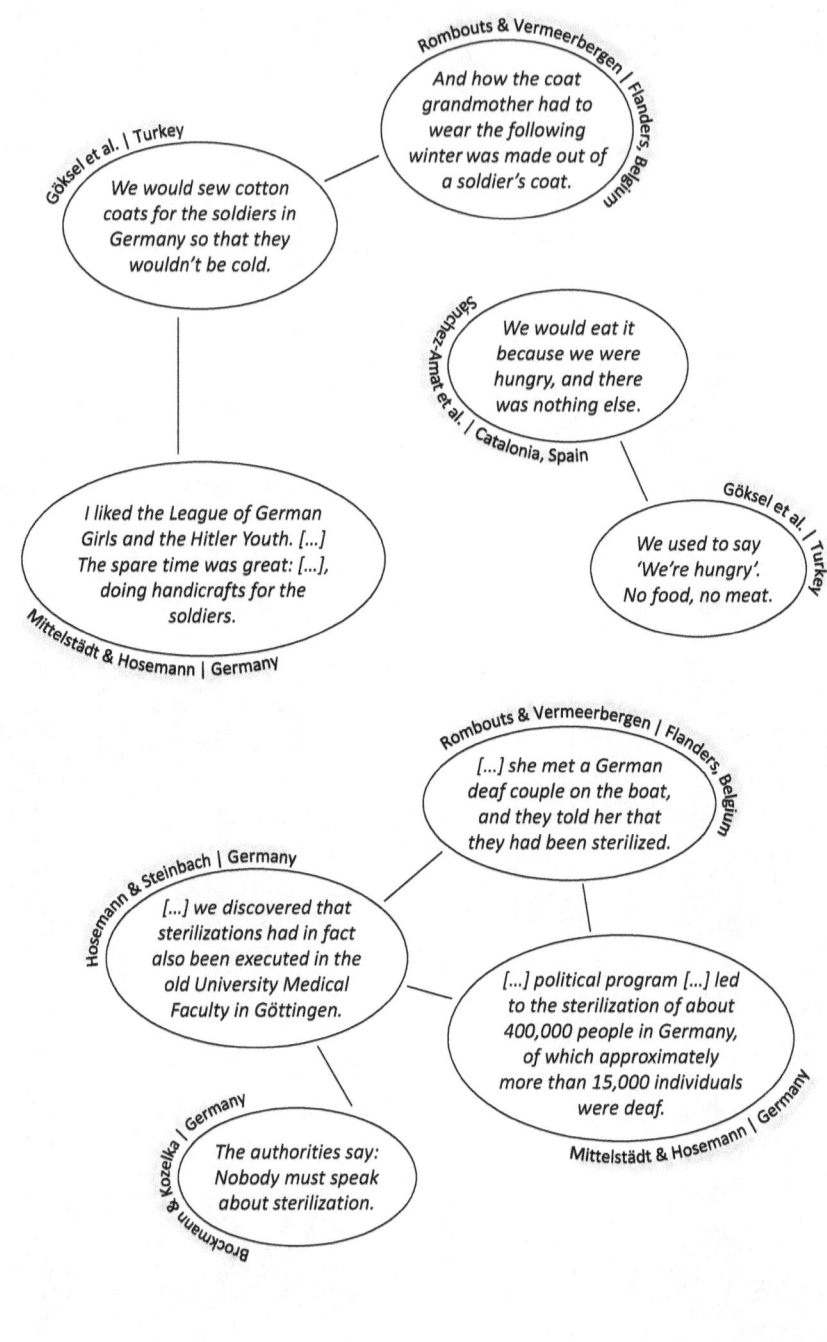

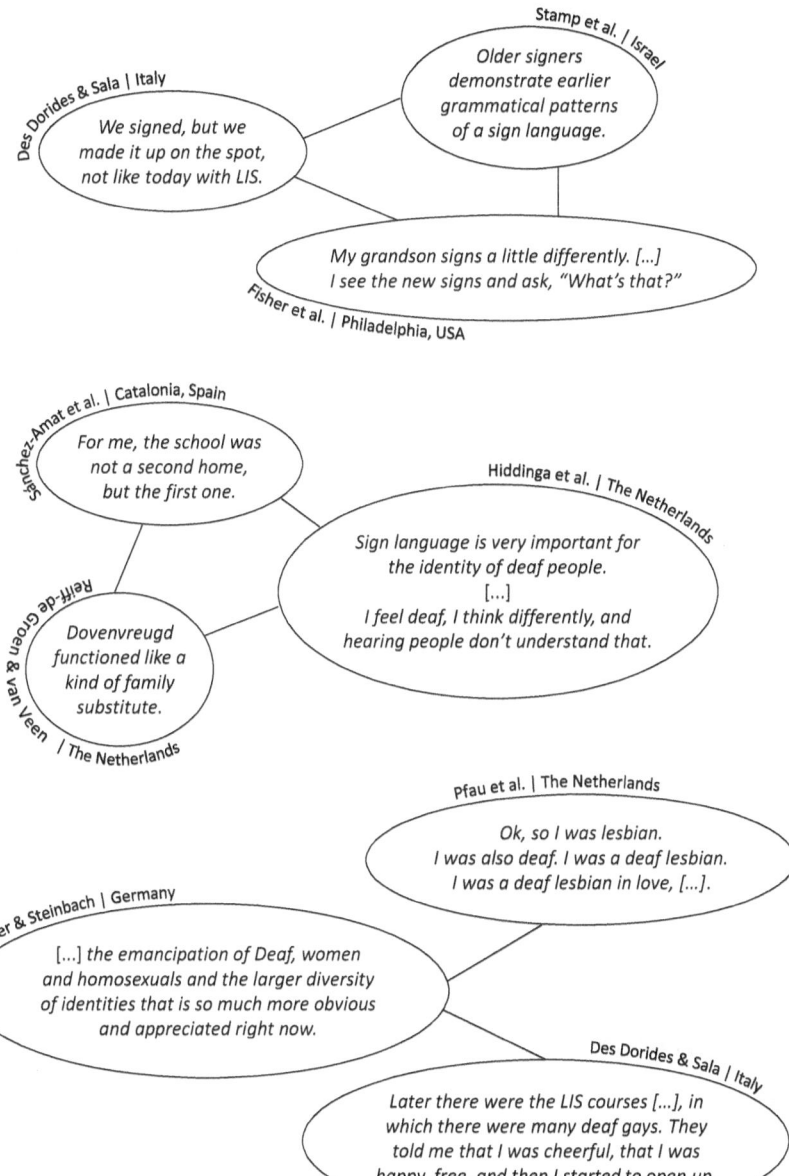

www.ingramcontent.com/pod-product-compliance
Lightning Source LLC
Chambersburg PA
CBHW031749220426
43662CB00007B/335